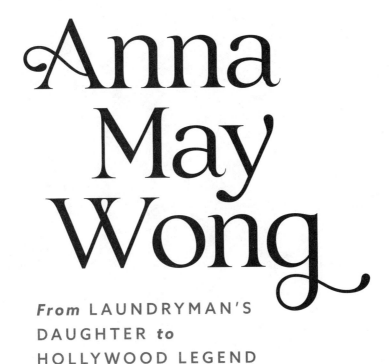

Anna May Wong

From LAUNDRYMAN'S
DAUGHTER *to*
HOLLYWOOD LEGEND

GRAHAM RUSSELL GAO HODGES

CHICAGO
REVIEW
PRESS

First edition published in 2004 by Palgrave Macmillan
Second edition published in 2012 by Hong Kong University Press
This edition published by Chicago Review Press Incorporated
814 North Franklin Street
Chicago, Illinois 60610
ISBN 978-1-64160-883-1

Library of Congress Control Number: 2022942745

Cover design: Preston Pisellini
Cover photo: ARCHIVIO GBB / Alamy Stock Photo
Printed in the United States of America
5 4 3 2 1

For Gao Yunxiang

I hold your hands
We take joy in each other
Our love transcends life and death
We will grow old together

Contents

Preface to Third Edition

In 1999, when I started researching and writing this book, attitudes about Anna May Wong were ambivalent. While film buffs, gay men, and a few Asian American writers were enthusiasts, most Americans wanted to forget her and the stereotypical film roles she endured.

Today Anna May Wong is honored as a pioneering Asian American cinema star. A Google Doodle in 2020 saluted her birthday. In 2022 the US Mint issued a commemorative quarter bearing her likeness in a series honoring five great women of American history. Now, celebrated actor Gemma Chan will produce and star in a biopic based upon Wong's life and this book. This twenty-year transformation into a national icon after decades of being a "no-name woman" is remarkable. There are numerous factors explaining it.[1]

First, knowledge of Wong has become more accessible through the growth of the Internet. Two decades ago only major productions such as *The Thief of Bagdad* and *Shanghai Express*, noted more for her costars than Wong, were available. Today twenty-seven Wong films and many snippets are accessible on YouTube, either for free or via inexpensive rental. She is regularly featured in documentaries on Asian American history. There are daily mentions of her on Twitter, Instagram, and Snapchat and constant sales of her pictures and other memorabilia on eBay. Artistic renditions of Wong from her lifetime have soared in value at major auction houses.

Second, original materials on Anna May Wong are now much more accessible on the Internet. As newspapers, magazines, and photographs are digitalized, knowledge of Wong has expanded globally. I have argued that Wong was a world star, made so by film distribution and magazines. Today, in addition to more

American and European newspapers and magazines, databases of historic periodicals from South America, the Caribbean, Africa, and China reveal the breadth of Wong's appeal during her career.[2]

There is now more appreciation of her as a cross-racial figure. Digitalization of African American newspapers helps us comprehend the affection Black Americans had for Anna May Wong. In addition to advertisements for her films and ongoing gossip, there was ample coverage in Black periodicals of her United China Relief efforts before and during World War II. Consider the fascinating moment reported in Black newspapers in 1942 when Billie Holiday, Hattie McDaniel, and the Nicholas Brothers joined Wong on stage in Los Angeles at a fundraising gala for China Relief sponsored by the local NAACP. In 1944 Wong joined Black celebrities Duke Ellington, Count Basie, and Josh White, along with six thousand attendees in New York City to celebrate Paul Robeson's forty-sixth birthday. The *Baltimore Afro-American* published a big picture of Wong and Robeson cutting a huge cake.[3]

More historical digital sources are now available from China. In 1931 a handbill published in Shanghai promoting methods to teach English language skills praised Anna May Wong's courageous battle against American racism. One key story suggests that Anna May Wong's efforts, after her visit in 1937, to recast her reputation as a loyal daughter of the nation were not entirely successful. During the Japanese invasion of China, famed journalist Zou Taofen repeated condemnation of her as a racial collaborator and an embarrassment to the "motherland" in a book intended to raise nationalist strength. Widely respected in China and among Chinese Americans, Zou was left wing and was honorably made a Communist Party member after his premature death in 1944. His harsh criticism of Wong in 1937 predates Madame Chiang Kai-shek's snub of her in 1943. I argued in this book that snub set the negative tone about Wong for the rest of the century. Zou's comments reveal that earlier hostility toward Wong extended after her trip to China and well before Madame Chiang's 1943 visit. Likely her family read commentaries on her by Zou and others published in the Chinese American press that colored their personal views, despite her valiant labors for United China Relief. Ameliorating that criticism is the newly discovered fact that Wong and famed Chinese actress Hu Die bonded by speaking Cantonese when they met. Adding further complexity to these cultural currents is the 1938 report in the *Chicago Defender*, a leading Black newspaper, that Anna May Wong had received a grateful cablegram from Madame Chiang Kai-shek thanking her for her generous contributions to China's benefits.[4]

There is also new material evidence of how Anna May Wong lived. Objects sold at the 2015 estate sale of Richard Wong, Anna May's last surviving sibling, offer glimpses of Anna May Wong's possessions. The gushing adverts describe boxes from before World War II and afterward of such chinoiserie as paintings, many jade Buddhas, several collections of silver dinnerware, large amounts of high-quality American and Japanese pottery and crystal, books about Chinese history, hundreds of record albums, costume jewelry, and multiple fur coats. They indicate that Anna May Wong surrounded herself with fine objects from China as well as Western art. Also sold privately were print collections now held in the Harvard Theatre Collection at Houghton Library. They consist of sheet music and original scores created by her and for her by Constant Lambert, Hans May, and Ernest Irving for her Austrian stage production and, significantly, for her vaudeville performances in Europe in the early 1930s. The sheet music and scores reveal that Anna May Wong planned to expand her annual circuits across the continent and to feature her singing voice as central to the act. May had already scored two of Wong's films, *Hai-Tang* and *The Road to Dishonour*, while Irving had worked with her at Ealing Studios and composed the music for Wong's 1929 production of *The Circle of Chalk*. Lambert was deeply infatuated with her, though she brushed him off the only time they met. He was noted for adapting the poetry of Li Po (Bai) to choral music. Lambert pioneered among British composers by incorporating jazz and blues into his work. Her possession of his sheet music indicates Wong considered using jazz rhythms in her routine in the 1930s, plans curtailed by the increasingly dangerous political situation in Europe. A fine example of her singing can be found in the 1939 film *Island of Last Men*.[5]

Anna May Wong's brief but ramifying encounter with Constant Lambert is but one of the rediscovered recollections about her from acquaintances. Bernardine Szold Fritz's time with Wong in Shanghai and Beijing is the subject of an essay by Susan Blumberg-Kason. Fritz met Wong first in Shanghai during the star's visit in 1936. Fritz had an active salon at which Wong met Austrian novelist Vicki Baum, Chinese intellectual Hu Shih, and British author Harold Acton, among others. Fritz helped Wong acquire fine silk for the cheongsam dresses the actor adored. The well-connected Fritz supplied Wong with letters of introduction to personages in Beijing.[6]

More attention is needed to Anna May Wong's family in China. This book remains the best source about her family, headed by matriarch Lee Shee (Woman Lee or Li, 李氏) and her son, Huang Dounan (黃門南, formal name Yuying, 黃預英). As with generations of ordinary women in a traditional patriarchal society, Lee Shee was nameless. Nonetheless, as the first wife, she held immense power in the Wong clan. Shirley Jennifer Lim argues in her 2019 biography, *Anna May Wong: Performing the Modern,* that the film Wong made of her trip demonstrates her Western modernity and alienation from China. While I showed earlier that Anna May Wong displayed tourist tendencies in China, the visit to Taishan had deeper meanings for her.[7]

In Chinese culture, the Taishan family, headed by Lee Shee, was paramount in the Huang hierarchy. As the first wife, Lee Shee held power over her son's destiny and the future earnings of Wong Sam Sing's second family, including Anna May Wong. Wong Sam Sing honored his obligations by sending money regularly to Lee Shee, financing their prosperity. Overseas remittances produced more income than the local agriculture industry and funded a railroad, the construction of better homes, and the expansion of education in Guangdong Province. Huang Dounan's father paid for his college education at Waseda University in Tokyo. One important factor in maintaining this familial arrangement was that Lee Shee and Lee Gon Toy, Wong Sam Sing's second wife and Anna May Wong's mother, never met, lessening any direct tensions between the two wives. Shortly after the accidental death of Lee Gon Toy, Wong Sam Sing traveled back to Taishan with his son, Richard, to rejoin his first wife after a forty-year separation. When Anna May Wong, making one of the most significant visits of her life, arrived in Taishan in 1937, Lee Shee's acceptance affirmed Anna's place in the first family. Lee Shee died in 1942 at the age of seventy-four. A large photograph of Wong Sam Sing (who died in 1949) hung in the family home near Taishan until very recently. [8]

Comparison of Anna May Wong's two families indicates the pernicious effects of American racism. Her American family, beset by hard occupational and educational racial ceilings, produced only two children in the next generation.

On the other hand, the three wives of Huang Dounan birthed four boys (one died as an infant) and four girls. There were seven boys and fourteen girls in the next generation. Among the great-grandchildren, eleven are now enrolled or have graduated from college. The daughter of Austin Yu, my informant about the Huang family, entered graduate studies in biotechnology at the University of Pennsylvania in 2022. Other members of the family settled in San Francisco. The two branches of the family have not met since 1937.[9]

Third, the gender-busting quality of her career is clearer. A character based on Wong appears briefly in four segments of *Hollywood*, Ian Brennan and Ryan Murphy's 2020 television miniseries. In the segments, Michelle Krusiec effectively portrays Wong's late-career bitterness, despair, and alcoholism as well as her later redemption and humble triumph. In an imaginative gesture in the final segment, Wong receives an Oscar for supporting actress in the fictive boundary-smashing film *Meg*. Other winners include a gay man, a gay and Black screenwriter, and a Black female lead. Augmenting the importance of these would-be accomplishments are scenes of Black and Chinese families listening to the ceremony on the radio and showing thrills at the announcements. For all Krusiec's talents, however, Wong's roles are ancillary to the main plot and never really mesh with the rest of the action.[10]

Fourth, younger Asian Americans now view Wong much more favorably. Yunah Hong's 2010 documentary, *Anna May Wong: In Her Own Words*, remains the best and most comprehensive cinematic examination of Wong. A brief 2020 documentary, *Searching for Anna May Wong*, directed by Denise Chan and Z. Eric Yang, takes a different tack, with interviews of young Asian American actors and the obstacles confronting their career ambitions. With cameos by Sandra Oh and James Hong, the film features several aspiring Asian American actors, most notably Natasha Tina Liu, who talk about fierce parental opposition to a career in drama and the sordid opportunities Hollywood pushed at them. The viewer is reminded of the opposition Anna May Wong faced from her parents and the casting couch relationships early in her career.[11]

Fifth, scholarly interest in Anna May Wong has grown in the decade since the second edition of his book. Some of it is innovative, others not so much. The better studies use Wong to create a new theoretical approach to the history of Chinese Americans. Yiman Wang essays Anna May Wong's linguistic cosmopolitanism by looking at some of her smaller pieces in which Wong recites Taishanese poetry, thanks audiences in multiple languages, and refutes white observers who wanted her to speak in broken English. Wang creatively argues that the MGM short film *Hollywood on Parade* gave Wong an opportunity to articulate her Chineseness, as a counter to arguments that her inadequacy in Mandarin made her less so. Wong was also able to make a small retort to the failure of MGM to cast her in the epic film *The Good Earth*.[12]

Shirley Jennifer Lim's 2019 book has useful comparisons of Wong with Josephine Baker and Lupe Velez. However, her poorly aimed arrow, that my book has too much detail and too little argument, flies by my ears. My book often comments on, among other topics later featured in Lim's book, Wong's importance in discussions of orientalism, international modernity, and celebrity. Lim acknowledges that my biography is helpful for following Chinese language commentary on Wong, but she neglects to mention that also included are critical views from Japan, England, France, Germany, Austria, Spain, Australia, and an assortment of other nations. Moreover, Lim is entitled to use and analyze the Wong correspondence with Carl Van Vechten and the interview that Walter Benjamin conducted with Wong in Berlin in 1928. Her use and analysis of these sources are interesting, but her suggestion that she discovered these sources, rather than learning about them from this book, is misleading at best.[13]

Scholarly comparisons of Anna May Wong cite Baker, Velez, and other Western stars. However, none have contrasted Wong's career with that of her Chinese contemporaries, Ruan Lingyu, Hu Die, or the tragic Wong Ying. The same is true for Asian American actors. Yunxiang Gao makes a fascinating distinction between Wong and Soo Yong, a Hawaiian-born contemporary actor, who was far better educated than Wong and more respected by the Chinese elite. Soo Yong had secondary roles in numerous big Hollywood productions from *Klondike Annie* with Mae West in 1933 to the Marlon Brando epic *Sayonara* in 1957. Soo Yong took Wong's place as the Auntie in the 1961 film *Flower Drum Song* when Wong was too ill to perform.[14]

Sixth, there is much more appreciation of Wong in the arts. Wong is now regarded as a fashion icon. Anna Sui and Vivienne Westwood, among many designers, cite Wong as a major inspiration for their designs. Critics have lauded her makeup and hairstyles. Actor Gemma Chan caused a stir at the 2021

Metropolitan Museum of Art's annual gala in New York by appearing in a Prabal Gurung–designed gown that was a tribute to the Travis Banton Triple Dragon dress worn by Anna May Wong in the 1934 film *Limehouse Blues*. Chan's hairstyle at the Gala recalled Wong's character in the 1924 film *The Thief of Bagdad*. Curators and collectors have paid increasing attention and cash outlay to acquire fashion photography featuring Wong by Edward Steichen, Man Ray, and Edward Hurrell.[15]

Wong's fashion style was evident in the epic 2015 Metropolitan Museum of Art exhibition *China: Through the Looking Glass*, in which Banton's Triple Dragon dress played a prominent role. Inspired, or perhaps dismayed, by the exhibit is Anne Anlin Cheng's impressive and insightful essay "Shine: On Race, Glamour, and the Modern." Cheng argues for the convergence of celebrity and allure with race. Cheng focuses on Wong's magnetic performance in *Piccadilly* (1929) as Shosho, a Cinderella character rescued from a restaurant scullery by its owner, who is then put on stage in a costume that emphasizes her "golden, palleted body" in blinding, eroticized light. Cheng identifies *Piccadilly* as the sole film in Wong's career that foregrounds her ascent to celebrity status. Wong clearly identifies with the main character, Shosho, even to the point of signing her real name. In a remarkable insight, Cheng argues that Wong's "shine" both attracts and deflects the male gaze. Anticipating a method Wong used extensively in 1930s Europe, Cheng says her dance in *Piccadilly* represents a choreographed soliloquy, a form of feminist ornamentation. Shosho's costume consists of stylistic fragments of Chinese, Korean, Vietnamese, Thai, and Indonesian references, much as Wong's career coalesced many Asian nationalities. Light and costume bring together the powerful tensions of Wong's iron rod of ambition and celebrity with the harsh, unyielding racism of her profession and times.[16]

Wong is now the inspiration for poems, short stories, and novels. Poet Sally Wen Mao makes Anna May Wong central to her work. In a series of poems initiated in the *Missouri Review* in 2015 and later collected in her 2019 book, *Oculus*, Mao creatively recovers Wong's early career, connects her with Josephine Baker, and then brings her into the present in the poem "Anna May Wong Makes Cameos." In the section implanting Wong into Gong Li's character in the 2005 film *Memoirs of a Geisha*, Mao writes, "I'm Gong Li's evil apprentice geisha. . . . Dew drips down my forehead, my jewels, in the confusion, I perish, of course."

Mao's use of this film in which the great Chinese star Li plays a Japanese geisha recalls how Wong's casting generalized Asians rather than specifying nationality. It's also a play on Wong's cinematic sexuality as a "China doll," a woman of pleasure who, having crossed boundaries, must die, loveless and unwanted, at the end of the film. Peter Ho Davies's 2016 novel, *The Fortunes*, uses Anna May Wong as a central character to express the Chinese American experience, as does Amanda Lee Koe in her 2019 novel, *Delayed Rays of a Star*.[17]

Finally, Anna May Wong's principal legacy is her perseverance over a five-decade Hollywood acting career. She had to endure terrible, racist casting, knowing that the best parts were reserved for white women made up as "yellow faces." Occasionally yellowface casting arises even today. Yet the pressing questions, evident anytime that Asian American actors speak, are whether the profiled casting suffered by Anna May Wong still exists and whether there are limits on Asian casting today. Veteran actors such as James Hong, who has more than 450 film credits, have far surpassed Wong's lifetime exposure. Since the 2018 success of the film *Crazy Rich Asians*, a younger, highly visible generation of Asian American actors, such as Constance Wu, Simi Liu, Awkwafina, and Jimmy O. Yang, has emerged. Even so, of the one hundred US films with the highest box office earnings in 2021, only *Eternals*, with Gemma Chan, and *Raya and the Last Dragon*, with Kelly Marie Tran, feature actors of Asian descent. They are among just eleven women of color starring in the top one hundred films. The worry is that, as with Black American actors, an elite emerges without a larger cadre of character actors who get steady work in film, television, and the Internet. Moreover, of the roughly twenty thousand working screen actors today, about 6 percent are Asian. Many of them gain only bit parts and smaller pay, a problem that Wong faced in the 1920s. As I have argued earlier, only political pressure will ensure Asian American representation in visual media. The efforts of Oh, Chan, Krusiec, and others will push political pressure for that representation, thereby fulfilling Anna May Wong's mission.[18]

In my travels in China over the past twenty years, I have found that younger women in particular are fascinated by her historical presence and inspired by her style. Anna May Wong is very much alive in the present everywhere and doubtless will be in the future.

Acknowledgments

I first encountered the mystique of Anna May Wong on Cecil Court off Charing Cross Road in London in the fall of 1999. There, I noticed in a bookstore window an autographed photograph for sale of a beautiful woman. Fascinated, I rushed into the shop and bought the framed image. It was expensive, and I wondered what I was doing. After checking capsule biographies of Anna May Wong on the Internet, I grew more engrossed. Soon I found myself buying other pictures and documents of her on eBay, the Internet auction house. Within weeks, interest turned into fixation. Soon after, Deborah Gershenowitz, my editor at Palgrave, Global Publishing at St. Martin's Press, focused my obsession by signing me to a contract with a deadline for this biography.

Following Anna May Wong through her film and stage career and tracing her travels around the world indebted me to many people and institutions around the world. In the People's Republic of China, I owe a great deal to scholars and friends. Professor Zhang Juguo of Nankai University spent many hours with me in the Nankai University Library and at the Tianjin Municipal Library. There I owe great thanks to the courtesies shown to me in the Department of Tianjin Historical Documents, Tianjin Library. Gao Chunchang of Ludong University traveled with me to Shanghai to sift through hundreds of Chinese movie magazines at the Shanghai Municipal Library. I benefited from the friendship and help of Shen Yulu of Beijing Foreign Languages University, who plowed through innumerable film magazines with me at the China Film Institute; the staff there was very helpful. Zhang Aimin of Eastern China Normal University spent many hours working for me at libraries in Nanjing and Shanghai. I am especially grateful to Professor Li Jianming of Nankai University for his skillful calligraphy for the dedication page. Xu Xiaohong of Beijing Foreign Affairs College was a wonderful friend and listener about Huang Liushuang, as Anna May is named in China. Wu Jinping of Jinan University, Guangzhou, China, along with his student Dai Fan, found valuable materials with me at the Guangzhou Provincial Library. Wu Jinping arranged for a memorable visit to Taishan City and to the village of Chang On, the ancestral home of Anna May Wong's father. Professor Mei Weiqiang of Wuyi University traveled with me to Chang On and acted as expert interpreter from the Taishan dialect to Mandarin and English. The party secretary for Chang On, Mr. Huang Xinyi, generously provided introductions to the village residents. I learned much about Anna May Wong's 1936 visit to Chang On from Cai Yongnian, Tan Haiqiong, and Huang Gaodian. The village genealogist Huang Shijin was extremely helpful. Also of great assistance were Raymond and Kathleen Lee of Hong Kong.

I am very grateful for the kindness and friendship bestowed upon me by the descendants of Huang Dounan, Anna May Wong's half-brother. I am grateful to Huang Xinyi and Luo Xinqiong for their hospitality in the ancestral house of Huang Liu Tsong. In Guangzhou, the family of the late Yu Paisui and Huang Cuixiang, the daughter of Huang Dounan, was especially helpful and gracious. In particular, Anna May's grand-niece, Yu Jinyan, and her husband, Su Xionghui, helped me gain access to many rare images of the Chinese family of Anna May Wong. Now this couple have become my dear friends.

Her American relative unfortunately did not match the exceptional courtesies shown to me by the Chinese side of Anna May Wong's family. As he did with other researchers, Richard Wong obdurately refused to assist this project in any way. It is troubling when a relative who benefited greatly from Anna May Wong's fame kept significant parts of her life locked away from the world.

His was the only such obstacle. Everywhere else, I received gracious assistance. In Tokyo, Seiko Kihira of the International Christian University helped me with great enthusiasm in finding Japanese stories and pictures of Anna May Wong. Sayaka Kosubuchi of Tsuda University traveled with me to Waseda University to read magazines. I owe much to the archivists at the Shochiku Film Library and to their counterparts at Waseda University's film collection. In Tokyo, Hunter, Suzanne, and Mary Catherine Hale provided a wandering scholar with a roof, good food, and conversation.

In Vienna, Alexandra Ganser proved to be immensely helpful as a researcher, contact, and friend. Alexandra became deeply involved in this project and came up with innumerable valuable leads from German and Austrian sources. I appreciate her enthusiasm and generosity, and her help on this project has been immeasurable. Dr. Gerda Barth of the Wiener Stadtund Landesbibliothek located several significant film posters. Heike Fernandez of the University of Maryland-Heidelberg shared her immense energy and contacts to help on this project. I thank Gunther Lenz of the Free University of Berlin and the late Dr. Kurt Mayer of the University of Vienna for their help. In London, I owe much to the archivists at the British Film Institute and the British Library. In Paris, I profited greatly from the assistance of the archivists at the Bibliotheque du Film.

I owe many thanks to the patient staff at the Billy Rose Theater Collection of the New York Public Library and to the Rare Book Room staff at Columbia University. Grants from the Faculty Research Council of Colgate University enabled me to conduct much of the archival work for this book and to pay permission fees. I am also indebted to Ann Ackerson and the rest of the Interlibrary Loan staff at Case Library at Colgate. I owe much to Ned Comstock, archivist of the film collection at the University of Southern California, and to the generous and patient staff at the Herrick Library at the Academy of Motion Picture Arts and Sciences. Charles Silver of the Museum of Modern Art, Mimi Brody of the UCLA Film Archives, and Theresa Schwartzman of UCLA were of great assistance in catching flaws.

I am deeply grateful to Michael Duckworth of Hong Kong University Press for commissioning the second edition. Let me raise a glass to Paul French, who brought Michael and me together. Thanks as well go to Jessica Wang of Hong Kong University Press and Alvin Tse for their skillful and patient copyediting.

Yunah Hong, an independent filmmaker in New York City, spent many hours talking to me about Anna May Wong, read several drafts, and generously shared with me the fruits of her own research. She has now created an expert documentary about Anna May. The manuscript archivists at the New York Historical Society were of great assistance.

I presented chapter five of this work at the American Historical Association's 2003 meeting in Chicago. I am grateful to Steve Rachman and Victor Jew of Michigan State and Tina Klein of the Massachusetts Institute of Technology for their valuable suggestions at this panel.

Several other friends in the United States graciously hunted down leads. Barry Maxwell of Cornell University told me of Walter Benjamin's article on Anna May.

Mary Lynn Weiss of the College of William & Mary found numerous articles in French archives and deserves great thanks. Bruce Kellner of the Carl Van Vechten estate was generous with time and information. Helen Harrison of the Pollock-Krasner House alerted me to the artist Ray Johnson's interest in Anna May. Colleagues who encouraged me and lent hands in other ways include Jill Harsin, Ray Douglas, Al Brown, Robert Nemes, Jing Wang, Yunte Huang, Peter Kwong, Helen Zia, and Wendy Wall. Eric Allini-Pisano and Ross Ferlito aided with rapid, precise translations. I am grateful to Poshek Fu and Gavin Lambert for their valuable readings of a late draft. Warren Wheeler made numerous prints of rare images for me. Lin Zeng, Colgate Class of 2003, was my invaluable student research assistant. Carolyn Lane, Colgate Class of 2003, helped with several expert translations from the French. Enormous thanks are due to my agents, Andrea Cavallaro and Elise Capron, for their able handling of this book on numerous occasions. Thanks as well to Gemma Chan for believing that this book and Anna May Wong's story might be translated into a film. Let me offer particular thanks to Jerome Pohlen, senior editor at Chicago Review Press, for arranging for this third edition of the book. Thanks as well to Frances Giguette, for her expert copyediting of the new preface, as well as the rest of the team at Chicago Review Press.

Finally, much appreciation is owed to my family. Carl Prince, my mentor, is a constant and highly valued supporter. I am continually inspired and invigorated by memories of the love and sound advice I received from my deceased parents, the Reverend Graham R. and Elsie Russell Hodges. I wish to thank my in-laws, the late Gao Zhen, Du Xiuhua, and Gao Yunpeng of Lanqi Village, Wu Meng District, Inner Mongolia, People's Republic of China for their readings of Anna May's palm. My wife, Gao Yunxiang, deserves the deepest appreciation. As she completed her dissertation in modern Chinese history at the University of Iowa and is a full professor of history at Ryerson University, Gao Yunxiang listened patiently to my ideas about this book and provided good cheer at all times. She read several drafts and helped me avoid numerous gaffes. Her comments on Anna May Wong's hairstyles, dress, dance, and other Chinese customs greatly enhanced this book. She alerted me to a number of Chinese sources unavailable earlier. Best of all, she is my partner, now and in the future. Since the first publication of this book, she and I have been blessed by twin sons, Graham Zhen and Russell Du Gao-Hodges, who have become inspirations for my life. I dedicate this book to her.

Introduction

Anna May Wong (1905–1961) remains the premier Asian American actress. In part this distinction stems from the historical rarity of Asian actors in American cinema and theater, yet her singularity derives primarily from her laudable acting in more than fifty movies, during a career that ranged from 1919 to 1961, a record of achievement that is unmatched and likely to remain so in the foreseeable future. During her time, Anna May Wong had significant roles in *The Thief of Bagdad* (1924), *Peter Pan* (1924), *Piccadilly* (1929), and *Shanghai Express* (1932), films that are acknowledged classics. Her feature debut in *The Toll of the Sea* (1922) at the age of seventeen, in the first Technicolor film, made her famous throughout the world. Throughout her career, Anna May Wong established a reputation for a high level of professionalism, personal grace and charm, and an unmatched film presence. No viewer could ignore Anna May when she appeared on screen. Her popularity was so widespread that she frequently graced the pages of movie magazines in America, Europe, Australia, South America, China, and Japan.

Anna May Wong meant many things to different people. During her career, her fame, abetted by the paucity of other Chinese in Euro-American capitals, gave her symbolic power as a Chinese woman. To her fans and film critics in the United States, Europe, and much of the rest of the world she personified Chinese womanhood. This supranational image angered Nationalist Chinese leaders, who regarded her as a puppet of Hollywood. Her family considered her at varying points a devoted daughter, a breadwinner, or a disgrace. Her American audience felt sympathy when she explained why she could never marry, even as they accepted loneliness and death as her cinematic fate. During her life and in memory, an underground audience of gay people regarded her as one of their own, even if her public image was that of the disappointed woman doomed never to marry. She was considered reliable and friendly by her costars and by journalists, and she was accepted in the top ranks of society in all the world capitals. Her strength in dealing with harsh criticism alone merits admiration.

Her durability and professionalism meant that Anna May outlasted numerous other actresses from her era, including Betty Bronson, Colleen Moore, Renée Adorée, Fay Wray, Louise Brooks, and Luise Rainer. Despite her achievements, Anna May Wong has become what Maxine Hong Kingston refers to as a "No Name Woman." Like her fictional counterpart, Anna May remained unmentionable. Although Anna May is included in the walk of fame on Hollywood Boulevard and is one of four actresses commemorated in a cluster of statues located at Hollywood Boulevard and La Brea in Los Angeles, there is little other coverage of her career. She is left out of standard books on women of silent film and omitted in memoirs and biographies of better-known actors. When she is recalled, Anna May is burdened by a reputation as someone willing to undertake roles in movies degrading to her people. Such was her status with the Nationalist and Communist parties in China, a perception then inherited by the political and artistic Left in the United States and among Chinese Americans generally. Li Lili, a Chinese movie star from the 1930s, when asked early in the twenty-first century about Anna May, retorted: "Fame and achievement are not the same thing." In the United States, Chinese American writers seldom insert Anna May into their novels, poems, and plays. She is controversial among scholars. When I first mentioned this book to a senior Asian American scholar, he angrily responded: "Why do you want to work on her? She was a Dragon Lady. A China Doll! She always died or committed suicide." The pain of her memory has poisoned her American family, who refuse access to her papers because they are ashamed of her.[1]

Anna May's descent into oblivion may seem necessary to a people anxious to forget how American cinema denigrated their culture. Anna May's life intersected with the period of the Chinese Exclusion Act, when Chinese Americans were few and badly oppressed by racism. Films with an Orientalist theme were common in early American features and invariably included an undercurrent of fear of interracial sex. For that reason, Anna May Wong and Sessue Hayakawa, the Japanese male actor, appear as sexually inviting to their white cinematic counterparts, a quality that always condemned such Asian characters to death by the end of the movie. Film codes forbade kissing between the races, severely limiting Anna May's career, since it meant she could not secure lead roles.

The temptation is to dismiss Anna May Wong as a product of American Orientalism. After all, she commonly signed her publicity photos, "Orientally yours." Her career intersected with the intellectual creation of the "Oriental" at the research institutes of the University of Chicago. Studies of the concepts of "Oriental" and "Orientalism" have been of immense interest to scholars in the past thirty years. In his powerfully influential treatise on Orientalism, Edward Said has described it as a combination of academic, political, and institutional power created first in Europe, and appearing more recently in the United States. Though Said has little to say about theater or film, his argument can certainly be extended to those arts. In his words, Orientalism justified the hegemony Western powers imposed upon the people of the East—"dealing with it by making state-ments about it, authorizing views of it, describing it, teaching it, settling it, ruling over it, in short . . . dominating, restructuring, and having authority over the Orient." Said has had specific influence on Jonathan D. Spence, a preeminent scholar of China, who has demonstrated how the West has long revealed singular attitudes about the Middle Kingdom in its literature. The recent remodeling and expansion of Said's "Orientalism" into the concept of globalism by Michael Hardt and Antonio Negri fit well into the history of the worldwide twentieth-century hegemony of Hollywood, Anna May Wong's chosen world. American films have dominated the world market since the early 1920s and, accordingly, Anna May Wong's personification of the Asian American woman had global reach, a fact angrily resented by Chinese nationalists, who disliked how Hollywood used Anna May Wong to represent the Chinese woman. Such controversies affected conceptions of gender in the movies. In Hollywood, males working as produc-ers, directors, casting agents, and cinematographers created Anna May Wong as the embodiment of the cinematic Chinese woman. As Laura Mulvey has argued, filmmakers constructed a "male gaze" that presented their own vision of the female body. Considered together, these methods of analysis reduce Anna May's life and career to that of a caricature of the Chinese woman who was the willing pawn of powerful men and nations. In so doing, such critics emulate the harsh denunciations made against Anna May during her lifetime. Just one example may suffice here: when Anna May traveled to Hong Kong in 1936, an angry demon-strator shouted that she was "the puppet that disgraces China."[2]

When she heard such condemnations, Anna May's face reddened and tears welled in her eyes. She was caught between caustic denunciations of her career and the hegemonic power of Orientalism. As a system, Orientalism had sig-nificant impact upon Anna May. American and Californian state laws curtailed her ability to marry a man of her choosing and regulated her movements in and out of the United States. As noted, motion pictures codes forbade her to kiss a westerner on screen and limited her to supporting roles. Local discrimination in housing and work restricted her opportunities and those of her family and friends. In childhood and as an adult, she felt personally the pangs of racial hos-tility. Though Anna May Wong suffered these insults and legal prejudices bravely, she occasionally spoke out defiantly and otherwise seethed inside. Several times her internalizing of discrimination made her physically ill. Although racism victimized Anna May, that mistreatment was not the whole story. Her courage, grace, and intelligence propelled her out in the world in search of love, career satisfaction, and happiness. She became a unique actor whose transnational life and career crossed political, racial, and sexual borders.[3]

The first task of this book, of course, is to rediscover her film career. Copies of about half of the films in which she appeared no longer exist, but fortunately most films with her in major roles are still available. As a star of the first rank, she was ubiquitous in film magazines around the world. Film magazines of the era were often the sole means by which fans could learn about their favorite stars. Through this glossy medium, Anna May and her story became standard fare for eager readers from the United States to Russia, from Sweden to Brazil and throughout the East. I rely on movie magazines to supply the reviews and arti-cles from many countries around the globe to give a nuanced understanding of her transnational career. In the pages that follow, I show how critics from many nations regarded her films differently. Their reaction to her films simultaneously elevated comprehension of her art while consigning the meaning of her career to Orientalism. Anna May added a personal quality to her celluloid and print repu-tation by visiting her fans throughout the world. Invariably her jaunts were of her own design rather than the efforts of the studio publicity machines. Star tours around the world were common, as were global reputations. Charlie Chaplin,

Douglas Fairbanks Sr., Mary Pickford, and Greta Garbo were popular every-where. Anna May was of their stature, but unlike the others, racial and nationalist politics colored her reputation wherever she went. Because of her unique fame as an "exotic" Chinese actress, Anna May caused controversy. She frequently intro-duced Chinese culture and identity to world societies whose contact with actual Chinese people was minimal.

Anna May also had much to say about her films and spoke freely about the casting dilemmas she faced. She wrote frequently about her unique position and expanded her comments regarding politics, fashion, career counseling, and her ceaseless anger at the racial codes that limited her success. Famous for her beauty and grace more than for the discouraging roles she endured, Anna May was the global representative of modern, articulate Chinese womanhood. As a star during the glory years of Hollywood's impact on American and world audi-ences, she reached out to her audiences in numerous ways. Independent of the studio wishes, she expanded her career to the stage and, later, to political action during World War II.

In books and articles published since the initial appearance of this biography, students of Anna May's life and career have accentuated her modernity, strived to complicate her symbol as Orientalist movie star, and associated her with the phenomenon of the modern girl. Early in her career, Anna May clearly identi-fied herself as a flapper through her dress, speech, love of cars, cigarettes, and personal independence. She became, as I note in this book, a model for young Chinese women. At the same time, Anna May struggled and then came to value her family and its traditions. China, as this book shows, became the lodestar for her values and aspirations. While Anna May came from an ordinary background, her multiple successes demonstrate her extraordinary drive and self-awareness as public vision of the Chinese woman. As I argue extensively in this book, Anna May was much more than a "yellow yellow face," as one recent scholar has described her.[4]

Anna May Wong was able to improve upon her film career by introducing Chinese culture in ways that often the director or screenwriter would not under-stand. She expressed Chinese traditions through her hairstyles, clothing, body movements, and language. Her contemporaries considered Anna May Wong to be among the world's best-dressed women, and she assembled a huge collection of Chinese gowns, which she often used in her films. By the late 1930s, when American attitudes about China had improved, Anna May was able to present positive roles of Chinese women on screen. During World War II, she made patriotic movies and visited Allied troops around the United States and Canada.

Much of her career is maligned or poorly understood as cinematic Orientalism. In this book, I contend that this view limits Anna May Wong to a superficial caricature. As a scholar of African American history, I am suspicious of theories that impose conceptions of power upon creative people. A Chinese expression acknowledges that every person has a thousand faces. Anna May's cinematic and personal reputations translated differently among the world's myriad nationalities.

A second task of this book is to uncover the breadth and depth of Anna May Wong's life. Her childhood was troubled, as she was caught between the traditional world of her home and the nasty racism of white Los Angeles. She found respite from her dilemma in motion pictures, a new cultural form created in the streets where she walked every day. After her debut in the movies, she became the "Chinese flapper," an ultra-modern girl who had rejected the ways of her parents. As Sucheng Chan has pointed out, second-generation Chinese American children were prone to such rebellion.[5] Anna May Wong was actually third-generation, but her parents' deep sense of tradition limited the acculturation she gained at home. Later, she tired of being a flapper and began a lifetime investigation of her roots. At first she merely longed to travel to China, then, after a sojourn in Europe, she adapted the styles of the famed Peking Opera. Her nine-month visit to China in 1936 was one of the highlights of her life. She returned fully identified with China and exerted herself constantly in film and philanthropic actions to improve the image of China in the United States and to raise contributions for China Relief efforts and the struggle against Japanese imperialism in World War II. The Cold War cut her off from China and, of necessity, she had to create the Chinese American personality that she used until her death in 1961.

Anna May Wong was expert in self-promotion and wrote articles in fan magazines and newspapers on significant topics including interracial love, Hollywood careers, and Japanese aggression. She never married, and so she took it upon herself to explain to the people of the world the dilemmas of a Chinese American artist during a time when her chances for love were limited by prejudice and demography. Anna May Wong was always courteous to newspaper writers, but she also gave time to such distinguished intellectuals as Walter Benjamin, who interviewed her in 1928. Anna May could converse as an equal with Benjamin and a host of other powerful intellects, regardless of setting. To use a term popular in Asian American studies these days, she was a transnational, who went from continent to continent in search of fulfillment.[6]

Significant to Anna May Wong's life were her relations with her family and with the close friends she accumulated over the decades. She actually had two families. One, the issue of her father's first marriage in China, was less known to her. Their story, however, provides a useful counterpart to her American kin. In the United States her father, Wong Sam Sing, and his second wife, Lee Gon Toy, had eight children, seven of whom survived into adulthood. Living in a country of hostile political and social institutions, family was critically important to Chinese Americans. As in any family, Anna May's relations with her parents and siblings were not always smooth. In fact, her older sister Lulu told one researcher in the 1990s that the family was ashamed of her. But as Lisa See has shown about her own family, which was friendly with the Wongs, such clan histories, told over many decades, can reveal much about the unfolding of Chinese American history.[7]

Anna May Wong's social world was not limited to her family. Her friends are also a substantial and informative part of this book. For example, she sustained a four-decade friendship with Carl Van Vechten and his wife, Fania Marinoff, which is preserved in a rich cache of personal letters. Their correspondence reveals Anna May's charm, humor, and appreciation for life. She befriended people everywhere and tried to maintain those contacts over her life. Because of racial and class restrictions, Anna May never married. She did conduct a series of long-term affairs by which she took what happiness the world would allow. She carried the pleasures and memories of her loves always in her heart and used these experiences in her films and writings.

These are the large themes of this book. I have divided Anna May Wong's story into seven chapters, with her film career as an organizing device. The first chapter covers her childhood and the early life of her parents in late nineteenth-century California until her debut as an extra in Nazimova's movie, *The Red Lantern*, in 1919. The second chapter recounts her early years struggling for stardom in 1920s Hollywood. Frustrated by the lack of promotion and angered by her roles, Anna May moved to Europe for three years, as I detail in chapter three. She came back to the States a star, lauded by critics and loved by fans all over Europe. As chapter four narrates, Anna May Wong spent the first years of the 1930s seeking to maintain her stardom in Hollywood but searching for independence by annual trips to Europe, where she made films and created her own stage show. In between appearances, she enjoyed the best of Paris, London, Berlin, and the rest of Europe until political unrest and war forced her to stop. In 1936, driven by personal desire and pushed by the ugly rejection by MGM of her pursuit of the lead role in *The Good Earth*, Anna May Wong made the hegira of her life to China. This remarkable return to her roots is the story of chapter five. In the years after her return in late 1936, Anna May made a series of remarkable films and, motivated by her China trip, devoted huge chunks of time and energy to China Relief and support of the Sino-American alliance in World War II. Sadly, what worked for Marlene Dietrich on the European front did not pay off in Anna May's career. The last, seventh chapter tells of her years battling obscurity, illness, and prejudice to buttress a dignified semi-retirement using her sage investments, diligence, and charm. An epilogue records how Anna May Wong's influence extends into the present.

Upon finishing this book, I hope the reader will discover Anna May Wong's saga to be as fascinating and courageous as I have found it to be in my years of research. Anna May Wong's life is testament to the uplifting example of the individual's will and strength against hegemonic powers, whether political, intellectual, or personal, that seek to oppress a misunderstood or forgotten creativity.

List of Illustrations

1. The Wong Family, late 1920s. Courtesy of China Film Archives, Beijing, People's Republic of China.
2. Lee Gon Toy, Anna May, Lulu, and Wong Sam Sing in traditional garb, ca. 1907. Courtesy of China Film Archives, Beijing, People's Republic of China.
3. Lee Gon Toy, undated. Courtesy of the Huang Family, Chang On Village, Guangzhou, Guangdong Province, People's Republic of China.
4. Wong Sam Sing, undated charcoal drawing, Chang On Village, ca. 1890. Courtesy of the Huang Family, Chang On Village, Guangzhou, Guandong Province, People's Republic of China.
5. Lee Shee, first wife of Wong Sam Sing, undated photograph, Chang On Village, ca. 1890. Courtesy of the Huang Family, Chang On Village, Guangzhou, Guangdong Province, People's Republic of China.
6. Huang Dounan, son of Wong Sam Sing and Lee Shee, and half-brother of Anna May Wong, ca. 1922 during student years at Waseda University, Tokyo. Courtesy of the Huang Family, Chang On Village, Guangzhou, Guangdong Province, People's Republic of China.
7. Early image of Anna May from *Dinty*, 1921. Photograph taken by James Wong Howe, the great Chinese American cinematographer. Courtesy of the Wisconsin Center for Film and Theater Research, Madison, Wisconsin.
8. Lon Chaney and Anna May in *Bits of Life*, 1921. Here Chaney introduces Anna May to the tortures she will commonly receive in her roles. Collection of the Author.

One
Childhood

By birth, Anna May Wong was a third-generation Californian, with family roots that traced back to the first years of Chinese arrivals in the Gold Rush years. Both sets of her grandparents arrived in California by 1855. Between that date and Anna May's birth in 1905, the Chinese in California went from initial acceptance to attempted exclusion in the 1880s to violent racial hostility at the close of the century. These historical circumstances shaped her life. Although she was a native Californian with roots as deep as any white person's, Anna May Wong faced harsh social prejudice and discriminatory laws. Her strong sense of family, nationality, and purpose helped her surpass racial oppression.

Anna May Wong's life began on January 3, 1905 at 351 Flower Street, a few blocks away from Los Angeles's Chinatown. Her father, Wong Sam Sing (his nickname was Liangren), had married her mother, Lee Gon Toy, in a Chinese ceremony in San Francisco on September 9, 1901. Wong Sam Sing and Lee Gon Toy had their first home and workplace at the Wong Laundry on 117 Marchessault Street in Chinatown. There, Lee Gon Toy gave birth to their first child, a daughter, Lew Ying (Lulu Huang), on December 21, 1902. The birth of a girl upset Wong Sam Sing so much that he did not come home for days. Domestic aspirations forced him eventually to move his small family to 351 Flower Street, where he founded the Sam Kee Laundry. Flower Street was an integrated block slightly outside of Chinatown. The family moved there right before the birth of their second daughter, Huang Liu Tsong, whom they called Anna May. The family name meant *yellow*; Tsong meant *frost* while Liu translated into *willow*. After Anna May arrived, the mother and two girls promptly caught the measles, adding to Wong Sam Sing's misery over the lack of a son.[1]

1

* * *

Wong Sam Sing belonged to a generation of Chinese men who had undergone much hardship in America. As work dried up in the gold mines and after the transcontinental railroad project was completed, Chinese men faced rising tides of violent reaction from white laborers. In the early years, Chinese could be found in small towns all over the West as workers in laundries and restaurants and on truck farms. As anti-Chinese violence erupted after the American Civil War, Wong Sam Sing and his generation fled into the larger cities, creating Chinatowns. These Chinatowns were unique to the United States in that residents were forced into cramped, decaying housing within narrow geographic borders. There they attempted to fend off the racism of the ruling race through reliance on traditional lifestyles and domination of property and local industries.

National political developments further diminished the status of the Chinese in America. After the Civil War, the marginal status of the Chinese paralleled the social and political decline of prestige of African Americans. In a process that one scholar calls the "negroization" of the Chinese, these once-valued laborers faced worsening legal, occupational, and social prejudice. Drawing on the US Supreme Court's controversial Dred Scott Decision in 1857, American nativists worked hard to ensure that the Chinese did not gain citizenship and called for their exclusion. Among the newer fears was "amalgamation," a loaded nineteenth-century term for mixed marriages. Such unions between whites and Blacks were considered unthinkable since the 1830s; after the Civil War, racists extended these anxieties to the Chinese. As Wong Sam Sing matured, he faced a larger society that increasingly ostracized him. He could scarcely be blamed if he regarded contacts with whites warily.[2]

Wong Sam Sing's travels back and forth across the Pacific identify him as a member of a new style of Chinese: the sojourner. As Wang Gungwu relates, Chinese people had migrated out of the Middle Kingdom before, but not in such large numbers. Until the large-scale migration to the Americas, never before had Chinese labor moved into host societies that regarded themselves as economically and technologically superior. Transit to the United States meant that Chinese sojourners now entered a working class, equally disadvantaged and untutored, that considered itself racially and culturally superior to the Asian arrivals. As a result, Chinese sojourners in the United States traveled from place to place in a vain search for a receptive community. Wong Sam Sing found his in Los Angeles. On the Pacific Ocean or around the United States, sojourners of his generation learned to accept a transient way of life. While his new American society, especially the laboring class, grew more hostile to sojourners such as Wong Sam Sing, his Chinese culture grew closer, despite the separation of the Pacific Ocean. Contact with "home" through diplomatic channels, newspapers, banks, and frequent visitors kept China foremost in his mind.[3]

Wong Sam Sing's Chinese ideals were his bulwark in a hostile world. Chinese sojourners in the United States had faced sharp discrimination since the 1870s. A series of laws starting with the Burlingame Treaty in 1868, through the Page Law of 1875, and culminating in the Chinese Exclusion Act of 1882 sharply curtailed the migration of Chinese men to the United States. Legislation also blocked the arrival of most Chinese men identified by the catchall identification of laborer, and barred most Chinese females on a presumptive belief that they were prostitutes. Families were disrupted because, unless the husband was American born, laws banned the immigration of wives. The US Congress amplified these laws over the next twenty years in a series of measures that specifically curtailed the rights of Chinese Americans. Such discriminatory laws made the Chinese the only ethnic group in the history of the United States to suffer restrictions aimed directly at them.[4]

Labor competition and legal restraints were not the only reasons for the racist violence that drove Chinese Americans into refuge in large cities. The last decades of the nineteenth century saw the rise of an American literary Orientalism. While such noted authors as Mark Twain and Bret Harte denied that their stories and poems were malevolent attacks on Chinese Americans, others construed their message as anti-Chinese. From their works emerged such stereotypical Chinese as Ah Sing, the expert card cheat, or Ah Song Hi, an entrepreneurial immigrant who is attacked by the police. Both writers attempted to re-create a pidgin or commercial English language that they heard from Chinese Americans. By the early 1890s, Harte and Twain had, however inadvertently, helped create a genre known as "Chinatown fiction," which portrayed Chinese Americans as insular, poorly acculturated, and often doltish. Whereas the two writers seemed to admire Chinese American talents, Jonathan Spence notes, their curious blending of stereotypes, myths, and self-fulfillment was matched with language filled with pure racial hostility. In one of Harte's plays, for example, Ah Sing is described as "slant eyed son of the yellow jaunders," a "sinful old sluice robber," a "jabbering idiot," and a "moral cancer." By the hands of other writers and during worsening political times came even nastier racial literature that relentlessly portrayed Chinese men as schemers—dangerous, unreliable, and vicious. In the aftermath of the Boxer Rebellion came a series of books that informed white American readers that the Chinese were a genuine threat to civilization. The novels of Sax Rohmer in the early twentieth century told his audience that even a brilliant Chinese such as his character Fu Manchu was evil, genetically incapable of any good. These stereotypes quickly translated into the new medium of film.[5]

The bulk of those films were made within a few blocks of Anna May's birthplace. Chinatown, Los Angeles, was a relatively recent development. The few Chinese who lived there before the 1880s had faced significant hazards. A major riot and massacre against them occurred in 1871; there were severe incidents of arson in 1886 and 1887. Despite these aggravated assaults, Chinese immigrants held a virtual monopoly on vegetable selling in Los Angeles. When the city of Los Angeles tried to tax them out of existence in 1878, the peddlers went on strike and forced the government to back down. Their early heroism helped such other businesses as laundries, restaurants, and herbalist shops to survive and prosper.[6]

In 1900, Los Angeles's Chinatown was a dense settlement of 2,111 souls, 90 percent of them male. Street peddlers crowded the sidewalks. Lo Sang, as locals called it, was architecturally composed of American brick and Mexican adobe buildings and Chinese mercantile and joss houses, and it appeared to outsiders as dirty and overrun with vermin. The nearby gas plant and railroad yards polluted the air, and on occasion the Los Angeles River overflowed through its streets. Because the neighborhood was constructed on private property, there were few such amenities as sewers, indoor toilets, paved streets, or gaslights.[7]

* * *

The Wong family's move to the periphery of Chinatown was not unusual. Lo Sang's squalid ambience had pushed out other ambitious Chinese families. The Asian population of Los Angeles, while segregated, was not as isolated as the

African American or Mexican. The neighborhood was mixed, with Germans, Irish, and Japanese families sprinkled throughout. Other families preceded the Wong clan's removal to the neighborhood's outskirts. Among their friends were the See family, who founded their dynasty of shops just outside Lo Sang on First Street, between Spring and Broadway. Despite the separation of a few blocks, Chinatown remained important for the Wongs. Within two years of Anna May's birth, her family moved briefly back to Chinatown and resided at 21 Private Alley. The Wongs lived there until 1910, when they moved back to the margins of Chinatown at 241 North Figueroa, where they would stay until 1934. This new district was multicultural; the Wongs were the only Chinese on a block composed primarily of Mexican and Eastern European families. Unlike the "bachelor" society found living in Chinatown, the Wong children, though they lived in a traditional home, came into contact daily with other peoples. Her childhood instilled in Anna May an awareness of, if not always a comfort with, a diverse population. In addition, North Figueroa was close to but separated geographically from Chinatown. To get to Chinatown, Anna May and Lulu had to walk several blocks down Temple Street, across North Main Street and Los Angeles Street to the crowded Chinese neighborhood. Prostitutes of all nationalities strolled the streets. Walking home involved going up at least two steep hills, which accentuated the distance between themselves and other Chinese. This geographic separation from other Chinese eventually created a psychological distance for Anna May. While her own neighborhood was diverse, the Los Angeles Chinatown was more ethnically homogeneous than others around the world, which tended to be populated by a polyglot mixture of Chinese sailors and laborers from all over China and the world. In Los Angeles, migrants from Taishan in Guangdong Province and Fujian Province predominated. Although she always identified herself as Chinese, her personality was open to and partly shaped by other Americans. Eventually her search for identity pushed Anna May into travel and the transient reality of film.[8]

Her parents' background added to that social complexity. Though their personal lives retained strong elements of Chinese traditions, Anna May's parents were American-born citizens. Wong Sam Sing was born in the gold region of Michigan Bluffs, California, on July 23, 1860. He was the son of A Wong Wong (Wong Leung Chew or Qiuxian), a merchant who owned two stores, the Fong

Lee and the Wing Chung Chung, in Michigan Bluffs, Placer County, with his wife, Pon Shee. According to the genealogy of the Huang family of Chang On, Guangdong Province, China, A Wong Wong (Qiuxian) was the son of Changhu, the patriarch of this branch. The date and location of Wong Sam Sing's birth suggests that A Wong Wong operated stores for gold miners, work that required some capital and indicated that A Wong Wong had arrived in California after 1853, as Chinese immigrants replaced Anglo-American miners. Burdened by discriminatory taxes and the targets of worsening racial attacks, Chinese miners survived an initial attempt to expel them.

Wong Sam Sing lost both his parents at an early age. Pon Shee died in 1865, and soon after the father took his little boy to his ancestral home of Wing On, a village outside Taishan, Guangdong Province, China. Wong Leung Chew, according to his son, died trying to save a woman who had fallen down a well. When he was five, the orphaned boy returned to the United States, then went back to Wing On from his ninth to his eleventh years. Wong Sam Sing also lived for a time in a joss (a Chinese medicinal) house in Fiddletown, another Chinese settlement, about twenty miles south of his birthplace. The Chinese mining camps in which Wong Sam Sing lived were segregated from the white towns. Although the Chinese borrowed older Euro-American forms of architecture, they quickly adapted them to their own customs. Joss houses in particular represented the strongest examples of the homeland, which these Chinese miners tried to re-create in California and other western states. Such cultural retentions mixed with the evolving aggressive hostility whites expressed toward Chinese immigrants surely made Wong Sam Sing feel far more Chinese than American. His experiences kept him from assimilating and prepared him for his life in Los Angeles's Chinatown.[9]

By the age of nineteen, Wong Sam Sing had saved sufficient capital to return to Taishan to search for a wife. According to statements he made to immigration inspectors forty years later, Wong Sam Sing voyaged in 1886, though this date does not tally with his age at that time. By now the Wong clan had founded a new village, Chang On, about one hundred yards from their old home. Wong Sam Sing used a marriage broker to arrange matters. Now twenty-six years old, Wong Sam Sing married Lee Shee, who was eight years his junior. Marital happiness enticed Wong Sam Sing to remain in China. Lee Shee gave birth to a son, Huang

Dounan (his local name was Jingshu), on February 29, 1893. Sometime after that, Wong Sam Sing moved back to the United States. Such partings were common in Taishan. The original home of a majority of Chinese Americans, Taishan was filled with filial wives who waited for decades for their overseas husbands to return.[10]

Wong Sam Sing told the immigration authorities that Lee Shee had died before his return. In fact, she lived to the age of seventy-eight in Chang On, supported by funds sent by her husband. There were many women like her in the village; Taishan's economy was dependent on funds sent back by husbands abroad. His memory of dates was equally shaky. He claimed to have returned to the States in 1889, something apparently he did not do until the late 1890s. When he returned, Wong Sam Sing opened a laundry, an occupation so common in his family that there was a Wong Laundry Association. Bolstered economically by his work, Wong Sam Sing wrote Lee Shee asking her to bring their son to Los Angeles. Lee Shee replied that she wished to stay in Chang On and maintain the clan there. If he did not like her answer, she wrote, he should find himself another wife. While Lee Shee may have been unwilling to come to America, US immigration policies virtually forbade any Chinese female, including wives, from entering the nation. Those who did come had to undergo extensive and often degrading personal scrutiny before they might be admitted. Even the famous Soong sisters, who were from the most elite family in China, were kept in a pen for two weeks. Ailing Soong (the sister of the future Madame Chiang Kai-shek) later complained directly to President Theodore Roosevelt about her mistreatment. Her account of this abuse became legendary and instilled terror in ordinary people. Not wanting to risk everything for an uncertain future, Lee Shee and Wong Sam Sing agreed that he would stay in the United States and, as was the custom, send cash back home. Wong Sam Sing was more fortunate than most Chinese males and could afford a second wife. Within a year, Wong Sam Sing agreed through a Chinese broker to marry the sixteen-year-old Lee Gon Toy.[11]

His lengthy absence from Chang On did not mean that Wong Sam Sing neglected his Chinese family.[12] According to his daughter, Wong Sam Sing owned quite a bit of property in Chang On. This property was given to Huang Dounan. In addition, Wong Sam Sing regularly sent over cash to subsidize his son's education. Huang Dounan proved to be a scholar and continued his education into his thirties. Wong Sam Sing later asked Anna May to give some of her earnings to Huang Dounan, although she refused. Eventually Huang Dounan graduated from the prestigious Waseda University in Tokyo and became a schoolteacher and a prominent figure in Chang On. His intellectual pursuits are an indication of Wong Sam Sing's early ambitions for his children, nearly all of whom eventually graduated from college, with the important exception of Anna May.

Wong Sam Sing's travels were common for a Taishanese American of his generation. As Madeline Hsu has demonstrated, Taishanese sojourners combined traditional practices and expectations of family life, along with loyalty to native place and to their kinship organization, while they traveled the world in search of their share of prosperity. Wong Sam Sing went to China at least three times in his life, and he lived in three places in California before settling in Los Angeles. His children doubtless heard many tales of life back in Taishan. The frequent letters and demands from Lee Shee made the old country all the more real to the Wong children. Anna May grew up in a family with a fundamental loyalty to China but with a daily attachment to Los Angeles. She would live with this cultural split her entire life. The psychological ramifications of this partition were manifested in her film career.[13]

Less is known about Anna May's mother. Lee Gon Toy was born on Clay Street in San Francisco on June 6, 1886, the only child of Lee Leng, the proprietor of the Fook Lee Cigar Factory, and his wife, Lee Shee (no relation to the other). Cigar making was a common if unstable industry for late-nineteenth-century Chinese in San Francisco. There was frequent turnover among the shops and small factories, often caused by competition from white firms. Anti-Chinese behavior was at its height during the 1880s, and cigar makers such as Lee Leng faced boycotts, riots, and problems raising capital. Like her future husband, Lee Gon Toy no doubt lived in a household that regarded whites with caution. Nonetheless, Lee Leng was a businessman, and the match must have seemed worthwhile to Wong Sam Sing. While Lee Gon Toy's new husband was the same age as her father, it was not unusual for a Chinese American woman to marry someone far older than she. Lee Gon Toy lost contact with her parents after they left for their home in Lung Jew Village, Yunnan Province, around 1913. Anti-Chinese repression began before her birth and continued throughout her life. Lee Gon Toy, like other Chinese American women at the time, did not dare to interact with European American society. She could speak and understand English, but she preferred to use the Taishan dialect. Doubtless, that is what she spoke at home with her children and husband. Her American birth lessened the likelihood that she had bound feet.[14]

Wong Sam Sing was fortunate to find a suitable wife in California. The bigoted perception that most Chinese females who arrived during the Gold Rush years were prostitutes propelled California legislators to pass the notorious Page Law in 1875. Under this legislation, Chinese female immigrants, even the most wealthy, entered California burdened by the presumption that they planned to work as prostitutes, a racist conception that was later dramatized in the cinema. Stemming in part from white workingmen's anxieties about the growth of Chinese families in the late 1860s and supported by white capitalists who feared that larger families meant higher wage demands, the Page Law targeted all Chinese women. Immigration officers routinely refused entry to Chinese women, and local police harassed respectable women with potential deportation. That Wong Sam Sing could afford to support wives in California and China attests to his prosperity.[15]

Wong Sam Sing and his large family were different in another aspect from other Chinese residents. The Chinese laundryman's life in the United States was a study of social isolation. The job was stigmatized. Among whites, the work of the Chinese laundryman was associated with dirty water and vile odors. As Iris Chang has described it, laundry work was harsh, unceasing, and physically exhausting. Wielding an eight-pound iron, the laundryman and his family labored on a wet, slippery floor, washing and pressing clothing. Finishing work, including starching detachable collars, cuffs, and shirtfronts, required meticulous attention and delicate treatment. Laundry workers commonly worked twenty-hour days and prided themselves on possessing "flexible" stomachs, ones that could go one or two days without food. Varicose veins and swollen legs were common ailments.

In Los Angeles, however, laundry work was so common among Chinese Americans that it approached the level of a social norm. One out of every five male householders operated a laundry, and Wongs accounted for almost one-third of all laundrymen. Wong Sam Sing employed a classic immigrant method of improving his lot; he had many children who could help in the business as they grew. In all, Wong Sam Sing employed a dozen people in the laundry, a number that included all the children. A laundry was a sure business prospect, provided a man worked long hours toiling with dirty clothing and boiling water. The exhausting work also tied a man down to the home, so that he rarely had the energy to gamble with the dice, faro, and fan games ubiquitous in Chinatown. The job could provide prosperity. One laundryman earned enough to buy a fifty-thousand-dollar hotel. If lucky, you could get a choice spot near a hotel and apartment buildings frequented by young Western businessmen who required clean shirts. But there were family benefits. The family lived behind the store. Clothing eight children cost little for Wong Sam Sing. And his job gave the father an exalted status. In his shop, Wong Sam Sing was, as his second daughter later recalled, "lord of his household." While Anna May would eventually escape the humid prison of the laundry, her work there fostered lifetime habits of exacting dress.[16]

There was no question of who was in charge of the Wong family. His Taishanese origins and membership in the Wong Association placed Wong Sam Sing higher up in the local hierarchy than his work would indicate. Old World ties reemerged in the family associations. Wong Sam Sing became an active member of the local Wong Kong Hor Tong, the family association, and the Chinese Laundry Alliance. Such ties also mandated that he continue to send support for Lee Shee and Huang Dounan back in Chang On.[17]

Wong Sam Sing now had two daughters but pined for a son. To please him, Lee Gon Toy placed a Chinese boy's cap on Wong Liu Tsong's head and arrayed her in the robes of a prince. Later, Anna May attributed her public confidence to this masculinizing influence.[18] The need for such deceptions ended when Lee Gon Toy produced the first son, Wong Yah Wing (James), on July 15, 1907. As Lulu and Anna May grew older, they helped their mother care for the infants who arrived like clockwork over the next few years. After the birth of Wong Lew Huang (Mary) on March 11, 1910, a second son, Wong Way Ying (Frank), arrived on March 12, 1912, and a third, Wong Suey Ying (Roger), was born on May 16, 1915. Another girl, Wong Lew Choon (Marietta), was born on April 27, 1919, but died in March of 1920. A fourth boy, Wong Kim Ying (Richard), rounded out the family on August 4, 1922.[19]

By the end of the second decade of the century, Wong Sam Sing had sufficient family labor. The girls worked the counter and delivered the clothing while the boys learned to iron shirts. Lulu and Anna May probably ironed as well, given that they later reported small burn scars on their hands. Laundry work had liberating effects on Anna May. In her tasks, she learned business principles and money management, and how to work with people, especially the westerners she encountered when delivering fresh laundry. She became far more acclimatized to westerners than many of her female classmates.[20]

Although his family status separated Wong Sam Sing from the overwhelmingly bachelor society around Chinatown, many of the common household patterns were universal. Dinners, predominately pork, beef, and rice, were cooked in woks over a clay stove. Fish delicacies from the Los Angeles market included cuttlefish, crab, clams, and oysters. Turtles came from local ponds. The young Wongs grew up eating rice from ceramic bowls decorated with bamboo designs. Main dishes were served from plates of more expensive designs of the Four Seasons or from celadon Double Happiness bowls. Tea was drunk from Chinese cups without handles. Anna May doubtless helped her mother prepare these dishes as she gained a lifelong love of cooking for herself and for larger groups.[21]

Chinese parents were famously conservative with money, but they never hesitated to lavish presents on their children. A family photo taken when Anna May was eighteen months old shows her posed with Lulu between her father and mother, each dressed in traditional Chinese garb. The clothing of the children speaks to the family's deep adherence to Chinese customs. It also shows a degree of prosperity, as such ceremonial garb was most commonly owned by wealthier families.[22]

Lulu and Anna May owned dolls, probably made in Germany, and later shared marbles with their brothers. Years later, Anna May told a Chinese journalist in Hong Kong that Lulu first had dolls and that Anna May asked her father for more. She remembered, "I did this on purpose. Taking my bed as a stage, and my dolls as actors, we performed our own play. Later one of my younger brothers joined us." The wealthier See children owned cast-iron trains and fire engines pulled by iron horses, toys that were enjoyed by middle-class children across the United States.[23]

Anna May's earliest memories involved a frustrated desire for luxury and a new awareness of racial boundaries. Her parents taught her to be decorous and to carry herself with dignity. An English family lived next door to the Wongs and invited young Wong Liu Tsong to their home, where they had a large upright piano. At first Anna May and the neighboring children "played games together and romped around with no thought of color or creed to disturb us." Then, the children's mother invited Anna May to touch the gleaming black and white keys of the piano. Enchanted, Anna May climbed onto the bench but lost her balance and fell clumsily to the floor. She recalled, "I was covered with humiliation. I felt that I was disgraced forever in the home of my friends and that I would not be permitted to play with them any more because of my unbecoming conduct." Had she been a Western child, Anna May believed, she would not have worried, but because of her upbringing as a Chinese child she felt that she had disgraced her parents. She told an interviewer decades later that the impression of difference was so great that "I have never forgotten it." Discouraged, Anna May never learned to play a musical instrument.[24]

Initially, Lulu and Anna May attended the California Street School, accounting for half the Chinese children enrolled. While they learned English and could write their names in the national tongue, the girls received a sobering lesson in American racism. To fit in, Anna May waved her hair and strained to hold her eyes open to round them. She was shocked when her "American" classmates chose her to "represent China because I was the most typically Chinese girl in the school. My attempts at disguise had merely made me stand out more." There were other, less friendly lessons. Western children did not hesitate to use slurs against the young girls, pulling their hair and shoving them off the sidewalk. In the schoolyard, "the great game was to gather around my sister and myself and torment us." When the sisters ran home in tears to tell Wong Sam Sing, he told them to be proud of their people and race. Their position in society was very difficult and perhaps it was best that they "find this out now." A boy sitting behind Anna May took matters further. He stuck pins into Anna May to determine if Chinese children felt pain differently from the way he did. The next day she wore an overcoat for protection, so the youthful sadist used a longer pin. Before long Anna May was wearing six coats as a barricade against him. The teacher insisted that she unbundle when spring arrived, instructions that made Anna May sneeze, then catch a severe cold that developed into a near-fatal bout of pneumonia. She never forgot these incidents, which made the pain of racism very real. It is hardly too much to speculate that the boy's racial torture, which Anna May made into a standard part of her autobiographical interview, instilled a general unease in her that contact with whites could have painful consequences. Fortunately they found that not every white person treated the girls with contempt. Rob Wagner, later a famous editor and writer, befriended Anna May when she was about eight or ten. He later recalled seeing Anna May and her sisters hauling bundles of clothing up and down the hill that separated their neighborhood from downtown Los Angeles. Wong Sam Sing would wait and watch at the bottom of the hill. Wagner's acquaintance, which later blossomed into a professional relationship, originated from Anna May's work for her father.[25]

Alarmed by the racism their daughters suffered, the Wong parents quickly transferred Lulu and Anna May to the Presbyterian Chinese Mission School at 766 Juan Street off Apablasa in Chinatown. There the girls studied geography, history, arithmetic, and English. The Presbyterians had been active in Chinatown since 1876 and used the schools, which the Chinese prized, as enticements to conversion. Children learned English and Cantonese. Such schools were the advance guard of what would later become a positive national policy toward the Chinese; during the first decade of the twentieth century, they were a bulwark for Chinese Americans against the dominant American racism. As acculturating forces, the Presbyterian schools created a wedge between their Chinese students and the rest of the community, which considered the English-speaking children outsiders. More positively, the Presbyterian schools were places of recreation where hardworking children such as Lulu and Anna May could relax away from the laundry. Anna May remembered the school with great fondness. She described herself as a "tomboyish creature" who played baseball and marbles and refused to learn sewing. Sometimes Wong Sam Sing would come across his second daughter playing marbles, "tousled, grimy, with hair flying, having a glorious time with my 'gang.' My actions troubled him," she remembered.

Such schools also gave the girls a heavy dose of Anglo-Christian values. Although the teachers were white, the students were all Chinese, thus alleviating the harsh racism of the public school. Displeased that his daughters were getting insufficient instruction in Chinese, Wong Sam Sing sent them to an afternoon and Saturday Chinese-language school, which was located above a Pentecostal church filled with wild-eyed worshipers. Anna May recalled how the schools were open all the time, except Sunday. Classes were conducted in a long narrow room in an old building down in Chinatown. She remembered how "The teacher sat at his desk, a bamboo stick beside him. If one of the pupils showed signs of restlessness or disobedience, whack went the stick across the hands of the offender. Serious disobedience was punished in a severe manner—and not across the hands either." Anna May had mixed feelings about the school. She enjoyed being with other Chinese students and felt comfortable in Chinatown with its "narrow streets lined with grimy buildings, the shops where Chinese herbs and rugs were sold, the gambling houses where white men and Chinese mixed, the overcrowded tenements where the Chinese lived, sometimes entire families living in a room, the gaily painted chop-suey restaurants with their lanterns a soft-many-colored blur in the dusk." She felt sorry for the schoolteacher, who lived in a small room behind the schoolhouse and who never seemed to leave the building and cooked his own meals. His efforts with her were unsuccessful, for after five years she was barely able to read and write Chinese. Still, her days in Chinatown instilled a powerful visual vocabulary in Anna May, which she later used in her acting.

Anna May and Lulu noticed how the schools were changing them. Anna May recalled how "outside of our own home, we were thoroughly American in dress, action, speech, and thought. Right and left we were smashing the traditions of our forebears." Americanization was causing her "to forget all my parents' teachings." As they grew older this process accelerated. Later, Lulu and Anna May returned to their old school, which welcomed them. They then matriculated into the Custer Street School (now Central Junior High Intermediate) and finally to Lincoln High. Lulu left after six months, but Anna stayed for two years in a vocational program.[26]

Future journalists' accounts of Anna May's childhood would portray Wong Sam Sing as a controlling, traditional father. Such parents required their daughters to obey without question and remain close to home. At the same time, Chinese girls had more value in America than in China because of their scarcity and the greater opportunities available to them. While Wong Sam Sing doubtless considered himself a traditional Chinese man, concepts of what that meant were changing rapidly. The fall of the Qing dynasty and the construction of Republican China excited Chinese American men, who considered the triumphs of Sun Yat-sen and other Republicans as proof of China's resurgent power. Chinese Americans were appalled at attempts to restore the monarchy in China.

At the same time, they staunchly resisted modernist reforms intended to elimi-nate Confucianism and argued against equality and freedom for women. Chinese American men desired to keep women subordinate to men and to keep children obedient, according to Confucian principles. Talk of freedom for women in the United States had, according to prevailing views, already made many Chinese American women unfit for marriage.[27]

While it was possible for their father to maintain charge over his growing family at the laundry, Lulu and Anna May experienced more of life by walking to school or riding the bus through middle-class neighborhoods. Delivering laundry for their father also brought them into contact with non-Chinese adults. Someone noticed Anna May's blossoming beauty, because by the age of ten she was modeling coats for a furrier. Her father was so impressed by a newspaper photo of her dressed in a mink coat and ankle-length pantaloons that he sent the picture to Huang Dounan. Her half-brother responded: "Tsong is very beautiful, but please send me the dollar watch on the other side of the page." Anna May retorted, "a fur coat doesn't tick." Her work for the furrier taught Anna May about fashion and instilled in her a lifelong love of fur coats. By the age of twelve, she had a steady job as a counter girl and model for a department store, Ville de Paris. Her father found her a secretarial job, which required a substantial commute. She hardly lamented when her poor shorthand skills prompted her dismissal.[28]

Family outings included going to Chinese theater. Chinese theatrical perfor-mances had been a staple of Los Angeles Chinatown since 1890 and were begin-ning to incorporate women into their companies, which was a major change from traditions in the old country. Chinese theater in America was largely based in San Francisco, but touring companies regularly visited Los Angeles. A traditional father such as Wong Sam Sing would take his family to see companies of actors performing traditional Chinese plays, often in serials lasting several weeks and accompanied by acrobatics and variety plays. Unlike the more famous Peking Theater, most of the Chinese American actors, plays, and performances came from Cantonese precedents and used Taishanese dialect. Costumes, stage props, and plays often came directly from China. Later, Anna May recalled these eve-nings fondly. She remembered that performances lasted four hours and that the audiences ate dried melon seeds and chatted constantly. She learned that a good actor had to know hundreds of parts, and be able to perform them at a minute's notice. However entertaining such evenings were for the Wong family, acting was not regarded as a potential career. No respectable Chinese father wanted a daughter to become an actress. Initially Wong Sam Sing did not have to worry, as female roles were rare in traditional Chinese theater.[29]

Wong Sam Sing was less pleased about a new form of entertainment. The motion-picture industry, which was less than fifteen years old, was laboring hard to appeal to a female audience with ornate theaters, white-gloved ushers, and melodramatic plots. On one occasion at the age of nine, Anna May received a handsome tip for laundry delivery and used the cash to go to the movies. Immediately, Anna May became a big fan of the flicks, often sneaking away from school to the cheap movie houses. She forged excuse notes for her teachers. Later she recalled using her lunch money to buy a ticket and sat in the front row, "where everyone looks funny and wrong-angled." Eventually, her poor eating habits resulted in illness, and her father had to intervene. Still she loved films. Dreams of stardom filled the young girl's mind. She dreamt "not like children dreaming of paradise with angels and toys and fruit—but I saw in my dream a wonder . . . wonderful, amazing sun city shining with golden light, where white palaces were erected and odorless gardens and [I] wander on white paths and dance and am overjoyed and throw blissful looks in the blue air." The dream addressed her: ". . . and opposite the palace and gardens—there is a man with short sleeves and a big horn in front of his mouth, shouting, 'Anna May Wong, now you come down the stairs and look like the prince was already approaching—we do a close up of that!' And then the other man comes near with a three-legged peep show box and winds and winds . . . and I have an overjoyed face because I feel the great happiness—and the important man says 'You did a great job, Anna May Wong—You are a film star!'" Then the dream ended and her father was looking for her with a bamboo stick in his hand.

Anna May recalled these beatings many years later. She remembered that the bamboo stick was talking to her and was long and that it itched when a strong hand used it on a certain part of her behind. "My father has such a muscular hand, and this burnt so much. Ouch, much! You have to go to school, father shouted at me! And not always play hooky."[30] Although Wong Sam Sing spanked her with a bamboo stick for these adventures, Anna May could not resist the thrill of the cinema. Her first sighting of a movie star occurred when she encountered

Alma Rubens in an elevator. She became first a fan of the films of Ruth Roland, and then, like so many American girls, became absorbed in the serial film, *The Perils of Pauline*, starring Pearl White and Crane Wilbur. Each week, parallel versions of the series appeared in film and in the Hearst newspapers. Such combinations were common ploys by newspapers hoping for increased sales. The films, in which White performed amazing stunts while she and Wilbur fended off marauding Indians, thrilled Americans in 1914. Joining the two lead characters in the film was a sinister Chinese criminal, Wu Fang. This character became the prototype of Chinese villains of the 1920s, culminating in the many stories of Fu Manchu, as written by Sax Rohmer. Anna May was hardly the only child to miss the explicit racism of these weekly serials. She learned to accept racism as part of the enchanting narrative up on the screen. She concentrated on White's virtuosity, which convinced her that actresses could perform multiple roles. Already literate, she doubtless could also make the connection between print and film stardom, which she later exploited thoroughly. Less inspiring were the theaters she attended, which were poorly ventilated and shabbily furnished and did not resemble the cinematic palaces found in upscale neighborhoods. An electric piano provided the music for the largely Mexican customers. Still, the films thrilled Anna May. Afterward she would retreat to her room and practice acting in front of the mirror for hours on end. Later, she recalled how she would rehearse the "scenes that appealed to me most." Characteristically, they were screen moments that required that she "cry in anguish, with tears streaming down my face; I would clutch the lingerie to my bosom, and then I would tear it in a paroxysm of sorrow." No one would disturb her, although "my mother saw me once in one of these scenes, but she said nothing." Later, she contended that her father was the principal opponent of her budding film career and that her mother was tacitly accepting. In those years of watching and practicing, Anna May combined a spectator's voyeurism with the imagination of an apprentice actor. As Miriam Hansen has argued, the Hollywood method of narration was creating a new kind of American hieroglyphic that marked a new universal language. For most people, spectatorship was sufficient; for Anna May it was necessary to incorporate the new language into her heart and mind. Sadly, Hollywood was creating an identity for her, and she would have to suffer its malevolent messages for years.[31]

Anna May's interest in films coincided with major transformations of the motion-picture business. One innovation was the emergence of the star system. As film productions gradually began to favor fiction over documentary films, and human performances outstripped mechanical fascination of the flicks, fans across the nation begged studios for information on favored actors. Such genres as vaudeville, opera, and minstrelsy had long depended on stars to boost box office receipts, so it was not surprising that the movies followed suit. Moreover, as stars became more famous and demanded higher salaries, which had soared into thousands of dollars per week by 1915, they represented to their largely female audience the height of success and consumer fashion. Building their fame were the movie fan magazines that were specifically tailored to females and their consumer dreams. Soon, American women were following the leads of their favorite actresses in purchasing clothing, changing their hairstyles, and demanding automobiles.[32]

Accompanying these modern themes were baser appeals to human emotion. In early cinema, anti-Asian themes were among the most profitable narratives. Beginning with a Thomas Edison short made in 1898 and entitled "Dancing Chinamen-Marionettes," the foreign, exotic quality of the Chinese became a staple of American filmmaking. One method that catered to that fascination was "rubbernecking," in which American tourists visited Chinatowns on buses equipped with a "megaphone man" who commented on the passing urban scene to his audience, who were seated in ascending rows similar to those in a theater. Chinatown residents angrily tried to halt the tours, but lacked the political power to do so. Bus tours were for the middle class who could afford the costly tickets; movies appealed to the working class and families eager for inexpensive entertainment. The first films about the Chinese and Chinatown were made in New York; the genre accompanied the industry's migration to Los Angeles in the 1910s. Soon, film writers, directors, and producers expanded their visions, incorporating misinformation and racial myths about China and focusing on urban slums such as the Limehouse district in London. By the time Anna May was a teenager, derogatory movies about the Chinese and their locales were standard Hollywood fare.[33]

There were some positive elements to the American fascination with China. The collapse of the Qing dynasty following the 1911 revolution encouraged

Americans to renew a moral commitment to democracy in China and to disavow the anti-Chinese discrimination in the United States. At the same time, American businesses pushed into China and offered such modern consumer goods and styles as cars, movie theaters, electric lights, bobbed hair, department stores, and photography. As Jonathan Spence has indicated, the rush to modernity in China created an emotional backlash in the States for traditional Chinese culture.[34] That focus on the future, however, manifested in the films more as costume design and set arrangement. Major films dealing with Asian issues pushed older anxieties about interracial love into the foreground.

Wong Sam Sing may have been aware of such currents only insofar as he, like other Chinese American adults, resented the insulting stereotypes offered by the cinema. Yet the danger to his parental authority was immediate. The motion-picture business was much closer than the cinema screens. The fledgling business transferred many of its operations to Los Angeles in the years before World War I. In addition to the constant sunshine, Los Angeles offered protection from a violent patents dispute over a key mechanism in the camera in New York. This battle was the latest installment in a long-term war over rights exclusively owned by the Edison Company. As the studios relocated to Los Angeles, a favorite locale for shooting was Chinatown. When the film actors actually appeared making movies on Chinatown streets, Anna May was hopelessly entranced. The first real actress she encountered in the streets was Mae Murray. Anna May was confused because Murray was "ragged and dirty" in her costume. In the child's mind, Murray should have been "dressed in ermine and blazing with diamonds." Nonetheless, Anna May hung around the film shoots as early as the age of nine, begging for a part. Soon, the actors noticed the pretty little girl and called her the "C.C.C.," or curious Chinese child. She in turn became determined: She *would* become a movie star.[35]

Anna's big chance came in a major production in 1919. Sensing that films with Chinese themes appealed to the Americans, Metro Pictures filmed *The Red Lantern*, produced by and starring the veteran actress Alla Nazimova. This extraordinary actress may be credited with introducing the now dominant Stanislavsky or "Method" acting to America. She was known as the First Lady of the Silent Screen and cultivated an image as a "foreign" sexual sophisticate, a role later borrowed by Pola Negri, Greta Garbo, and Marlene Dietrich. Nazimova was keenly aware of the importance of "racial portrayal" on screen. She wrote in an article for *Moving Pictures Stories* of the need to be sensitive to how racial types would respond to emotional demands—for example, how a Chinese girl or a French girl would experience rejection by her lovers. *The Red Lantern* featured a sympathetic reading of tragic interracial love. Nazimova plays an illegitimate Eurasian woman who falls in love with an American missionary. When he does not return her affection, her character condemns hypocritical westerners who teach the Chinese but allow racial prejudice to interfere with genuine love. Angry, she joins the Boxer Rebellion. Watching this great artist perform, the fourteen-year-old Anna May learned that her own "racial portrayal" had equal value to others and so she could emphasize her own experiences.[36]

In the film, Nazimova plays a dual role as half-sisters, the high-yellow Eurasian Mahlee, born to an English father and his Chinese mistress, and the pure white and blonde Blanche Sackville, the child of the same father and his English wife. Soon the sisters fall for the same man, an American diplomat who chooses the English girl; the father soon disowns Mahlee. Her love for the American unrequited, she swallows poison after he is killed in the Boxer Rebellion. As Mahlee dies on a peacock chair, the titles reveal her final words: "East is east and West is west," a message that proclaimed the mournful fate of mixed-race lovers.[37]

The film inspired a popular theme song and gained generally favorable reviews. One less positive notice, which foreshadowed future criticisms, came from a Chinese student who wrote in *The Baltimore Sun* that no Chinese woman would bare her legs as Nazimova did in key scenes. Such commentary about Hollywood's misrepresentation of Chinese women would dog Anna May through much of her career. Though Anna May received no credit for her work as an extra, *The Red Lantern* was more than a minor debut. It exposed her to the talents of a major star and to the practice of Euro-American women as "yellow faces" who played Asian roles. Mahlee's suicide introduced Anna May to the type of cinematic death she would endure. At the same time, it brought young Wong Liu Tsong to the attention of Hollywood directors, paving the way for her next major role. Anna May placed her account of getting the part in the Nazimova film into her personal mythology and retold the story many times. Nazimova seems to have liked the young actress, and the two became friends.[38]

Nazimova Productions used Euro-American actors in the main roles. Joining Nazimova were Virginia Ross, Frank Currier, Winter Hall, and a youthful Noah Beery. The sole credited Asian actor was the Japanese Yukio Ao Yamo. *The Red Lantern* was set in Peking, thereby mandating large numbers of Chinese extras and locale. One sequence required three hundred Asian extras. There had been appeals to Hollywood producers to use Anna May before. Harry Carr and Rob Wagner, who had known her since childhood, urged the producers to give her a chance, only to be frustrated by "that old squawk about racial prejudice," which they believed existed primarily in the producers' minds. It took the Reverend James Wang of the Baptist Church, who often acted as a go-between for Hollywood producers and Chinese extras, to secure a job for Anna. An influenza epidemic put many Chinese actors out of work, so Anna's dreams seemed more real. She approached Wang and poured out her heart to him, telling him of her adoration of Crane Wilbur, Pearl White, Mary Pickford, and others. She told him of cadging nickels to sneak into "bad-smelling North Main Street movie theaters." Although he acceded to her pleas to get her a role as an extra, he warned her that she would be lost among the hundreds of Chinese faces. Still, he mused, "I am sure that you will not go unnoticed, for your face is like a tangerine, your ears and your nose are large, and your eyes are big." His clairvoyant talents then failed him, for he worried that "you will not be photogenic enough." Wang knew Marshall "Mickey" Neilan, a prominent director, through his own roles as a Chinese man in westerns. Through this contact, Anna May got her start. Excited at the chance, she rushed home, stole into her mother's room, and rubbed her cake of white Chinese rice powder all over her face. Her face was then too pale, and so she colored it with the red paper found in any Chinese home for wrapping "lucky money." Anna May noticed one of her eyebrows was now obscured, so she quickly crayoned in a black line. Highly pleased with herself, she presented herself to the studio. The makeup man was aghast, grabbed her by the hand, and flung her into a chair. In two minutes the mask was removed and a more suitable one affixed in place. At first hurt and annoyed, Anna May soon became accustomed to and enjoyed the skills of a makeup artist. Later, she remembered her first day on the set. She did not feel any fear, "because I had acted in front of myself every day . . . so when I acted, it was a wonderful feeling, as though I was just playing myself."[39]

Her enthusiasm was not shared at home. Wong Sam Sing was upset that his second daughter was in the films. Initially, she did not listen to him at all, preferring to bask in the happiness of filmmaking and convinced that the "camera didn't look at anyone but me." Wong Sam Sing warned his daughter that Hollywood made other films besides those about China and that she would not be needed in those productions. Within a few days, she realized that he was right: "No film . . . No dream . . . They didn't need a Chinese girl in that film." Anna May now understood that even with her beauty, she could only get parts in films with Asian themes. Hollywood's rigid racial casting, which exists to the present, had boxed her into a limited number of roles. For the time being, she lost face only within the family. Fortunately for Anna, parts for Chinese actors became fashionable again and she was able once more to find herself immersed in "the place where film enchants people." For the next eight months, she was the "one-hundredth or two-hundredth among Chinese women." Anna May's recollections indicate that she was probably in many more films than she is credited with today. Working as an extra gave her valuable experience and, little by little, more exposure.[40]

Her future in film was still not settled at home. What Chinese films were made were vexing enough to Wong Sam Sing. In addition to Nazimova's production, D. W. Griffith's film, *Broken Blossoms* (1919), established a cinematic vision of the Chinese as spiritually peaceful and unable to compete with the stronger, more masculine Western cultures. Similarly alarming for the father was the reputation of actresses. In China, popular perceptions ranked actresses with courtesans. Nor could the American screen world offer much comfort. Sexual scandals plagued the industry throughout the early years. Not until Douglas Fairbanks and Mary Pickford glamorized the profession in the 1920s did Americans regard actors as more than low-class rabble. The glory of their marriage still had to compete with an underworld that helped drugs circulate freely on sets. Hollywood divorce and sex scandals played well in the newspapers; more prosaic and tragic were the fates of thousands of girls who flooded into town, anxious for the chance of a lifetime. The studios were far apart geographically and often isolated from the overburdened trolley lines. Hitchhiking made women vulnerable to wolfish males. Successes were few, and suicide and starvation were common. Anna May was not frightened by the hazards of her new profession. Showing how Americanized she had become, Anna May confronted her father about the career she wanted. In interviews conducted a few years later, she remembered how he said that she was disgracing the family. She retorted that she wanted to be independent and not like the submissive girls in China.

Many years later, just before meeting her father in Taishan and going to the ancestral village, Anna May recalled that her parents held traditional Chinese thoughts that "a good man will not be a soldier, and a good girl will not be an actress." Such proverbs, overheard by the teenage actress, revealed the tensions between her ancestry and her Chinese American identity. She also remembered that her father was reassured in 1919 by the sudden arrival at his doorstep of about one hundred and fifty Chinese coming to Los Angeles to perform in the movie. He knew some of them, "so he did not stop me any longer." Her mother, she claimed, was even more difficult, because Lee Gon Toy believed that cameras captured the soul. Home life was saddened further when a daughter, Marietta, born on April 27, 1919, died the following March. The baby's death and her parent's disapproval of her career made Anna May ripe for melancholia. That despair coalesced with her own confusion over her identity. While Anna May lived in a Chinese home, she worked in a Western industry, one whose product further alienated her from her birth culture. Parental tensions, domestic grief, youthful rebellion, and celluloid fantasies pushed Anna May far into hidden racial and personal grief. It is no wonder that she emerged from childhood unable to speak the language of her parents.[41]

Her father's disapproval did not keep Anna May from the lure of Hollywood. She was among many American ethnics who found that films provided a passageway, intellectually and monetarily, into American society. Cinema helped non-white Americans such as Anna May find a forum for her fantasies for a different future than the one envisioned by her father. She later acknowledged that her first years working as an actress were tough, but the cinema, with its abilities to absorb older hopes and modern dreams, gave her the promise of abundance and self-transformation. She could appropriate movie stardom for herself and thereby insulate her feelings from the eventual betrayals by men and the studios.[42]

But before Anna May was able to focus on her chosen career there was the matter of her education. She recalled the two years at high school as among the happiest of her life. She took up tennis enthusiastically and in her second year won both singles and doubles tournaments. She overdid her exercise, however, and collapsed while attending Camp Estelle for girls on Mount Baldy. She was brought back into town suffering from St. Vitus Dance. Wong Sam Sing took her to a Chinese physician who tried a number of unsuccessful remedies. Anna May lamented that Marshall Neilan and the other directors who had taken an interest would now forget about her. Finally, the doctor tried an unusual method: he scraped her arms with a gold coin until she bled. He repeated this treatment every few days until she recovered. According to Anna May, her return to health had more to do with her aversion to the treatment than the treatment itself. She had missed months of school. There was some talk of college, but Anna May decided to end her formal education in favor of the full-time pursuit of a career in acting.[43]

Anna May's illness and her response to its cure reflect the extraordinary pressures she faced in life. Wong Sam Sing had made it plain that he disliked her new career. Her response to him and to Chinese culture indicates the psychological gulfs within the family. Unable to withstand paternal insistence, Anna May came close to an emotional collapse. Her mysterious illness resembles those suffered by characters in Maxine Hong Kingston's memoir, *The Woman Warrior*. Therein young Asian American women suffer inexplicable ailments that derive from conflicts at home over identity. As with Kingston's characters, Anna May's illness struck her during a period when her imagination was filled with conflicts over ethnic identity and the racial roles she played or observed in Hollywood cinema. Those conflicts would recur.[44]

The battle over her soul affected her physical beauty. At seventeen, Anna May was on the verge of stardom yet deeply resented in her home. Her father anxiously tried to marry her off, nearly pushing her into a nervous breakdown. An extraordinary photograph made by W. F. Seeley for *Photoplay Magazine* at that time reveals the tensions right under the surface of the beautiful young woman.[45] She is wearing a flower-embroidered dress, a tightly bound collar, and a Chinese country girl's "Child Flower" hairstyle, signifying her unmarried, virginal status. Underneath these reassuring customs are blunt, rebellious eyes, Western eyebrows, and pouting lips. The caption for the image tells the audience that she "is a true daughter of the lotus land," a dismissive reference to China. The writer's overt racism toward this third-generation American girl missed the troubled truth of a Chinese country girl openly defying her traditionalist father. This tension is most apparent in her hands, which are posed palm up below her belly, opening the flowers on her dress, and presenting her purity to a tawdry world.

Wong Sam Sing's aversion to the film world was rooted in Chinese culture. The idea of a female film actress was new in China, and the job had low prestige and poor wages. Before the intrusion of Hollywood films in Chinese cities forced the use of actual women in female roles, men performed such parts. Their meager wages made actresses in China shuttle back and forth from work as "dancing girls," a euphemism for prostitutes. Print images of actresses were generally based upon older portrayals of "calendar girls" and demimondaines, using languorous, sexually alluring poses. The model's eyes looked directly at the viewer, with no modesty. Other aspects of the introduction of women to Chinese cinema were subtler. Regional origins were important. Cantonese (the general area from which Anna May's family came) women were considered by other Chinese to be more lively and liberated. Wearing their hair drawn up into tufts in the fashion of slave girls, they were more useful to Shanghai producers than the northern girls, who were regarded as chaste, living by ritual propriety, and subservient. In short, Anna May's adolescent rebellion against her father shaped her for undesirable stereotypes in Chinese eyes and rendered her fair game for wolfish American cinema executives.[46]

Just how much Chinese Americans disliked the screen world can be discerned in the story of Fong Fat, a peanut seller in San Francisco. Allen Holobar, producer of *Hurricane Gal!* for First National Pictures in 1922, recruited Fong Fat for a part in the film. Fong Fat refused, advising the director that Chinese were averse to the film world because of its depictions of them as villains. When Holobar promised Fong Fat that his role would not be negative, the young peanut seller demanded that the Chinese consul in San Francisco, who gave him permission to take the part, settle the issue. After that, Fong Fat refused to come by boat to Los Angeles, fearing that he would be kidnapped. Only when a train fare was arranged was he willing to take the role.[47]

Anna May Wong did not need travel expenses. She grew up amid moviemakers and was enchanted by them by an early age. Despite her family's traditional ways, young Huang Liu Tsong was ready in her early teens to convert her fantasy world into stardom. She was hardly alone in that aspiration. Hollywood was filled with young, eager, and unformed children who often had no experience with the theater before their careers started. Few of them had much in the way of "reality" behind their stardom. Many came from poor backgrounds and broken homes, and they lived in the public eye at an early age. "Stars" were often tabula rasae, malleable to authoritarian directors. Their roles shaped their personalities. A necessary quality was a plasticity of character and a willingness to shape oneself according to the demands of the public.[48] Anna May's home life was more substantial than that of many of her contemporaries in film. Her father's fierce traditionalism was a bulwark upon which she could lean in times of distress. Her Chinese culture provided the self-esteem needed to navigate the shark-filled waters of Hollywood. In the years to come, she would learn to rely on her family and her culture to buffer her from the hardships of her career.

Two
Seeking Stardom

Following her debut in *The Red Lantern*, Anna May gained small, unaccredited parts in several films. First she had a tiny bit in a Priscilla Dean feature, *Outside the Law*, directed by Tod Browning for Universal Pictures. This film was the first of eight screen collaborations between Browning and Lon Chaney, who was ascending into stardom. The film was set in San Francisco's Chinatown. Chaney played two roles, that of Ah Wing, the servant of Chang Low, and the mobster Black Mike. Dean played Molly Madden, daughter of "Silent" Madden, a mobster trying to go straight with the advice of Chang Lo (E. A. Warren). Black Mike, worried that the former will exchange evidence for his freedom, frames "Silent" Madden with a shooting. His daughter, alienated by this treachery, plans a jewelry robbery with one Dapper Bill (Wheeler Oakman). Though they succeed, they are doomed to a life of crime. The film climaxes in a thrilling gunfight in which Black Mike is killed. Molly and Dapper Bill are arrested, but Chang Lo gains their release by returning the stolen items. If her role lacked billing, Anna May gained valuable attention from director Browning and from Chaney, an actor on his way up. Whereas *The Red Lantern* had given her a somewhat positive view of Chinese history, this next introduced her to the dismal perceptions westerners had of Chinatown and its residents. One side of the plot taught Anna, as she would learn over and over again, that Chinatown harbored treacherous gangsters of many nationalities. The example of Chang Lo offered some consolation and taught her that Chinatown was a state of mind where marginal characters could share lives across racial lines.[1]

The strength of her performance earned Anna May a spot in a Samuel Goldwyn production, *A Tale of Two Worlds*. This was the first time Anna May crossed paths with Goldwyn, an encounter that would resonate throughout her career. In this instance, she was able to work in a major production, staged in San Francisco's Chinatown. An antiques dealer named Carmichael gains possession of a priceless Ming dynasty scepter. Boxer rebels in China murder Carmichael and his wife, so his daughter, Sui Sen (Leatrice Joy) is brought up by Ah Wing (E. A. Warren) in Chinatown. The Boxer leader Ling Jo (Wallace Beery) covets both Sui Sen and the Ming scepter. She, however, falls in love with Dr. Newcombe, a wealthy young American. Newcombe saves Sui Sen, who is, incidentally, white, and kills Ling Jo. Anna May is relegated to the sidelines for most of the film, which nevertheless introduced major themes that would dominate her career. Sui Sen represented the white female captive taken by barbarians, a theme as old in American culture as the seventeenth-century Indian wars. In this melodrama, Anna May could see how desires of a Chinese villain threatened to corrupt a white woman, even if she seemed to be Chinese. The costs of love and sexual desire across racial boundaries were already a major theme in Hollywood's Orientalist dramas and became major factors in Anna May's career. The physical setting of the film in antique stores introduced Anna May to the more subtle Orientalist theme of nostalgia for the past. Only sixteen years old, Anna May was entranced by the antiques, which suggested sophisticated Chinese culture, and soon she began collecting them for her own home.[2]

She then signed with Selig-Rork Productions for a little-known film entitled *The White Mouse*, playing a Chinese wife victimized by a villainous "Oriental" depicted by Wesley Barry. Later she claimed to have had an extra role in the major hit, *Lilies of the Field*.[3] But her big break was in 1920. After two years of playing only the "one-hundredth or two-hundredth servant," she was informed that her next part would be as "the servant!" She reminisced later that the moment she heard that she would be the only Chinese in the scene "still throbs in my pulse." The movie, *Dinty*, directed by Marshall Neilan, was set in San Francisco, and featured Wesley Barry as youthful newsboy and son of a scrubwoman. The plot centers on the kidnapping of the daughter of a prominent judge by a Chinatown gangster, Wong Tai. Dinty (Barry), with his keen knowledge of the streets and criminal behavior, quickly takes the police to capture Wong Tai. As a reward the kindly judge adopts Dinty, whose mother had recently died of tuberculosis, and helps him toward a better life. The film was largely shot in San Francisco's

Chinatown at the end of November 1920. This meant that not-quite sixteen-year-old Anna May, even with her small role, had to travel with the cast, far away from parental supervision. San Francisco at least was the center of Chinese theater and she could slip away to enjoy its illustrious actors. The film did reasonably well in the United States and in Europe. There filmgoers got their first impressions of Anna May's talents, beginning a romance that would last nearly two decades. The film gained her some credibility at home when she returned with a big check in her hand. Anna May felt the "greatest happiness—like a rare flower, when it doesn't grow everywhere and always—only in fields of sun or white gardens."[4]

Now a casting regular, Anna May next appeared in *The First Born*, starring the distinguished Japanese actor Sessue Hayakawa. For the third time Anna May worked in San Francisco. Using a mixed cast of American, Chinese, and Japanese actors, *The First Born* told the story of Chan Wang, a boatman forced to marry Chan Lee when his beloved, Loey Tsing, is sold to a wealthy merchant in San Francisco. Chan Lee soon gives birth to a son, Chan Toy. When Chan Wang meets his former love in San Francisco, her jealous husband lures Chan Lee and Chan Toy to his home. The boy falls from a window and is killed. The revengeful Chan Wang kills his beloved's abductor, and then returns to China with Loey Tsing. Anna May's movie gained favorable reviews in Europe, though her part, in which she carried a teacup to Hayakawa, was not specifically mentioned.[5]

Anna May's exposure to Sessue Hayakawa is noteworthy. Hayakawa became a significant Hollywood player in Cecil B. DeMille's 1915 production, *The Cheat*. Before coming to the United States he was a major actor in Japan and prided himself on his mastery of Shakespeare. American film magazines featured Hayakawa and his wife, Tsuru Aoki, as top-ranked representatives of Asian acting in American settings. Hayakawa assumed roles of many nationalities, including Chinese. Hayakawa's parts often dealt with the hazards of interracial love; whatever the context, disaster and tragedy followed love between races. Hayakawa's male performances, matched by similar acting by "yellow faces," or white actors in Asian roles, established a path that Anna May would have to follow. At the same time Hayakawa had several advantages in his career over Anna May's. He was male, married, and Japanese, all qualities that granted him a stature she could not attain. He had a substantial home at which he and his wife entertained large numbers of Hollywood players, social behavior that undergirded the success of his career. Anna May, who still lived at home, could not compete at that level.[6]

Marshall Neilan gave Anna May her first billing in the four-part Chinatown chronicle, *Bits of Life*. Neilan had a good reputation for working with child actors, having introduced Wallace Berry to national prominence. The production, set in San Francisco's Chinatown, gave Anna May her first significant role working opposite the Man of a Thousand Faces, Lon Chaney. Previously she had worked with Nazimova and Hayakawa, both powerful actors. Chaney had noticed the youthful extra when they worked together in *Outside the Law*. Now Anna May was on screen with Chaney, who was a master of pantomime and makeup. Her success with him displayed her extraordinary maturity as an actress. In the episode featuring Anna May, Chaney portrayed Chin Gow, a young Chinese boy who, upon arriving in San Francisco, becomes the proprietor of several opium dens. Anna May plays his wife Toy Sing, who bears him a baby girl. Displeased, Chin Gow beats his wife mercilessly and vows to kill the child. Surviving stills of the lost film portray Chin Gow choking a terrified Toy Sing. A friend of Toy Sing brings a crucifix from the local priest. As the friend nails the cross to the wall, the spike penetrates the skull of Chin Gow and kills him. Despite the violence of his screen character, Chaney became somewhat of a role model for Anna May. He was a tireless worker who appeared in dozens of silent movies, playing a broad gamut of roles, a trait that Anna May openly admired. It was her goal, she told one reviewer, to play a variety of Asian roles. She later recalled her role in *Bits of Life* wistfully as the only time she got to play a mother.

Her work in *Bits of Life* secured a nice citation for her American resume when *Motion Picture Classic* paired her with the Chinese actress Winter Blossom in an article with the unfortunate title "The Yellow Peril: China Invades the Screen." There was international coverage as well. Anna May had to be pleased when the British cinema magazine *Picture Show* put her on the front cover. Significantly, Anna May was now playing supporting roles to major stars and working with famous directors. Impressive to her family was that she earned about $150 per week on the film while attending to her bookkeeping duties in the laundry. She now felt confident enough in her career to order head shots of herself. Photographing these early images of Anna May was James Wong Howe, who had come from Taishan in 1904 at the age of five and who was now achieving fame as a cinematographer.[7]

Not all members of her family were pleased. It may have been *The First Born* that sent alarms through the family in China. Huang Dounan, who saw the film in Tokyo, where he was attending Waseda University, wrote Anna May's mother anxiously, pleading "to take [her] out quick" from the movies. Lee Gon Toy paid no attention to him. Perhaps the family should have listened to Huang Dounan. Mickey Neilan, the film's director, was a notorious playboy who spent his salary of $125,000 per picture on wild parties and presents for his many girlfriends. Though more than twice her age, the jaded Neilan had no qualms about seducing the teenage Anna May Wong. Neilan's partner, Allan Dwan, reported that their affair was an open secret in Hollywood and that Neilan and Wong planned to travel to Mexico for a quick marriage. Neilan's friends reminded him of the laws of California, which forbade unions between Euro-Americans and Chinese and that Hollywood big-shots, already tired of Neilan's cavorting and drinking, would dump him fast. Neilan dropped Anna May, divorced his wife, and married Blanche Sweet. Despite Neilan's lack of courage, Anna May never stopped caring for him. Over a decade later, after Neilan's career was in shambles and Anna May had become a major star, she returned to Hollywood after an absence of over a year with a present for him. She brought a cross an Irish maid had given her in London, a talisman guaranteed to give the owner luck. Neilan became the prototype of Anna May's male lovers: white, older, and hierarchically more powerful in the business.[8]

Anna May's second billing came shortly after with the release of William Fox's production of *Shame*. Set in Shanghai, the movie featured veteran actor John Gilbert in the title role of William Fielding, a westerner entangled with a Chinese woman, Li Clung, who cares for his son following the death of his wife. Foo Chang, a Chinese trader, kills Fielding in a fit of jealousy over Li Clung. Li Clung takes the boy to San Francisco, where he grows up to inherit the family estate. Foo Chang attempts to bribe the son, played also by Gilbert, with a cargo of opium. He tells him that he is a half-caste. Young Fielding then flees to Alaska, to be followed by his wife, his son, Foo Chang, and Li Clung. The faithful Li Clung kills Foo Chang and informs the youthful Fielding that he is purely Caucasian. The family, including Li Clung, all return to happiness in San Francisco. *Shame* introduced Anna May to German audiences. *Das Kino-Journal* in Vienna gave the film a strong review, calling it "an original and extremely thrilling theme."[9]

Now a credited player, Anna May Wong's next film was one of her greatest. *The Toll of the Sea*, directed by Chester M. Franklin with a story line by Francis Marion, borrowed heavily from Puccini's opera, *Madame Butterfly*. The opera was among the most popular in early twentieth-century America and was a staple at the Metropolitan Opera House in New York. An earlier version, starring Mary Pickford, was a huge success. Various versions in book, opera, and film made the story into a classic statement of American Orientalism. It is impossible to discuss the place of Asian Americans in American films without allusion to the plot of *Madame Butterfly*. Here the fates of two nations—America and Japan—are bound up in the identity of two people. The original and succeeding versions are archetypes of the Western construction of "the Orient" as a sexualized and sexually compliant space ripe for conquest and rule.[10] The 1922 film, while altering the locale from Japan to China, is substantially the same as the others. What is significant is how Anna May subverts the tragedy and makes the movie a vehicle for her own interpretation of Chinese culture.

Frances Marion, a pioneering female screenwriter, admitted later that the film was "practically the step-daughter of *Madame Butterfly*." In Marion's interpretation, Lotus Flower, played by Anna May, rescues an American man, Allen Carver, played by veteran actor Kenneth Harlan, washed up on the rocks of the Chinese coast, ostensibly near Hong Kong. Although warned by a wise man that the sea takes more than it gives, she nurses him back to health.

As the plot of *The Toll of the Sea* unfolds, Lotus Flower and Carver fall in love. In these scenes, Anna May appears blissfully happy. There are clear signs that at seventeen, she was creating a screen persona and appearance that overwhelmed the other actors in beauty and intensity. In the rescue scene, she is dressed in a traditional Chinese girl's outfit and has a Child Flower hairstyle cut straight and low across the forehead, like a virginal country girl. She clasps her hands together girlishly at her throat. *The Toll of the Sea* was shot in Technicolor and is considered the first color film. Anna May's clothing used bright yellows and reds, made radiant in Technicolor. However, color could not mask her sorrow. Her joy is short lived. Life's exigencies intervene. A family emergency calls Carver back to the United States. His friends easily convince him that taking Lotus Flower along would be inappropriate. During the scene in which he breaks the bad news to her, Lotus Flower wears an antiquated Victorian dress. As the meaning of Carver's treachery becomes real to her, Lotus Flower's eyes fill with sadness and pain, real emotions dredged from the broken heart of a woman deserted by the gutless Neilan the year before. In *The Toll of the Sea*, Lotus Flower has a son during Carver's absence, and, though taunted by other Chinese women, clings to the belief that Carver will return. Lotus Flower resorts to counterfeit letters to maintain the illusion of marriage. In one letter she tells her "husband" that his son has grown a "big little chicken," a tender adult Chinese term for a baby's penis, and a euphemism for maleness that appears nowhere in dictionaries of English slang. While Frances Marion was the screenwriter, clearly Anna May was giving her more authentic lines. While Lotus Flower waits, her hair is drawn back in the *binzi* style of a Chinese wife. Ominously, her clothing is now dull browns and blacks, garb more appropriate to a widow. She holds her hands pensively in her lap, without any of the joy of the earlier scenes. Later, as the years go by, her hairstyle speaks to her predicament. As her comprehension of Carver's abandonment becomes unavoidable, Lotus Flower now cuts her hair across her forehead. One-half is a young virgin's cut; the other is that of a married woman, epitomizing her dilemma. She is "married," but not legally.

When Carver does return, he does so with a white wife, Beatrice, a friend of his since childhood. Not knowing she has been supplanted, Lotus Flower greets him in a wedding outfit richly tailored in red and blue colored silks. Her hands are held across her lower belly, a mark of a married woman welcoming her spouse home. Carver tells her of his new life. Heartbroken, Lotus Flower maintains a stoic appearance and gives her son to Carver and his wife to raise in America. She then throws herself into the sea.

The Toll of the Sea was a star-making vehicle for Anna May. *Variety* generally dismissed the use of color as gimmickry, but it praised Anna May as "extraordinarily fine," and "an exquisite crier without glycerin." The *New York Times* declared that Anna May was "naturally Chinese," and that she succeeded in a difficult role. It demanded that "She should be seen again and again on the screen." The reviewers were especially taken with Anna May's talents, and the film's tragic themes allowed Anna May to display them well. Silent film acting relied on combinations of pantomime and gestures. From the opening scenes in which she motions to the fishermen to save the drowning westerners, Anna May uses economical but expressive gestures. Similarly, her hands reflect her joys, sadness, and despair. Her crying scenes overwhelmed viewers. While Harlan's several attempts to comfort her about his racial infidelity fall flat, Anna May's sobbing wrings every sad emotion from the scenes. It would not be the last time that Anna May upstaged her male acting counterpart, and fans and critics remembered to watch for her teary scenes. Crying on cue was considered a rare talent in Hollywood, and Anna May was considered among the best. Many years later, she acknowledged that she lacked acting technique in this and other early films. She remembered that she "drained [her] emotions trying to live the part out." Her emotions were, of course, based upon her Chinese childhood in Los Angeles. By using her emotions, hairstyles, choice of costumes, gestures, and words, she was staging a Chinese persona on the screen in ways that the Western director and screenwriter were unlikely to understand. As a teenager, Anna May manipulated the Western myths of *Madame Butterfly* to represent Asian cultural currents. In the midst of this newfound glory, there were troubling signs. Her role as a sexually available Chinese woman, ready to be exploited by an older American businessman, would eventually earn her resentful criticism in China.[11]

Those complaints were still in the future. *The Toll of the Sea* helped Anna May's stature in Hollywood. Her acting made her known to a number of key industry players, who hired her for parts throughout her career. Studio executive Joseph Schenck oversaw the entire project for Metro Pictures and later signed Anna May for several movies. Adolph Zukor of Famous Players-Lasky Corporation was enormously impressed by Anna May. Soon, Famous Players-Lasky signed Anna May to a regular contract; in the 1930s, its successor, Paramount Pictures, became her main studio. Similar accolades came from the esteemed artists Maxfield Parrish and Charles Dana Gibson, who were among the first painters in the United States to try to capture her beauty on canvas. Other painters and photographers followed suit. Finally, the film was a major success. Shot on a low budget, it played in thousands of theaters across the country and abroad and reaped large profits for its productions. Later American cinema writers hailed the film for its important introduction of color and Anna May's powerful acting. Frances Marion, the screenwriter, was a good association for Anna May. No longer an actress, Marion was among the most celebrated screenwriters.

Photoplay Magazine extolled her intelligence and her "fair skin, soft-golden blond hair and youthful-looking dark brown eyes." Anna May made an additional connection when Frances Marion's best friends, Mary Pickford and her husband, Douglas Fairbanks Sr., attended the premiere. Fairbanks would remember Anna May's tour de force performance.[12]

The Toll of the Sea gained Anna May favorable overseas press. The English critics praised her for "practically carrying the film," and noted that she made a very attractive figure of Lotus Flower. The critics noted that the performance was delivered with "real restraint and subtlety that only a true artiste can attain."[13] Similar praise came from the other side of the world. Notwithstanding its racial themes, Japanese critics praised *The Toll of the Sea*, calling the film and its star "full of beauty and romance." One critic stated that "Japanese movie stars can't compare with her." The Japanese response to Anna May was racially neutral and seems very close to the Orientalist interpretations found in Western nations. In fact, Japan distanced itself culturally from China. Japanese commentary on Anna May demonstrates multiple perceptions of Orientalism, even among Asian nations. One factor was political. There were restrictive quotas in Japan against Chinese immigration. They were not as severe as the American laws, and there had been some loosening of restrictions in recent years. Still, the Chinese population in Japan numbered only 16,936 in 1922, a figure that was double the total ten years earlier and about half the number in 1931. Careful accounting of the Chinese population in Japan during the interwar years showed annual fluctuations and a sharp downturn after the Japanese invasion of China in 1931.[14]

One review had limited circulation but held long-term importance for Anna May. *The Chinese Students' Monthly*, published for the several hundred elite Chinese students in American universities, reviewed the film in late 1922. The magazine was the organ for the eastern branch of the Chinese Students' Association and was filled with serious debate about the relative importance of railroad versus military modernization in China. Its membership was composed of innumerable current and future leaders of China: Among them, for example, was Wellington Koo, who had graduated twelve years before from Yale, but still maintained contact with the association. Koo was already a successful diplomat. The journal's film critic Chung-Shu Kwei admired the Technicolor method and called the film "easily the best that ever purports to portray on the screen the daily life of the Chinese." His attitude toward Anna May was mixed. He regarded her as "creditable," though he disparaged her mix of old-fashioned costumes and modern gestures. A few paragraphs later, Kwei noted that her costumes represented a "stage in the highly developed Chinese art of embroidery." Overall, he judged her acting to personify Chinese womanhood. Though she may not have read it, the review was an important one for Anna May as it initiated a favorable view of her persona that would help protect her against future attacks in the Chinese press.[15]

International fame did not substantially change Anna May's status at home. After leaving high school in 1921, she still lived behind the laundry and kept the books for her father. The outside world, eager for information about this fascinating young woman, came to the family home. After the release of *The Toll of the Sea*, reporters began visiting the laundry to ask questions. They sufficiently annoyed Wong Sam Sing that he now insisted upon an arranged marriage that could end his daughter's distressing notoriety. Just as her liaison with an older white man had instructed her about the high boundaries of mixed race love, so her father's pressure highlighted the other side of her romantic predicament. In Chinatown's bachelor society, in which single Chinese men heavily outnumbered women, Wong Sam Sing could undoubtedly have arranged a profitable match. After all, women constituted only 12.6 percent of all Chinese in America. The numbers of Chinese women admitted to the United States in the first decades of the twentieth century were minimal; in 1920, for example, only 429 Chinese women were allowed into the United States. A union arranged by her father would immediately end Anna May's career, for in the traditional Chinese world women were child bearers, rarely appearing in public. Legal sanctions also inhibited her chances for marriage. The restrictive California and federal marriage laws further would doom her career. A law passed in 1907 stated that an American-born woman who married a foreign national had to take her husband's nationality. This law became part of the Cable Act of 1922. Under this law, if the prospective groom was "ineligible" for citizenship, a woman such as Anna May might lose her citizenship. To avoid nosy immigration officials, she would have to live a secretive, private existence. Iris Chang has indicated that mixed-race marriages between whites and Chinese were common in 1920s Los Angeles. Few of them involved people with profiles as high as Anna May's.

Legal and family injunctions pushed Anna May to refuse to consider any marital plans. She admitted part of her dilemma was personal. She acknowledged that she could only respect a man with her father's ambitions; at the same time, she feared that such a husband would dominate her and keep all her earnings to himself. Staying unmarried did not alleviate family pressures. There were Chinese women, primarily elite students, who chose single status, but Anna May's family did not see her in that role. Anna May was as realistic as she was defiant. She knew that Chinese American men preferred Chinese-born women, who they felt were less spoiled than their American-born counterparts. Nor was there much likelihood that Anna May could find a husband among the male Chinese students in the United States. Largely from the elite and Mandarin speakers, they tended to regard the Cantonese in the United States with disfavor; linguistic and class differences seemed insurmountable. She also had the wrong kind of job. While Chinese students knew of her, it is doubtful that any one of them would have risked his career by marrying an actress. Her father would have to be satisfied with her large financial contributions to her family's welfare. Over the course of the next two decades, Anna May paid for the higher education of her brothers and sisters. She balked at paying for Huang Dounan's schooling in Japan, but indirectly she subsidized him, because Wong Sam Sing now could send more money overseas. To satisfy her longings for romance, Anna May had to turn to Euro-American men, who seemed unthreatened by her fame, stature, and intelligence. Anna May became a prototype for Chinese American women who needed to step outside of their people to find a match. Sadly for Anna May, the men she loved lacked the courage she possessed and forsook her.[16]

Anna May faced additional pressures to get married. Her unmarried status hampered her career. Films of the 1920s explored all aspects of marriage and divorce. Fan magazines amplified these obsessions and spread the word across Hollywood and into at least twenty-four other nations. Weekly and monthly publications were filled with stories of the raptures and tragedies of star marriages. Fans eagerly inquired about the marital and amorous worlds of their favorites. Legal and cultural strictures against Anna May's chances for marriage made her peculiar in the eyes of the adoring public. While many Hollywood players never married, Anna May's high profile and the unconscious public anxieties about her single status were costly to her reputation.

Still, Anna May's notoriety was widespread among Chinese Americans. A fascinating instance of mistaken identity around this time indicates one effect of her fame. An advertisement appeared in Los Angeles newspapers asking her to come to 908 North State Street and telling her, "This is a matter of Life and Death! Your Mother." Anna May knew that Lee Gon Toy was fine and living on North Figueroa Street. When Anna May went to the house at 908 North State Street, two detectives met her. They represented a "troubled old Chinese woman" whose own daughter had disappeared two years before. The woman had looked everywhere for her child and upon seeing Anna May's picture in the newspaper had hoped that the image was that of the missing daughter. The old lady apologized to Anna May and told her, "I'm sorry if I scared you, but I was so happy about this new hope to find my child. Now this is gone, too." The woman cried so bitterly that Anna May was deeply moved by the incident.[17]

Anna May's real-life inability to find a suitable husband found confirmation in her film roles. Prohibitions against on-screen kissing and off-screen indications of interracial romance curbed her potential stardom and chances for finding the "right guy." Given the national controversy surrounding a kiss actress Mary Blair placed on the hand of her on-stage husband, Paul Robeson, in Eugene O'Neill's play, *All God's Chillun Got Wings*, Hollywood studios were not about to buck the sexual racism in the United States by giving Anna May a romantic lead role. She could not hope for the "heavenly" union enjoyed by Mary Pickford and Douglas Fairbanks Sr., or love with a wealthy man such as Marion Davies possessed with William Randolph Hearst. No big wedding meant no great house to entertain friends, and being alone cut her off from the Hollywood party circuit, with its heavy emphasis on husbands and wives. Her single status also meant no babies and temporary retirement into the bliss of family life. Rather, she had to labor constantly to maintain her image.

Anna May publicly discussed her marital dilemmas. Because of her height and large eyes she was not, she contended, attractive to Chinese men. Her independent attitude and modern behavior also, she believed, scared off men of her ancestry. As for American men, although they were good company and seemed to like her, she questioned the "use to let one's heart go when nothing can come of it." In another article, she declared that she wanted to marry a Chinese American man, because "the only happiness is with one's own race."[18]

As Anna May was still in her teens, such concerns could be ignored for a while. Meanwhile, she lived the life of a flapper to the hilt. One Hollywood writer recorded a visit to the Sam Kee Laundry. She was surprised that the counter girl, "a lovely little combination of ivory and jet," was the recent star of *Bits of Life*, Anna May Wong. The journalist Myrtle Gebhart returned to the laundry to interview the actress. Anna emerged from the store dressed in a sport suit, her facial complexion resembling mellowed ivory flushed with rose. Her lips, gushed Gebhart, seemed to be a "Yuan Chen poem stepping from the embossed covers of a book of old lyrics." When Anna opened her mouth, however, her modernity spilled out: "My, that's a nifty car. It's the kitty's eyebrows, what?" Now that each understood the other to be a modern flapper, the two set out "to worry traffic cops." The article brought readers up to date on some of Anna's off-screen activities. She had taught Constance Talmadge how to use chopsticks for *East Is West* and she ran mah jongg games for a local theater wishing to capitalize on her new fame, provided that she could keep her winnings. Anna May refuted those who criticized her for living at home. "I was born here," she asserted, and contended that her father would never allow her to be corrupted by Hollywood, so she was investing her savings in real estate. For the first time, Anna May publicly expressed a longing to visit China, but admitted she was afraid because "over there, they're not so particular and marry you off without much preliminaries." Anna May was proud that she had scored a lead role in the new film, *Drifting*, to be directed by Tod Browning, a well-established director. She had won the role despite her initial encounter with Browning. The director apparently did not remember the extra's tiny role in *Outside the Law*. When he arrived to meet her, she had been standing in the rain in a soaked fur coat, "looking very much like a drowned seal."[19]

Her public image as a flapper was partly studio publicity combined with a personal bid for sophistication. While the flapper is considered to be largely a Euro-American phenomenon, Anna May appealed to new consumers among young Chinese women in the United States and across the Pacific Ocean. In the United States, Chinese American men considered their female counterparts as "regular flappers," and often believed that the young women's searches for personal freedom made them less preferable as wives to women born in China. Even there, sophisticated young women such as Hui-Lan Koo, wife of the noted diplomat

Wellington Koo, delighted in dressing as flappers and jump-starting fashion trends that swept through Shanghai and Beijing. Of course, Anna May could be both a flapper and a traditional Chinese girl. That ambivalence is present in a dazzling screen snapshot in *East Is West*, which was produced around this time. In the opening scenes Anna May is dressed in a heavy Chinese robe and delicately dances on her toes in a moon gate doorway. At the close of this exhausting traditional dance, Anna May smiles at the camera and morphs into a young flapper girl in a modern black dress cut just below the knees. She beckons charmingly with curled finger and then vanishes stage right. An intertitle announces, "Presto! Chango!" Anna May bursts into a Charleston as the camera moves down to her knees, where her beautiful hands crisscross rapidly. At the end of the dance, she flounces onto a swing and chirps happily with characteristic good humor: "That was tiring. But it was worth it!" Anna May demonstrates the fun she is having as a westernized Chinese girl. Just as she had done in the dialogue in *The Toll of the Sea*, Anna May inserts humor that only her Chinese audience could appreciate. An intertitle exclaims: "It's enough to make Li Hung Chang turn over in his grave." This reference to Li Hongzhang, the famous modernizer of Chinese industry, military, and education in the last decades of the Qing dynasty, was unmistakably Anna May's contribution. Li Hongzhang was famous among the Chinese but known only to Western experts on Chinese history. Li's credo of modernization was that the Chinese nation should adopt Western industrial skills but nurture a Chinese soul. Anna May's joke plays brilliantly with that motto, by implying that her performance of the Charleston is far more radical a gesture than reformer Li had ever proposed. Certainly Li had never envisioned a Chinese woman adopting Western dance. At the same time, Anna May's impish humor left unanswered the question of her own cultural identity.[20]

In her own life, Anna May seemed to tire of her flapper image and longed to identify with Chinese culture. There were rumors of an offer from a wealthy Chinese in Beijing to finance a star vehicle for her. Anna May told reporters: "I wish I had been born in China," because she had such great respect for "my people, the world's oldest gentlefolk." In her films, she hoped to "represent them worthily," a clear signal that she considered herself Chinese in culture.[21]

Browning's *Drifting* was not much of a vehicle for Anna May's talents, although the recreation of Shanghai was quite authentic. The film starred Priscilla Dean as an opium smuggler named Cassie Cook who was under surveillance by Capt. Arthur Jarvis (Matt Moore). Cook and her confederate, Jules Repin (Wallace Beery), try to kill Jarvis, but Cassie falls in love with him and reforms. Except for some scenes of Chinese villages, critics found Browning's direction and the cinematography rather dull and termed the production wishy-washy. The one bright moment, *Variety* noted, was the "performance of the little Chinese girl, Anna Mae [sic] Wong, who walked away with all the honors and who handled a death scene magnificently." The *New York Tribune*'s critic confessed that he watched dispassionately while Dean was locked in a burning bungalow and that "in reality we were slightly wishing that she would get burned up and leave the hero for Anna May Wong." The film did quite well in Japan, where it was described as doing "a beautiful job capturing the atmosphere of China."[22]

A surviving still from *Drifting* shows Anna May dressed in a Chinese robe, ripped down the front and nearly exposing herself. While Anna May's face is filled with terror, her hair drapes erotically over her breasts. The suggestiveness of the image was mirrored by her relationship with Browning. Almost a quarter-century her senior, Browning's career was plagued by alcoholic binges and marital discord. For the second time in a few years, Wong found herself involved with an older, married man. Their sexual affair was an open secret and some regarded it seriously. "He was in love with her," said the MGM production manager, J. J. Cohn. Cynics regarded the tryst as typical of Browning's irresponsible taste for something different. His wife was most vexed, knowing that the dalliance with Wong was, legally, statutory rape. Shortly after, she walked out on the troubled Browning.[23]

Anna May's popularity was growing rapidly, and she was now regularly featured in fan magazines in the United States and Europe. She dressed smartly in Western style. One article described her wearing "a tip tilted hat, pure Parisian heels, sheer silk stockings, and a Persian lamb wrap." Magazine photos in this period captured her in men's suits. As a display of her new prosperity, Anna May bought a Willys-Knight six-cylinder car, then wrecked it on a bridge trying to evade a motorcycle cop. Involved in the crash was a young writer named William Cliffords, who had published a collection of essays entitled *The Movies from a Worm's Eye*. Cliffords, who was apparently at fault for the accident itself, though not for Anna May's flight from the cop, apologized and promised to write a play for Anna May. After a while, she forgot about the promise and never expected to hear from Cliffords again.[24]

Anna May made one more movie in 1923. *Thundering Dawn*, directed and produced by Harry Garson, starred Anna Q. Nilsson in a humdrum South Sea tale of a young American going to hell in the Far East. Jack Standish, played by J. Warren Kerrigan, is guilt-ridden over the failure of his father's business. To assuage his feelings, he travels to Java, where he is first seduced by Lullaby Lou, a vamp, and then exploited by a merciless plantation owner. Fortunately, his fiancée, played by Nilsson, rescues him and nurses him back to health. Anna May had a minor role as the Honky Tonk Girl, which made explicit the notion of prostitution slightly veiled in her previous roles.[25]

The tawdriness of such minor parts did not, fortunately, blind the world to her talents and beauty. Moreover, *The Toll of the Sea*, no matter how unfortunate the story, served as a prime vehicle for her talents. The other movies merely showed that she was a true professional willing to put much energy into whatever role the studios allotted her. These professional qualities attracted one of Hollywood's biggest stars, Douglas Fairbanks Sr., when casting started for his next epic. "Doug," as he was known throughout the world, was a major box-office draw and one of the founders of United Artists, with his equally popular wife, Mary Pickford; the universally appealing Charlie Chaplin; and D. W. Griffith, then king of the directors. For his next film Fairbanks planned an epic set in medieval Baghdad. The fantasy incorporated irrepressible humor, Fairbanks's own athletic stunts, and a number of magical special effects. Directed by the talented Raoul Walsh, the story line of *The Thief of Bagdad* was slight, but fans of Fairbanks all over the world marveled at the spectacular stylized sets, his dashing, charismatic athleticism, and his personal charm. Fairbanks had seen Anna May in *The Toll of the Sea* and insisted in casting her for his new epic. He had to get past Wong Sam Sing first. The avuncular Fairbanks told the *New York Times* with obvious condescension how he had to promise her father that Anna May would be protected on the set. No doubt, Fairbanks had already heard the gossip about Anna May and Neilan and Browning, so he assured Wong Sam Sing that he would personally chaperone his teenage daughter.[26]

Anna May was cast as a "Mongol slave" who betrayed her mistress. While her role was brief in a very long movie, her effect was sensational. Although her hair was cut in the virginal Child Flower style, her costume revealed much of her torso and legs. Fairbanks and she were the only characters in the movie with ample sections of bare skin, making her in effect as interesting to the viewers as the international star. She played a key part in uncovering the secret identity of Fairbanks as the thief. When the bare-chested Fairbanks intimidates the cowering Anna with a sword pressed to her naked back, the effect was unforgettably erotic. As he holds the knife against the small of her back, she pivots her body so that her face looks back with fear while the rest of her trembles with a mixture of terror and sensuality. This interlude lasts for many seconds. Some felt that Anna May had upstaged Fairbanks, though his constant presence in the lengthy film ensured that he could not be ignored. Fairbanks's popularity and the film's magic guaranteed that *The Thief of Bagdad* would be a worldwide hit. The biggest movie of the year in America, the film played for months throughout Europe, dominated downtown theaters in Soviet Moscow for nearly six months and Russian provinces for years, and attracted thousands of fans in Hong Kong and Shanghai before the Chinese government banned it as a "ghost film." Anywhere in the world where motion pictures were screened, Fairbanks's epic was a must-see. It sustained his stardom and sent Anna May's popularity soaring.

International critics adored her as a "fine actress." Curiously, the European premiere occurred in Brussels. P. L. Mannock, an English journalist, scooped his colleagues by watching the show on his way back from Germany. Once home, he was the first to announce the arrival of a new "glamour-sensation, the American-Chinese Anna May Wong." Now on notice, other London critics gave her much credit for playing her part "with remarkable understanding." *Picture Show* magazine gave her a two-page spread reviewing her career. The popular French magazine *Mon Ciné* put Anna May on the front cover and devoted a lavish article to her career. In Austria, Anna May benefited doubly when *The Toll of the Sea* was revived in Berlin and Vienna. Because of the film's origin in Puccini's opera, the German and Austrian press initially thought that Anna May was Japanese and declared her the "famous Japanese tragedy actress." After that cultural misunderstanding was clarified, Anna May became even more popular in Austria. Advertisements clearly using her popularity in *The Thief of Bagdad* touted her older movie as "Anna May Wong in natural colors." The review also indicated that *The Toll of the Sea* had become a regular part of the weekly programs "in other

European capitals." Between her supporting roles in *The Thief of Bagdad* and the upcoming *Peter Pan*, along with her featured part in *The Toll of the Sea*, Anna May now had a solid reputation in Europe. Similarly, *Cinelandia,* the magazine for the South American film fan, described Anna May soon after as the "bonita mucha cha Chine," and reminded readers of her part in *The Thief of Bagdad*.[27]

Favorable treatment of Anna May continued on the other side of the globe. In Japan, The *Tokyo Movie Times* critic generally disparaged *The Thief of Bagdad*, but told readers: "Only the beautiful limbs of Anna May Wong remain etched in my memory." *Tokyo Play and Movie* featured a large picture of the barely clad Anna May cringing before Fairbanks's sword. In Australia, newspapers announced the arrival of a major new talent. Around the world, the effect on her fans was electric. Postcards, lobby cards, and photos of a sleek Anna May, still only nineteen years old, frightened by Fairbanks's sword, perched vulnerably on a bed, or curling into a ball with her rear end tantalizingly exposed quickly circulated through Europe, Russia, and Asia.[28]

While much of the world admired her beautiful figure, the revealing costumes scandalized her family and caused consternation in China. Her father felt betrayed by Fairbanks and disgraced by his daughter, who had caused him to lose face. The reality was much worse. According to his daughter-in-law, Fairbanks Sr. bragged about an affair with Anna May, despite Wong Sam Sing's surveillance. If their words were available to him, magazine writers in his native land would have intensified his anguish. The film critic for the *Dianying Zazhi* (Shanghai Movie Magazine) described the film as having "grand scale, but the art is not much good." He singled Anna May out for criticism, stating that "Huang does not satisfy Chinese peoples' hopes." Overall, he found her performance "degrading," a common taunt over the next few years. Another magazine, *Dianying Huabao* (The Screen Pictorial), ridiculed Anna May as merely a "cat's paw, who plays minor roles." Compared with Sessue Hayakawa, who had established himself as a major star and a credit to Japan, Anna May did not, according to this critic, "respect her identity and [she] seems content to play the roles of Mongolian or Egyptian girls." He urged Anna May to turn over a new leaf so that her fellow countrymen could learn to respect her.[29]

Anna May was too busy trying to fulfill her dreams to pay much attention. Later that year, she had a minor role in a slight production, *The 40th Door*, of which the best thing that can be said is that it was set in New York City. While she was there, she dated the actor Brent Romney. Peter Arno, the *New Yorker* cartoonist, recalled that Romney was suddenly scheduled to meet Richard Rodgers. But then the actor "had a date with this beautiful, beautiful, Oriental actress, Anna May Wong. Well, if you think I could get him to break that date to go see Richard Rodgers, well, not at all."[30]

After that Anna May played Keok, a minor player in the Famous Players-Lasky production of *The Alaskan*. Popular at the time as a vehicle for lead man Thomas Meighan, the film was actually shot in the wilderness of Alaska. Publicity documents referred to Anna May as a "featured player," a title that represented a promotion. Shooting the movie required that Anna May make her first trip outside the United States, when she traveled through Canada to get to the film's site. As a gift for her brothers she brought back three suits made of the finest English material.

While the plotline was a fairly modest story, *The Alaskan*'s spectacular cinematography included Kodiak bears, mountain sheep, deer, and gorgeous mountains, all photographed by the legendary James Wong Howe. In fact, his cinematography was about the only thing worth mentioning about the film. *Variety* condemned the film as a flop after its first week and the film quickly sank in the United States, though it did have a decent run in Britain and in Japan.[31]

After these deflating efforts, Anna May's next assignment brought greater acclaim and association with a major picture. Paramount Pictures' 1924 version of James M. Barrie's *Peter Pan* is now considered among the best productions of this classic American fantasy. Beautifully photographed by James Wong Howe, the film starred Betty Bronson as the boy who never grew up. Other featured actors included Ernest Torrence as Captain Hook and Virginia Brown Faire as Tinker Bell. Anna May held fourth billing as Tiger Lily, an Indian girl. Her most memorable scene was a dance she performed in a clearing. As Karen Leong has pointed out, Tiger Lily leads the Lost Boys in an attack on the English and the virginal Wendy. After the failure of this ambush, Tiger Lily is exiled to Never Never Land, the only female among the primitive boy-men. Despite her secondary role, the film helped restore her reputation as a popular attraction. Released around Christmastime 1924 with two major premieres in Kansas City and Los Angeles, the film was the biggest hit of the season. Adolph Zukor proudly announced to

European vendors that *Peter Pan* was a smash in 250 theaters across the United States and described the film as sure to break all records. His words proved prophetic. The movie was another international credit for Anna May. Foreign distribution spread all over the globe. An extravagant publicity campaign in Australia, for example, included photos, caps, and statuettes featuring Betty Bronson, Anna May, and other stars of the film.[32]

Anna May's international fame suggested to her that foreign travel might be in order. She had some travel experience already. Her role in *The Alaskan* meant that Anna May had to apply for and receive Immigration and Naturalization Service Form 430, a certificate of identity applicable only to Chinese citizens of the United States, to reenter the nation. The paper trail established by this first permit continued until 1943. Any future applications for trips outside the United States began by reference to the 1924 application, which served as the first page in a voluminous file, issued in triplicate. Form 430 from 1924 served as an official passport, which Anna May had to produce every time she made a new application to travel. Furthermore, Anna May, the rest of the family, and any other Chinese Americans had to keep the immigration inspectors continually aware of their residence. These procedures were not automatic, and there were instances of courts rejecting women with solid qualifications. No matter how great her fame, she had to check in with the local inspector, J. C. Nardini, any time she wanted to leave the country. Forming a positive relationship with the immigration inspector was important. Many of the white males working for the immigration service held racist views of the Chinese and viewed them as illegal arrivals until proven otherwise.[33]

These forms unintentionally provided key personal information. Anna May was now nineteen and had reached her adult height of five feet six inches. According to her document trail, she had black hair and brown eyes, a mole on the back of her neck, and a pit mark on the forehead of her otherwise flawless face. Her hairstyle changed according to the demands of fashion or her whims, though she generally maintained the "Child Virgin" cut in her films. Now that she was fully grown, her father once again demanded that Anna May find a husband. Wong Sam Sing had signed a long-term lease for the laundry with his landlady, which gave him proprietary rights in eight years. A curious clause in the lease made the laundryman pay rent directly to the Socialist Labor Party. More stable than ever, Wong Sam Sing doubtless wanted to find a good match for his second daughter. His pleas soon drove Anna May out of the house. She used her earnings from *The Thief of Bagdad* to invest in real estate. She soon learned that Hancock Park, where she had ridden on buses as a child, was off-limits to Chinese. The same was true for Beverly Hills. She finally purchased a bungalow in the 1400 block of North Tamarind. Her father's pressure was probably not the only reason she left home. James Wong was now in high school, Mary was in junior high, Frank and Roger were in lower grades, while Richard was still an infant. The small home behind the laundry was doubtless too small for the maturing family. To maintain filial affection, Anna May arranged for the entire family to travel to Mexico. A second and more significant reason for the trip was to establish files for each member of the family and obtain certificates of identity, just as she had done the year before. The Immigration Act of 1924 provided for the exclusion and possible expulsion of any "alien ineligible for citizenship." Even though all members of the family were born in the United States, the Wong family apparently regarded the acquisition of identity papers as protection from future legal problems. Mexico was a safe destination because of its porous border with the United States. Many Chinese immigrants arrived in the United States through Mexico. The Wongs probably reasoned that if there were any legal problems, they could easily reenter from Mexico. Parents and children all trouped down to the immigration office for interviews with J. C. Nardini. For James and the younger children, the interviews became a rite of passage. Each child had to give precise answers to Nardini's questions about the family. Any discrepancy in addresses, schools, teachers, birth dates, and other minutiae of individual lives could cost the family considerable inconvenience. It is a testament to their maturity and poise that the children could recite faithfully the significant markers of family life. Nardini's approval of their application gave each one bureaucratic imprimatur and eased the way for further applications.[34]

Life on her own as a westernized Chinese woman soon bore heavily on Anna May. Once again, she became emotionally upset. As she related to her Chinese film audiences a few years later, she was deeply grateful to her father when he invited her to come home and built a small bungalow for her behind his laundry. There she relaxed back into the life of a traditional Chinese woman, albeit a highly famous one. Novelists and journalists soon began tramping into her house for interviews. She served them tea in her brocade clothing amidst an exquisitely chosen Chinese interior and told them many eastern stories, beliefs, and philosophies. She had, as she told her Chinese fans, returned to her natural style.[35]

After frequent interviews, Anna May synthesized the elements of her life story, published as an autobiography in *Pictures* magazine in 1926. Unfortunately limited to two issues and ending prematurely with the start of her screen career, her narrative enabled Anna May to create a standard recitation of her early life. Later she would add to her story with appropriate comments on a contemporary movie, but her retelling of her early life remained the same. Much of the narrative accentuated her Chinese heritage. She began by noting that, although she was considered Chinese, in fact she was a native-born American for whom English was her first language, which she felt made her "original" among Chinese Americans. She acknowledged that her father began their family in Michigan Bluffs, California. Wong Sam Sing, she said, was a traditionalist and after making a fortune in America went home to China to find a wife through a marriage broker. She then described the traditional Chinese wedding and the place of the woman in the home. Her father, she recognized, had two wives and a son by his first wife in Taishan, Guangdong Province. After Wong Sam Sing returned to America, he found another wife and had eight children with her, including Anna May herself. Wong Sam Sing regularly sent money back to China to support his first wife, Lee Shee, and to help his son Huang Dounan become a great scholar. Lee Shee, as the first wife, commonly wrote the family with domestic instructions, which Wong Sam Sing tried to enforce.

Anna May felt troubled by such behavior. She contended that: "The Chinese child is born with ages of superstition, beliefs, and traditions in the his [sic] blood." It was no easy task to rid oneself of them, and Anna May was clearly struggling with her open defiance of Wong Sam Sing. She "wondered where my course will lead me. I puzzle over things a great deal." Her confusion existed within the boundaries of ethnic identity. The subjects she placed in the foreground of her life story indicate that the Chinese Flapper was more Chinese than a modern girl.

Her ethnicity did not mean that Anna May passively accepted her father's domination. She continued her narrative by discussing Wong Sam Sing's dismay over the birth of two daughters in America. Rejected at birth, she learned humiliation in the piano incident, acknowledging that a Western child would have laughed off the fall and subsequent bruise, but that she felt she "had disgraced myself and my family." Becoming acculturated was a mixed blessing. Anna May spoke of working hard at English and her fun with other children. Then came, she told, the treachery, the harsh racism of the other schoolchildren and vicious attacks from the boy behind her. She and Mary sobbed together at the racial insults heaped upon them by their classmates. The two sisters felt enormous relief when their parents took them from the American school into the Presbyterian Chinese Mission School, an institution that combined sympathetic American paternalism with Chinese culture. Anna May had a split understanding of gender. She told of her happiness at playing boys' games, of the pleasures in being with Chinese children, and her discovery of the movies, watching the *Perils of Pauline* serial and encountering real stars in the streets of Chinatown. From then on, her history headed to the movies. As she related, Anna May was eventually helped by Reverend James Wang and given an extra's role in *The Red Lantern*, starring Nazimova. From then on, the struggle was to integrate her fledgling movie career, the demands of her parents, and schoolwork, which she candidly admitted she failed to do. High school was happiness because of tennis and camp, not studies. Anna May finally spoke of how Marshall Neilan hired her for *Dinty*. After returning to school, she had an emotional collapse, from which she took months to recover. After so many absences, she decided to leave school forever and capitalize on her film career, much to the dismay of her parents.[36]

Anna May's worldwide stardom did not ensure her success. It was hard for Anna May to capitalize quickly on her burgeoning fame. She was still a studio contract player, and her role in *The Thief of Bagdad*, while sensational, did not break her out of the casting line of degraded women of the Orient or help her to the big contracts other stars garnered. At this point, there was not much she could do. The studios held immense power over actors, locking them into contracts, threatening them with suspension if they refused a role, or loaning them out profitably to other companies. Hollywood had typecast her as an Orientalist performer and burdened her ambitions with the prejudices of the era. As a studio star, Anna May's plight mirrored that of many other actresses. As a Chinese American talent, she possessed singular problems. She had become the standard for Asian beauty and "was invariably conscripted when a moving picture needs

Oriental intrigue." There were strict limits on her roles because "her appearance will never let her be the heroine, although she occasionally manages to achieve a sympathetic role." Anna May now provided authenticity to films with Oriental themes and validated the performances of "yellow face" actresses, who, because they were white, could take the lead roles and get the guy.[37]

There were bright spots. She had established herself, if not as a star, at least as a significant actress. She had all the requisites: personality, a growing resume, and a portrait portfolio. She seemed to have passed the journeyman stage and was poised for stardom. And she had an international following. Criticism in China notwithstanding, *The Thief of Bagdad*, along with her other films, gave her a global popularity. She remained frustrated by limitations in American film industry, but her worldwide fame would later prove to be a significant and liberating asset.[38]

Anna May planned, earlier than previously known, to produce stage and screen productions that highlighted Chinese culture. In 1924, Anna May and her manager, George M. Martin, contracted with promoter Forrest B. Creighton that he would raise $400,000 in thirty days to fund a series of films "accentuating Chinese legends." The contract stipulated that Anna May would be liable for debts Creighton incurred. After Creighton altered the contract and apparently used Anna May's name largely to broker stocks, she won a temporary injunction against him and eventually disassociated herself from the venture. In addition to showing her desire to promote Chinese culture and demonstrating her tough business mind, Anna May looked to the stage to enlarge her repertoire into theater work. She opened a vaudeville show in San Francisco in late 1924 that included singing a Chinese lullaby and a popular ditty called "Sally." Anna May announced that she would perform "nautch" dances as well. Nautch-girls were barely-clad, professional dancers from India, who performed intricate, erotic performances. Ruth St. Dennis had helped popularize nautch dancing in the United States. Perhaps also piquing Anna May's interest was a sensational trial taking place in Bombay in early 1925 involving the disfigurement of India's most famous and beautiful nautch-girl and murder of her lover by thugs hired by the Maharajah of Indore. Anna May declared that she was doing the vaudeville production "as a step toward real dramatic work."[39]

During the late winter and early spring of 1925, Anna May went on the road with a group of other silent stars including Bryant Washburn, Cullen Landis,

Ruth Stonehouse, Phyllis Haver, and Helen Holmes. The tour fared well in its initial shows in Texas in mid-February. Ten days later it appeared in New York City. After that, it was back to the Midwest for a night at the Kansas City Convention Hall. Admission was two dollars, but promised dancing with the stars after the show. Despite the fanfare of a marching band and police escort, the actors arrived at the convention hall to find eighteen thousand empty seats. The presence of reporters convinced them that the show must go on. They performed for no pay as the local promoter put a lien on the meager gate receipts. Disaster continued at the next stop in Atchison, Kansas, where the orchestra conductor's check bounced. He quickly grabbed the admission fees. Following that fiasco, Anna May and the rest fled back to the safety of Hollywood. It was her first barnstorming tour, and despite this first financial flop, she could see the possibilities of stage performances. Anna May became an avid theatergoer herself and started saving the playbills of the performances she attended. Her collection tells of the many shows she saw and indicates her constant movement.[40]

After turns as a Mongol slave and an Indian princess, Anna May next played a Eurasian villainess in *Forty Winks*, the screen adaptation of the novel *Lord Chumley*. Anna May's role in this film was slightly larger and more key to the plot than previous efforts. As Annabelle Wu, she gets the foolish young Lieutenant Butterworth drunk, steals his keys, and steals the plans for the defense of California. Lord Chumley, expertly played by Raymond Griffith, is initially blamed for the fiasco, but through a series of shrewd efforts, he gets back the plans and reveals the innocence of Butterworth and the treachery of Annabelle. Her performance was described as "very convincing as a calm seductress" in Japan. In England, critics described her as excellent. Austrian reviewers called her "outstanding." She then made a very brief appearance in the opening shots of *His Supreme Moment*, a screen adaptation of a popular novel by Frances Marion, her writer for *The Toll of the Sea*. Now a lost film, *His Supreme Moment* featured many scenes filmed in Technicolor.[41]

Anna May appeared in four films in 1926, none of which were of great consequence. Producers and filmmakers tried to capitalize on her fame from *The Thief of Bagdad* by giving her high billings, advertising her part in the film, and then using her briefly in their productions. This method brought free advertising and attracted her fans but cost little because she was paid on a weekly basis. An example of this was the movie *Fifth Avenue,* produced in New York City in the spring of 1926. The plot involved a southern girl who arrived in New York to start a career as a fashion designer. After several escapades involving mistaken presumptions about her and prostitution, she inevitably winds up with the leading man. Anna May, who played the part of Nan Lo, appears briefly in scenes that have little to do with the main plot. In other films, she appeared to justify an Orientalist flair in otherwise ordinary plots. Such was the case with *A Trip to Chinatown,* made by William Fox and released in June 1926, in which jealousy among white Americans is played out in San Francisco's Chinatown. The locale is nothing more than scenery, and Anna May's part as Ohtai has little to do with the unfolding plot.[42]

Anna May's next production had different intentions from most Hollywood fare. She starred in a lost and possibly never released eight-reeler from Fairmont Productions, *The Silk Bouquet,* with Jimmy Leong. Information drawn from a German film magazine notes that, supported by "the rich Chinese people of San Francisco," the China Educational Film Company was producing this movie "to improve the bad opinion that America has about Chinese people." Only licensing materials indicate that this film ever existed. Its production plan tells something about Anna May during this period. While Hollywood seemed disinclined to offer her anything more than small, degraded roles, she was anxious to break this mold and make a film that would show positive aspects of Chinese life. She was willing, moreover, to declare her independence from the studio system and take parts with unknown and even amateurish companies to attain that goal.[43]

At the same time, she was not ready to give up her substantial Hollywood career. She finished the year by playing Oneta in *The Desert's Toll,* a western produced by MGM. Anna May's part was minor and her presence seemed irrelevant to the plot. Still, viewers of her scenes as the Native American woman, Oneta, marveled at her beauty. Her salary for this film was two hundred dollars per week; her small role and careful accounting limited her actual pay to $125 for one week and $208.33 for the second, significantly less than the five hundred dollars per week earned by the star, Francis MacDonald, and far less than the six thousand per week earned by Paramount star Gloria Swanson in her films.[44]

Anna May was now twenty-two and had eight years of experience in Hollywood films, including two major films and a brilliant showcase. Yet she was still confined to unimportant parts in production fodder. Her first movie of 1927 was more of the same. She joined the great Japanese actor Kamiyama Sojin and Matt Moore in the Hal Roach production of *The Honorable Mr. Buggs*. In this somewhat larger production, Anna May's pay jumped to $250 a week; her total earnings amounted to $666.67, substantially less than the $3,000 earned by star Priscilla Dean, but much more than the $91.67 paid to Sojin. A second film that spring was *Driven from Home*. Produced by Chadwick, it was a stale melodrama that happened to include Chinatown as a backdrop and Anna May as the attraction in scenes, that in the *Variety*'s reviewer's opinion could easily have been omitted. Later that spring, Anna May had a small part in a Laurel and Hardy short, entitled *Why Girls Love Sailors*.[45]

Around this time, Anna May found a new amour. She had a love affair with cinematographer Charles Rosher. Twenty years older than Anna May, Rosher had a life filled with adventures (he photographed the Pancho Villa revolution in Mexico) and was among the leading innovators in Hollywood cinematography. At the time he met Anna May, Rosher was working on *Sunrise*, a classic silent film that earned him his first Oscar. This gorgeous film, which unfortunately opened within days of Al Jolson's talkie, *The Jazz Singer*, was the Hollywood debut of German director F. W. Murnau with a featured score by Hugo Reisenfeld. Rosher's career lasted until the mid-1950s, and he was later famed for such pictures as *Little Lord Fauntleroy* (1936), *The Yearling* (1946 and his second Oscar), *Ziegfeld Follies* (1946), *Show Boat* (1951), and *Kiss Me Kate* (1953). During the 1920s, Rosher was a member of the Lofty and Exalted Order of Uplifters, a gentleman's club founded in Rustic Canyon just north of Los Angeles by a group of wealthy businessmen. Hal Roach, who had teamed Anna May up with Laurel and Hardy, was also a member. Club members could lease land and build fairytale bungalows. Rosher filled his with Oriental antiques to please Anna May. This affair brought her greater happiness than the tawdry entanglements with Neilan and Browning. Anna May became popular with the Uplifters, who encouraged her interests in exotic plants. By 1927, the club recognized her achievements by naming a portion of the landscaping as "Anna May Wong Garden." Later, a member named an orchid after her. Today the room in which Anna May stayed during their tryst is still called the Anna May Wong room. There was much to do at the Uplifters Club. The club offered amenities including horseback riding, archery, cricket, and dart tournaments, all skills Anna May would later use. The Uplifters Club was all about contacts. Rosher was the personal cameraman for Mary Pickford, the leading female star in Hollywood, a close friend of Frances Marion's, and the wife of Douglas Fairbanks Sr. Pickford and Fairbanks were known as America's favorite couple. Her relationships with Marion and Rosher drew Anna May closer to the most powerful people in Hollywood. It is doubtful that Anna May tried to revive her brief affair with Fairbanks Sr. Certainly, Rosher's own English background and his connection with Murnau and other German expatriates helped Anna May to develop her international contacts.[46]

While frolicking with the Uplifters, Anna May sustained her film career. After a year of dreary productions, Anna May must have been relieved to land a part in the MGM production of *Mr. Wu*, starring Lon Chaney and Louise Dresser. The story concerned the seduction of the daughter of a Mandarin by an Englishman. Chaney, playing Mr. Wu, learns of his daughter's love affair with the white man and, "according to Chinese custom," executes her by chopping off her head. Chaney was among the most intelligent and enlightened Hollywood stars. Anna May and Chaney acted together in one of her first roles and they had remained friends. His attitudes about China reveal the difficulties Anna May faced even among friends and sympathizers. In an interview published in Germany, Chaney spoke of the difficulty playing a Chinese Mandarin because his "soul will always remain a secret to us." Acculturation was unreliable because the "Chinese who studies abroad and then returns to his home country after a couple of years remains largely untouched by the sentiments of the foreign country." Chinese pride, Chaney continued, leads to tragic endings. Using classic Orientalist ideology, Chaney described the characters he played as having "refined cruelty," by which "upbringing, education and knowledge are erased." Such were the feelings of even Anna May's most devoted allies.[47]

MGM's script indicates how the narrative and camera angles purported to demonstrate negative Chinese attitudes toward the mixed love affair. In the script, Basil Gregory (Ralph Forbes) is flirting with Nang Ping (Renée Adorée), Mr. Wu's daughter. In attendance and thereby complicit was Loo Song (Anna May, adapting her real name for the part). In one scene Basil sighs, "If only you could understand my language." Nang Ping winks at Loo Song and replies, "We understand him very well, don't we, Loo Song?" Basil comes again and again to meet Nang Ping in the Lotus Garden. Complicating their relationship is an invitation from Mr. Wu to have Basil's parents over for tea. Although the curmudgeonly Mr. Gregory uses crude racism to grumble that he "did not want to drink tea with a Chink," the family goes anyway. At Mr. Wu's home, Mrs. Gregory, incapable of understanding the relationship between her son and Nang Ping, talks of her desire for a blue-eyed, white-skinned grandchild. Hearing this, Nang Ping tells Loo Song, "There is no place for me in the West." When Nang Ping and Basil slip away to the Lotus Garden, the cameraman intersperses shots of Loo Song to reveal a Chinese horror of mixed love. As Nang Ping and Basil embrace, the camera records Loo Song gasping three times, her body shaking in horror at the lovers. By repeating that shot the film alludes that the American revulsion for mixed love matches that of a true Chinese. That Anna May, already a lover of three white men in real life, had to convey this message made it doubly ironic.[48]

Variety, which otherwise gave the film a grudging review, noted that Anna May played her part in a "loyal and sympathetic way." *Photoplay* gave Anna May credit for the film, but its writer displayed discomfort about the open love scenes between Adorée and Forbes. The article's title "Pletty Chinee Maid Likee 'Melican Man,'" indicated its concerns about how the film attempted to bridge "the ancient barrier of East and West." Anna May had to suffer similar slights in the media. An article on wax figurines that featured her was entitled "Beautiful but Dumb." Despite these petty insults, Anna May's new film did well for MGM. The company also spent ample amounts of cash on publicity, including stories about how Anna May taught her fellow actress Renée Adorée how to use chopsticks and speak Chinese. Such images captured the problem for Anna May. Adorée, who was far less talented and pretty, was given a larger and more significant part simply because she was a white woman playing a "yellow face." Her performance revealed Western caricatures of Chinese females, through her portrayal of Nang Ping as childishly vulnerable while sexually ambitious. Meanwhile, Anna May, at twenty-two years of age, was reduced to coaching Adorée in simple Chinese skills. The crux of the issue was that even in this cinematic indictment of interracial love, only a white woman could play a romantic lead opposite Ralph Forbes, the Englishman. Adorée, who otherwise barely appeared to be Chinese, could dress up in Chinese gowns with her eyes taped back and acceptably kiss Forbes. Anna May, whose Chinese origins were obvious and whose beauty was never more evident, could only watch as Adorée stumbled through her scenes. She did have at least one fan. Emil Jannings, who rarely had good things to say about anyone, raved about her performance. The kindly Chaney also encouraged her. When she told him of her frustrations, he replied that she should stick it out, promising: "You are bound to get a break some day." The film received generally good reviews in the United States, Europe, South America, and Japan.[49]

Anna May needed Chaney's encouragement. Matters proved worse in *Old San Francisco*, produced by Warner Brothers and released in May 1927. Remembered primarily as an early experiment in using the human voice as part of the musical score, *Old San Francisco* was considered a major film at the time. In this tale of land grabbing at the end of the Spanish era in California, Warner Oland played Chris Buckwell, a merciless persecutor of the Chinese and corrupter of the Vasquez family, which personified the genteel Spanish. Buckwell plays a dual role. On the outside he is a white man committed to "keeping the Mongol inside Chinatown." In secret, he was Chinese by birth and wore Chinese robes and worshiped Buddha. He also kept his dwarf brother hidden in a cage. The film featured superb photography by Hal Mohr, a great score by Hugo Reisenfeld, and employed such excellent actors as Oland, Dolores Costello, and Sojin, who played the leader of the Chinese community. Anna May had an unsympathetic part as Lotus, the treacherous lover of Buckwell. Her introductory scene in the film is telling. The 1920s was a decade in which filmmakers learned to emphasize the beauties of the human face. When Anna May appears on screen, she is visible only through the steel mesh of a door; in effect, the cinematography bars her face (and beauty) from the audience's vision. Similar injunctions occur against kissing. Though Buckwell is frequently described as secretly Asian, taboos against interracial love prevent any physical contact. In one scene, she and Buckwell come within inches of kissing. As James Moy has demonstrated, Anna May's part fits the stereotype of the sexually available Asian woman. And once again, her race condemns her to death. Lotus and Buckwell are part of the Chinese underworld and deal in opium. After Buckwell kidnaps the Vasquez daughter, played by Costello, and tries to sell her into white slavery, the earthquake of 1906 destroys the city and "eliminates" Buckwell and Lotus. Throughout, commentators announce that once Sojin's character and the other Chinese discovered Buckwell's true identity, they would torture him and his wife in ghastly fashion. The film portrays the Chinese in the worst light and today appears to be filled with unrelieved racism. The Chinese in San Francisco are victims of race traitors whose cruel fantasies include the kidnapping and rape of white women. They collaborate on opium sales or are stereotypically cruel. Despite elements that seem tawdry and racist today, the film was well received at home and abroad. In no way were studios penalized for racist appeals or for misusing Anna May.[50]

The dilemma for Anna May Wong was increasingly obvious. Despite her triumph in *The Thief of Bagdad* and continued good reviews in mediocre productions, her career was stalled in Hollywood. True, she was now a staple in the movie magazines, with full-page spreads appearing regularly. But her chances of moving up from supporting or featured player to star were improbable. Production codes against interracial kissing meant that she could not graduate to star billing, even in film with Orientalist themes. Rather, she had to watch as less talented white women took the roles that might have given her more fame, and, at least, more sympathetic parts. Despite her great beauty, she was cast as a prostitute, an opium dealer, or simply as insignificant local color. Her final scenes featured suicide by knife or death by overdose of opium.[51]

Ironically, censors and directors who denied Anna May the right to kiss another actor (and thereby secure more significant roles) highlighted how her career veered from Chinese traditions. Anna May openly complained about code injunctions against kissing on screen, and magazine writers sympathized with her. Within the Chinese theater, however, attitudes were different. The Chinese theater, whether Peking or Cantonese style, did not allow on-stage busses. In Chinese cinema, pronouncements against kissing were fierce. One contemporary commentator argued, "Kissing is a more primitive way of expressing intimacy." He continued: "As humans further evolved from their animal stage, they embraced more civilized and healthy forms of intimate contact. For instance, the Chinese usually expressed their intimate feelings through eye contact."[52]

If there was any consolation, Anna May was performing with fine actors who could prove good friends outside. Emil Jannings, one of Germany's major actors, who had come to Hollywood fairly recently, regularly asked her to his parties. Sojin and his wife made her a frequent guest in their home. On such occasions Anna May often sang a ballad written for her:

I'm Anna May Wong
I come from Old Hong Kong
But now I'm a Hollywood Star
I'm very glad
Dream in the nap, Bagdad
I look oriental
I am kind to other players
I make them smile
Good luck to China
As there is nothing more
I can do to become beautiful
They invite me by ship on the Pacific
The silk and rice in China
You will surely like
Please think I'm as beautiful
As them
I'm Anna May Wong
From Old Hong Kong
I will love her forever

When Anna May sang this tune, Sojin reported, "she [broke] people's hearts." He remarked that she had captivated the world when she appeared naked in *The Thief of Bagdad*. To Sojin, Anna May's greatest assets were her eyes: "Her big eyes, bright and clear, are her best feature. When she makes her eyes narrow, they express the mystery of the Orient." Anna May's heart was already broken, but her bright, stylish personality carried her through. Just as Anna May charmed her friends, so she could fascinate a crowd, as she did when she appeared dressed in Chinese gowns in the audience to see Ronald Colman in *What Price Glory* at Los Angeles's Forum Theater, or *Lady Precious Shen* with an all-Chinese cast.[53]

There were other moments of public fame in Los Angeles. *The Thief of Bagdad* had a gala, highly memorable opening. Anna May joined Norma Talmadge on January 5, 1926, in turning the first spadeful of earth, using a gold-plated shovel, at the groundbreaking ceremonies for the construction of the fabled showman Sidney Grauman's Chinese Theater. Anna May looked stunning in a full-length silk Chinese coat, similar to the one she wore in *The Toll of the Sea*. Her presence lent an air of credibility to the ballyhooed event. The theater, when completed a year later, was a monument to Orientalism. Seating 2,258 spectators, Grauman's Chinese Theater featured ushers and usherettes in elaborate outfits copied from ancient Chinese costumes. The box office was a pagoda; the roof was jade green fashioned from bronze. Between two huge columns was an immense stone dragon modeled in relief thirty feet square. Chinese vines and verdure draped the walls. Inside, the center of the ceiling, sixty feet in diameter, was entwined in immense silver dragons in relief bordered with a circle of giant gold medallions. Throughout the immense theater a riot of faux-Chinese culture was displayed. Despite her contribution, Grauman neglected to ask Anna May to place her hands and feet in cement, a publicity stunt quickly adopted by white actors. Later the theater did display a wax statue of Anna May in its lobby.[54]

If her handprints were not in the cement sidewalk in front of Grauman's, her face was everywhere. Quality photographers lined up to shoot her portrait. Some were Hollywood regulars. Clarence Sinclair Bull caught her extraordinary eroticism in a publicity shot for a Ramon Navarro movie. Shortly after, Ruth Harriet Louise, a legendary photojournalist, took a lovely series of images of her in 1927 for *Theatre Magazine*. Others worked in different milieus. The English photographer E. O. Hoppé took a number of images of Anna May, which were soon adapted into postcards. The fashion world found her irresistible. *Vanity Fair*, whose photography editor Edward Steichen and critic, novelist, and aspiring photographer Carl Van Vechten took notice, published a lush image of the "melodramatic Anna May Wong" a year later. Soon after, Steichen himself did the first of several lovely portraits of Anna May. This time he presented only her head near a white flower, using a method popularized by Man Ray in his image, *Noir et Blanc*. Cecil Beaton, then an aspiring fashion photographer, shot a portrait of Anna May "in a grotto of gypsophilia and cellophane suspended from billiard cues." As Anna May's Hollywood career stalled, her fame among an elite group of artists soared.[55]

Anna May attracted attention as a model and a designer of innovative clothing. Images of her in a bathing suit made of Chinese fabric circulated in Japan and China in 1927. As lovely as the fabric may have been, the eyes of her fans went quickly to her bare legs, a scandalous revelation in the East. In America, bare legs were more acceptable. Eventually, Chinese filmmakers promoted Li Lili as the "athletic star" and were thereby able to portray her in short shorts. Anna May crossed another boundary and displayed her unique taste the same year with an eye-popping kulak suit, described as the first business suit made for women. She displayed her own creativity in the design of a jacket made out of her father's wedding coat. Anna May called the coat her favorite article of clothing. It was all the more unusual because Chinese women customarily adapted their mother's wedding outfits. Anna May's highly individual sense of style attracted attention in Europe.

Anna May's global fame surged. British film magazines gave her full-page coverage. Japanese film magazines regularly noted that she was in a film, however briefly, a sign that her fans there were numerous. *Tokyo Stage and Screen Magazine* gave her a full-page color layout in a "swimming suit with oriental style" just months after it featured a beautiful portrait from *Mr. Wu*.[56] In China, *Liang You Huabao*, the most popular women's magazine in Shanghai, featured Anna May on the cover. Inside, an image guaranteed to promote her fame in China showed Anna May, Wu Liande, the editor, and Douglas Fairbanks Sr. in a friendly clasp of hands. Wu Liande was a valuable friend. As founder of the Liang You tushu yinshua gongsi (good-friend and book company), he oversaw a small empire of film, literary and sports journals, and several book imprints. In Shanghai's booming cultural world, he had the power to keep Anna May's visage before an eager public.[57]

Anna May kept up a steady routine of work throughout 1927. She had a small role as a nautch dancer (prostitute) in *The Devil Dancer* with Gilda Gray and Clive Brook, two talented actors, for United Artists late in the year. Gray was one of the highest paid actresses in Hollywood and received $250,000 for the movie. Anna May would encounter Gray and Brook in the near future. Sojin and Anna May teamed up again in *Chinatown Charlie* in early 1928. This movie also attracted the attention of censors in New York State who demanded and got cuts of any suggestions of interracial sex along with a scene that featured the rape of a white woman by a Chinese man. One benefit Anna May gained from *The Devil Dancer* was working with Gray, who was known as "The Queen of the Shimmy." Gray's dancing, along with that of Anna May and the other nautch girls, was enough to make New York State's censorship board require heavy cuts of close-ups of the half-clad women. In January 1928, Anna May appeared in *The Chinese Parrot*, directed by Paul Leni for Universal. This film was the first Charlie Chan movie, the title role of which was later popularized by Warner Oland but here is played by Sojin. Anna May's part was predictably brief as a nautch girl. Perhaps the only benefit of the film for Anna May was working with Sojin and Leni, who introduced her to more members of the German cinema community in Hollywood, among them the great star Conrad Veidt and the screenwriter Carl Vollmoeller. Soon, these friendships would have a major effect on her.

The Chinese Parrot did well in England, where Anna May's stardom continued to rise. French and Austrian critics praised the film. When the film was shown in China, however, critics condemned it. In late 1927, one magazine published an image emphasizing her bare back, a scandalous exposure. Initial comments about the film stated that Anna May was losing face for China again. By the time the film actually appeared in the Shanghai movie houses, the movie reviewer for the *Pei-Yang Pictorial Weekly* of Tianjin had read her narrative published the month before in *Liang You Huabao* in which she spoke of her respect for the motherland. He was disappointed to see that nothing had changed. He wrote: "In the movie, I saw Miss Wong dancing in a crowd of naked natives, violently twisting her bottom and her dance displayed no other movements." He concluded that her performance would be unacceptable to Chinese audiences.[58]

Three films made shortly thereafter pushed Anna May to exasperation with Hollywood. In *The Streets of Shanghai*, she had to contend with a mediocre script; also appearing in the film was Kenneth Harlan, her costar in *The Toll of the Sea*. If it was inconsequential, *The Streets of Shanghai* was less troubling than her next two films. In *The Crimson City*, released by Warner Brothers in July 1928, she got only a minor part and had to instruct Myrna Loy in how to use chopsticks. Loy had the decency later to say that she felt terrible acting as Onoto, a Chinese girl about to be sold into slavery. The difficulty, said Loy, was that playing a Chinese woman in a film with Anna May Wong made [Loy] appear about as Chinese as "raggedy Ann." Wong's other spring offering was an unbilled part in *Across to Singapore*, starring Ramon Navarro and Joan Crawford. In this South Sea adventure, Anna May played a barroom seductress who drapes herself first all over Mark Shore (Ernest Torrence), the older brother of Joel Shore, played by Navarro, soon switching to Joel. In the surviving American version, Navarro and she barely touch, but in stills preserved at the Herrick Library, extraordinarily passionate scenes between the two wound up on the cutting-room floor for screenings in the United States. In advertisements for the South American market, where presumably mixed-race love was more accepted, Anna May is portrayed in tight squeezes with Navarro and Torrence. Anna May's passion is apparent in surviving scenes in which she appears with wild eyes, lush hair askew, and bare belly. Her legs are barely covered with a see-through gauze, and she wears a necklace made of shark teeth. She embraces both men with abandon and at one point kisses the older man on the face. It was not a major breakthrough to be sure, but the on-screen kiss passed the censors. In publicity shots taken by Clarence Sinclair Bull for the film, Anna May used only her lush hair to cover her breasts. At the age of twenty-two, Anna May was openly confident about showing her body and creating an air of on-screen sensuality.[59]

Production notes for *Across to Singapore* reveal how Hollywood studios carefully excised any materials that suggested mixed-race love. In his original story, which formed the basis for the film treatment, Ben Ames Williams describes the character Anna eventually played as "a lovely slut, and when she came through the door of the place with her head held high . . . the golden rings on her dark arms and ankles clinked. She sat on Mark's knee, ruffled his hair. He pinched her arm, smelled her hair, bit her thumb and then he kissed her." When they stood embracing, they were "like two lovers long parted." Softening this sensuous exchange in the first treatment, written on November 8, 1927, writers Lawrence Sterling and Ted Shane changed her skin to "yellow" and placed her on Mark's knees, "Mark kissed his trull with a boisterous smack." Other lusty elements remained. When Joel (Navarro) arrives, the girl makes a face at Mark and kisses Joel fully on the mouth. Later, in a street fight, Mark is stabbed. The girl tells him, "This time I will never let you leave me," then helps him up the stairs to her home. As she walks, she pulls strips of silk from her scanty costume. By the time the cameras rolled, all these steamy scenes were deleted. The girl, now identified in the script as Anna May (other actors were called by their parts), kisses Mark softly on the cheek. Later during the fight, she helps him up the stairs to her home, without the striptease.[60]

Disgusted at how Hollywood studios were keeping the brakes on her career, Anna May Wong announced that she was leaving to work in Germany. She had contemplated this move for some time and had gone to apply with her older sister Lulu for Form 430 on June 7, 1927. Her decision was helped when UFA officials passed over thirty other starlets to give her the part in a forthcoming production. Anna May was friendly with a number of German film people. Carl Vollmoeller recommended Anna May strongly to director Richard Eichberg, who worked for UFA. In an interview several years later, Anna May recalled, "I sought the advice of many relatives and friends. I considered all they said. Many of them advised against such a difficult and uncertain venture. Then I made up my mind—I would go." To alleviate family concerns, she agreed to take Lulu along with her.

Soon after her arrival in Europe, Anna May described her reasons for leaving America. First, although she was making good money, she dreamed of becoming a great actress and felt limited by Hollywood casting decisions. Second, American racial conventions required that if she felt any romantic interests, which were always present in Hollywood productions, she had to die by the end of the script. Unsurprisingly for a girl of twenty-three, she had become bored with her inevitable cinematic demises: "I think I left America because I died so often. Pathetic dying seemed to be the best thing I did." A final reason for leaving had to be personal freedom. Living with her family had many advantages, but the ability to move freely, a prized quality for any twenty-three-year-old, was absent. Racist conventions about interracial love in the United States meant that, as one writer put it, "it was hard to go back to the little house behind the laundry—alone!" Anna May spoke openly about this before she left for Europe. Doubting that she would ever marry, a deeply pessimistic attitude in one her age, she lamented that she had never "found a Chinese man whom I could love." Such men, she worried, "demanded complete authority," and her education, work, and personality clashed with such requirements.[61]

There were clear dangers, however, in the move. After years of disinterest in foreign markets, Hollywood studios had begun their domination of world cinema by the mid-1920s. Paramount Pictures already had made significant inroads in England and France and dominated the market in Asia and South America. Although Germany, in particular, attempted to stem this onslaught with its own national cinema, there was danger that Anna May's career would be eclipsed by association with lesser-known cinema studios. Moreover, the talent stream, even from Germany, was moving toward Hollywood, not away from it. Her decision to buck international trends indicates the depth of Anna May's despair with her status in Hollywood, her single-minded rejection of American racism, and her courage to set out on her own. On March 28, 1928, Anna May, accompanied by Lulu, left Hollywood for a new career in Germany.[62]

The Wong Family, late 1920s. From left: Lulu, Roger, Mary, Lee Gon Toy, James (in rear), Richard (in front), Wong Sam Sing, Anna May, and Frank.

Lee Gon Toy, Anna May, Lulu, and Wong Sam Sing in traditional garb, ca. 1907.

Lee Gon Toy, undated.

Above: Wong Sam Sing, undated charcoal drawing, Chang On Village, ca. 1890.

Right: Lee Shee, first wife of Wong Sam Sing, undated photograph, Chang On Village, ca. 1890.

Below: Huang Dounan, son of Wong Sam Sing and Lee Shee and half-brother of Anna May Wong, ca. 1922 during student years at Waseda University, Tokyo.

Early image of Anna May from *Dinty*, 1921. Photograph taken by James Wong Howe, the great Chinese American cinematographer.

Lon Chaney and Anna May in *Bits of Life*, 1921. Here Chaney introduces Anna May to the tortures she will commonly receive in her roles.

Anna May Wong, by W. A. Seeley. This publicity image from around 1922 reveals Anna May's extraordinary beauty mixed with rebellion against the traditions of her parents.

Allen Carver (Kenneth Harlan) tells Lotus Flower (Anna May) in *The Toll of the Sea* that he is leaving for America without her. Anna May is unsuccessfully fighting back the tears.

Right: The image that titillated the world. Anna May curls her body in terror from the knife that Douglas Fairbanks, Sr. thrusts into her back in *The Thief of Bagdad.*

Below: Douglas Fairbanks, unknown writer, Wu Liande, editor of *Liang You Huabao* (The Young Companion Pictorial), China's foremost women's magazine, and Anna May on the studio lot of *The Thief of Bagdad.* The association with Fairbanks, whose fame was matched only by that of Charlie Chaplin, helped Anna May's reputation immensely, especially with Chinese audiences.

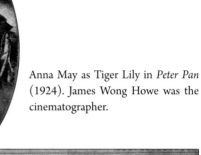

Anna May as Tiger Lily in *Peter Pan* (1924). James Wong Howe was the cinematographer.

Cover of *Liang You Huabao,* June 30, 1927. An early example in the nation's leading women's magazine of Chinese enthusiasm for Anna May, soon to be replaced by sharp criticism.

U. S. DEPARTMENT OF LABOR
IMMIGRATION SERVICE

LOS ANGELES FILE   Los Angeles, Calif.,
NO.27160/291
                                                June 2, 1927   192

To _____ Walter E. Carr
        Officer in Charge, Immigration Service,

        Los Angeles, Calif.

Sir: It being my intention to leave the United States on a temporary visit abroad, departing and returning through the Chinese port of entry of _____ New York, N.Y. _____, I hereby apply, under the provisions of Rule 16 of the Chinese Regulations, for preinvestigation of my claimed status as an American citizen, submitting herewith such documentary proofs (if any) as I possess, and agreeing to appear at such time and place as you may designate, and to produce then and there witnesses for oral examination regarding the claim made by me.

This application is submitted in triplicate with my photograph attached to each copy, as required by said rule.

Respectfully,

Signature in Chinese   (Wong Lew Song)
Signature in English   Anna May Wong
Address   241 N. Figueroa St.

RECEIVED

JUN 15 1927

CHINESE BRANCH, U. S. I. S.
New York, N. Y.

                    Chinese Branch,
OFFICE OF _____
                    NEW YORK, N. Y.
                    June 16, 1927

Respectfully returned to
        District Director
        Commissioner of Immigration,
        Inspector in Charge.
                    Los Angeles, Cal.

with the information that I have _____ Approved _____ the application on the basis of the evidence submitted herewith.

                    Inspector in Charge.

Anna May's application for Form 430, which would allow her to return to the United States after a trip outside the country. No matter how great her fame, Anna May always had to apply for and gain confirmation of her American citizenship.

Above: Anna May modeling one of the first examples of a pants suit designed for and worn by an American woman. Unlike the self-conscious adaptation of men's outfits used by Marlene Dietrich and Greta Garbo, here Anna May reveals how stylish she can be in a suit made just for her.

Left: Anna May in her favorite coat, fashioned from her father's wedding suit.

Right: Anna May with Warner Oland on the set of *Old San Francisco*. The pair collaborated in many of Anna May's greatest films and were good friends.

Below: In this important scene from *Piccadilly*, seen through the eyes of Wilmot (Jameson Thomas), the owner of the Piccadilly Nightclub, Shosho dances for the maids in the scullery room. Anna May's fusion of Chinese and Western dance captivated her European audience.

Viennese poster for *Piccadilly* displaying the openly erotic quality of European Orientalism and Anna May's greater sexual freedom abroad.

Marlene Dietrich, Anna May, and Leni Riefenstahl at the Berlin Press Ball, January 1929. Photo by Alfred Eisenstadt. This famous image is variously interpreted. In the late 1930s, Americans used it as a rebuke of Hitler's racial attitudes. Later, gay scholars used it to indicate an intimacy between the trio. Unquestionably it shows the personal freedom Anna May found in interwar Europe.

Above: Anna May with Jacob Feldkammer in the Viennese opera *Die Chinesische Tänzerin* (The Chinese Dancer) in August 1931. Anna May was always proud of this casting coup.

Anna May in *Daughter of the Dragon*, Paramount Pictures' big-budget Fu Manchu film and her welcome back to the United States in 1931. Anna May's extraordinary sense of style was never so evident.

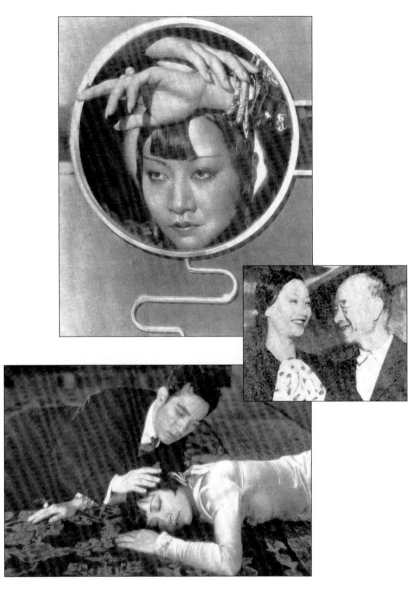

Above left: Anna May's hands were considered the most beautiful of all Hollywood actresses, and are fully on display in this still from *Shanghai Express*.

Inset: Anna May and her father, ca. 1932. "I was always looking for my father in my films," she once said. Here they are reconciled.

Left: Sessue Hayakawa and Anna May in a scene from *Daughter of the Dragon*. Here Anna May performed one of the many deaths her characters suffered in her films.

Above left: A postcard showing Anna May dedicating a willow tree for the new Chinatown in Los Angeles. Anna May frequently posed for such commemorative shots and benefited her old community in many ways.

Above right: Anna May's palm, as found in Charlotte Woolf's popular treatise on palm reading. Woolf's reading uncovered deep tensions in Anna May's personality.

Right: Triple Dragons! Anna May does the Apache Dance in *Limehouse Blues* with George Raft. From a Chinese perspective, Anna May's body, her dress, and the ceiling decoration accentuate the power of the dragon as the symbol of China. From a western viewpoint, the elements signify the dreaded Dragon Lady.

Paul Robeson, Anna May, and Mei Lanfang on the streets of London in 1935. Photo by Farina Marinoff. Anna May's internationalism is fully apparent in this candid, friendly image.

Anna May, Carl Van Vechten, and Farina Marinoff in New York, late 1930s. Photograph at a party by Nikolas Muray, one of the gang Anna May always visited with the Van Vechtens in New York City. Note the modified Peking Opera headdress Anna May is wearing.

Hu Die (Butterfly Wu) and Anna May, Shanghai, 1936. China's first lady of the cinema with the greatest Chinese American actress. After a difficult beginning, they became good friends.

Anna May carries out the body of a boy killed by Japanese gunmen during an air raid of Chungking, the Nationalist capital-in-exile during World War II. This still from *Lady from Chungking* de-emphasizes Anna May's beauty in favor of her patriotism for the Chinese cause.

Three
Europe

Anna May and Lulu arrived in Hamburg, Germany in April 1928. Their arrival there occurred at a time when the nation's film industry was trying to challenge the dominance of American moviemakers. To German filmmakers, Anna May was a major star who would guarantee attention for any production. Berliners were passionate moviegoers, attending films for the newsreels and to be entertained by beautiful women such as Anna May. Germany's largest cinemas were on the Kurfürstendamm and near Potsdamer Platz in Berlin. There were regular screenings throughout Berlin's suburbs and in thousands of small movie theaters around the country. Attendance was so constant that cinema owners regularly scheduled morning shows. Berliners were ready for Anna May's appeal. While later film critics and scholars would hail Fritz Lang's direction in *Metropolis* or Marlene Dietrich's starring role in *The Blue Angel*, the average Berliner preferred, as Alexandra Ritchie has put it, the "light entertainment" created by UFA, the largest German film company. Other popular themes included dramas about the dangers of Berlin or cross-sections of its society, such as in *The Adventures of a Ten Mark Note*. The American films Anna May had taken part in were always popular, and Berliners did not demand high art of her. In particular Anna May appealed to modernized working-class females who saw in her a pioneer in raising hemlines, smoking cigarettes, driving and wrecking cars, and in demanding as much personal freedom as a movie star could secure.[1]

At the time, Berlin was perhaps the most modern city in the world. Its theater was unquestionably the best in Europe and offered spectacular plays and performances. Bertolt Brecht's *Threepenny Opera* was the big hit of 1928 along with Franz Lebar's *Friederike* with Richard Tauber as Goethe. Musical revues were common and widely patronized. At the Kurfürstendamm, Marlene Dietrich lay on her back on stage and pedaled in the air with her gorgeous legs. Berliners were accustomed by now to what they considered exotic. Black performers introduced jazz to the metropolis after 1924. The Americanization of Berlin culture began after World War I and was powerfully influential by the mid-1920s. Berlin was crazy for jazz and fox-trots. At the same time, Berliners were capable of the worst sorts of stereotypes and demanded routines by Black performers to match their own racial fantasies. Germans frequently used derogatory words to refer to Blacks and reveled in racial fantasies about their sexual capabilities. At the same time, Black performers, of whom Josephine Baker was the greatest, subverted these racial images and often parodied Germanic mores. Baker first arrived in Berlin in 1925 and divided her time and performances between there and Paris for years. Not all Black performances were permissible, however. The police quickly closed two nude shows involving Black men with white women. If interracial sex was off-limits, Berlin offered sexual pleasures for other predilections. Prostitutes mobbed the streets. As Anna May walked around the metropolis or went to clubs at night, she could easily see hundreds of young women dressed flapper-style and available for the choosing.[2]

Yet Anna May Wong and Lulu entered into a society in which Chinese people were rare. Germany's capital city may have been a world center for an artistic avant-garde, but not even sophisticated Germans had much contact with Chinese people. While small numbers of Chinese had visited Germany for centuries, they came as seamen and street vendors and made little impression on the country. There were few Chinese institutions in Berlin. The city's first Chinese restaurant had opened only in 1925. Unlike American Chinatowns, in which sizable numbers clustered together against a hostile society, Europe's Chinese neighborhoods were more integrated into the urban world. There were only a handful of Chinese in all of Germany. The census for that year counted only 747 Chinese in the entire country, of which 312 lived in Berlin and only 30 of those were female. Anna May was not only enhancing Germany's film reputation, she greatly enlarged its national public comprehension of China.[3]

Anna May's first job was to act in *Song*, a movie produced and directed by Richard Eichberg. Film production began in the first week of May 1928. Barely remembered today, Eichberg was the most popular and successful German director in those years, surpassing such now-famous names as G. W. Pabst, F. W. Murnau, and E. A. Dupont. Eichberg was noted for his turbulent and sensational action, spectacular optical effects, and exotic genre films. Considered the "most American" of European directors, he was a natural match for Anna May, who was used to the efficient American studio system. He also worked as an independent and had a contract with UFA, the nation's largest film company and an affiliate of Paramount. He already had a deal in place to produce films at the British International Pictures' Elstree Studios. Eichberg had excellent contacts throughout the European movie industry. He was respected for working with already-famous actors in ways that helped them express their unique characteristics.[4]

Anna May's intentions encountered a German film consciousness that contained particular advantages and pitfalls for her. German expressionism was perhaps waning by 1928, but its lessons remained strong in the works of a commercial director such as Eichberg. Narrative techniques accentuated travel and transient lives by setting scenes in ports, ships, and taverns, all locales Anna May knew well from her past films. These images of transport helped Anna May to link her emotions to her film character. Anna May could thereby join her emotions in such transitory, urban milieus and make her films her life story. Add the narrative of mixed-race love to the film's plot and Anna May fused her psychology with the story line. Eichberg's American style created a marriage between a generalized racial exoticism, borrowed from Hollywood, with a far more sensitive use of Anna May's talents and physical appearance. Eichberg's embrace of Hollywood, combined with the unfamiliarity of Germans with the Chinese, created a dangerous exotic quality that marginalized Anna May's characters and doomed their fates as surely as would happen in any American production. Eichberg's fusion of older expressionist methods with faster American techniques had a pragmatic origin. As Germany's studios fell on hard times in the 1920s, their American competitors, sensing an opportunity, flooded the market with films. Eichberg, concerned with profits, was merely adapting to the times.[5]

Anna May spent the first few months in Berlin, working with Eichberg and taking an eight-hour-a-day crash course in German. German photographers and publishers quickly lined up to shoot portraits of her. Soon she was featured in a major 1929 collection of German film stars. Lotte Jacobi, a rising star of German photography, shot a number of spectacular images of Anna May from *Song*;

these pictures circulated around Europe for years. Jacobi's images, along with other spectacular poses of Anna May, were published in such prestigious French magazines as *Ciné Miroir*, *Ciné*, *Pour Vous*, and *Cinéa*, or in cheap but popular weeklies such as *Mon Ciné*. Anna May received ample coverage in magazines all over the continent from England to Holland, and from Spain to Italy, Hungary, and Romania.

Such continental images caught the eye of high-gloss American magazines, whose editors quickly responded by inserting Anna May into upcoming issues. During this period, Edward Steichen, the famous photographer, introduced several more images of Anna May in *Vanity Fair*. The French magazines and *Vanity Fair* could be found all around the globe. Film enthusiasts in China, for example, could easily obtain them in the French concessions of Shanghai. Such international exposure boosted Anna May's global reputation. Similarly, souvenir postcards made her face ubiquitous. Ross, the German postcard company, published dozens of cards of her in various poses and outfits, borrowing a number from images shot by E. O. Hoppé. These cards were printed throughout Europe, Russia, and the East. Other artists made more personal images of her. The Viennese sculptor Felix Weiss sat Anna May down to do her head; she playfully demanded to do one of him at the same time and "did it commendably well." Ross-Verlag was also partners with the Menasse Studio of Vienna that was notorious for its erotic photographs. Menasse was perhaps responsible for the nude images of Anna May sent from Europe to appear in Chinese newspapers.[6]

Making herself more comfortable, Anna May began to explore Berlin. She became a regular at the theater and opera. She moved easily among Berlin's intellectual elite. Berlin had an advanced café society; artists and intellectuals met their adherents in chosen coffee venues. Anna May hopped from one to the other, sure to encounter famous artists or writers. Going more deeply into intellectual circles, she began making the rounds of private parties. In June, Anna May spent an evening in Berlin with Walter Benjamin. The philosopher had recently returned to Berlin from Moscow and Paris. He was now writing essays for *Literarische Welt*, translating Proust into German, and beginning his Arcades Project, now recognized as one of the great philosophical treatises of the century. He described his meeting with Anna May in the July 6 issue of *Literarische Welt*. Her beauty dazzled the philosopher, who searched the boundaries of his poetic imagination to describe her. Benjamin characterized her name as "like the specks in a bowl of tea that unfold into blossoms replete with moon and devoid of scent." As they talked, Anna May told Benjamin about how Lulu and she arrived in Hamburg's train station, knowing no German, listening to the knots of people and hoping to hear the word "Berlin." They felt so lost, a sensation, according to Benjamin, that no longer pertained, since now all Berlin was watching Anna May. She was optimistic about the Eichberg film, saying that the part was perfect; "it is more mine than any role I have had before." She loved the sad scenes; workers from all over the studio were coming to watch her cry. Benjamin was clearly charmed by her. He said that Anna May's "open, joyful demeanor does not lie, and that her deep admiration of heartrending drama betrays a balanced and cheerful daily life. . . . Indeed, with a serious and comradely gaze that looks past every charm, this fit and upright girl has nothing of a movie star: An ample face like a spring breeze /Round in form, peaceful in Spirit."

Benjamin's narrative is one of the best descriptions available of Anna May in a private setting. He closely observed her physical presence in a sitting position: "she constructs a swing from questions and answers—she leans back, reappears, sinks down, and I feel as if I am pushing her a bit from time to time." Anna May recalled the first time she had ever been in a theater. In previous interviews, she had told of playing hooky. School was closed, she told Benjamin, because of an epidemic. She used her pocket money to buy a ticket. When she returned home, she acted out everything she had seen in front of a mirror. In this way, she decided upon her acting, for "one's career in life is a matter to which one must turn one's thoughts early on." Once her mother noticed her in front of the mirror, her passion was discovered and the incident did not pass without scolding. Benjamin and Wong went into another room. Comfortable now with his queries, she told Benjamin she no longer wanted to play flappers. She spoke of her desire to play a mother: "The best are mothers. I've played one before, at fifteen. Why not? There are so many young mothers." Her own mother, pregnant at fourteen after a marriage brokered by her father, would confirm this.

Wong and Benjamin talked about critics, whom she said mattered little to her. Wong told Benjamin of her own proverb, that "the truth, if it is bitter, is only heard from enemies. I want to hear the bitter truth from my friends also." She reclined on a couch, loosened her long hair, and arranged it in the manner of a "dragon romping in water," pushing it back over her forehead. Enchanted, Benjamin stared as the hair fell down over her face; he wrote that in the middle "it comes down a bit lower, cuts into her face and makes it the most heart-shaped of all. Everything that is heart seems reflected in her eyes." He learned that her favorite garment was cut from her father's wedding coat. The enraptured philosopher observed that "the fabric was donned divinely / But the face was even finer." Such admiration is clear proof that the twenty-three-year-old actress could hold her own with one of the century's great geniuses.[7]

Had Walter Benjamin been less overwhelmed by Anna May Wong's beauty, he might have enlarged his creative interpretation of Baudelaire's concept of the *flaneur*, or urban observer. Discussion of the flaneur remains a hot topic among film, literary, and urban scholars, who have identified male painters, photographers, novelists, and cinema workers as examples of this quintessential urban observer with the "male gaze." Leo Ou-fan Lee, a premier scholar of modern China, recently used the flaneur to interpret Shanghai in the 1930s. Feminist scholars have sought to find female flaneurs. Among the constraints are legal prohibitions against the female presence in the urban night, the perception that any women out were prostitutes, and that women were always gawked at. Yet Weimar Berlin housed many young women who felt no barriers. As the young psychology student Charlotte Woolf put it: "We had no need to be helped to freedom from male domination. We were *free*. . . ." Woolf was a good friend of Benjamin's and probably was with him when Anna May visited. If so, she could have recognized a brave, cosmopolitan woman who was willing to make her own direction in the world and was creating her own narrative. Anna May's acting gave her special freedom to fashion her own story. Coming to Berlin was her first big step in making her own transnational identity, which surpassed the keen, city-bound observations of the flaneur.

After finishing *Song* for Eichberg, Anna May traveled to Paris. As in Berlin, she made an immediate impact upon a nation whose exposure to Chinese people was minimal, though in different ways from that of Germany or England. French cultural attitudes toward the Chinese embraced the gamut of Orientalism. Dating back to the eighteenth century, French adoration of Chinese grace and delicacy began with the appreciation of silk, porcelain, and temple architecture, as Jonathan Spence has remarked, to form the basis of an entire aesthetic. This sensual taste expanded into an intoxication with Asian bodies, with perceptions of the hidden cruelties and barbarism of China, finishing with a vision of China as the realm of melancholy, with a lost past now compounded by its weakness and poverty. Opium was the narcotic of this melancholic languor. To the French, Anna May personified all they envisioned about the Orient.[8]

Anna May's initial sighting in Paris came on June 21 when she visited Ramon Navarro backstage at the Ballet Russe after his performance. Shortly thereafter, she brought a reporter along with her on a visit to the Louvre. She informed her infatuated scribe and his readers that she was returning to the museum for a third look at *The Road to Sevres* by Corot, a painting she believed helped her to transcend personal sadness and to understand the French people. If Anna May was trying to understand the French mentality, her subjects had larger problems trying to understand her. As in Britain and Germany, the history of the Chinese presence in France was minimal. The French had joined with England in importing about 100,000 Chinese laborers, mostly from Shandong Province, during World War I. These men built barracks and roads, unloaded ships, made ammunition, and exhumed dead soldiers. About 2,000 Chinese died during the war and were buried in France, Belgium, and England. Nearly all survivors were repatriated after the war, but about 3,000 Chinese men remained in France during the 1920s, including about 1,900 skilled metallurgists. Enlarging the Chinese population in France were students. Even so, by 1926, the French census enumerated only 2,863 Chinese, of whom just 233 were female. To the French public, as in other European countries, Anna May seemed to be uncanny.[9]

She may have seemed unusual to the Chinese in France. French Chinese were not from Canton, as in London and the United States, but hailed from the northern provinces and spoke Mandarin. Unlike those living in Germany and England, the Chinese in Paris were skilled workers in luxury and decorative objects, chiropody, catering, and furniture making. France hosted some exceptional Chinese people. Future revolutionaries Zhou Enlai and Deng Xiaoping created radical organizations and put out newspapers and magazines. Unlike other European nations, France attracted a number of educated, ambitious Chinese women. They included the artist Fang Junbi and Tcheng Soume, who in 1925 became the first Chinese woman to graduate with a degree in law from the Sorbonne. Other Chinese women students, whether rich or poor, formed associations and prepared for distinguished careers later in China. The presence of sophisticated Chinese in France provided a sound basis for Anna May's love affair with the City of Light.[10]

All the while, Anna May kept her American and Chinese audiences in mind. When Dr. Tien Huang, the "Lindbergh of China," announced his plans to fly from Los Angeles to Hong Kong, the ever-vigilant Wong quickly wired him, asking if she could accompany him. She also made sure that American audiences knew that she was achieving stardom in Europe. In the United States, *Screenplay Secrets* ran featured images of her, touting her new stardom across the Atlantic.[11]

From Paris, Anna May moved to London, where she began shooting *Piccadilly*, directed by E. A. DuPont. She was an immediate sensation in London. Anna May rented an apartment in the Mayfair District in the Park Lane Hotel, where rooms overlooked Hyde Park. Lulu and she received guests there with an American enthusiasm. They made trips down the Thames to Maidenhead and visited Limehouse, where London's Chinese population resided. She told reporters she liked London enormously because everyone was friendly to her. Her impact on the public was immediate. People mobbed her everywhere she went, making her forays into the city difficult. English girls tinted their faces ivory with ochre color to get the "Wong complexion." They cut their hair with bangs in the front to achieve the "Wong haircut." Gorgeously embroidered coolie coats blossomed among the theater crowds in Piccadilly Circus. Anna May began to make the rounds of London theaters, seeing Fritz Kortner, a German actor she had befriended in Hollywood, in one performance, and Tilly Losch, the Viennese sensation, in another.[12]

Lulu left for America in late July, so Anna May was on her own. Soon after, journalist Annesley de Silva interviewed Anna May in her London residence at the elegant Park Lane Hotel. His account is useful for understanding Anna May's life on the road and for understanding how she appeared through the Orientalized vision of a Western journalist. A "spectacular Chinese servant" ushered the writer into Anna May's sitting room. Expecting to find the "opulence of the East," he was mildly disappointed at the simplicity of the room, although he noted books, pictures, Chinese vases, and easy chairs near the fire. More catching to the eye were "cushions of daring colors leap[ing] over one another.

A heavily embroidered Chinese shawl was spread across to its full length and breadth and caught the most careless gaze." Anna May entered the room "softly, silently and greeted me with a melodious 'good morning.'" She put him at ease with the "winsome smile of the pretty little dancing girl of the pictures—the smile that thrilled a hundred thousand hearts." Anna May offered him a Players cigarette, which he found ordinary "from a hand which should have held a gold case inlaid with jade." Anna May then related to him over the next half an hour her standard autobiography, which differed little from similar narrations given over the years to myriad numbers of journalists. Yet, even in the written edition, her verve and lovely personality lifted the timeworn tales of the tortured girl, paternal disapproval of her career, and constant rehearsals before the mirror at home. The journalist discerned two women before him. One was the international star, the other a "simple Chinese girl, unmoved by the honors that have fallen thick upon her." He left enchanted, as so many other journalists before him had done and after him would do.[13]

Journalists were not the only ones enamored of Anna May. Londoners flocked to see Anna May because of her exotic qualities. Despite its far-flung empire and imperialist intrusions into China, Britain had few Chinese residents. Virtually all of the Shandong Province laborers who toiled in British ports during World War I had been repatriated. In 1930, census counters found only 1,934 Chinese in England and Wales. About half of them were either seamen or laundry workers. Despite their small numbers, the Chinese loomed large in the English imagination. Labor unions were vigilant against Chinese competition, especially on the waterfront; eugenicists warned against dilution of English blood through intermarriage with Chinese; and the popular press stoked feverish anxieties about racial purity, drug abuse, and potential Chinese political power. Two results occurred. Like those in the United States, British laws restricted Chinese immigration and forced out Chinese residents. The second effect sustained a xenophobic popular imagination that identified the Limehouse district (London's Chinatown) as the locus of the "intrinsic evil of sexual contact." As in the United States, the racist impulse behind these forces produced the roles Anna May labored under in her movies. Nonetheless, Anna May liked London despite such attitudes and told friends that she felt most comfortable there. She usually said that about any place she visited.[14]

Under her contract with Richard Eichberg, Anna May had film work to do. She returned to Berlin at the end of the summer for the gala debut of *Song*, which opened on August 21, 1928, at the Alhambra Theater in Berlin. *Song* was her first starring role since *The Toll of the Sea*, six years earlier. In *Song*, Anna May plays a "human piece of driftwood," as an intertitle described her, who falls in love with a tough cabaret artist and professional knife-thrower who exploits her. Some preliminary scenes introduce the relationship of John Housenhat, a famous music hall artist, and his mistress, the beautiful dancer Gloria Lee. When John discovers Gloria in another man's arms on a ship, he and the adulterer fall overboard during a fight. Their bodies are lost in the current and both are declared dead. In fact, John washes up on the shore near Constantinople. Saved from drowning by some fishermen, he goes into hiding in Constantinople and makes his living by dancing in disreputable dives. One night on the beach, he saves a lovely Chinese woman named Song (Anna May) from rape by two brutes. Song quivers next to his chest and swears she will be his slave if he keeps her. They live happily until one day when Gloria Lee, now a big star, comes to Constantinople to dance at the Grand Theater. The sight of her astounding beauty reinvigorates John's love for her. In a failed attempt to get sufficient cash to attract Gloria, he tries to rob a train. When the police chase him, he hides under the train and is blinded by its cinders. Song then saves him and takes him back to his home to nurse him. Anna May's character shows her sexual availability in two ways. Her hair is completely loose on her shoulders; her costume, earlier made up of proletarian rags, now features a grass skirt, as if to emphasize a primitive sexuality. In a fit of jealousy, Song pours tea on Gloria's picture and then rips it apart. She then retreats to the loft and prays to a small Buddha. Because she understands the origins of his madness, Song begins to wear Gloria's type of perfume and invents dramatic stories to deceive John. Such efforts fail and John angrily denounces her devotion. He then sets out to find Gloria, who quickly dismisses him because he is without "cash." Song then begs Gloria for the money to pay for an eye operation for John and winds up stealing twenty pounds from her. After the theft is discovered, Gloria's manager, Praeger, searches for Song, not to arrest her but to offer her a chance to become a star at the Palace Theater. She agrees as long as the money goes to help John. Song is featured at the theater, dancing in a gypsy outfit. In several quick scenes, Song pays for an operation for her lover and quits the stage. Praeger then convinces her to return to the stage. After beseeching the gods, she accepts his offer.

Song's new act is sensational. She marches onto the stage in a gypsy outfit, surrounded by African dancers and carrying a giant knife. In contrast to her earlier scenes, her hair is now done up in an elaborate knot with a scepter-shaped crown. Amidst stunning, shimmering lighting on a revolving stage with rows of staircases, Song dances to jazz. She becomes a beautiful, seductive torch of a woman. At the pinnacle of her triumph, John walks into the club. Overcome by shame, she falls on the knife. John and others fight over her body. He carries her home and recognizes that Song was his true love. She dies in his arms as he sobs. Although Anna May told reporters that this was the greatest role of her career, still she had to die, as in American films, at the end of the story.[15]

The beauty of the film astonished German, Austrian, and French reviewers. Ernst Jaeger, the German film critic, spent most of his review lavishing praise on Anna, acclaiming her experience in "the erotic gardens of California to know how to set her mimic powers against the style of conventional film." Anna May danced to a "strange rhythm, the rocking of the plum blossom dance of her country of origin." Her eyes were "dark [treasure] chests. Their lashes hang over them like branches from a tree." The critic stated frankly that Wong had to die because of her love for a man of another race. Yet he described her tragedy as "Dostoyevskian" and asserted that Anna was one step above all her colleagues in that the "mask-like rigidity remains fixed, even when her eyes are screaming, when her lips go up in flames. She is chosen for the camera."[16] Overall, the film is a showcase for Anna May. Gorgeous cinematography offers close-ups of her face in isolation; show numbers feature her dancing, and costumes reveal her physique, albeit apart from those of the other actors. Austrian critics hailed her "great performance." Commercially, the film seems to have done well. Its producers put out full-page advertisements filled with Anna May's image or with rave testimonials from Berlin newspapers and magazines. Within two weeks, ninety-four cinemas across Germany screened the film.[17]

Critics of other nationalities were not quite as kind. The English literary film magazine *Close Up* was less charmed by the film's effect. Its reviewer acknowledged himself to be a "fan" of Anna May and believed that Hollywood was "blind to the grace of the little creature" and had hoped that someday she would work with people who "might appreciate her charm." Eichberg was not the right type, because "paradoxical as it might sound, Anna May has gone to Germany only to be Americanized." The review blamed Eichberg for wasting her talents, punctuating stock Hollywood scenarios with close-ups of the star. American reviewers were generally negative. While *Variety* described her as "charming," the *New York Times* sourly ignored the film's plot and reminded readers that German journalists neglected to mention that Anna May was born in America, preferring to emphasize her Chinese heritage.[18]

The newspaper's grouchy complaint was accurate. Anna May was moving toward a stronger identification with China. Film critics all over Europe regularly labeled her as Chinese, even when they recorded that she was born in California. Anna May encouraged this label herself. This was clear in an article she published in *Rexall Magazine* in May 1930 explaining why "The Chinese Are Misunderstood." *Rexall Magazine* was distributed gratis at pharmacies throughout the United Kingdom to an audience composed primarily of housewives. The article demonstrated her increasing concern with the effects of her screen image on the global reputation of Chinese people. She noted that Western misperceptions of the Chinese started with negative representations of them in film. In fact, Anna May informed her readers, Chinese people were good-natured lovers of life, characteristics that were represented in their clothing, pottery, costumes and feasts. The Chinese valued friendship and family above all else and were extremely trustworthy. Best of all, she claimed, Chinese women could maintain their youthfulness and beauty because they seldom worried: "[The Chinese woman] believes that worry is a non-productive institution, and is therefore inclined not only to put it off continuously, but eventually to relegate it to someone else." At this time, of course, Anna May had never been to China. Her audience was equally provincial, so her words came across as authoritative. Anna May's naive, uninformed opinions suggest that in Europe at least, she reveled in being Chinese rather than Chinese American.[19]

Anna May stayed most of the autumn of 1928 in Berlin. Josephine Baker brought her revue to town in early September, and it seems plausible that the two women crossed paths. Anna May did encounter another twentieth-century icon sometime during the fall. Marlene Dietrich was a rising star. Sexually voracious and, as one account puts it, "the busiest and most passionate bisexual in theatrical

Berlin," Dietrich loved seduction not for power or advancement but for the excitement and emotional joy of sex. Dietrich sang a popular song with Margot Lion, entitled "Wenn die beste Freundin" (When My Best Girlfriend), which became the theme song of lesbians in late 1920s Berlin. Anna May and Marlene began appearing in public together. Alfred Eisenstadt, long before his halcyon years at *Life* magazine, captured Anna May, Marlene, and Leni Riefenstahl together at the Press Ball in January. At this and other festive occasions, photos made of Wong and Dietrich reveal an intimacy and warmth beyond a publicity friendship. In the most striking image, reproduced in a recent film about Dietrich, the photographer recorded Anna May pouring liquor into Marlene's mouth. In Chinese culture, placing food or drink in another's mouth in public signifies deep intimacy. Were they lovers? Biographers of Dietrich have assumed so and stated that Dietrich seduced Wong because she was an exotic personality. According to one biographer, "Dietrich openly discussed her casual amours, which included . . . Anna May Wong." No doubts are ever expressed; rather Anna May was simply another conquest for Dietrich, who used sex to express casual friendship rather than deeper affection. Wong's reputation suffered greatly from rumors of this liaison. It was one principal reason for the shame her family felt toward her career. There is no definite proof that Dietrich and Wong, or for that matter, Wong and Riefenstahl, were ever lovers. At the same time, Dietrich probably would not accept less of a public companion. Gay women were everywhere in Berlin, and arriving at a party with someone of the same sex simply proved one was modern. The clear intimacy found in Eisenstadt's photos strongly suggests that Anna May had a fling with Dietrich and possibly Riefenstahl, though the latter denies ever seeing Wong after that night. Having a quick affair with so willing a partner as Dietrich does not, as some have suggested, make Anna May gay. Generally, she seems to have preferred men. Certainly, a long-term relationship with Dietrich was not a realistic possibility. If anything, the tryst demonstrates Anna May's adventurous character and willingness to cross boundaries.[20]

As Anna May flourished in Berlin, writers around Europe hailed her arrival as proof that the continent's cinema would soon rival that of Hollywood. However naive an idea this was at a time when American films dominated the world market, it was evidence of the hopes placed upon Anna May's featured roles. Anna May did her best to charm local reporters. Stanley Fitzmaurice of the French film magazine *Pour Vous* visited her on the set of *Piccadilly*. He found her charming, not capricious like other stars. Anna May, he wrote, was "a real woman," who hummed the ditty composed for her by Hollywood friends: "Anna May Wong /From old Hong Kong /She can't be wrong." Anna May told him of her childhood, her discovery, and showed off baby pictures of her youngest brother, Richard. She avowed that she liked Europeans because they accepted people of color. Then, to the writer's sorrow, Dupont called her back to the stage. Fitzmaurice concluded his article by recognizing her for what "she is—a great actress. Not only is she talented, but she is friendly and simple, and she has this independence of mind that only real artists have and that those stars are lacking."[21]

Her European isolation from Hollywood made Anna May ponder her career. She wrote articles for the French magazines about life in Tinsel Town. For the March 7 issue of *Pour Vous*, she wrote a lengthy letter from London in which she told readers about the real Hollywood. It was a place where many dreams met with a harsh reality. Although the town was based upon entertainment, there was, she opined, perhaps no other place with less "amusement" in the conventional sense of the word. For many aspirants, the great chance never arrived. Young girls worked in restaurants and stores for years and years, longing for the parts they never would play. Yet Hollywood was not always grim, but a place for idealists who earned their way up to a good position thanks to hard work and intelligence. She claimed that everybody understood the necessity of such trials and encouraged struggling actors. She told of a beautiful young woman who had worked for ten years in a Hollywood restaurant; Anna May believed she would soon be famous.

Anna May understood the fragility of fame. She told one French interviewer that "success is not a jewel that you can purchase and keep for your entire life. On the contrary, the brightest star can fall down at any time for short-lived reasons and can miserably fade away into the dust. The audience is an implacable judge." It is to that public judgment that the actress must appeal: "She has to please millions of people with her personality, and her success depends only on the changing tastes of the audience."[22] Anna May also understood how fleeting was her youth. Accordingly, she dropped two years from her age. She apparently even changed her birthday. One German magazine listed it as September 21, 1908, shaving off nearly three years. Her actions initiated misconceptions about the year of her birth that last to the present day.[23]

Anna May explained to her readers the fates of the idealists who made up Hollywood society. In order to remain close to the action, older actors became managers of apartment buildings, tearooms, beauty salons, flower shops, and garages. In general, they lived regular lives. The last place to look for famous actors was in the nightclubs, where tourists wound up staring at other tourists. In fact, she wrote, famous stars relished steady lives with their families, or had hobbies such as Noah Beery with his farm or Douglas Fairbanks with his creation of a Spanish village. It was a remarkable description, which revealed Anna May's own hopes for a full family life and her recognition that someday she would have to stop chasing her film dreams and find alternative work. As she toiled in films thousands of miles away from home, Anna May doubtless realized that her destiny was Hollywood.[24]

Despite its intentions, the European community had its own limitations. Like their counterparts in the United States, European filmmakers commonly used "yellow faces" to act in Asian roles. Charles Boyer, the veteran French actor, recalled how making his eyes slanted and adjusting the curve of his cheeks gave his eyes an impassive look "that our western faces do not have."[25] At the same time, Europeans were deeply aware of the need to appear "white." An article on women's hands that appeared in *Pour Vous* declared that "whiteness [was] one of the most essential qualities that the standard beauty code requires of women's hands." To satisfy this need, perfume makers created ointments and expensive lotions to make hands whiter. The color of nail polish had to accommodate this need for whiteness. Nail polish had to match the lipstick, and red, a favorite color of Anna May's, was particularly hard to match. Women with lesser hands than hers had to be content with pastel colors to avoid notice of their ordinary hands. They could, however, paint their toenails red, when walking through the rain or mud, as it makes a woman happy to know that you have "carmine nails shining like sultans' nails of 'The Arabian Nights,' inside your shoes and your stockings." Anna May, whose hands were considered the most beautiful in Hollywood, enhanced a rose-hued skin with a stunning sense of fashion. Anna May had, in French eyes, achieved a kind of whiteness. The French were astonished at her beauty, intelligence, grace, and success. At a time when other Chinese were barely marginal characters in European society, Anna May was extraordinary and gave through her public persona a positive glow to her ethnicity. It is not enough to say that she was a product of colonialism. Her public stature in France transcended that.[26]

The French were especially aware of how American filmmakers denigrated China in their movies and seemed determined to do better. French writers commented that while the real worlds of China and Japan were doubtless ordinary and boring, American films portrayed a cinematic vision of "a cheap world of Doctor Fu Manchu and Madame Butterfly, and the world of crimes and kidnappings." French writers observed that in the Chinatowns in this racial vision "blonde young girls were held captive in secret rooms below laundries." Later these same blonde women became Shanghai Lily or Sal of Singapore. In such American films, sexual love was the boundary to Anna May's attempts to sustain a stardom unchecked by race. The same was unfortunately true in France. Despite her Chinese ancestry, the French regarded Anna May Wong as mixed race and fated to become involved in a fatal love saga with a European. Her end had to be violent. Even if a "real white woman" was able to stay faithful and live in the strange existence she had chosen, that was the exception. Most of the time, Americans and French took very seriously the privileges and duties of white people. None of these hoary themes had changed at all.[27]

Despite these underlying prejudices, the climate for Chinese actors was different in France. Chinese actresses had already entranced Parisians. They seemed to have an "undeniably exotic charm with their slanted eyes, their ebony hair, and their silk dresses with large foliage." Parisians found such names as "Miss Moonlight, Miss Weeping Lily, Miss Ivory Legs" poetic and charming. A reporter from *Pour Vous* reported on the Shanghai movie scene and found the actresses "supple when dancing our European styles." One difficulty was that traditional Chinese opera used men for female roles, which meant that the actresses were all inexperienced. They were far less convincing to the writer than the incomparable Anna May Wong. She, the French writers claimed, possessed a beauty that transcended national boundaries and was the hallmark of a successful film star. They called her eyes universally lovely.[28]

Writers in Europe enhanced Anna May's reputation in the East by dispatching articles about her. Magazines in the Far East dutifully recorded her travels to

Europe. *Screen and Stage* of Tokyo depicted Eichberg and Wong talking pleasantly. In another, she posed for a painting by a Professor Michallow in Berlin, an event recorded in Shanghai film magazines. Anna May helped the cause by writing personal letters to magazine editors about her travels. Writing from Paris, she told Wu Liande, the editor of the pioneering Chinese magazine *Xinyingxing* (Silverland), about her career and her life in Hollywood. Other Chinese magazines gave her mixed coverage. The popular *Pei-Yang Pictorial* from Tianjin put her on the cover in August 1929 and featured her in other issues after denouncing her risqué dancing the previous year. When nude photos of Anna May circulated from Germany, the *Pei-Yang Pictorial* promptly published them, along with snide references to her as "Huang A-Mei," a term that Chinese readers denoted as prostitute.[29]

As soon as *Piccadilly* became the most talked about film in late 1929, prestigious and popular magazines on the continent vied to include images of her in their publications. In England, *Film Weekly* put her on its front cover. *Das Magazin*, one of Germany's most sophisticated and stylish journals, featured her on its cover. The Swedish magazine *Filmjournalen* devoted four pages of stills to *Piccadilly*. *Cinémonde* and *Ciné-Miroir*, two prestigious French magazines, featured her twice on their covers. An Austrian critic hailed her as "The Wong," an accolade reserved for the highest ranked stars and one that suggested that she had become an institution. American studios, sensing Anna May's high popularity in Europe, re-released a number of her silent films from the mid-1920s, hoping to cash in on her fame. In November 1929 alone, *Old San Francisco, The Devil Dancer*, and the English talkie *Elstree Calling* hit the screens in Portugal, Germany, and Austria.[30]

Posters for *Piccadilly* emphasized Anna May's exotic beauty. The most extravagant of all was a fifteen-foot-high poster by George Pollak for Austrian cinemas. The poster, which borrowed an image of her from *Across to Singapore*, featured Anna May in a topless gypsy outfit with large bangles. Her limbs and breasts have a yellow hue and her legs and posterior are larger than life. Behind Anna May the artist Pollak drew an expressionist vision of Piccadilly Circus replete with cinemas, dance halls, restaurants, and theaters, while cars and cabs circle the streets. Portraying Anna May topless was not scandalous in Vienna, but it would have rocked her audiences in America and in the East. The poster suggested only a measure of the personal freedom she enjoyed in Europe.[31]

As the opening night of *Piccadilly* loomed in London, Anna May traveled to England and luxuriated in the comfortable rooms of the Claridge Hotel. Her English fans were numerous and vocal in their approval of Anna May. Her arrival was hailed as proof that the nation's studios were attracting international talent. For some reason, the release of *Piccadilly* was delayed in London until February 1929. The leading film journals called Anna May's acting "brilliant," though the intellectual review *Close Up* was harshly critical of the film. *Picture Show*, however, put her on its cover twice within one year. It also gave ample coverage to the shooting of *The Road to Dishonour* and gushed that Anna May had "applied herself assiduously to the study of English elocution and the miraculous change she has effected in three months is the marvel of all her friends." The magazine touted her singing voice as well. Another magazine spoke of her hard work learning French. In short, English magazines notified readers that Anna May Wong was prepared to survive the "talkie" revolution. The same seems to be true for French film critics. *Hebdo-Cinéma*, one of the most nationalist journals, honored her with a front cover and gave the film extensive coverage.[32]

Piccadilly, considered among the best of films from the silent era in England, was a marvelous credit for Wong. The script was based upon a famous novel by Thomas Burke; Anna May claimed to have read every book of his. The locale was the Piccadilly Club, one of the most elegant nightspots at the famous London crossroads. From the outset of the film, the club was a favored hangout for London's elite because of the modern dancing of Vic and Mabel, played by Anna May's old friend, Gilda Gray, who perform "The Piccadilly Shiver." Gray was also credited with inventing the Charleston and the Black Bottom. In the film, Mabel's professional relationship with Vic soon became personal, to the anger and jealousy of the owner, Wilmot, expertly performed by the veteran English actor Jameson Thomas. After Vic kisses Mabel in public, Wilmot confronts the dancer and fires him. Unfortunately, Mabel can't carry the show by herself and customers quickly move to other locales. One night as he surveys the emptiness of the once-crowded tables, Wilmot has to put up with the drunken antics of a customer, played by Charles Laughton in his feature debut, who complains loudly about dirty dishes. Wilmot then marches into the kitchen for answers, only to be ushered down to the scullery. There he finds all the dishwashers entranced by the erotic dancing of a young Chinese girl, Shosho, played by Anna May. Shosho's hairstyle signifies the innocent virgin; her pigtail wrapped around the back of her head in the style of a country laboring girl. Her face is filled with innocence. Shosho's dance, in which she places one hand below her hips and the other arm cocked before her made-up forehead, recalls a Tang dynasty dance, *Si Lu Hua Yu*, about the Silk Road that connected China to Western culture. Her dress, on the other hand, combines a working-class skirt with a chic, broad-striped sweater. Wilmot orders the dishwashers to get back to work. As business worsens, his thoughts return to Shosho and her slow gyrating hips. After "interviewing" her in his office, Wilmot decides to put her on stage. During this scene, the talented Thomas actually sketches Anna May. His decision to replace Mabel with Shosho signified a sexual victory for the former scullery maid over the vaunted inventor of the Shimmy and implies an English preference for authenticity. Gray, a talented, gracious actress, played the part of the abandoned woman expertly.[33]

To convince Shosho to perform, Wilmot has to accede to two significant demands, presented by Anna May with hands defiantly on hips. First, Wilmot has to purchase an elaborate costume from a shop of her choice down in the Limehouse district. Second, he had to employ Shosho's dour friend, Jim, played by King Hou Chang, in real life one of London's most famous Chinese restaurant owners, to play the Chinese musical instrument *erhu* for background music. Throughout this scene, Anna May uses a masculine style, even crossing her face with splayed fingers, a Chinese man's mark of negotiation. During this episode, her hair is tied loosely on her nape, but allowed to fall freely down her back. One disconcerting note is the constant emasculation of Jim throughout the episode. Much taller than her partner, Shosho dominates and diminishes him. Anna May's influence on the script is overt. While in Hollywood, Anna May's demands were often discreet; in this film, her influence was written into the story line.

Shosho's dance is a mixture of traditional Chinese and Anna May's own ultra modernism. Her use of fluttering hands and slow swaying of the upper body combines Mongolian traditional and palace dances. Her thighs are not part of her dance and show Anna May's willingness to expose her body to gain further notice. Her costume is that of a warrior. In the movie, Shosho's dancing rapidly captivated the fancy crowd, who were in fact Anna May's friends among the English royalty. Although Mabel soon makes her unhappiness known to Wilmot, he is now in love with Shosho. Anna May plays this part in a manly style, particularly during contract negotiations when she stands over Wilmot and to Jim, when she closes the door on him while jousting with the nightclub owner.

One night Wilmot takes Shosho, now wrapped in furs and with a distinctly modern hairstyle, to a jazz club where they watch interracial carousers. A tight hat covers her hair, with curls slipping down by her ears. After they go nightclubbing, she invites him back to her rooms, which are filled with Chinese antiques. It was the first of many times in which the sets of Anna May's movies were filled with priceless antiquities. At home, Shosho changes into a seductive gown, lies on a couch, and obscures her face with an arm adorned with silk veils. Her hair is slicked back against her head. In one of the most erotic scenes from the silent era, Shosho entices the aroused Wilmot to come closer and gradually lets her veil drop from her pliant face. Although the censors cut the ensuing kiss, their sexual embrace was inescapable. This scene was the closest Anna May had come to an on-screen kiss since similar embraces with Ramon Navarro in *Across to Singapore*. Thomas later contended that Anna May and he agreed the scene should be cut because although the English were more tolerant than Americans about interracial kissing, "we were very careful to handle such scenes tactfully." Should there be any doubt of their intention, the photoplay book, penned by Arnold Bennett, included a still photograph from the scene with a caption in which Shosho tells Wilmot, "Kiss me . . . I like you." Despite the overt fantasies English writers and actors had about Anna May, she sadly accepted that they lacked sufficient courage to embrace her fully. Later in life, a friend suggested that they go to a screening of *Piccadilly* in Los Angeles. She refused, stating that she was in a terrible emotional state when the film was made and did not want to be reminded of her suffering. The episode with Thomas convinced Anna May that despite London's seeming liberality, its codes matched American injunctions against interracial kissing on screen. There were a few dissenters. *Social Magazine*, a prominent arts journal from Havana, printed a lovely picture of Anna May sometime after and declared that many believed the ban on kissing her should be lifted.[34]

After that erotic scene, the plot takes a violent turn. After Wilmot leaves, Mabel enters the apartment to beg Shosho to let her man alone. Shosho retorts that she is unwilling to give back what Mabel was unable to keep. Humiliated, Mabel pulls a gun out of her purse and threatens Shosho, who takes a dagger from the wall. During the scramble it appears that Shosho is killed and later police find her body. Because Wilmot refuses to admit where he was on the night of the murder, he becomes the principal suspect, based partly on the testimony of Jim. At the inquest, Mabel testifies for Wilmot, making the case more complex. When the judge demands that Jim return to the witness stand, he is found mortally wounded in a nearby toilet. As he dies, Jim admits that he was Shosho's husband and was furiously jealous at Wilmot's dalliance with her. Because Shosho had made him suffer so much, "I took my revenge."[35] The film's trite conclusion does not undermine Anna May's achievement. Unlike American films in which her sexuality was suppressed, here she openly vamped Wilmot. No viewer could deny her extraordinary sensuality. Despite fine performances from Thomas and Gray, Anna May carried the film and established herself as a leading lady. The picture also gave her the chance to showcase her fusion of European and Asian fashion.

At the same time that *Piccadilly* opened in London, Anna May made her stage debut as the star in a Basil Dean stage production of *The Circle of Chalk*. This was an adaptation of a thirteenth-century classic from ancient Chinese theater called *A Hundred Pieces* that Klabund first brought to the West by translating it into German. James Laver then converted it to English. Anna May was proud to play the role of Hai-Tang, the second wife of the Lord Ma and the mother of his son. Opposite her was the treacherous, first Mrs. Ma, played by Rose Quong, a Eurasian actress from Australia who was well known to English critics. In a supporting role and making his West End debut was a young Laurence Olivier. In the play Mrs. Ma uses the knowledge that her successor, Hai-Tang, once worked in a brothel to damage the younger woman. She then poisons her husband and casts blame on Hai-Tang on the grounds that the latter has taken a lover. She is even able to convince the court that Hai-Tang's baby boy is actually hers. As Hai-Tang sings of her tragedy, she is beaten and nearly hanged. Ultimately she is saved by the intercession of a powerful nobleman. The play featured a technique by which each actor revealed his or her plans to the audience, who could anticipate the unfolding of the plot. Despite its overt appeal to Orientalism, the play was highly poetic and offered Anna May several opportunities to sing of her plight and salvation.

The Circle of Chalk opened in March 1929, during the critical transition period from silent to talking movies, a process Robert Sklar has called the most significant innovation in the history of film. Although the house roundly cheered Anna May when she made a speech in Chinese, by the end of the first performance the critics had turned on her. While allowing for her beauty, success in films, and general acting ability, theater critics lambasted Anna May's voice and singing. One writer scorned her "Yankee squeak." The *Sketch Magazine* critic wrote "to behold her is a pleasure, to hear her just a little strain." Another scribe claimed that she could not act at all and forecast the end of her career as talking movies came to dominate the industry. The threat to Anna May was ominous. The careers of such stars as her old friend John Gilbert were already in a tailspin because of weak or grating voices.[36]

Nor did her director defend her. Basil Dean, one of England's most distinguished directors, described his casting of Anna May as a "miscalculation" and called her California accent as "thick as the smog that smothers their cities." He did credit her with professionalism and talent, noting that she had even read Bertrand Russell's *Essay on China* to understand English attitudes toward the Chinese. Eventually, the play settled into a routine and finished a successful run. Anna May paid a Cambridge University tutor £100 to help her gain an upper-class English accent to please the critics and to ward off potential career anxieties. Toward the end of the play's run, Basil Dean gave a luncheon for newspaper critics at which Anna May was asked to speak. Ever sensitive to the importance of the press, she rose and remarked how she appreciated the kindness of the English newspapers, but "wished they could make up their mind whether she had a New York or Hollywood accent." She then announced she would speak so that *no one* would understand her and rattled off sentences in Chinese. As she sat down, the journalists broke into applause. Anna May made sure that American newspapers reported the success of the play and not her vocal problems. Later Bertolt Brecht borrowed much of the play as the basis for *The Caucasian Chalk Circle*.[37]

Anna May and Richard Eichberg next collaborated on the film entitled variously *Pavement Butterfly* or *City Butterfly*, which was filmed in March 1929 and released in May of the same year. Eichberg shot the film in several parts of France and Monaco including Nice, Monte Carlo, Mentone, and Paris. In Nice, Eichberg included scenes from the famous carnival, and in Monte Carlo he filmed night scenes in the terrace of the Casino and on the Mediterranean Sea. He used the streets of Paris for night scenes. Anna May played the role of

Butterfly, a Chinese dancer at street fairs, who falls afoul of the law when she is unfairly accused of causing the accidental death of an acrobat. Fleeing a mob that threatened to lynch her, Butterfly finds refuge in the studio of a young and struggling painter, Serge Kushmin. After he welcomes her into his studio, Kushmin paints a portrait of Butterfly, which he quickly sells to the count of Nauve for 4,000 francs. He gives Butterfly the check to cash; a circus clown, who is the actual murderer, then robs her of the check. He also threatens to kill Kushmin if she informs on him. Later Butterfly is able to regain the money from the clown, but Kushmin, now in love with another woman, rejects her. At the end of the movie, Butterfly leaves Kushmin and his new bride and "walks away to make happy the man she will never forget." Critics in France, Austria, and Germany lauded *Pavement Butterfly* as "a very beautiful movie," and proclaimed Anna May's performance as "amazing." The normally cautious *Hebdo-Cinema* described her as "ravishing" and someone who acts with sincerity. The contrast across the Atlantic could not have been sharper. In the United States *Variety* dismissed the film as forgettable.[38]

Anna May spent September and the first week of October 1929 at the Hotel Esplanade in Berlin. She wrote the American novelist and photographer Carl Van Vechten that she was enjoying a "holiday on salary," with many friends coming and going. She told Van Vechten: "Hello and goodbye [is] a continuous performance" during this "glorious time." Her major accomplishment "is speaking German like nobody's business and I have to speak German and English in the new films. It's been most interesting to master what formerly seemed like an impossibility but we sometimes even surprise ourselves at what we can do." By October 10 she was off to England to make a "talkie" for British International Pictures.[39]

Her first venture into the new technology of talking movies was in an all-star production for Elstree Studios. Her cameo was a send-up of *The Taming of the Shrew*, which had recently been released in the United States with Douglas Fairbanks Sr. In *Elstree Calling*, Anna May's bit involved appearing through a door and flinging custard pies at everyone while denouncing them in Taishanese dialect. Directed by Adrian Brunel with assistance from Alfred Hitchcock, the film was a British version of an American musical revue organized loosely around a cover story that offered a pretext for a number of musical, dance, and comedy performances. One scene cut from the film but appearing later in the 1930s in another all-star show portrayed the misogynist Hitchcock plastering Anna May with a pie.[40]

Anna May and Richard Eichberg's last film together was shot in three languages in three nations as *The Road to Dishonour* (English title), *Hai-Tang* (German title), and *L'Amour Maitre des Chases* (French title), which did not appear until 1930 as a "talkie." Despite the name of the lead character, the film bore no other relationship to *The Circle of Chalk*, in which Hai-Tang was the feature role. Anna May did her dialogue in all three languages, each time with an entirely different cast. In addition to learning several languages, Anna May also journeyed to Budapest to learn traditional Hungarian folk dances. She later returned for the opening night of the film.

The plot revolved around a love affair between Boris Ivanoff, an officer in the Russian army, and Hai-Tang, a Chinese dancer, played by Anna May. Boris gets into trouble for lateness on duty and is imprisoned for two weeks. His paramour catches the attention of his superior, who warns him that further antics could cost him a trip into exile in Siberia. Fortunately, Boris has a friend in the grand duke, who takes a fatherly interest in him. Still smitten, Boris takes the grand duke to the theater where Hai-Tang is performing. Her charms soon conquer the duke, who has tired of his own mistress. Boris is dispatched to invite her to dinner with the duke. She, Boris, and her father, Wang-Ho, recognize the trap into which they have fallen. To refuse the duke is impossible; to accept his blandishments is to accept disgrace. Impulsively she decides to sacrifice herself to save Boris. At the dinner, the duke's attentions become increasingly obvious. As he moves in, Wang-Ho appears with a gun. His shot goes amiss and the duke lives. Wang-Ho is arrested. Now Hai-Tang desperately needs to sacrifice her honor and goes to the duke to convince him through her charms to save her father. Yvette, the duke's mistress, enters the intrigue. She determines to steal the pardon the duke awarded to Wang-Ho, rationalizing that his execution would embitter Hai-Tang toward the duke. Enter Boris, who steals the pardon back and saves Wang-Ho at the last minute. Tragically, Hai-Tang's loss of honor makes marriage to Boris impossible. Facing a bleak future, she takes poison and dies in Boris's arms.[41]

The English version of *The Road to Dishonour* is particularly distinctive for its kiss between Anna May and costar John Longden, one that unfortunately wound up on the cutting room floor. It was a full kiss, and the newspapers made the most of it. It became a national sensation, and many called for its removal. Longdon made some equivocal comments about the controversy, calling the ban on kissing between Chinese and English "stupid and inconsistent" and a "ridiculous anomaly." At the same time, he admitted that he preferred not to kiss Anna May and felt that the film would work best if "the climax were left to the imagination. The kiss is more beautiful as a vision, than as a length of film." The kiss may have stayed for a while, but the surviving copy does not include it. American newspapers enjoyed reporting the English discomfiture over the removal of the kiss. Ever the assiduous worker, Anna May did her part by making personal appearances each evening during the opening run of the film in London.[42]

That famous buss may have been the reason why *Variety* dismissed the film as wholly wrong for American audiences and voiced considerable doubt about Anna May's drawing power, forecasting that the film would go directly to "the cheapest grinds or the double-feature neighborhood bills through cheap rental." The reviewer disparaged Anna May's voice as "flat American," a fatal dismissal for someone allegedly playing a Russian character. The review concluded by stating the film was: "Just an error all around." Curiously, the *New York Times* gave a favorable review to the French version, but not the English film. Abroad, one obscure censor doubted the film's authenticity. Budapest authorities banned the movie because of the sexual relationship between the duke and Hai-Tang, stating that "such a performance could never have occurred in real life, and was offensive to monarchist feelings." French reviewers were much kinder. *L'Amour Maître des Choses* inaugurated the first luxurious cinema on the Champs Elysées. The prestigious film magazine *Cinémonde* recalled her wonderful role in *Song* and was grateful for "another amazing performance from this beautiful and voluptuous woman, this strangely sincere and fascinating interpreter." *Hebdo-Cinéma* described her French as "impeccable diction." Even more extravagant in their praise were the German magazines. Anna May was featured on the front cover of several film journals when *Hai-Tang* hit the screens. This coverage was far greater than the exposure given to Marlene Dietrich's films of that year.[43]

Anna May kept up her German popularity by writing letters to *Mein Film*, a widely distributed fan magazine. In one article, which was accompanied by an autographed photo to her fans, Anna May addressed the revolutionary transition to talking movies. She recounted how the first word she uttered in a talkie was *"Mitleid"* (pity), which was followed by a plea to the king to save her brother's life. She heard her voice "swallowed by the ear of the microphone," and she worried that it did not sound good to the producers. She felt it was one of the most important moments in her career. Her knees shook just as they had during close-ups in silent films. Gradually she relaxed and "with every word . . . my fear vanished and my voice found its firmness again and I was proud and happy." She compared it to the sensation of swimming alone for the first time. Ever the professional, she was not satisfied, and took to "studying voice and speech in order to control the modulation of the tone, which is so important in dialogue."[44]

Maintaining her rigorous work schedule, Anna May played a small role in a film production entitled *Sabotage*, directed by Ernö Metzner, a Hungarian who had made films for the German Social Democratic Party and who had worked with G. W. Pabst on *Diary of a Lost Girl*, with Louise Brooks. He directed *Überjall* (Accident), an avant-garde classic, in 1929. He was widely respected for his "daunting versatility" as an art director, costume designer, and director. Best of all from Anna May's perspective, his co-writer and frequent star was his wife, Grace Chiang, a European Chinese. Their marriage was proof to Anna May that interracial unions could work. Made years before the famous Alfred Hitchcock film of the same title, *Sabotage* was an action-packed film about sports car racing and featured Bob Stoll in a double role as both villain and hero. The plot involved the murder of a royal family member by the deceitful side of Stoll's character. Improbably, the better side gives chase and catches the evildoer in a frantic car-chase. Anna May had a brief role as a mechanic who is also killed in the fatal car crash. The film debuted in Paris in July and had a short run before disappearing.[45]

By the end of 1929, Anna May reveled in her new life in Europe. She arrived three weeks before the start of the French production to spend the spring in Paris. She stayed at a lovely hotel with a perfect view of the Tuilleries Gardens, the Place de la Concorde, and, in the distance, the "glistening Seine with its river boats." She studied French every day for several hours and then enjoyed lunch in a typically French restaurant. At night she went to the theater to attune her ears to the language. She talked about the necessity of getting vocal tones right for the new technology: "I had to learn German and to take speech lessons in English because English people did not like my accent." She contended that she did not mind working hard if it meant that she could be "something more than a young girl still living at her parents."[46]

The English were not wholehearted in their love for Anna May, as their criticism of her performance in *The Circle of Chalk* indicated, but she did enjoy enormous popularity. English men pursued Anna May avidly, and she admitted that she did not pay for a dinner for months. She explained that the English experience in the Far East made marriage with a Chinese woman more possible than in America. Members of the royal family extended invitations to Anna May. Prince George, the brother of the Prince of Wales, sent word that he wanted to be introduced to her. Her appearance in the gallery of Parliament stopped proceedings so that the peers could gape at her. One of the king's cousins gave her a dinner, and there were even hints that she might be presented to the royal court. Later, she mused that no Chinese woman had ever been introduced at the royal court. Unfortunately, her schedule would not permit it.[47]

She did get a second chance at London theater in April 1930, playing the Chinese mistress of a Chicago gangster in Edgar Wallace's adaptation of his novel, *On the Spot*.[48] During this stint, she helped out her fellow American Paul Robeson, who was starring in a difficult production of *Othello* with Peggy Ashcroft. Robeson had done well in London in 1928 with *Show Boat*, but taking on Shakespeare's Moor was theater on a different level. His producers were patronizing and the press was often hostile, especially because the play ran during the controversy over Anna May's kiss in *The Road to Dishonour* and because Ashcroft was white. By opening night, May 19, 1930, Robeson's nerves were screaming. Anna May came to the first night dressed in an extraordinary Chinese outfit and visited her American friend backstage several times during intermissions to give him moral support. Apparently her kindness helped and Robeson got ten standing ovations, though critical reception was tepid.[49]

From London she traveled to Paris, to film *L'Amour Maitre des Choses*. She fell in love with Paris again, and its citizens matched her affections. Two leading French film magazines, *Ciné-Miroir* and *Mon Ciné*, put full-page photos of her on their covers. J. M. Airmont, writing in *Carnet*, put Anna May at the top of the acting world. He claimed, "Anna May Wong inspires the imagination better than Greta Garbo, Joan Crawford, Anita Page, or Lupe Velez, better than any actress who embodies the different and perfect facets of feminine seduction which worry and disturbs men." Her attitudes "charm us and make us think differently." He declared that in her presence "genuine magic emanates from the moving picture." The French were deeply impressed by her professionalism, which was described as "consistently excellent; she is as diverse and secret as one can possibly imagine." In a later article, one writer remarked how well European artists were received in the United States. Yet very few Americans could claim European fame. It was true that Joan Crawford and Jeanette MacDonald could pack movie houses, but still they were considered only guests in Paris. The only exceptions to this rule were Adolph Menjou, who was quite popular on the stage and screen in Europe, and Anna May Wong. The praise for Anna May was a counterpoint to Parisian resentment of the many Americans sporting in their city and of the baneful influence of American films.[50]

In the Parisian spring of 1930, Anna May felt deeply happy, if homesick. She felt free to talk about America and spoke of the advantages of being Chinese there: "After all, I am very lucky to be born in Los Angeles. If I had grown up in China, I would probably have never been free or independent." Anna May's wistfulness mixed easily with her strong sense of professionalism. Unlike her life in the United States, where her fame was marred by the racial roles she had to endure, in Europe she spoke of her joy in her career: "I like seeing myself on a screen, and reading the nice things that critics wrote about me. And I also like making money." Anna May wondered if she could actually work in Paris, as she preferred to spend the entire day outside, "in your pretty city, which is the prettiest city I have ever seen. I know it can sound common, but I really mean it."[51] Anna May allowed herself many small dreams. She fantasized about buying a Hispano-Suize, a fancy sports car, that year. She mused about becoming a pilot, though Paramount refused to let her because of the risks. While not dreaming of planes and cars, Anna May went to theaters in Paris. She watched the French chanteuse Yvonne Printemps one evening, enjoying the show so much that Anna May faithfully went to hear the singer any chance she could. Anna May went to the Theatre Negre to see the show *Black Flowers*, featuring Louis Douglas, one of her favorites, and the Jubilee Singers. Her attendance at these shows is notable for her support of African American artists.[52]

She enjoyed French interviews because they were not as inquisitive as the Americans and rarely did they ask her about love affairs. Although she had heard that politeness was vanishing in France, "everywhere I go in your country I am left in peace and welcomed. I am not different from anybody else." The French, she claimed, did not reject her because of her skin: "My skin is yellow and I have slanted eyes." She openly spoke of becoming European: "What if my soul is different from yours? Is that my fault? I am not completely Chinese and not completely European yet. It is a tragedy! The two halves of my soul are fighting like cats and dogs."[53]

In her interviews, she regularly revealed personal charm and wit. A German reporter met her in the hotel lobby and was astounded by how she had become the "most Parisian of women because of her charming movements and her exquisite genuine elegance." Anna May had learned something of Parisian philosophies of beauty. She told the scribe: "You can forgive a woman for a face that is not beautiful" more easily than for a dress that isn't. A beautiful woman, she added, had to be "pleasing to the eyes, then to the ear, through nice sounding speech and laughter, but a bit of intelligence doesn't mar the picture either, and finally a woman shall smell like a flower." The reporter was impressed, telling his readers that in her childhood, Anna May had played hooky to go to the cinema, while now "[s]he is hard-working, studies the vocabulary and sentences of her role." At that point, the "French teacher had appeared, and had a dissatisfied look through her horn-rimmed spectacles." Off went Anna May to her lessons.[54]

Hai-Tang was the last European film for Anna May on this trip. She worked primarily with Eichberg, who is not remembered for great films. Her performances for him do provide new light on an old controversy: whether German and other European films of this period foreshadow the coming of Fascism and eventually World War II. Siegfried Kracauer was the first to call attention to the significance of German film as mass psychological preparation for Adolf Hitler and his Nazi Party. Kracauer argued that films, more than any other medium, were group projects that inclusively addressed the anonymous multitude. Lotte Eisner later modified Kracauer's brilliant insights and, recently, Thomas Elsaesser has pointed out that Kracauer's analysis depended on a few classic films rather than more popular efforts by such directors as Eichberg. As Tim Bergfelder has pointed out, Wong's German films are shot through with racial exoticism. Though I have taken pains to demonstrate how Anna May Wong strove to alter the racial fantasies of the directors, she could not change everything. Her films indicate that the accomplishments of such directors as the immensely popular Eichberg uncover his nation's racial delusions and enhance their burgeoning beliefs of national superiority. Anna May's films, brave as her struggle was, unwittingly reveal the coming racial storm in Germany, just as her American movies demonstrated deep racial tensions in that society.[55]

While Anna May was in Paris, the Viennese director Jakob Feldhammer approached her about possible performances in Vienna. Feldhammer and his associate, Otto Preminger, had convinced major industrialists to invest in the Volksoper/Neues Wiener Schauspielhaus theater in Vienna, but the theater was struggling to survive. Unemployment plagued the city, and few people had the cash to buy tickets; cutting prices attracted more patrons but slashed profits. Feldhammer and Preminger believed that booking famous Hollywood talent might attract larger audiences than the classic productions, contemporary comedies, and foreign theatrical ensembles that played for a week or so and then moved on. The duo decided that Anna May could save the theater. Her nationality would be a novelty, as there were only thirty-three Chinese in all of Vienna in the early 1930s. Anna May seemed open to the possibility, and the only thing needed was a script. Re-enter William Cliffords, who had helped wreck her car in Los Angeles in 1925. He surprised Anna May by sending a complete manuscript for a play entitled *Tschun-Tschi*, which he had written while working as a props assistant in Hollywood. When she received the manuscript, Anna May telegraphed the management at the Neues Wiener Schauspielhaus in Vienna with whom she had been negotiating about an appearance. She told the managers: "I will bring a play with me, it's called *Tschun-Tschi*, and was written for me." Despite the uncertainties of her film contracts, Anna May agreed to a guest engagement in the fall in Vienna. She arrived there on either July 11 or 15, staying at the Hotel Hübner. As always, her hotel choice was top-grade. The Hotel Hübner was no longer a retreat for diplomats and industrialists. Now it advertised as the rendezvous of top entertainment stars and boasted of such guests as Rudolph Valentino, Paola Negri, and tenor Richard Tauber, who now was a good friend of Anna May's and might have recommended the hotel to her.

First performances of the opera, now called *Die Chinesische Tänzerin* (the Chinese Dancer) were planned for August 14. For the rest of July, Berndt

Hoffman of the Theater St. Gallen in Switzerland directed the rehearsals. Joining Anna May on stage were Feldhammer as the male lead, Reinhold Bent of the Berlin Lessing Theater, and Ria Rose as the "white woman." With the approach of opening night, ambitions ran high. Anna May planned to act in local performances until October 2, followed by tours through Germany in the fall, then engagements in Paris and London. She made sure that newspapers in the United States were aware of her coup.[56]

Anna May, as always, charmed most reporters. Erwin Reisler, the correspondent in Europe for several Chinese newspapers and a fluent Mandarin speaker, met her at the theater for an interview. Reisler compared Anna May favorably with historic Chinese beauties and described her eyebrows as *O-mei* (tender moth caterpillars) and her eyes as *Hsing-Yen* (kernels of an apricot). He spoke to her in Mandarin until he realized that she knew only Taishanese dialect. Soon, Anna May sang a South Chinese folk song for him, which moved everyone in the room.[57]

The opera's plot had familiar elements for Anna May. She played a Chinese temple dancer who falls in love with an American millionaire and saves his life from a cruel priest. Eventually, he abandons her for a white film star. As she often did, Anna May had opening-night jitters. The critic for *Wiener Zeitung*, the daily newspaper, blasted the entire enterprise and belabored Anna May's failures. Her German was atrocious, he claimed; she "had no voice, at least not a voice suitable for the giant hall of the Neues Wiener Schauspielhaus; she often sings painfully out of tune—we would almost like to say she meows like a kid you place on stage." Many Viennese children, the critic claimed, could have done much better. He also ridiculed the plot, contending that such exoticisms were repellant to proper Germans and that the device of attracting a film star to the stage simply did not work, as it was a "mixture of film, revue, and dramatic kitsch." Further upsetting the critic was that the adoring audience made "thunderous applause during the opening of each scene and after each scene, finally even some words of thanks by the darling of all moviegoers were the signature of the evening." Another critic, this time from *Mein Film*, found such adoration fascinating. The critic wrote that "when she sings Chinese songs, strangely sad songs written by herself, in her sweet voice, the theater falls silent. And then a thundering applause breaks free, and Anna May Wong stands onstage—she is a little embarrassed, but happy as a child. The Viennese carry Anna May Wong in their hearts." Such veneration continued into September. Despite the critics' sour commentary, the audiences found Anna May sensational and kept up the applause long into the twenty-fifth performance. She apparently tired of the effort, however, and the theater announced that the opera would close on September 19 because Anna May had cinema engagements she could not forsake.[58]

Stating that she was homesick, Anna May announced her intention to return to America. There may have been practical reasons to return as well. While she may have missed the California sunshine, she had to be concerned with her career as well. Europe had become a second home to her, but her movie career was languishing without the powerful Hollywood machine behind her. Her European films, however artistic, had received poor reviews and limited, if any, exposure in the United States. While she may not have been aware of it, the loss of Paramount's publicity mill meant much less advertising for her films in Japan and China. If she wanted to continue her film career (and, at the age of twenty-five, she was aware of its fragility), the reality was that the US studios called the march for the rest of the world. She had gained prestige in her European venture. Now was the time to go back and capitalize on it. She departed from Europe on October 19, 1930.[59]

Anna May offered a more personal reason for coming home a year or so later to *Screenplay Secrets*. She told magazine writer Ted Le Berthon that she had a dream one night in London that she was standing under a willow tree with her friend Grace Wilcox, a New York writer and translator. Anna May explained that her name in Chinese means willow. Wilcox and she "stood beneath willows, and wept, but held no speech." She knew that Wilcox was in New York at the time. Anna May interpreted the dream as a warning that her family was in danger. She wired Los Angeles and got a response telling her everyone was fine. So she went on to Vienna, Berlin, and then Paris, where she completed *L'Amour Maître des Choses* in Paris. Anna May arrived in New York at the end of October. She was still filled with foreboding about the dream. She told the reporter that Grace, who "is a dear friend of mine, I knew in my heart, was in no trouble."[60]

Initially all was well. Anna May Wong got her first job back in the United States before she even landed. Producer Lee Ephraim was casting Edgar Wallace's latest play, *On the Spot*, for opening on Broadway. It occurred to Mr. Ephraim that it might be a good idea to cast Anna May in the role of a Chinese woman. Hurriedly, Wallace met Anna May in London. As she landed, Ephraim met her at the pier with the script and contract, which she signed before she even made it through customs.[61]

After Anna May signed the contract, there occurred an amusing event that became apocryphal among New York City journalists. In the quarantine room, reporters bombarded Anna May with questions about conditions in Europe, to which she gave the amusing anecdotes they loved to hear from her. As they finished, one scribe remained.

He stumbled through his queries: "Uh, Miss Wong, uh, well, you see, there was—I mean . . . to be frank about, there was one other thing I wanted to ask you, and—."

Anna May smiled and interrupted him. "It's not true," she said. At least six different reporters told the story for years afterward. It was the kind of quip that made Anna May so endearing to journalists all over the world.[62]

Anna May's European trip was a major success. It established her as a star, created impressive credentials for her resume, and gained her a huge number of new fans and friends. She learned to speak with an upper-class English accent, something sure to impress the nouveau riche in Hollywood. She expanded her repertoire and prepared herself for future visits to England and the Continent. It also impressed her old employer. When Paramount Pictures learned of her return and of her contract to do *On the Spot* on Broadway, its executives rushed an agreement to her to act in *Daughter of the Dragon*, based on the new hit novel by Sax Rohmer. Soon Paramount extended that single contract into a long-term agreement. While Paramount may have finally recognized Anna May's enormous talent, others seemed to believe that her European success made her whiter. *Motion Picture* magazine editorialized shortly after her return "Anna May Wong has been away three years. In that time she has learned German and French and acquired an English accent. She has made three successful pictures in German, two in English, and one in French—and has been a sensation on the stages of the Continent, London, and New York. She is glad to be back. She went away a Chinese flapper—and now many tell her that she no longer looks Oriental." They did not know the woman of whom they spoke. Anna May returned to the United States determined to be more Chinese than ever.[63]

Four
Atlantic Crossings

Anna May's turn on Broadway in the fall of 1930 was a rousing success. Edgar Wallace, a successful contemporary novelist, had adapted his work into a play called *On the Spot*. The critics were not universally kind—the *New York Times* called her "an inscrutably loyal jade"—but the play was a success and drew large enough audiences to move after the Broadway run to a Brooklyn theater. During its run on Broadway, *On the Spot* became the biggest hit ever for the Royale Theater and ran for 167 performances. There was an amusing incident in the New York run of *On the Spot* that Anna May added to her repertoire. During a poignant moment in the play, when she lay "dead" on the stage, production directions required that a "gramophone recording of Gounod's 'Ave Maria' fill the theater with sadness. One night, an inexperienced stagehand mistakenly put on a selection of 'Negro melodies,' which caused the normally professional Anna May to lie on the stage convulsed with the 'most inopportune laughter.'" The show then prepared to tour across the country. Anna May intended to join the troupe, but a tragedy at home was calling her back to Los Angeles.[1]

Her success gave Anna May no comfort, for the fearful dream in London had come true. Shortly after Anna May's arrival in New York a tragic accident back home killed her mother. Lee Gon Toy was crossing the street in front of the home at 241 North Figueroa. A passing car, driven by one Joe Rondoni, hit her. Lee Gon Toy, aged forty-three, died from a fractured skull and internal injuries at Georgia Street Receiving Hospital on November 11, 1930. The police did not charge Rondoni, who claimed that Mrs. Wong had stepped in front of his automobile and that he could not avoid hitting her. Lulu purchased a family plot where her mother could be buried and arranged for transfer of the infant

Marietta's remains to the plot. A few months later, the Wong family filed suit against Rondoni for $50,000 in damages. What happened within the family is a matter of debate. Anna May did not leave her play in New York to come to the funeral, which reportedly infuriated Wong Sam Sing and other members of the family. A second version is that Wong Sam Sing had his wife's body kept in a mausoleum until the spring when Anna May was able to return and did not hold a deep grudge against her.[2]

A year later, *American Photography*, among the most prestigious magazines of its kind, published a full-page portrait of Anna May by Dorothy Wilding, taken around the time of Lee Gon Toy's death. Earning an honorable mention in the magazine's annual contest, the picture might easily serve as Anna May's portrait of grief. Unlike her publicity photos, which often featured a gay smile or seductive glance, Wilding's image shows a downcast, pensive Anna May.[3]

Anna finally arrived in Los Angeles on June 1, 1931. She had not forgotten the frustrations of previous years and was unsure if she was going to do more films in Hollywood. She told journalist Doris Mackie: "I was so tired of the parts I had to play. Why is it that the screen Chinese is always the villain? And so crude a villain—murderous, treacherous, a snake in the grass. We are not like that. How could we be, with a civilization that is so many times older than the West?" She had to swallow her suspicions. Impressed by her European credentials, Paramount Pictures, her former and new employer, gave her a first-rate role in the thriller *Daughter of the Dragon*, derived from the Sax Rohmer novel *Daughter of Fu Manchu*, which was a bestseller the same year. Paramount purchased the rights to the book for $20,000 and lavished more than a quarter of a million dollars on the production. Paramount shot the film at the end of June 1931. Joining Anna May in star billing were Warner Oland as Fu Manchu and Sessue Hayakawa as Ah Kee. Anna May had worked with both men before. Oland had become a rising star as Charlie Chan, and Hayakawa had a very respectable star resume dating back to the early teens. Although Anna May and Hayakawa acted together earlier in her career, *Daughter of the Dragon* marked the first film featuring two major Asian stars. Also in the cast was Anna May's sister, Mary, who was making her film debut. It was good working with old friends. Like Anna May, Oland, who had played opposite her in *Old San Francisco*, had a good sense of humor. When he met Anna May on the first day of the shoot for *Daughter of the Dragon*, he asked her what they were playing this time. When she told him, he responded: "Husband and wife? Father and daughter? This is getting pretty incestuous." Oland received the top salary for the picture, earning $12,000 at a rate of $2,500 per week. Anna May earned $6,000 for four weeks' work; Hayakawa earned $10,000. Paramount also spent a thousand dollars, far more than the costume costs of any other player, for Anna May's elaborate Chinese gowns. She was still underpaid in relation to her costars, but her earnings were much better than before she traveled to Europe.[4]

In the film, Anna May, as Princess Ling Moy, a famous Limehouse dancer, is at the center of the action. When first viewed, Ling Moy is finishing her triumphant performance. Her costume was divide between a Peking Opera headdress and Western bare legs, a combination that Anna May used frequently in these years and that reflected the continuing divide in her personality between China and the West. Ling Moy attracts the attention of Ronald Petrie (played by Bramwell Fletcher), an attraction that worries his fiancé, Joan Marshall (played by Frances Dade). Meanwhile, Detective Ah Kee has traced Fu Manchu, long thought dead, to London. Fu Manchu has sworn vengeance against the Petrie family. Discovered, Fu Manchu is mortally wounded but escapes through a secret tunnel to Princess Ling Moy. In his last moments, Fu Manchu tells Ling Moy that she is his daughter and that she must avenge his death. In an evocative scene, Ling Moy swears that she is the son of Fu Manchu and will take revenge on the Petries. Fu Manchu dies thanking the spirits that he has a "son." Even though Ling Moy has fallen in love with Petrie, she plots to kill him. In a love scene with Petrie, Ling Moy uses a Western hairstyle and costume. They almost kiss. Ah Kee thwarts the plot and tells Ling Moy that he loves her and begs her to return to China with him. She plays the *pipa*, a Chinese stringed instrument, and softly sings a Taishanese dialect song for him. She drugs his wine, captures Petrie and Marshall, ties them up, and reveals her identity. When Ah Kee, abetted by Scotland Yard, intervenes in the ensuing tangle, he and Princess Ling Moy are both killed and the English couple live happily ever after. The film's trite plot and overwhelming message of the dangers of interracial love recalls those plots Anna May endured before her flight to Europe. Although the production was big budget, Hollywood's racial anxieties still burdened her career.[5]

The plot device by which Ling Moy declares herself to be the "son" of Fu Manchu has led one scholar to argue that Anna was "cross-dressing" in the film as a man. Ling Moy's roles switch between male and female characteristics and blur binary differences between the sexes. Even Anna May's female outfits were powerfully cut and mannish and provide coded meaning to homosexual viewers.[6]

Released on September 5, 1931, the film received strong reviews in the United States. The *Los Angeles Examiner* called Anna May's acting "splendid" and her voice "excellent." Even the *New York Times*, so often critical of Anna May, admired the film's lavish sets with secret panels and the elaborate garments worn by the players. It admitted that Anna May often "did quite well," and that Oland "makes the most of his part." There was no mention of any problems with Anna May's voice, an absence that allowed her to slip past the critical test of the talkies. *Variety* thought less of the film, though it did recommend it for "the kids," a reference that never hurts a movie. Oddly, the Latin American press dismissed the film, designating it mediocre entertainment.[7]

Reaction to the film in Portugal was equally curious. *Cinéfilo*, the nation's leading film magazine, had earlier misidentified Anna May as Japanese. Although Paramount Studios regularly advertised in the magazine, its writer admitted knowing very little about Anna May, her age, origins, or past experiences. Based on her photographs, the journalist argued that she could "without great effort, extinguish many Hollywood stars," and was the "only genuine thing" in *Daughter of the Dragon*. After these admiring comments, the article lapsed into Orientalism, suggesting that many people "don't reject her talent, rather the opposite, they adore the yellow [skin]." The writer was convinced that as Anna May became more familiar to Portuguese audiences, they will "long for the Chinese, dreaming of oriental scenes, full of opium-smokers and peaceful faces." The article concluded by imagining that readers would want to "write her mysterious notes in strange letters, copied from crates of tea." The article is an instance of pure Orientalism, made up of Portuguese unfamiliarity with Anna May, and with Chinese people in general, racial fantasies derived from skin consciousness, and blatant stereotyping. Unlike the Germans, English, or French, whose racial understanding had benefited from Anna May's persona, the marginal character of Portuguese filmmaking sustained Portuguese misconceptions of her.[8]

Working for a major studio meant that Anna May's film once again received a potent publicity campaign. Such was the case for Paramount's media offensive for *Daughter of the Dragon*. Its press kit included some fascinating twists on the use of "yellow faces." In the publicity for a movie that included real Asian stars, Paramount, perhaps made mindful of the spontaneous emulation of Anna May by English girls, suggested to local theater owners that they use publicity stunts to make Euro-American girls look Chinese. In an article entitled "Peroxide China Dolls Rare," Paramount's publicity office suggested hiring "a good looking girl with flaxen tresses and a straight bob." Technicians were to use egg white or gum arabic to slant her eyes, wax her lashes black, and to do "her hair swirled or looped with a tiny forehead pigtail, to make her more Chinesque." To advance this illusion of a blonde Chinese girl, add spiked heels to her shoes, and a silken robe or pajamas of Mandarin red, and put her in a store window. For added effect, she could be given a parasol. Then put advertisements for the movie on "the little packs, which are commonly strapped on the backs of Chinese ladies." The copy on the pack should read, "You never saw a Blonde Chinese Maid." Such a girl, the promoters assured, would bring "scads of attention to any store."[9]

For all of Hollywood's anxieties about "mixed blood" and myths of racial purity, fears that had limited Anna May's rise to stardom in the 1920s, public conceptions of beauty in the 1930s veered toward the exotic and the multicultural. Even as Hollywood used "yellow faces" to avoid, however clumsily, suggestions of mixed-race love, American women were gradually rejecting the boredom of Anglo Saxon visions of beauty and accepting nonwhite skin as equally lovely. The introduction of suntan lotions and heavier makeup meant that any Euro-American woman could appear exotic. While such plans hardly disturbed the color line in American cinema and society, nonwhite or ethnic beauty was becoming acceptable. Still, while Greta Garbo and Marlene Dietrich could become "Orientalized" in film, there was really only one genuine article, Anna May Wong.[10]

Notwithstanding the relaxed views of facial color, Americans recognized the genuine nonwhite actors. American magazines played up the return of Sessue Hayakawa and Anna May Wong to Hollywood, noting that each of them had slipped away for a number of years. Anna May's sister Mary also received some publicity for her film debut. While Hollywood writers were impressed by Anna

May's Continental resume, made much of her upper-class English accent, and even contended that she no longer looked Oriental, Anna May's response was mixed. She acknowledged that people told her that "I don't even look like a Chinese girl anymore. . . . I believe that the mind and spirit show through the features. My face has changed because my mind has changed. I think like the people in the West, except in some moments of despair and stress. Then I'll fall back on Oriental philosophy, which is to accept, not to resist. There's no use to struggle. That philosophy gets you through a lot of tight places."[11]

This ambivalence showed that Anna May was trying to seize the moment. The early 1930s also saw a revival of Orientalist fashions. Popular since the late eighteenth century, combinations of Chinese silks and Indian cottons, Turkish gowns and Arab burnooses, when worn by stars like Greta Garbo and Joan Bennett, were associated with luxury, female sexuality, and stylistic modernity. New makeup introduced by Elizabeth Arden and Helena Rubenstein featured Chinese Red lipstick and rouge. Emphasized in films such as *The Bitter Tea of General Yen*, makeup and clothing allegedly transformed Euro-American actresses into more realistic "yellow faces." Technicolor, used in big-budget films of the 1930s, augmented this new "realism." The treatment did not extend to Anna May, who had been wearing genuine Asian costumes since the beginning of her career. Anna May was in fact too authentic for Hollywood or for fashion designers. Although her 1922 movie *The Toll of the Sea* was a landmark in Technicolor technology, she would not appear in color again in a big-budget movie until close to the end of her career.[12]

After finishing *Daughter of the Dragon*, Anna May returned to her role in *On the Spot*, which opened in Los Angeles in the middle of August 1931, after the New York cast made its way across the country. Her reviews in Los Angeles were especially strong, evidence of how her reputation had benefited from her European sojourn. During the run, she was a regular at parties in Los Angeles, sometimes accompanied by her friend Carl Van Vechten. After the run of *On the Spot*, Anna May decided to return to the road. As *Daughter of the Dragon* hit the screens across the United States, Anna May contributed to its success by performing at a series of vaudeville theaters, hitting such towns as Oakland, Salt Lake City, Kansas City, Detroit, and Pittsburgh. In Philadelphia's Mastbaum Theater, after an introduction by Master of Ceremonies Dick Powell, she sang

"Boys Will Be Girls and Girls Will Be Boys," and thanked an appreciative audience in five languages, including Yiddish. At New York's Capitol Theater, she was the headline act in a large show that included Jack Benny, Lew Cody, and Abe Lyman's orchestra. By the end of October, she was back in Los Angeles, where she was seen at a party in Malibu. There she captivated the other guests with her outfits purchased in flea markets in Budapest. She spent the winter enjoying road versions of new plays, including an all-Chinese version of *The Yellow Jacket*, an introductory showing of the Chinese play *Lady Precious Stream*, and Noel Coward's *Private Lives*. Soon she began to incorporate Coward's songs into her own shows.[13]

Emboldened by the freedoms she had experienced in Europe, she began to make political statements in the United States. Late in 1931, angered by the Japanese invasion of Manchuria, Anna May wrote one of the few overtly political pieces of her career. Entitled "Manchuria," and published in her friend Rob Wagner's *Beverly Hills Script*, the article contrasted China's ancient, patient wisdom with the modern, aggressive, and bellicose society of Japan. The piece was inspired by the 1931 Mukden Incident, which she contended violated the League of Nations Treaty. In an early example of what would later become her dominant cultural affiliation, Anna May spoke of China's traditional independence and the patient resistance of its millions, qualities which guaranteed its eventual success. She wrote:

> Never has the world so felt the need of spiritual rejuvenation to relieve it of the weariness of the whirl and clock of machines and the nerve-strain of speed and crushing size. Thus we are witnessing the greatest renaissance in history, which will culminate in a new interest and happiness in the philosophy of life. Just as fate destined the exquisite lotus to bloom above the polluted torrents, thus, despite the iron heel of Japan, will the endangered bud of Chinese culture bloom forth in its consummate moral purity and spiritual elegance above the mire of blood and destruction.[14]

The article demonstrated Anna May's evolving Chinese nationalism. She spoke glowingly of Chinese inventions and revealed pride in that national language with "its metaphors, similes, and vignettes that a literal translation into [another] language [makes] meaningless." China had become, she declared, more open to the West since the fall of the Qing dynasty. She enumerated the scholars "Hu Shi, Fon See, Wellington Koo, Alfred Sze, T. Z. Koo, Tiangfan Lew, all of whom have achieved high honors in western colleges." Their success was appropriate, she argued, because "the Chinese nation has held the scholar-class in high esteem," far more than it did its warriors. She noted that distant scholars were always welcomed in Peking, perhaps reflecting her hopes that someday she too would gain a favorable audience. That combination of scholarship and spirituality promoted the resistance, which would consign Japan's aggression to oblivion and fuel a Chinese cultural renaissance. Anna May's statement approximates the passive resistance that Poshek Fu identified later in Shanghai under Japanese control. Anna May was not in an occupied zone in the United States. At the same time, she had experienced constraints in her freedom in the past and had to feel dominated by Western attitudes. In time, she would expand her methods of resistance.[15]

* * *

With no roles in sight in the fall of 1931, Anna May prepared to return to Europe. *Screenplay* magazine reported to its readers that "neither the American stage or screen could give her the parts she wanted to play." Suddenly a new role turned up that gave her third billing in a major new movie entitled *Shanghai Express*. Production began in late 1931. The film was produced by Adolph Zukor, directed by Josef von Sternberg, and starred Marlene Dietrich, Clive Brook, Anna May, and Warner Oland with excellent support from a number of character actors. The film's locale was China during the Civil War in 1925. Some footage, taken by cinematographer James Wong Howe during his visit to China in 1928, was authentic. The action occurs on a passenger train from Peking to Shanghai and focuses on "Shanghai Lily" (Dietrich), a famed prostitute who had destroyed many men in China. The film quickly introduces the first-class passengers who include a number of stuffy European types, each with a secret to hide. Also on board are two Chinese: Henry Chang (Oland), a warlord traveling incognito, and Hui Fei (Anna May), a prostitute. Several Europeans, including leading man Captain Donald "Doc" Harvey (Brook), refuse to acknowledge Hui Fei. One, a Presbyterian minister, even insists she be put off the train, a demand not made of the equally notorious Shanghai Lily. Anna May's dialogue punctures such pretensions. Mrs. Haggerty (Louise Closser Hale), owner of a Shanghai boarding house and a silly, pretentious fraud, steps into Hui Fei and Shanghai Lily's compartment. Mrs. Haggerty gives the pair her business card, pompously announcing that her boarding house is "only for the most respectable people." Shanghai Lily arches an eyebrow and pretends to believe that Mrs. Haggerty runs a bawdy house. Hui Fei is even more cutting, remarking that she does "not know the standard of respectability you demand in your boarding house, Mrs. Haggerty," sending the prissy lady back into the aisle in a fury.

En route, the train is stopped and soldiers of the Chinese army capture a rebel spy. Discreetly, Chang wires ahead to have the train stopped again. In a major scene, Captain Harvey and Shanghai Lily rekindle a lost love. After the train is hijacked, Chang steps forth as the commander-in-chief of the rebel army, interrogates all the first-class passengers, and holds Harvey for ransom. That night, Chang diverts himself by raping Hui Fei. Chang's reason for stopping the train, however, was to demand a trade of his spy for Captain Harvey. The deal is made, though Chang also requires that Shanghai Lily stay with him. Intervening, however, is Hui Fei, who stabs Chang to death in retribution and a $20,000 reward. At the end, Shanghai Lily and Harvey embrace in a crowded train station as Hui Fei walks away, alone but alive.[16]

Although von Sternberg used Expressionist techniques to highlight Dietrich's blonde hair and angular face, Anna May's talent lifted that of her character into significance. Her often understated, ironic tone mediates the uncovering of the dark past of the European characters. Her brisk, economic acting underscores her open contempt for many of the European travelers. Her quiet dignity, for example, when Captain Harvey refuses to shake her hand, exposes his character's racist hypocrisy. While the doctor rejects any contact with one prostitute because she is Chinese, his love for another, Shanghai Lily, drives the romantic story of the film. Ironically, he can overlook the fact that, as Dietrich famously remarks, "It took more than one man to change my name to Shanghai Lily." As notorious as Dietrich's epigram might be, Anna May delivers the toughest line in the movie. After she gains revenge by stabbing Chang, Hui Fei confronts Harvey in the hallway and tells him to save Lily by warning him "You'd better get her out of there. I just killed the general." Delivered deadpan, Hui Fei's advice rivals any film noir lines. Later, Shanghai Lily tells Hui Fei, "I don't know if I should be grateful to you or not" for killing Chang. Hui Fei's sardonic response: "It's of no consequence. I didn't do it for you. Death canceled his debt to me." The film also marks the first time since *Peter Pan* and *The Thief of Bagdad* that Anna May did not have to die at the end of the movie. Although her character was clearly a prostitute, von Sternberg's ambiguous finish to the movie allows Hui Fei to walk away alive.

While von Sternberg and the talented Paramount costume director Travis Banton clearly limited her costumes in order not to overshadow Dietrich, Anna May skillfully used hairstyles to develop her character. When first introduced at the station, Hui Fei wears her hair down her forehead in a long, thick slab, a hairstyle called in Chinese the *Cha Hu Gai* (lid of the teapot). Combined with sharp locks down the side of her face and dangling earrings, her look presents a tough, worldly woman. In later scenes, such as the rape scene, Hui Fei's hair is completely loose, signifying sexual desirability. Anna May as Hui Fei also uses this style when she and Shanghai Lily are awakened in their compartment and forced outside by the rebels. When dealing with the rebels, she pins her hair back up, though it comes loose after Chang rapes her, again. After that, the rebel soldiers toy with her, understanding that her wild hair reveals her sexual status. Later, when she takes out a dagger and stabs Chang to death, her hair is combed into the maidenly Child Flower style. At the close of the movie she returns to the worldly *Cha Hu Gai* hairstyle and prepares to go back into the world. When reporters crowd around Hui Fei with questions about the assassination, she brushes them aside, saying, "I don't want to talk about it."[17]

Anna May did have many last words about her role, though she could not utter them in the movies. As she roamed about Europe in the next few years, Anna May created a monologue about Hui Fei and regularly performed it in the language of the nation she was visiting. Its words revealed how Anna May regarded her role:

> The sun doesn't shine for a woman like me.
> My work, as you can see, begins at night.
> In winter or summer, if it's raining, thundering, or freezing
> For me it's all the same, I'm waiting for clients.
> There's a young man from the fleet! "Hello, old chap, how's it going?
> It's good to see you. Hurry, let's go, come on."
> Young and old, rich and poor, all kinds of men.
> Those who cry and those who laugh, they all come by.

They come to buy. And since I sell, it's their right.
They call this love, but I call it hell.
"Good evening, sweetie, are you happy with life?"
"What's going on, little guy? Go ahead, I'm leaving."
Long ago, I loved deeply with all my heart. He loved me.
It was a passionate love! We weren't going to leave one another ever, ever
One night, he sold me for two bills, less
Love is such a beautiful thing! Oh, how unthinking we are when we're
in love
But some day, by chance, I'll meet my lover!
How sweet vengeance is! How I am waiting for that moment!
I'll smile at him, I'll flirt with him. I'll be very sweet
When he's in my arms, I'll draw him close to me:
"How beautiful life is! What happiness, my love!"
Die, you wretch! Oh, yes, everyone gets his turn!
The police will find me, of course; there won't be any reason for me to hide.
They're always after me anyway, following me; they're so cruel
Anyway, what difference does it make! Nothing really matters.
So, then, it's better to laugh than to cry! Right?
Hello there, officer. It's ok, I'm tired
Let's go, here are my hands. I'm not complaining. It's life![18]

This remarkable soliloquy revealed Anna May's bitterness toward the men who had deserted her over the years, doubtless starting with Mickey Neilan and continuing on through Browning, Rosher, and others. Anna May identified with the prostitute's plight as an actress condemned by those closest to her, by her nationality, and by those men eager to love her but too gutless to make a commitment. Spoken to audiences in Italian, French, Spanish, Swedish, German, and Norwegian, Anna May's words voiced the tragedy of women about whom men fantasize, but whom they cannot love. As Anna May aged, she must have understood that her love was in vain.

She could comfort herself with a good payday. Anna May earned $6,000 for the film, a fraction of Dietrich's salary of $78,166, which was half of the German star's salary from Paramount that year. Dietrich's wardrobe cost about double that of Anna May's. Even a cursory viewing reveals that Anna May's outfit in *Shanghai Express* was much less elegant than her usual costumes. In a medium in which clothing counted for so much, the Blonde Venus could not afford to let Anna May distinguish herself in her extraordinary Asian outfits.[19] Immediately hailed as von Sternberg's best film ever, *Shanghai Express* became a hit. Had there been such an award then, the consensus is that Anna May would have received an Oscar for her supporting role.[20]

Chinese reactions were less positive. The Nationalist government was conducting a campaign against "spiritual pollution" and was targeting American films as especially offensive. Earlier von Sternberg had visited Shanghai to seek out locales, but with the knowledge of the Chinese government. Despite his preparation, there were aspects of *Shanghai Express* that the government found offensive. For one, the Embassy objected to the line "Time and life have little value in China." A second problem was Anna May's role. As the film was being made, the *Pei-Yang Pictorial News* of Tianjin, China, shouted in its headline that PARAMOUNT USES ANNA MAY WONG TO EMBARRASS CHINA AGAIN. Paramount studio executives sought to assuage the Chinese ambassador about the film, but the outcry in China continued. A big problem was Anna May's portrayal of a prostitute. A Shanghai tabloid derided Anna May as "the female traitor to China" for her role as Hui Fei. When the film opened in the French Concession area of Shanghai, Hong Shen, a director and writer with strong Nationalist beliefs, watched the film during the afternoon. Hong Shen had studied at Yale and doubtless had greater familiarity with Anna May's films than other Chinese had. Like most Chinese who were educated in the United States, he was sensitive to films insulting to China. Moreover, he was a leading composer and director of modern Chinese theater, which made his animosity toward Anna May all the more tragic. Hong Shen was not new to international controversy and had made a name for himself as a critic in 1929 by denouncing a Harold Lloyd film as insulting to China. After watching the matinee performance of *Shanghai Express*, Hong stood up in the front row of the theater at the start of the evening show and attacked the film to the audience. At his behest, the Nationalist government quickly banned the movie.[21]

The film offended Chinese nationalists in ways Paramount and even Anna May probably did not understand. Putting two prostitutes in leading roles was already intolerable, but to mock revolutionary forces in the midst of Japanese attack, as the film did, was ill advised. Beyond these political reasons lay deeper Chinese antagonism toward the film. The studio had just attempted to buy all of the Chinese studios, thus establishing a monopoly over movies in the nation.

Paramount Pictures symbolized American cultural imperialism; the buyout nearly succeeded until the government objected, and Paramount's films were then placed under sharper scrutiny. Then came issues of political personality. Hong Shen was the leader of a Nationalist movement ever on the prowl for offensive foreign movies and was out to publicize his beliefs at any opportunity. Finally, Anna May's background and appearance were Cantonese, an ethnicity held in disfavor by the Nationalist government. For all these reasons, film censors quickly banned *Shanghai Express* and suspended Paramount's license to show films in China. It took US diplomatic intervention to restore the company's business.[22]

Had Hong Shen and other Nationalists not been so sensitive to perceived insults to China, they might have heard pro-government pronouncements from Anna May's character. When the rebel warlord Chang takes over the train and begins bargaining to ransom one of his staff held by the British, Hui Fei mulls over the $20,000 reward for his head. She remarks to the other passengers, "The government has offered a price of twenty thousand dollars for his capture, dead or alive," and concludes: "It will be a great day for China when that price is paid." Hui Fei, though a prostitute, is a patriotic follower of the Kuomintang, the Nationalist government attempting to subdue such warlords.[23]

Anna May was more popular in China than Hong Shen and the Nationalists may have recognized. In addition to her friendship with Wu Liande, which resulted in frequent coverage in *Liang You Huabao*, other Chinese magazines and newspapers including *Pei-Yang Pictorial News*, *Shen Bao* and *Ling Long* routinely published images from her latest films. A surprising source produced a prestigious honor. *Mein Film*, the German fan magazine, reported in an article entitled "Fräulein Doktor Filmstar" that Peking University, far and away the most famous Chinese university, had awarded an honorary doctorate to Anna May. The magazine described the news as "probably unique," since European (and for that matter, American) universities did not confer doctorates *honoris causa* to actors. In so doing, Peking University recognized Anna May as providing "honor to her home country and [that] she has served the arts." The magazine argued that Peking University's action showed that it did not regard film as a "second-rate art." Given the Nationalist outrage against Anna May, this honorary doctorate is all the more unusual. What it demonstrated is that Anna May had likely attracted favorable regard from liberal intellectuals in China who wanted to show their appreciation to her. In the future, such intellectuals would provide her with support and succor.[24]

On the set of *Shanghai Express*, Anna May renewed her acquaintance with Marlene Dietrich, whom Paramount was now molding into a major star to rival Greta Garbo. In her autobiography, Dietrich failed to mention Anna May. But as her daughter recalled, at the time Anna May and the Blonde Venus became "chummy." Maria Riva remembered: "Between takes they talked, not rehearsing their scene, just soft conversation, smoked, sipped cool coffee through their straws." Marlene fussed with Anna May's square bangs and had the costume designer redo one of her kimonos so that it would be more flattering. Anna May and Marlene sometimes relaxed in the latter's luxurious dressing room, where they enjoyed the German actress's extensive collection of Richard Tauber records. Marlene clearly preferred the company of Anna May to her leading man, who turned out to be "exactly as predicted—a photogenic jaw, British, and little else."[25] European magazines followed suit, giving yards of coverage to Anna May's role in *Shanghai Express* and to her friendship with Dietrich. Indeed, French and Portuguese magazines featured Anna May rather than Dietrich.[26]

That association, in the eyes of some critics, occupied the center of the film. Dietrich's cinematic love affair with Brook lacked conviction, partly because of the stiff manner of the English actor, but mostly because their interaction did not have the chemistry found, for example, a decade later between Humphrey Bogart and Ingrid Bergman in *Casablanca*. More tantalizing in *Shanghai Express* was the interaction between Dietrich and Anna May. Their characters, Shanghai Lily and Hui Fei, share a compartment, separate from the other travelers. Their occupations explain why. Their relationship emerges, as Gina Marchetti shows, through costume, makeup, lighting, framing, and placement in space, all of which hint at more profound intimacy. Shanghai Lily always wears black, while Hui Fei complements her by dressing in muted colors.[27] Anna May's costumes in her other movies during this period often rival Peking Opera style. In *Shanghai Express*, Anna May wears simple gowns. When Shanghai Lily moves in with Hui Fei, she draws the curtains, as if to shut out the world. However, later, after Hui Fei kills Chang as revenge for her rape, she dismisses Shanghai Lily's offer of thanks. Clearly, Hui Fei acted on her own motives rather than to save Lily, whom

Chang was kidnapping. Lily ends the movie in the arms of the chilly Doc, while Hui Fei walks off into the crowd alone. In her career Dietrich joined the center of the Hollywood crowd and seemed to personify the cosmopolitan clique within Tinsel Town. Anna May, the genuine sophisticate, returned to her solitary travels around the world. Her departure relieved Dietrich of competition. Once, a friend watched *Shanghai Express* with Dietrich. After the screening, the friend remarked about Anna May's magnificent performance, which caused a distinct chill in the air. There are no accounts of further encounters between Dietrich and Wong.[28]

These scenes in *Shanghai Express* are often cited as proof of revived sexual relationship between Marlene Dietrich and Anna May Wong. It is unlikely that the truth will ever be known. While the studios protected their stars from gossip as much as possible, actors were expected to behave themselves. Hollywood officials let it be known that any homosexual activity would be met with immediate dismissal. Stars who had gay relationships had to travel to safer towns outside of Los Angeles. In Hollywood, gossip columnists Louella Parsons and Hedda Hopper operated out of restaurants opposite the major studios and effectively policed the movie community. Both columnists liked Anna May and gave her appreciative publicity; both had spies everywhere to dig up any clue of gay activity. Lesbian chic, so popular in the 1920s, was now going underground in the newly conservative era. Anna May especially had to be completely above suspicion. Nonetheless, her scenes with Dietrich offered coded signals to gay people about her own sexuality. Gay love among actresses of this era was hardly news, and if Anna May and Dietrich did have an affair, it would offer yet another example of Anna May's courage in crossing boundaries, in blurring the lines that divided human behavior. Just as Anna May had to travel to Europe to enjoy the company of white males, if she desired a female companion, international travel was the safest option. It is telling that Anna May was not invited to make a publicity tour with Dietrich, lest she offer competition, however indirect, to the rising German star.[29]

Although the film was a financial success, Anna May's featured role in *Shanghai Express* did not bring new contracts, even when a script called for an Asian character. There were parts for which Anna May was rumored to be the lead actress; these did not pan out, sometimes fortunately. The first was *The Bitter Tea of General Yen*, in which she was scheduled to play the mistress of a corrupt Chinese general. Although the film eventually opened at the new Radio City

Music Hall, controversies plagued it. The Chinese embassy to the United States, now more vigilant than ever about films insulting to its national image, objected to the line "Human life is the cheapest thing in China," and to the depicted treatment of war prisoners. American critics were upset over suggestions that a white woman might offer herself sexually to General Yen to protect another woman (actually Wong's potential role). *Variety* voiced American concerns by stating crudely, "Seeing a Chinaman attempting to romance with a pretty and supposedly decent young American white woman is bound to evoke adverse criticism." The film's violation of American sensibilities against mixed-race love lowered the film's profile and doomed its return years later. The studio's preference for "yellow faces" enabled Anna May to avoid further contact with the contaminated product. Still, the old prejudices remained. She did a test for MGM in 1932 for the leading role in *The Son-Daughter*, which was adapted from a David Belasco Broadway play. She heard through the grapevine that MGM considered her "too Chinese to play a Chinese."[30] Later in the year, Helen Hayes was miscast in the lead role of *The Son-Daughter*. MGM's decision turned out to be doubly disastrous. Hayes's performance was embarrassing, and the Chinese government banned the film as demeaning to its people. The 1933 remake of *Madame Butterfly* featured Sylvia Sidney and Cary Grant; another film entitled *The Honorable Mr. Wong* improbably starred Edward G. Robinson and Loretta Young.[31] Anna May was able to inject some culture into a Tinsel Town production when she performed a Chinese poem in Taishanese dialect for the short subject *Hollywood on Parade*. Paramount's slide into bankruptcy in 1933 could not have helped; and that was it for Anna May's year in Hollywood. Her poetry reading indicated that as far as Hollywood was concerned, Anna May's provincial dialect epitomized the Chinese idiom, a position the Nationalist Chinese government, intent on imposing Mandarin as the official language, found infuriating.[32]

Anna May was more concerned about work than the politics of language. Quickly grasping her predicament, and with little in the offing in Hollywood, Anna May returned again and again to New York City as well as to Europe. She remained popular with the European film journalists, who spotted her at the Casino de Paris watching Josephine Baker. Anna May's face adorned the covers of magazines in many countries after her return to Europe in early 1932. *Daughter of the Dragon* and *Shanghai Express* received rave reviews in British and German magazines. In May, she did *On the Spot* again with Crane Wilbur in the Grand Opera House in London. English journalists chronicled her latest appearances, mentioned upcoming projects, and generally kept her in public view.[33]

Her trips to the East Coast and to Europe now had a familiar routine. In New York, she stayed at the Algonquin; in London, the Dorchester was her regular haunt. Back in Los Angeles, she stayed in the fashionable Park-Wilshire Apartments. She normally took the train back and forth. One incident in the spring of 1932 reminded her of her shaky legal status. When her overnight car stopped at the Canadian border, she stepped out to reminisce with some friends. The Canadian immigration officials refused to allow her into their country. She was forced to wait in Detroit and take an all-American route. And, Anna May was constantly in search of work.[34]

Looking for employment involved seeking the succor of cosmopolitan places and people. After arrival in New York City, one of her pleasures was a photographic sitting for Carl Van Vechten. Best known today for his role as photographer of the Harlem Renaissance, the critic and novelist was just then starting his new career as chronicler of the artistic world. Anna May had become friendly with Van Vechten and his wife, Fania Marinoff, exchanging holiday greetings and warm telegrams for special events. She had met them in May 1930 and went to parties at their house in October of that year. Through Van Vechten, Anna May gained access in New York City to an urbane, intelligent, wealthy, and racially tolerant society eager for excitement. Its members did not recoil from interracial love or homosexuality, and matched the liberal salons that she had found in Europe. At one such party, Anna May mixed with fellow star Fredric March, his wife, Blanche Knopf, writers Sinclair Lewis and Zora Neale Hurston, and Ethel Waters. On another occasion in New York City, she met Eric Maschwitz, the producer of the BBC show *Radio Times*. Maschwitz was immediately smitten, recalling later that he could still envision the moment she opened the door, "a slender, exquisite person in a white blouse and white skin." His marriage to Hermione Gingold was on the ropes and Maschwitz, ever the Lothario, was charming to Anna May, but years would pass before they became lovers. He sailed back to London with her face in his memory and a fragment of a song in his heart. For the present, Anna May had to content herself with outings with Van Vechten, with whom she went to a six-day bicycle race at Madison Square Garden, an event she probably had learned to enjoy in Berlin. Friendship bred a correspondence that lasted the rest of her life. On this occasion, he caught her lovely face and black hair in a cloche hat made of white feathers. She liked most of his images very much, though several in a tuxedo displeased her. She would sit for him on numerous occasions.[35]

Anna May's letters to the Van Vechtens reveal much about her personality. Usually sent on her personal stationery with her name in embossed Chinese characters, the warm, friendly missives are written in a clear, intelligent style. The letters, while chatty, demonstrate Anna May's sincerity toward her friends; her mature, sophisticated understanding of life; and her cheerful optimism. The Van Vechten letters are the largest cache of Anna May's correspondence available to researchers. Their sizable number (more than two hundred over thirty years) show that Anna May worked assiduously to maintain contact with those she considered valuable friends. Not relying on studio publicity alone, she used personal letters to sustain her contacts, to thank those who reviewed her favorably, and to drum up support for her projects.

The sophistication Anna May reveals in her letters was matched by her career skills. She was a consummate actress who could perform tragedy, comedy, horror, and stock melodrama. As she told the Van Vechtens in one letter, she felt "so fit, I could tackle most anything, and even the prospect of vaudeville doesn't frighten me." Vaudeville, with its constant traveling, was wearing, but it allowed her to feature her talents in singing and dancing. Her peers looked at Anna May with great respect and affection, high praise in a town known for jealousy and hypercompetitiveness. Hollywood players loved to rub shoulders with writers, intellectuals, and visiting royalty in order to acquire more status. Anna May was one of the very few who could easily move in such circles without any pretense. During her European travels she regularly visited artists in their studios and could be absorbed in art at major museums. She was very well read. Anna May told *Screenland* magazine that she was an avid reader of Shakespeare and had recently enjoyed Anatole France's *The Revolt of the Angels*. Widely regarded as the owner of the most beautiful hands in filmdom, she was also considered the most cosmopolitan of the Hollywood players. Studios respected her professionalism, noting that she was always prepared, and never muffed her lines. Journalists found her charming, accessible, and witty. If other women chose to be divas, Anna May Wong understood that career survival could be found in professional cooperation as much as in hauteur. It is not too much of a jump to argue that Anna May Wong, the laundryman's daughter, was one of the most sophisticated women in the world.[36]

She had picked up a few life skills along the way. Anna May was multilingual and prided herself on her hard work picking up a new tongue. Critics sometimes admonished her for her poor command of German, for example, but her use of idioms was impressive. Oddly, her weakest language remained Chinese, though, as many autograph collectors know, she could ably write her name in characters. Her English handwriting revealed much about her personality to at least one observer. During Anna May's visits to London, she gained, or perhaps renewed, an acquaintance with Charlotte Woolf, a refugee psychoanalyst from Berlin. Woolf had two primary specializations. The first was chirology, the study of mental health through analysis of the human hand, a subject on which she later authored two distinguished works. The second covered bisexuals and lesbians, a subject about which she wrote several pioneering books. Woolf was herself a lesbian and usually dressed as a man. She moved among intellectuals in Berlin, where she was good friends with Walter Benjamin; in Paris, where she knew Ravel, Duchamp, and innumerable others; and now London, where the Society of Friends gave her succor from the Nazis. Woolf was engaged in putting together a popular book of the palms of celebrities, and probably met Anna May through their mutual friends, Aldous and Maria Huxley, who sponsored Woolf's entrance into London society and introduced her to the English publishers Chatto and Windus and the American Alfred Knopf.[37]

After her move to London, Woolf needed to earn cash and, with Huxley's help, composed the book of celebrity palm readings. Knopf published Woolf's book, *Studies in Hand-Reading*, in New York in 1938, a year after its London imprint. Aldous Huxley wrote an admiring preface for the work, which included his palm print along with those of such luminaries as Man Ray, Balthus, Maurice Ravel, Cecil Beaton, Antonin Artaud, John Gielgud, and Anna May. Woolf was a serious scientist and her insights into Anna May's personality are unique. She described Anna May's palm as "resembling Chinese calligraphy." Unlike Europeans, Anna May, like other people from the East, "have their emotions under control from their youth onwards, and really order their lives according to the views of the great Eastern philosophers." She contended that Anna May's emotional life was subordinated to "a spirit of contemplation," which alone "provides a counterbalance to her nervous irritability and fits of depression." Anna May's personality was formed primarily by "imagination and instinct" and by the special influence that she had on others, which accounted for her successful acting. Woolf went on to say that the "chief ethical motive in Anna May Wong's character is the idea of freedom and liberation, which she has followed from youth onwards." Her hand also revealed a "very early developed intellectual life, which combined with particular susceptibility to erotic influences, results in an overstrain of nerves in youth." Anna May's luck-line is "deeper and more uniform than the line of destiny," which meant that her life was determined less by work and free will than by chance. Whatever one might think of Woolf's science, and there are many skeptics, her discussion of Anna May's personality often rings true. Aside from Woolf's Orientalist musings, her portrait of Anna May reinforces the impact she made on other people, that she believed in personal truth and dignity, and that she mixed intellectual pursuit with sex (a factor plain in her early flings with directors and cinematographers). Woolf also revealed that Anna May's success was not without cost. As had been occasionally apparent since her teenage breakdown, Anna May was prone to depression and could be rude and irritable without warning. Those qualities would punish her later.[38] As a check on Woolf's findings, I asked several Chinese friends, who knew little about Anna May, to comment on her palm. Their insights were quite similar to Woolf's and accentuated early nervous diseases, trouble in school and with parents, and an unstable, irritable personality mixed with an artistic, optimistic sensibility. They worried that she would later have liver and gallbladder problems, comments that proved prescient.

Despite her "nervous irritability," Anna May knew how to be charming. She was good to her fans and regularly held autograph sessions to boost sales of her movies. Her openness may have had some bureaucratic benefits. Anna May had been to Europe so often during the 1930s that she doubtless knew American consular officers well. Eventually, her chumminess with them paid off. That and her fame enabled her to secure a precious American passport, #9389, issued to her by the Department of State through its consulate in London. While she had to continue to apply for Form 430, she now could do so with the certainty of an American passport.[39]

Anna May customarily left from New York City to sail on to European voyages. Taking leave of America from the giant steamship docks in the city was a romantic affair, just as the sea passage allowed her to befriend other personalities in first class. Her life in the city was also top of the line. In New York, Carl Van Vechten was an invaluable ally to Anna May, just as he was to dozens of other literary and artistic figures. His awareness of the best of New York taught Anna May to stay regularly at the Algonquin Hotel on Forty-third Street, where journalists, artists, poets, and novelists went frequently for lunch or for long-term residence. Anna May enjoyed the hotel so much that her testimonial in owner Frank Case's memoir of the hotel read: "I like the friendly atmosphere of the Algonquin. I dislike nothing." Through Van Vechten, she could meet such visiting celebrities as Gertrude Stein, who stayed at the Algonquin the same months that Anna May did in the winter of 1934–35. Such meetings were invariably publicized in the newspapers, which never hurt one's career. Van Vechten also taught Anna May how to use a Leica camera, which she carried with her to record her many stops around the world. In all, the Van Vechtens provided Anna May with the kind of cultural and artistic camaraderie in New York City that she had loved in Paris and London. Though he remained steadfastly loyal to Anna May, Van Vechten was critical of her in one aspect. As he informed his biographer, Bruce Kellner, he considered Anna May unreliable about keeping appointments and even rehearsals because of her nighttime drinking. Although not yet a serious problem, her alcohol consumption was starting to raise alarms. Anna May knew how to party. One hotel porter told a newsman that she never returned from social activities until 7:00 AM.[40]

Anna May's partying had not yet affected her health, in part because she remained athletic. Wherever she went, Anna May took part in sports. In Los Angeles, she played tennis; in England, she rode horses; in Switzerland, she skied; in warmer climes she enjoyed swimming. Postcards from this era show her slim, in an elegant and modern bathing suit. Ever the female flaneur, Anna May walked about the cities she visited, partly to gather attention and partly to learn more about the ordinary life of her new home.

Alcohol abuse and incessant smoking were signs, though hardly uncommon ones, of the personal costs of Anna May's stardom. As read in her palm, she suffered deep bouts of depression, and from some reports, could have sudden seizures of pent-up anger. Questions about her marital status bothered her, and her stock response to reporters was that she had fantasies about marrying a Chinese scholar. In reality, her love affairs were invariably with older, intellectual white males who ultimately let her down. Sadly, her chances of marrying a Chinese scholar were poor. Chinese students who studied in the United States generally kept a distance from Chinese Americans. There were class and language issues, and students coming in the 1920s held Nationalist views that made them resent and despise her film portrayals. Despite her romantic difficulties, Anna May was no pushover and sued her studio and threatened litigation against the *New York Times*. She was sharp in real estate deals, as befitting her experience as a bookkeeper for her father's laundry. While she seemed to be loving toward her family and extended financial help to each sibling for his or her education, her dilatory arrival after her mother's death showed Anna May could be distant. Her reasons for not going to Los Angeles immediately will never be known.

Anna May was now twenty-seven years old, highly successful and the toast of two continents. Her mind seemed filled with thoughts of love. In early 1932, she gave *Hollywood Magazine*'s reporter, Ralph Parker, an insightful, thoughtful interview on love and morals. She contrasted Chinese conceptions of love with American notions. In China, she noted, love was a deeply private matter. When Chinese visitors arrive in America, they do not understand its national sexual behaviors. In China, she argued, "There is no public display of affection as there is in this country. Orientals do not indulge in public kissing because to them it is a very private act." She compared true love to nature: "A tree with a bent body, a woman with a twisted soul, may love more nobly than others who are physically and morally more fortunate." The Chinese, she continued, know that "love, like most beautiful things, is fragile." Parker then changed the subject to European men, because, he explained, "There are few people who could more intelligently compare the characteristics of various people, for she has traveled so much." Anna May did not disappoint him. She spoke of how "Europeans have a certain ability to separate passion and love," which enables them to maintain paramours more easily than Americans, who regard immorality negatively. Europeans look upon adultery as inevitable and amusing. The Chinese, however, accept immorality "with philosophical calm, knowing that it is part of the unsolvable mystery of existence."

Anna May's own code consisted of knowing herself and basing everything she did upon that knowledge. That helped her avoid making mistakes, especially in an occupation in which the opportunities for "night life and immoral people" were so high. Yet she had never, she contended, "run wild." Her self-knowledge enabled her to have the "faithful following of my own conception of goodness." That strength came from "an Oriental consciousness of my ancestors and my obligation to them." She always planned her life, believing that self-knowledge gave her direction and helped her avoid the common problem that made most people "blunder along, going the way the wind of the hour blows. Then they complain because they are neither successful nor happy." Now that Anna May was famous and successful, she looked to new goals: "For always there is ahead study and self-improvement. I want to become mentally and spiritually all that is possible for me to be." She spoke of these admirable goals to an American audience.[41] To a different set of fans, Anna May Wong wrote an evocative article on the passions and dangers of mixed-race love.

During a return visit to Paris in the summer of 1932, Anna May wrote an extraordinary piece on interracial marriage for the *Revue Mondiale*. One of the fullest explications on the controversial subject ever written by a public figure, the article deserves extensive quotation. Anna May began the piece by questioning the famous Rudyard Kipling line "East is East, and West is West, and never the twain shall meet." She stated that Kipling's sensational and rhythmic words "[do] not make any sense," for she was "born and raised in the eastern world, but the western world is present in every moment of my life." When she married, Anna May declared, "that magical bridge" would fulfill her across East and West, which merge for "a lifetime of perfect happiness and harmony." Who the man or what his race was did not matter, she wanted only "to be free to love, get married, and start a new life with anyone from anywhere." Nevertheless, people of mixed marriages had to be exceptional because their lives "shall not be like the ones of people who live and die with no adventures and who always remain the slaves of 'appearances,' while being the exact same person as their next-door neighbor."

Her inspiration was W. Somerset Maugham's novel *The Moon and Sixpence*, about Gauguin, who lived a loveless existence with his wife, then rebelled, sailed to the South Seas, and married a charming native woman. She herself knew of a contemporary Euro-American who now lived happily in Malaysia with his

Chinese wife, who had rejected a Chinese nobleman to marry him. Such people prove that love can overcome anything. She would give herself only to a man who "will be good-hearted and brave, a man who will protect me and love me." But even so, she would remain Chinese, "because I do not really like those people who change their nationality." She preferred to be like Charlie Chaplin, who worked away from home most of his life but was faithful to his country. She did not want a man, and here she singled out the English for criticism, who wanted to remake their wives into "mere images of themselves." In order to keep alive a husband's interest, the wife must remain mysterious.

Anna May spoke frankly about prejudice in Los Angeles and America. Although the Cable Act had been rescinded in 1930, there were few Chinese men whom she could marry. There were still laws against intermarriage with whites. She remembered Chinese friends from school who married "Americans" despite the disapproval of their parents. A mixed marriage required a "couple to be dauntless, brave, and intelligent." Unless both parties were willing to admit their differences, the marriage would end in failure. At the same time, they would have to build their lives around their marriage. For that reason, she was not ready to marry because of the demands of her career, which made her happy and satisfied. Anna May's excuse revealed more than she intended. Racial legal restrictions intimidated her white lovers from marrying her, it is true, but, as she noted in her article, a legal union would cost her as well. Marrying a white man would mean the end of her career in Hollywood and probably would exile her from the United States and Britain as well. Home and career meant so much to Anna May that long-term affairs were more suitable for her.[42]

As Anna May pondered the travails of mixed-race love, she knew that a reputation was a fragile blessing. She was always vigilant about the errors of journalists that could compound her career anxieties. As one example, Anna May had to battle American newspapers over a case of mistaken identity in late summer of 1932. Composer Rudolf Friml and a Chinese female companion were driving to Vienna in early September 1932 when their car struck a bicyclist and badly injured him. A few days later the cyclist died. The Austrian police quickly arrested the pair and took away their passports. In the furor, the police mistakenly decided that they had Anna May Wong in custody. Excited by their arrest of an international celebrity, they quickly told the story to Austria's newspapers, which broke the news to the world. It took a day or so to sort out the accident and to determine that neither party was at fault and that, contrary to published reports, Anna May was not in the car or on her way to Vienna. The police issued an apology. Still, many Austrians believed that the woman really was Anna May, disguising herself to avoid heavier penalties. When Friml and the woman arrived in Vienna on September 13, a crowd of several thousand people gathered in expectation of glimpsing Anna May Wong. The crowd displayed its disappointment by rioting until the police used truncheons to disperse them. Shortly after the couple went to the Semmerling, a famous resort for artists. The *New York Times* ran daily reports on the accident, and, although it eventually published the exoneration of Anna May by the Austrian police, she was furious with the newspaper. She complained to Carl Van Vechten that the *New York Herald Tribune* had had the decency to check the story, but the *Times* simply printed what came over the wires. Through her lawyers, she demanded an apology from the newspaper. Dissatisfied with the results, she wrote Carl Van Vechten to inquire if he knew of another lawyer. Apparently, Anna May decided not to return directly to America in the fall, but stayed in London to study dramatic arts with veteran actresses Kate Rork and Mabel Terry Lewis, niece of the famed actress Ellen Terry. The Terrys were cousins of actor John Gielgud and his brother Val, who was the head of the BBC drama department and a novelist. These associations later brought Anna May further contacts and friendships within the elite of English arts.[43]

On April 26, 1933, Anna May returned to Europe for the third year in a row. Just before she departed for Europe, her whole family gathered for a group photo that showed Wong Sam Sing grinning happily in front of his brood. Then the family dispersed throughout the world. According to immigration records, Anna May did not return to the United States until July 1934; she departed for Europe again in October of the same year and stayed on the Continent until June 1935. Her brother Roger accompanied her on the second trip. Counting part of the three years between 1928 and 1930, she had spent most of the last seven plus years in Europe, a pattern of independence she would maintain throughout the rest of the 1930s. One writer marveled that no other actor could sustain such independence without finding studio doors shut. He concluded that it was Anna May's unique blend of Asian mystique and Western independence, and argued that she played the Hollywood game well. He found her to be one of the cleverest, most gracious women he had ever met, a quick learner, an accomplished and perhaps unique linguist, and a conscientious businesswoman. Her business acumen aside, Anna May's travels occurred between the ages of twenty-two and thirty-four, which are critical years for any actress. Anna May made a conscious choice to reject as much as possible the limitations placed on her career by the vulgar racism of Hollywood. Europe was not perfect, but its paternalist attitudes were more palatable. Its fascination with her allowed her to capitalize on her screen career with long-running stage shows and cosmopolitan living.[44]

As she told immigration inspectors, Anna May did not live cheaply. She traveled first class on ocean liners and stayed at the best hotels in New York and London. Anna May was not indifferent to economic woes back home. After she returned to England in 1933, she spoke frankly of the economic depression in America, observing, "There are so many things up in the air there at present, although everyone goes on making pictures. It's strange, but when there's a depression on and you are working you scarcely notice it, while in the good times if you are out of jobs, you suffer a great deal from your own depression." Anna May knew how to make the best of hard times and had a knack for unusual publicity stunts. For example, she caused a sensation on May 10, 1933, when she arrived at the House of Commons in a striking Chinese gown. The peers stopped their debate to stare at her. After that, she enjoyed the London theater and stayed at least until early June before sailing to Germany on the *Europa*. Going to Berlin in the summer of 1933 seems in retrospect to have been misguided. Attacks on and legal injunctions against Jews had sharply increased as Hitler consolidated his power. Aryan clauses pushed Jews out of the civil service, arts, newspapers, and commerce. Anti-Semitic violence was not as apparent in cinema, cabaret, or café society, which still retained the façade of Weimar freedom. Anna May's trip to Germany did not last long and perhaps she understood the national sickness spreading throughout her beloved Berlin. Or perhaps she was just protecting her market share in a city and nation that continued to favor her for years into the Third Reich.[45]

There was talk of a South American tour, which did not materialize. Instead, Anna May returned to London to do cabaret at the Embassy Club for about two weeks in early May. She greeted Fritz Kreisler, the famed violinist, at a London recital on May 28, then made more personal appearances at the Holborn

Empire Theatre in June 1933. After that she went to the south of France and to Majorca for a short vacation.[46] Returning to London, Anna May went over to the Dorchester Hotel, where she partied with Duke Ellington and his band during their European tour of 1933. She commenced her own stage show that October in Dublin. The show was called *Tuneful Songs and Intriguing Costumes*. After warm-up acts including acrobats, trick dancers, comedians, and other singers, Anna May started off her show by singing "The Jasmine Flower," a Chinese folk song, in a style local journalists found haunting. During this performance, she was dressed in a sensational Chinese costume. She then switched into the native garb of other countries as she offered an aural tour of global melodies, accompanied by a small orchestra. In a fashionable European gown, Anna May sang a lively tune entitled "Any Time Now" and concluded the evening with her characterization from *Shanghai Express*, which had recently screened in Ireland to much applause. After wowing Dublin, Anna May returned to London for two weeks, then took her show up to Leeds in early November and then to the Midlands, and on to Scotland. During her stay in Leeds, Anna May even took in a football match. She headed south and did stage shows in Rome, Naples, Florence, and Venice in the winter of 1933–34. By now she had to avoid her old haunts in Berlin. Though its café society still remained, the rise of Adolf Hitler and the Nazis to power had driven out or killed much of her old crowd as the German nation headed toward cataclysm.[47]

London remained safe and hospitable. With her Hollywood career in limbo, Anna May found film work in England. Her first movie of 1933 had a curious origin. *A Study in Scarlet*, an adaptation of Sir Arthur Conan Doyle's Sherlock Holmes story, was initially distributed by the Poverty Row studio, World Wide Pictures, in May 1933. Almost as soon as the film was finished, so was World Wide Pictures. Still, *A Study in Scarlet* was a top-flight production and, fortunately, Fox Pictures picked the film up, recognizing that any Sherlock Holmes story would be a sure hit. Anna's costar, Reginald Owen, had just finished a film entitled *Sherlock Holmes* for Fox and hoped to star in a series devoted to the master detective. Robert Florey, a French American, initiated direction but then bowed out in favor of Edwin L. Martin.[48]

The plot revolved around a series of suicides in London by members of the mysterious Scarlet Ring organization. After one member joins the suicide club, the others gather in the Limehouse district to disperse his property. Eileen Forester (June Clyde) joins the group to learn the fate of her father, who was the most recent victim. While she talks to the group, still another member, Mr. Pyke, staggers into the room, mortally wounded. After a third murder, the group asks Sherlock Holmes and Dr. Watson to investigate. Holmes soon encounters Mrs. Pyke (Anna May). After the locale shifts to the Pyke country estate, Eileen is imprisoned and other members are killed until Holmes finally deduces that Pyke, abetted by his wife, has faked his own death to gain complete control over priceless Mandarin jewels. After the couple's arrest for murder, Holmes reveals that in fact they were not actually married, thus reducing the suggestion of inter-racial marriage to a more acceptable concubinage. As the film closes, Eileen and her fiancé, John, are happily married. *A Study in Scarlet* has some interest-ing features. Shot in the Continental style, the film's suspense comes as much from camerawork, lighting, and atmosphere as from the plot. Characters meet in abandoned buildings in strange gatherings arranged by secret codes. Murders occur in fog-bound streets. The murderer is unknown during most of the movie, though through an innovative device the murders are seen through the killer's eyes, as a giant shadow suddenly looms over the victim, who shouts, "It can't be you!" The next scene shows a hand checking off the name of another victim. The camera angles for the climactic scene are through the killer's eyes, as he smokes a cigarette before the lens. While reviewers did not consider it the greatest Holmes movie ever, they gave Anna May credit for a good job and recommended the film overall.[49]

The success of the Holmes movie encouraged Anna May to stay in England and make more films. *Tiger Bay* was the first of three films she did in England in 1934. The project got off to a rocky start because the original script placed the action in London's Limehouse district, disguised slightly as Tiger Bay. By this time, Limehouse as a symbol of Chinese exoticism in London seemed played out. British censors denounced the script as the "worst type of American gangster film," and stated that it had no potential value for British audiences. Only after the locale was moved to a nameless South American port was the project approved.[50]

Anna May had the starring role in *Tiger Bay*. Done by A.T.D. Studios at Ealing, produced by Ray Wyndham and directed by J. Elder Wills, the film also featured Henry Victor and René Ray. The first important scenes are in the streets of Tiger Bay, a mythical port city made up of the castoffs of many nations. In scenes now common in Wong's European films, Blacks, whites, and Asians carouse and dance. Interracial couples are common. Liu Chang (Anna May) owns a nightclub in this district where races mix freely. She has decorated the place beautifully with Chinese antiques. Her gowns are exceptionally lovely. There is trouble in this little paradise, however. Olaf (Victor) and his gang are determined to shake Liu Chang down for protection money. When she rebuffs them, they start fights on the dance floor and drive all her workers away. A subplot involves a love affair between two young whites, Letty (Ray) and Michael (Victor Garland), a union that Liu Chang defends against the thuggish Olaf. In one amusing scene, Olaf and his toughs return to the nightclub, demanding dinner. Liu Chang serves them herself. When asked why, she informs the gang that as they have driven all her workers away, she now has to cook and wait tables herself. As they gorge themselves on the food, the gang suddenly understands her method of revenge and rush home, holding their stomachs and fighting diarrhea. After his gang kidnaps Letty, Liu Chang kills Olaf. Since she knows the police will punish her, Liu Chang then slits her own wrists and waits for death to come.[51]

The morbid ending notwithstanding, Anna May had a good time making the film. She wrote to the Van Vechtens, telling them how much she enjoyed working on *Tiger Bay* at the Basil Dean studio in Ealing. Making *Tiger Bay* meant more parties in London. At one she met the Prince of Wales. Flustered, she forgot to curtsey, but did manage to address him as "Sir," which is all an American is expected to do. At other parties, she sat with W. Somerset Maugham and met Wellington Koo, the Chinese ambassador to England, and his wife. Their friendship would later prove invaluable to her in China. Other alliances developed in less glamorous ways. In May 1934, Anna May hired Katherine DeMille, the adopted daughter of Cecil, to help her create a dance. Katherine, struggling with her own career, was unimpressed with Anna May's skills. DeMille wrote: "She can't dance and she can't sing. But she has the world's most beautiful figure and a face like a Ming princess, and when she opens her mouth out comes Los Angeles Chinatown sing-sing girl and every syllable is a fresh shock." Apparently, DeMille got over these unfavorable insights, and she and Anna May became friends for life.[52]

Anna May's next English film was *Chu Chin Chow* for Gaumont British Picture Corporation in London in April 1934. *Chu Chin Chow* was a legendary play that ran for 2,338 performances on the London stage and had run on Broadway from 1917 to 1919. English critics considered the film version to be a major event. Although her role as Zahrat, the faithless slave girl, was fairly minor and her screen time less than usual, magazines and newspapers featured Anna May in a revealing costume on their front and back covers. Anna May did not even make an appearance in the film for the first twenty minutes, yet the cover of the publicity program featured her in her outfit and playing a lute. The cast included the veteran music-hall comic George Robey as Ali Baba and the great Fritz Kortner, one of Anna May's old German friends, as Abu Hasan, the robber chief. An Arabian Nights fantasy, the film used the original songs from the West End show and added new ones. Ballet dancer Anton Dolin arranged some of the dance numbers. Critics praised the film's lavish sets and considered Anna May, despite her limited role, a major asset to the film. Later, she showed her business grit by winning a suit against the studio over paid appearances. Despite her brief involvement, *Chu Chin Chow* was a good credit for Anna May in England, which now rivaled Hollywood as a base of her operations. American reviews were generally dismissive. On the Continent, she received front-cover publicity in the leading movie magazines and excellent reviews. Kortner's presence in the film ensured attention in Germany and Austria. There, critics singled out Anna May for her "delicate and three-dimensional appearance."[53]

Java Head, Anna May's third English film of 1934, was generally a dud, though it had interesting racial aspects. In the film, Anna May played Taou Yuen, a lovely Chinese princess who travels with her English husband, Gerrit Ammidon (played by John Loder), back to his home in Bristol in the 1850s. Her appearance scandalizes his family and local townspeople and breaks the heart of Gerrit's first girl, Nettie Vollar, played by Elizabeth Allen. Particularly noteworthy is the overwhelming difference between the plain, Victorian attire of most of the cast and the spectacular gowns worn by Anna May. A special moment occurs early when Ammidon and Taou Yuen kiss on screen, a first for Anna May after years of censorship. Her character naively thanks her husband for "the way you say hello," a line used to undercut any sense of eroticism. As the film unfolds, Ammidon gradually tires of his Chinese wife and openly flirts with his first love. Eventually, Taou Yuen commits suicide and the English couple is happily reunited.[54]

Anna May's makeup in *Java Head* is noteworthy. Her hair and eyeliner were created in spectacular Peking Opera style. Hair and eyes signify royal status amidst the common English people, who openly gaped at her. When the Ammidon patriarch suffers a heart attack upon learning that his family business had been involved in the opium trade, Taou Yuen rearranges her hair in mourning style and prays to Buddha. Her disaffected husband coldly mocks her "pagan ways." Overall, Taou Yuen's role was that of a Qing dynasty princess trapped among common people; her suicide by eating opium is predictable and couched in traditional Chinese fashion for such horrific developments. By her own choice, Anna May's Hollywood career had nearly vanished. She had a brief cameo in early 1934 in the lightly regarded *Hollywood Party*, derided in *Variety* as "one big short." Anna May had probably filmed her cameo several years before. The only notable aspect of this film was that James Wong Howe was the cinematographer.[55]

It is a testament to her durable star quality that Paramount Pictures was willing to feature her again. After an absence of fifteen months from the United States and even longer since her last US film, Anna May returned on July 24, 1934, to the Paramount stable to make *Limehouse Blues* with George Raft and Jean Parker. The London Limehouse district had been a part of Anna May's oeuvre since *Piccadilly* in 1929, and this movie can be considered as the culmination of her fascination with London's mixed-race district made up of transients of all nations. It was a good credit for Anna May and paid $8,000 for what turned out to be a week's worth of shooting.[56]

As in *Java Head*, the opening credits included a gong emblazoned with the Chinese character for *Shen*, the spirit of all things. *Java Head* was produced in Britain, while *Limehouse Blues* was made in Hollywood. Anna May was the only connection to and likely the reason for this prayer to *Shen*. In the film, Harry Young (played by Raft with pulled-back eyes) runs a smuggling business out of his pub, the Lily Gardens. His rival, Pug Talbot (Montagu Love) is bitter about Young's success and takes his anger out on his beautiful daughter, Toni (Parker). A practicing pickpocket, Toni escapes from an angry victim into Harry Young's private office. Young defends her to the inquiring police because he is attracted to the young woman. Pug Talbot hears of his daughter's friendship with Harry and beats her. Knowing that Harry is falling in love with Toni, Harry's mistress, Tu Tuan (Anna May), warns him to stay away from the "white flower" who "cannot bring happiness to you." When he refuses, Tu Tuan replies, "The yellow flower obeys her master," and then warns him again: "One Day you will know the difference between East and West." Later, she tells Toni to stay away from her man. Anna May uses hair to convey character. Tu Tuan wears a *ji*—a bun at the back of the head, a married woman's hairstyle. In moments when she confronts Harry, she modifies this hairstyle to signify that she is *Kuo Taitai*, or a tough, rich wife who talks with her hands placed on her hips.

Harry and Tu Tuan have praying sessions to *Shen*, in which Harry asks for wisdom while Tu Tuan beseeches the god for love. Tu Tuan is not praying to a Buddhist god, but to a Chinese folk deity of the countryside of Taishan. In this movie, Anna May reveals more of her acceptance of the spirit of her family and childhood society. Sadly, this happens in the context of a very tough film.

As the action continues, Harry sets up Pug and kills him. An investigator visits the Lily Gardens just as Tu Tuan is singing "Limehouse Blues," one of the first instances in which Anna May sings in a film. The lyrics of the song are bitter. Tu Tuan is heard singing "Vivid Nightmares that never seem to fade / What are they made of? / And why am I afraid of Limehouse Nights? / Must I join those burlesques of humanity / Drifting along until I doubt my sanity?" These words were fitting for the toughest of African American blues songs; after the film, "Limehouse Blues" became a favorite of Black jazz and blues musicians, an indication of Anna May's crossover appeal.

As she sings, Tu Tuan wears a *qipao* embroidered with dragons and dances in a serpentine style similar to a dragon's movement. The façade of the stage bears a third dragon. Western observers could easily interpret Anna May as a dragon lady. She, however, routinely chose her costumes. Anna May thus intended her beautiful dress to signify the dragon as the symbol of China's power. After several years in Europe, Anna May doubtless felt greater confidence in her screen presentations and used her garments to make potent cultural statements that were not otherwise allowed in Hollywood scripts. Her impeccable and widely recognized sense of style permitted Anna May to give homage to her spiritual homeland. The dress, designed by Travis Banton, is now considered one of the most beautiful women's garments of the twentieth century. Anna May donated it to the Brooklyn Museum in 1956. Subsequently, the dress was gifted to the Metropolitan Museum of Art, which put it on display in a major exhibition in 2010. The dress's iconic status derived as much from Anna May's persona as its own beauty. It was the right dress at the right time on the right person.

Tu Tuan's warnings to Harry about racial differences were realized in the plot. Toni falls in love with Eric, a nice boy from the West End, a development that gives Tu Tuan more reason to mock Harry for stepping across the racial divide. In the most riveting scene in the film, Harry and Tu Tuan do an Apache Dance on a tiny stage at the nightclub. Although Tu Tuan wears a *qipao* on which is embroidered the Chinese characters for *shuangxi* (double happiness), or wedding, Harry is very cruel and flings her down three times. Anna May's wide-open eyes eloquently reveal her emotional pain.[57]

After her father's death, Toni is dependent on Harry Young's charity. But Harry learns of Eric's existence from Tu Tuan, and is determined to kill his young rival. Tu Tuan warns Toni and Eric, then kills herself. Harry realizes the folly of his ways, but too late; in a gun battle with the police, he is shot to death. Again, the young white couple escape to glorious happiness while the Chinese protagonists suffer violent deaths.[58]

Despite the excellence of Anna May's acting, singing, and dancing, the movie received tepid reviews in the United States and in England. Her friend Rob Wagner used the film to remind his Hollywood readers that her "hometown has never been hospitable to Anna May's brains and fine artistry." Wagner contended that the locals were lucky to get Anna May to come back from Europe, where she had earned the kind of social position that "Doug [Fairbanks] craved but was never accorded." Wagner went to Paramount's publicity party for the film "not because we were needed to boost Anna May, but because we love and admire her."[59]

Admiration was not how the Chinese regarded the film. The Chinese press blasted Anna May for making *Limehouse Blues*, a film that "again disgraces China." Paramount had consulted with the embassy's "technical advisor," who had suggested a number of small changes, but the film was fundamentally offensive to Chinese nationalists. *Diansheng* (Movietone News) of Shanghai ridiculed George Raft's portrayal of a Chinese man: "Look at the way he dresses himself and you can imagine how disgraceful his performance must be to China." *Diansheng* kept up its criticism of Anna May throughout 1935 by mentioning that she had undergone a crash diet because she was overweight. It introduced a new Chinese actress in Hollywood, Soo Yong, and prayed that she would not emulate Anna May's "craziness, being a puppet, and all kinds of disgraceful behavior."[60]

While Anna May was filming *Limehouse Blues*, her family embarked for China. Wong Sam Sing's laundry had been destroyed along with the rest of the neighborhood during the construction of Union Station. Forced into retirement, his second wife dead, the old man decided to spend his days in the family village of Chang On outside of Taishan in Guangdong Province, China. Traveling with him were Lulu, Mary, Frank, and the twelve-year-old Richard. Lulu and Mary had some aspirations to make films in China, while Frank and Richard were on their way to Chang On with their father. On August 5, 1934, Anna May waved goodbye as they left Los Angeles harbor aboard the *President Wilson*. She had not seen them for over a year and now they were parting once more. She promised to visit China the next year, but it would be almost eighteen months before they would reunite. After his arrival, Wong Sam Sing announced his pride for Anna May in a brief article in *Xinning* magazine, the monthly publication for overseas Taishanese.[61]

Anna May was not about to hang around Hollywood waiting for parts. After finishing *Limehouse Blues*, she set sail again for Europe. On December 24, 1934, she journeyed from Paris to Rome, where she gave several shows. Then it was back to London for many nights of theater. Among the shows she attended were an evening with Richard Tauber, a special performance of *Porgy and Bess, Before Sunset* with Yvonne Printemps, and a presentation of *Lady Precious Stream*, a traditional Chinese play with costumes by Mei Lanfang. (The actors were entirely white.) Then Anna May toured across Europe the rest of the winter, appearing in Oslo, Norway, from February 16 to 18, and in Sweden in early March 1935. From there she went to Italy, followed by Spain, Switzerland, and back to Scandinavia. In each case, Anna May visited a European nation with only limited exposure to Chinese. Immigrants from China to Scandinavia, Spain, and southern Italy were either sailors adrift from their ships, or a scattering of laborers and street hawkers who peddled dolls, kites, wood carvings, and other exotica. It is unlikely that any of these European nations had ever seen such a cosmopolitan Chinese woman as Anna May. Her stage show reflected her sophistication and international experiences. On these occasions, she sang a number of songs, including

"Jasmine Flower," "Parlez Moi D'Amour," "Ingre," "Dragon Dance," and "Street Girl," finishing with her signature tune, "Half-Caste Woman." In each country she customized her songs. For example, in Sweden, she sang about "A Swedish Girl," in Norway, she had a song about a Norwegian Girl, and so on.[62]

Anna May's choice of "Half-Caste Woman" reveals something of her temperament in these years. Penned by Noel Coward for Charles B. Cochran's 1931 *Revue*, the song was adopted by torch singer Helen Morgan for *Ziegfeld Follies* the same year. In Coward's view, the tune was a flop, but Anna May decided it was perfect for her show. Its first lyrics proclaimed:

> Drink a bit, laugh a bit, love a little more
> I can supply your need
> Think a bit, chaff a bit, what's it all for
> That's my Eurasian Creed.

The song continues with a dreamy lovelorn lament asking a "half-caste woman, what are your slanting eyes / Waiting and hoping to see?" The song evokes the contemporary despair of the Eurasian woman caught between two cultures and doomed to a solitary life, played out in bars and taverns around the Continent. The set design for "Half-Caste Woman," for Cochran's *Revue*, featured several flappers languorously decorating a near-empty bar lined with whiskey bottles. Though Anna May was not a half-caste woman by birth, her years wandering Europe doubtless made her feel like one. She was accepted by nearly all in Europe, but she was still exotic. Moreover, wherever she went around the Continent, Anna May felt a racial loneliness. As the song suggests, she may well have drowned these sorrows in alcohol and fleeting romances.[63]

During the middle of her winter tour of Italy, France, Scandinavia, and Switzerland, Anna May took a two-week vacation in France. By spring, she was in London, where on May 11, 1935, Anna May met two people who would help her immeasurably in the next year. At a reception at the Chinese Embassy in London, she was introduced to Mei Lanfang, the lead Peking Opera star, and Hu Die (Butterfly Wu), China's leading film actress, who was called the Empress of Film at home. Hu Die remembered the night in her memoirs. The two Chinese actors were exhausted after a whirlwind tour of Europe and had just arrived that day from Rome. Initially indifferent to meeting Anna May, Hu Die described her clothing as "reminiscent of soldier's outfits in the Qing dynasty." Because Anna

May spoke only Taishanese dialect, Hu Die could converse with her only through a translator, which inhibited deeper exchanges. If Anna May and Hu Die did not immediately become friends, Anna May did better with Mei. She discussed the Peking Opera with him and they agreed that if she visited him in China he would teach her techniques. She showed the great star around town. There are photos taken by Fania Marinoff, the wife of Carl Van Vechten, that portray Mei Lanfang, Paul Robeson, and Anna May on the streets of London, images that reveal Anna May's cosmopolitanism. She could be helpful in small ways as well. Marinoff was unhappy in London and was fortunate to have Anna May's friendship. Marinoff and Robeson had a difficult friendship and doubtless Anna May had to mediate between them. Also, Marinoff's hotel was under construction and she could not sleep. Anna May was able to secure her a room at the Claridge. Anna May then took Marinoff down to Brighton and up to Eton for several nights. Later they voyaged back across the Atlantic together. Marinoff wrote her husband of her great pleasure in Anna May's friendship.[64]

Anna May had known Paul Robeson for years. When they met again in London in 1935, Robeson was rejecting an offer from Republican Party National Chairman, John Hamilton. The Republican official proposed that Robeson return to the United States and campaign among Blacks for Alf Landon against President Franklin D. Roosevelt. Hamilton told Robeson that if he accepted, he could write his own ticket for any future Hollywood contracts, since the film magnates were all staunchly Republican and hated Roosevelt. Robeson declined. He may well have related this story to Anna May, giving her some food for thought about her own roles. Certainly, she wanted to upgrade her own film profile.[65]

Anna May returned to the United States in June 1935 with a major ambition in mind. She wanted to star in the biggest and most favorable Hollywood production about China ever. After several years of delay, MGM was ready to film Pearl Buck's Pulitzer Prize-winning novel, *The Good Earth*. Although Buck's powerful novel did not eliminate unsavory American Orientalism, its adaptation into film promised to be a major improvement upon past racism in movies. As Jonathan Spence has noted, the novel is best in its descriptions of farm labor, harvesting, and childbearing. At the same time, as Mari Yoshihara has argued, Buck homogenized the Chinese people and infantilized their characters, qualities which became more pronounced in the film version. Nevertheless, Anna May initially had high hopes for the book's transition into a motion picture. Anna May read Buck's classic when it first appeared in 1931 and immediately wanted to play the part of O-Lan, the heroine of the book. Perhaps O-Lan's taking of a cache of jewels, a theft that eventually financed her husband Wang Lung's descent into sexual decadence with another woman, resonated with her own ambivalence about the meaning of her career. The character of O-Lan epitomized Buck's perception of the Chinese woman as self-abnegating and servile. But despite these stereotypical features, Anna May probably recognized that the part of O-Lan was among the fullest characters Hollywood would ever offer to a Chinese woman.

MGM owned the rights to Buck's novel, and the writer did what she could to convince the studio to use Chinese actors in China. Touchy negotiations with the Chinese Nationalist government and the logistical problems of getting Chinese American actors back into the United States delayed the project and hampered Anna May's chances of getting the key role. MGM already had a long track record of preferring "yellow faces" to Anna May; another factor was that MGM considered Paramount a far less prestigious studio, although it had borrowed Anna May's skills before. The Chinese government did little to help her. General Tu, the official Chinese government advisor to MGM about the movie, told Rob Wagner that in China Anna May's reputation was "Very bad . . . Whenever she appears in a film, the newspapers print her picture with the caption 'Anna May again loses face for China.'" The general expressed some sympathy for Anna May, but concluded that the parts she played as prostitute or slave antagonized the Chinese public: "China resents having its womanhood so represented." The Nationalist government's attitude about Chinese American actors was not entirely accepted. While the studios were quick to curry favor with its officials, local Chinese actors had recently protested the actions of the vice consul. Led by Walter Wong, a cousin of Anna's, and Frank Tang, head of the Chinese Actors' Association, about forty actors and actresses protested to the embassy. They were especially angry that their agent, Tom Gubbins, sometimes called the "Mayor of Chinatown," had been blackballed by the vice consul because he worked in movies that the Chinese government deemed unfavorable to the nation.[66]

Undeterred by Chinese nationalism, Los Angeles newspapers mounted a publicity campaign as early as March 1933 to secure the part for Anna May. O-Lan, as found in the film's working synopsis, was a passive character that followed her husband, Wang Lung, slavishly. Anna May would be acting against type but doing so in a major role. Anna May maintained a public dignity about her chances for the lead part. When she returned from Europe in August 1934, Louella Parsons asked her about doing screen tests for the film. Anna May laughed and replied that she was not going to do any more screen tests for "*The Good Earth* or any other film for that matter." Showing her usual sense of humor, she noted that "I know I look Chinese and so does everyone else." She then touted her sister Lulu for the part of O-Lan, arguing: "She has been a mother to us all, although she isn't much older than we are."

Unsurprisingly, the studio bosses determined that European American actors could do the parts as well as authentic Chinese. When Paul Muni was cast as Wang Lung, Anna May's chances for the O-Lan part vanished, as the production code prevented her selection for the part of a wife of a white man, even if he was impersonating a Chinese. That left the part of Lotus, a sensual twenty-year-old, and the fifth most important role in the film. Anna May reportedly told Irving Thalberg at MGM: "If you let me play O-Lan, I will be very glad. But you are asking me—with my Chinese blood—to do the only unsympathetic role in the picture, featuring an all-American cast, portraying Chinese characters." Thalberg was unmoved by her plea. Moreover, there were reports in *Daily Variety* that "various censorship angles" would be deployed if "anything approaching miscegenation" were to occur through casting an Asian in such a prominent role. The studio took the easy way out. There are conflicting reports over whether or not Anna May ever received an offer to play Lotus. While she later denied that she would have accepted the part, studio files indicate that the production heads regarded her as too old and insufficiently pretty. They preferred the Austrian ballerina Tilly Losch for the part of Lotus. The part of O-Lan went to the German actress Luise Rainer, who won the second of her two consecutive Academy Awards for her performance. Had Anna May gotten the part and gone on to win an Oscar, as her talent indicated was likely, her future fame would have been secured.[67]

Anna May Wong was in Europe during most of the casting for *The Good Earth*, but it is unlikely that anything would have helped her desire to play O-Lan. MGM handed casting duties to Irving Thalberg's assistant, Albert Lewin, whose notes on Anna May and other Asian actors indicate the problems such thespians had breaking into the major studios. Initial plans seemed promising. Casting notes for the film as far back as 1933 indicated that the studio wanted Mandarin speakers. Type and ability were, the notes said, the only concerns. The role of O-Lan was, according to the film's writers, including Frances Marion, the most important part in the film. The actress should be between twenty to thirty years of age, with kindly eyes and mouth. Lotus, in contrast, should be about twenty years old, beautiful and sensuous with the most stunning figure in the picture. Lewin gave Anna May, now thirty years old and a sixteen-year veteran of films, a screen test on December 10, 1935. It is clear that Lewin considered Anna May not for the lead, but for the part of Lotus. He wrote to his superior that he was "a little disappointed as to looks. Does not seem beautiful enough to make Wang's (the lead male character) infatuation convincing; however, deserves consideration." In a second test four days later, Lewin again reported his concerns about Anna May's beauty. In his reports on tests for Mary Wong, Keye Luke, and other Chinese actors, Lewin consistently argued that, despite their ethnicity, they did not fit his conception of what Chinese people looked like. Therefore, Lewin recommended that they be used primarily as "atmosphere" and not as principal actors. The irony of his comments cannot disguise his racist undertones or those of his superiors who accepted his advice without question. Anna May later told her Chinese fans that MGM was making big mistakes by not hiring more Chinese actors; in fact, she told them, "I felt this was not right, so when they asked me to act in the film, I had to refuse." Her fate was consistent with other Chinese actors who seemed not the right ethnicity for the studio. As Victor Jew has argued, Alfred Lewin and his superiors were not looking for authenticity, but for "MGM Chinese." If it was any consolation for Anna May, MGM also rejected famed cinematographer James Wong Howe despite his excellent credentials and lengthy experience with Chinese locales.[68]

Whether Anna May refused the part or was rejected cannot be determined. Given Anna May's long track record of playing marginal parts in Hollywood films, some will ask if she had the range to play the role of O-Lan. As I have endeavored to show throughout this book, Anna May was a consummate professional. As a Chinese American woman who had pondered her identity for years, she had the talent and intelligence to portray a good wife, mother, worker, and, unquestionably, the victim of her husband's pomposity and deceit. Her personal experiences qualified her for the part far more than Rainer's. A more appropriate query should be if Anna May could have played the role worse than Rainer. The Austrian actress spoke her part with a thick Central European accent, rarely changed her expression of doleful passivity, and employed a narrow range of emotion through the entire movie. Her body movements were wooden and unrevealing; her hairstyle was entirely inappropriate. Her fellow actors fared equally poorly. A "yellow face" extravaganza, *The Good Earth* is now painful to watch. Just a few of its racially offensive features include Muni using gibberish to represent the Chinese language, crowds of character actors who look and sound as if they belong in a western, and Losch as a sing-song girl wearing outfits and performing dances that she undoubtedly learned from watching Anna May in Europe in previous years. Actual Chinese actors are primarily restricted to background extras. Although *The Good Earth* played well to American and European audiences, as a cultural bridge between the United States and China it stands as a disastrous missed opportunity.[69]

Anna May could not have understood the studio's plans for the movie. MGM's rejection of her hurt immediately and in time came to symbolize Hollywood's misuse of her career. Courageously, she decided to fulfill a lifetime dream by going to China. There were many indications that her reception there would be better than at MGM. Her hopes had substantial support. Her friend James Wong Howe spoke of how well he had been treated. Another friend, "Newsreel Wong," was on assignment there and promised to cover her visit. Benjamin Chan, the editor of *Dianying Huabao* (Shanghai Screen Pictorial), met Anna May in Hollywood and in Germany and extolled the hospitality of the motherland.

Anna May also had artistic reasons for going to China. Since the earliest years of her career, the Peking Opera had fascinated her. Her meetings with its most famous actor, Mei Lanfang, in London in 1935, had reinvigorated her interest. Her disappointment with Hollywood further alienated Anna May. Now she declared that she wanted to go to China to learn acting from Mei Lanfang, perhaps start her own theater there, or, more likely, return to the United States and dedicate herself to popularizing Peking Opera in this country.[70]

The most compelling call may have been the general relocation of Anna May's family to China. Her father had now been in Chang On for over two years. Her brother James was teaching at the prestigious St. John's College in Shanghai. Lulu had a job with the Chinese customs office in Hong Kong. Richard was studying in Chang On with his father. Only Mary, who took a minor part in *The Good Earth*, and Roger stayed behind in Los Angeles. The other Wongs were using the education Anna May had paid for to return to China. They joined the 1,600 or so Chinese Americans who each year sought better opportunities in China. Going to China had become a career option and a spiritual motivation for Chinese Americans coming into maturity in the 1930s. Anna May was ready to join them. On December 16, 1935, she wrote to the Van Vechtens that she had made two tests for MGM for the Lotus part and that Luise Rainer was "definitely set for the part of O-Lan." She admitted there was "no use bucking up against a stone." The same day, armed with her American passport, she went down to the immigration office to apply for Form 430 to ensure her reentry after a visit to China. Hollywood producers, undoubtedly tiring of Anna May's frequent absences, began grooming a new Chinese star. Hollywood's leaders surely felt that Yuen Tsung Sze, known as Mei-Mei, the daughter of the Chinese ambassador to the United States and a graduate of Wellesley, would be more acceptable to the prickly Nationalist government. Anna May seemed ready to abandon a career that had made her prosperous, but that had also burdened her with infamy. In a letter to a devoted fan, Fitzroy K. Davis, Anna May wrote, "I am leaving for China on the 21st of January to stay a year and study the Mandarin dialect and Chinese Theater, and I hope that I will be able to bring back something unusual." She was going home at last.[71]

Five
China

As the cameras rolled for *The Good Earth*, Anna May was preparing her own production. While the Hollywood magazines were ablaze with stories about the filming of Buck's novel, Anna May celebrated her thirty-first birthday with preparations for her trip to China. She knew that, above all, living well is the best revenge. She arranged with the Hearst Corporation to have the skilled cameraman Newsreel Wong travel with her in China, signed a contract to do several articles for the *New York Herald Tribune*, packed her trusty Leica, took all the cash she could afford, and set sail for the Middle Kingdom. Newsreel Wong was a top cameraman and had strong political connections with the Nationalist government in China. Before Anna May left Los Angeles, Harry and Tai Lachman gave her a big farewell party, with "all Hollywood there." At the party, Warner Oland joked that it would be amusing to go to China with Anna May, "But I am still Charlie Channing. This time in *The Circus*." He did have plans to meet her over there. Anna May wrote to Carl Van Vechten on January 7, 1936, thanking him for his birthday telegrams and hoping that she would receive the latest batch of his photos before her departure from San Francisco for Hong Kong through Honolulu on January 24. That was the Chinese New Year, which she considered a very good omen. Her departure, however, was delayed until January 26 by a dockworkers' strike. While she waited, Anna May took in a few nights of ballet and theater. She made sure her departure was well publicized. The Hearst newspapers, especially the *Los Angeles Examiner*, gave her lots of ink.[1]

Anna May publicized her reasons for going to China largely in family terms. She wrote that she was fulfilling a lifelong dream of visiting China and planned to learn its language and culture. She added that most of her family waited for her there. Just before she departed from San Francisco, Anna May announced that she wanted to visit Peking Theater with Mei Lanfang in hopes of returning and building a theater company to tour the globe. She told reporters that "I want to study the Chinese theater—I'll be a neophyte there, for all of my stage experience. I want to work with the old Chinese plays, and, eventually, I want to select two or three of them, find good translations, and take a group of English-speaking Chinese on a world tour."[2]

Anna May armed herself intellectually for the trip to China by reading Lin Yutang's famous book, *My Country and My People*. Lin was a highly respected compiler of Chinese dictionaries and had emerged as a leading philosopher. *My Country and My People* was published in the United States in 1935 and immediately became an important source on Chinese customs and beliefs. Anna May reveled in Lin's interpretations of Chinese character and found much of herself in them. Lin's discussion of the importance of mellowness and patience in life reflected her relations with Hollywood. His emphasis on femininity resonated in her writings. Lin's discussion of women's contemporary status had to impress Anna May. Lin argued that, after centuries of oppression, Chinese women now controlled their homes. Men dominated public society, Lin acknowledged, but the "married women with their fat handbags" were the envy of "salesgirls in the department stores of Shanghai," his reference to the Modern Girl. Fashion did not matter. Modern independence, Lin argued, did not amount to much, compared to the private freedoms of the married women, who controlled their homes, their sexuality, and their motherhood. Lin's historical analysis and philosophy directly challenged Anna May's public life and had to make her wonder if she would not have lived better in China as a mother, rather than sparkling in the illusory fame of Hollywood. Lin's recommendation that each person rely on humor was advice Anna May had taken for many years. Lin was in Shanghai and openly discussing a trip to the United States; Anna May looked forward to meeting and befriending him.[3]

Anna May's first reports back to mainland America arrived soon after her departure. She seemed ambivalent about her visit because she was traveling to a "strange country, and, yet, in a way, I am going home." She recalled her father's descriptions of his village and the gods who were worshiped in the home; but in words more appropriate to a tourist than to a pilgrim. She wondered how to deliver all the messages that Chinese Americans had entrusted to her for relatives on the mainland. She was most impressed on a visit to steerage class where ordinary Chinese travelers lodged. There she met Chinese men and women on their way home, some on their way to die. Others took along prized canaries as presents for relatives. Passage through Hawaii was uneventful. Anna May confessed to the Van Vechtens that after all the farewell parties, she slept "around the clock twice between San Francisco and Honolulu." She found Honolulu a clean city, enjoyed bird's nest soup, and took a swim in the Pacific at Waikiki Beach, which thrilled her the most since skiing in the Swiss Alps.[4]

Anna May arrived in Yokohama, Japan, on February 8. During a sightseeing visit, she toured Kyoto and Tokyo before departing for China a day later. She wrote to Van Vechten that her visit to Tokyo was unimpressive, though she did find the temples and shrines in Kyoto "really lovely." Anna May probably had no choice about the stopover in Japan, but her instant publicity use of it is curious. Sino-Japanese relations had been at a flashpoint since 1931 and Shanghai was awash with anti-Japanese pamphlets. Fortunately for her, knowledge of her quick tour of Japan seems to have been limited in China. Those who did know had other agendas. Wires from Madame Wellington Koo convinced Anna May that she should alter her plans and stop first in Shanghai, where the leading citizens planned a bevy of parties in her honor.[5]

Not everyone looked forward to her arrival. Even as the S.S. *President Hoover* sailed across the Pacific Ocean, waves of controversy about Anna May crashed hard along China's coast. Numerous magazines openly questioned whether she should be welcomed at all. The familiar charges that she had disgraced China filled their pages. Some openly questioned her character, for example, *Diansheng* (Movietone News) compared her unfavorably with Li Shimin, a Chinese actor in America, who had recently refused a demeaning movie role. Compared with his stance, Anna May's obedience and submission to the studio bosses showed a lack of national pride. *Shidai Dianying* (Shanghai Film Age) argued that she should be required to stay in China for five or ten years to learn more about its society. Unless she complied, its writer urged that she should be expelled. There was so much vituperation against Anna May that her brother James wrote an article defending her and asking that the Chinese people and press accept her. He focused on her desire to learn Chinese, her wish to visit famous sites in China, and her warm feelings of patriotism.[6]

Other issues had little to do with her personally but nevertheless created a hostile climate for her visit. Collective campaigns sponsored by the Kuomintang government against such antisocial and undisciplined acts as spitting, urinating, and smoking in public extended quickly to reactions against the female modernism that had emerged since the end of the Qing dynasty. Spokesmen for the government harangued young women to accept a modest political position and withdraw from public gatherings. Women generally were urged to accept the "four virtues" of chastity, appearance, speech, and work. Anna May's free display of her legs in films conflicted with the fully clothed styles of national stars Hu Die and Ruan Lingyu. Now the Chinese government presented the minimum lengths for hemlines. In such an atmosphere, Anna May's cinema presentations suddenly seemed politically dangerous.[7]

This new conservatism spilled over into film criticism. The furor over a film released in 1935 entitled *The New Woman* and the fate of its star, Ruan Lingyu, had not abated on the eve of Anna May's arrival. Filmmakers had yet to toe the government line, but unmistakable signs of retrenchment were there. Representations of career women and sexually independent females had become fairly common in Chinese cinema by the early 1930s, but only with caveats. Invariably, women who stepped out of traditional roles paid a heavy price, including disaster and death. So it was with the film *The New Woman*, which opened during the lunar New Year festival in Shanghai in 1935. Wei Ming, the lead character, is a divorced mother, schoolteacher, and would-be writer, who strives to survive in the big city. Her success as a writer does not lead to happiness, because her life is "exposed" by gossip magazines. The character's life was allegedly based upon the career of Ai Xia, a newcomer to the Shanghai movie scene who killed herself after starring in *A Modern Woman*, which she had also written. A second, powerful influence was the immense popularity of Ibsen's play *A Doll's House*, which was so ubiquitous in Shanghai that 1935 was locally called "The Year of Nora," after the tragic protagonist. In the new movie, ensuing public disdain also pushed the film character of Wei Ming to suicide. The film's semiotics revealed a fierce clash between the Shanghai studios and film journalists, who dissected every scene for moral and political meaning. Further complicating matters was the personal life of the star, Ruan Lingyu, who was a major Chinese idol in the early 1930s. Even more than Anna May, Ruan Lingyu transformed her own unhappy life into brilliant enactments of woman's fate. In her short career, she had already been raped twice and committed suicide in four films. Now, her own marriage had begun to unravel. She had had an open marriage with Zhang Damin, whose upper-class family disapproved of the union. After a short time together, the couple separated but remained married. As her star rose, she paid him to accept her new lover. When Ruan Lingyu asked for a divorce, Zhang took her to court. The scandal sheets seized upon her misfortune, and in despair, Ruan Lingyu committed suicide. There are estimates that over one hundred thousand people, or about one-tenth of Shanghai's population, attended the funeral, which was even reported in the *New York Times*. In the months and years that followed, pamphlets and magazines were devoted to the reasons behind Ruan Lingyu's death. Since then, her image has remained bright and controversial.[8]

The message for Anna May from *The New Woman* controversy was that her career and her life would, in the eyes of Chinese journalists, inevitably lead to her own death. Ruan Lingyu had accepted her "guilt." As she famously said, "Gossip is a fearful thing." Another association was that *The New Woman* was a silent film at a time when talkies were finally eclipsing the earlier technology in China. Although born in Shanghai, Ruan Lingyu spoke Cantonese, and her chances of competing in a Mandarin talkie were dim. Anyone in China who had seen *Shanghai Express* knew that Anna May spoke only elementary Cantonese, a fact that would ensure the death of her career in China. Anna May had complained bitterly about her movie roles, but had never openly contemplated suicide. Anna May shared with Ruan Lingyu and other outspoken Chinese actresses terrible fates in her movies. Her response, however, was the ironic observation that the epitaph on her tombstone should read: "She died a thousand deaths." While the Shanghai sharks of journalism sharpened their teeth for Anna May, she was ready for them as well.[9]

Fortunately for Anna May, the critics were not the only people in China who had seen her movies. Thousands of people were reported to flock to the pier to greet the world's most famous Chinese star. As Leo Ou-fan Lee has noted, most criticism in China came from a Left perspective and either followed or pushed further the Nationalist curbs on fantasy in movies and on female modernism.

Intellectuals, artists, and elite members of society had followed Anna May's career for years. For select and mass Chinese audiences, Anna May was a major star whose films had enthralled them.[10]

There was much for Anna May to do in Shanghai, a vital, dynamic, and cosmopolitan city. The city boasted a number of cinemas and department stores; its fashion magazines were filled with images of glamor and modernity. Its journalists and film critics addressed contemporary politics. Shanghai was also a party city. As a contemporary guidebook explained, nightlife in Shanghai started with tea and cocktails, followed by dinner and more drinking. After midnight came "Joy, gin, and jazz. There's nothing puritanical about Shanghai." Cabaret abounded in every hotel and restaurant down to "Blood Alley, playground of the navies and armies." Shanghai had developed a distinctive popular music composed of American jazz, Hollywood film music, and Chinese folk music known as *shidai qu* (modern songs). American jazz musician Buck Clayton, who arrived in Shanghai in 1934, was enchanted by the town's cosmopolitanism and by *qunzhong yinyue* (yellow music), as hostile critics called this hybrid genre. Clayton was not alone is his estimation of Shanghai. Called the "Paris of the East," Shanghai in fact rivaled its European sister city. Shanghai was not a provincial, colonial city, but an international center in its own right. Anna May had prospered in such towns before. It was the perfect place to start her Chinese journey.[11]

Anna May finally touched Chinese soil on February 9, 1936, when the S.S. *President Hoover* anchored in Shanghai. Actually, she began filming her arrival in China before she even landed. Anna May recorded her tour on a home movie, which she began as the *Hoover* entered the bay of the Whangpoo River. She shot several scenes of sampans and junks. Waiting for her on the dock were thousands of her fans. Before she could salute them, her brother James and a small squad of reporters rode by ferryboat to the ship to greet her. They waited in a ballroom until she appeared. James spoke to the reporters about his sister's career. When she first met the reporters, Anna May wore a black dress, which some interpreted as respectful to China. On her head was a black hat with a very sharp angle. She had designed the hat herself and called it a tiger hat. Caustic reporters noted that despite cosmetics it could be easily seen that her youth had disappeared. She called out to her brother to take a photo with her. Reporters quickly sensed that Anna May could neither speak nor write in Mandarin Chinese. The unflappable

Anna May then put on a form-fitting fur coat for the short ferry ride to the customs wharf. She obligingly posed for a number of photos from many different angles, which graced the newspapers and magazines in the next few days. Newsreel Wong recorded the entire event for the Hearst newspapers; later Anna May filmed the family reunion at the Cathay Hotel.

There were conflicting reports about who greeted her after her passage through customs. Some newspapers reported that no one from the Shanghai film industry greeted her and that she seemed troubled by this slight. Hong Kong dailies, by contrast, reported that not only famous people from the film world were waiting, but also Ambassador Wellington and Madame Koo, Anna May's older sister Lulu and Mei Lanfang. Anna May gave impromptu interviews in which she reiterated her desire to learn to speak Chinese, to study "my motherland's scenes and customs, my fellow Chinese, and all other things concerning China." The newsmen quickly cut to controversies over her movies, asking why she had made films insulting to China. Anna May's face reddened as she replied that often she had no choice. If she did not take a role, it would go to a "Japanese woman or Korean woman and . . . I would lose the chance to change partly the image of China." Moreover, if she refused, she would have to return her salary to the studio. She asserted that she had made few movies since 1933 and spent most of her time on stage in Europe.[12]

After her triumphant embarkation, Anna May became the focus of lavish dinner parties. Ambassador Wellington Koo and his wife gave a dinner in her honor. Such an invitation placed Anna May right at the top of Chinese society and amidst members of an international elite. Koo was about to depart to become the Chinese ambassador to France, and his wife was considered a great beauty. Anna May was stunned by the fifteen-course meals. Pictures of her with the Koos and other celebrities appeared in the local newspapers and in the *New York Herald Tribune*. Anna May told the Van Vechtens with obvious delight that Lin Yutang and his wife came to the reception; the famous author told her that the prospect of a trip to New York "frightened him into a state of inaction." Anna May and the Lins would become strong friends; when they moved to New York later in 1936, Anna May introduced them to the Van Vechtens, who immediately ushered the Chinese writer into the upper ranks of the New York literary world.[13]

Anna May continued her journey through Shanghai's elite circles. The night she met the Lins, she attended a banquet for the Norwegian consul general in Shanghai. On Saturday evening, she was the focus at a festival of Shanghai's "best-dressed women." During the day, she walked through the city. Madame Koo took her to her personal *qipao* tailor. Later, Anna May credited Madame for her "oblique suggestions" about Chinese fashions.[14] Anna May strolled through Shanghai's streets. Newsreel Wong filmed picturesque scenes of the streets and people, including shots of beggars, street tailors, fortune-tellers, and young girls. One day she encountered her friend Mei Lanfang, the famous Peking Opera actor, who invited her to dinner. She was also asked to visit the national film board in Nanking, an invitation she felt she could not ignore.

Anna May gave more extensive interviews with favored magazines. *Liang You Huabao*, the famous women's journal, had covered her career since the mid-1920s, and the editor was a personal friend. *Liang You* publications included five magazines, and each editor wanted an exclusive interview. Some had been openly hostile to Anna May in past issues, but now promised to allot her several pages of the next issue to tell her story in her own words. She told them familiar parts of her narrative, but she also accentuated her desire to visit China. She described how, during the height of her fame in Berlin, she felt the isolation of being the only Chinese person in crowds of supporters and that "she had longed for this day for many years." She wrote that the more she learned in France and Germany, the more she "missed China." She claimed that anywhere she went, her favorite reading material was about China. She especially cited Lin Yutang's *My Country and My People* as an influential book. She described how she had recently met a teacher from the Youth Association in Shanghai and how she "adored his refined and cultivated attitude, displayed especially on a Chinese scholar."

Anna May also spoke of the ways in which she tried to emphasize to audiences that her roles could not possibly represent the Chinese people and that they needed to study more about her nation. She tried in Europe to develop a "philosophy in the traditional spirit of our ethnic culture to comfort myself. Now I find it easy because I have really stood on the ground in my native culture."[15] One unpleasant incidence reminded Anna May that a few bigoted whites regarded her as inferior. According to Emily Hahn, a sophisticated observer to Shanghai, during Anna May's visit to Shanghai, a friend invited her to go bowling at the exclusive Western Columbia Club. The manager, arguing that he had to be careful, refused to allow Anna May access to the club quarters. Anna May learned that, even in roaring Shanghai, her Chinese ancestry made her no more acceptable than ordinary citizens. This was a city, after all, where signs in parks announced "Chinese and dogs not permitted."[16]

Despite Anna May's fond appreciation of China, hostile film writers kept up their attacks on her. They mentioned, with relish, that she was about thirty years old without a husband or even a boyfriend. *Manhua Jie* (Modern Puck) satirized her bewilderment that the Chinese people would not accept her and suggested that she was far less popular in China than Warner Oland. Another point of criticism was that she preferred to stay in the finest international hotels. Several emphasized that she was just a tourist who spent her time eating dinners with the elite of China and little time with ordinary people, who, one magazine claimed, did not really like her. These accusations were not entirely misplaced. Newsreel Wong's films showed her leaving luxury hotels and getting in and out of limousines. Even when she strolled through the streets, Anna May posed for the cameraman, just as she might in Hollywood or Europe. Her visits to the *qipao* tailor and the flower garden seemed more the actions of a wealthy tourist than someone seeking deeper insights into Chinese culture. Unlike a sightseer, however, Anna May behaved as a female flaneur, a self-conscious observer of urban culture around the world. Anna May had encountered Walter Benjamin, Charlotte Woolf, and other flaneurs in Berlin. Now she practiced the art of studious observation of the city. As recently discussed by Anke Gleber, the flaneur, male or female, digressed from packaged routes and pursued solitary, drifting avenues through the globe's cities. While some of Anna May's actions, such as sightseeing, resemble tourism, actually she was creating her own experience with an eye to improving her art. As an actress, Anna May was aware of the discontinuous movement of films. In her walks around Shanghai and other cities, Anna May sorted out the bombarding stream of images in order to fashion her own aesthetic. Even her shopping for elaborate dresses combined consumption with research and planning for future roles. Anna May's ability to combine her career and her emotional needs made Shanghai part of her visual consciousness.[17]

External events demonstrated that her trip was more than tourism. The pleasing quality of the newsreels disguised the complexity of local attitudes about

Anna May's visit. The tempestuousness of popular feeling became soon apparent. After six weeks in Shanghai, Anna May prepared to travel to her family's ancestral village in Guangdong Province. Her arrival in Hong Kong on March 26, 1936, promised to be a festive occasion. The Taishan Association of Fellow Provincials along with managers of the Duguan Film Company massed together to meet her at the wharf. The filmmakers, who hoped to convince Anna May to be the leading actress in two movies, bought eight flower baskets emblazoned with pink satin with her Chinese name "Welcome, Huang Liushuang—the Flower of Film" across them. Anna May, either suffering from a flu or upset following an argument with another passenger, was uncharacteristically rude to her fans. When the delegation from Taishan sensed her coldness, their reaction was swift and devastating. Someone shouted: "Down with Huang Liu Tsong—the puppet that disgraces China. Don't let her go ashore." Anna May understood their angry words and began crying. The flower baskets and satin ribbons were destroyed in the stampede.

The crowd's ferocious anger did not die quickly. Guangdong Province was experiencing high unemployment, and people were restless. Addressing him as Liangren, the angry leaders of the demonstration sent a joint telegram to her father in Chang On, urging him to tell his daughter not to come home. If she insisted on coming to Chang On, they warned, the entire family might be expelled. The leaders of the protest also telegraphed the local newspapers telling them not to publish any reports of her visit. Anna May by this time had gone to her sister Lulu's home, where she stayed for two days, undisturbed by reporters. Sadly, whenever she ventured outside, there were taunts from angry crowds. After three days, Liangren telegraphed Anna May telling her not to come to Chang On soon. Quickly she planned a trip to the Philippines, hoping that the tension would subside.[18]

Originally, Anna May had no intention to visit the Philippines, but giving a bad cold and fever as her reason, she booked a quick trip south. Though she arrived unannounced on Tuesday, March 3, traveling under the pseudonym of Liu Tsong, the island's press quickly spotted her. Declaring that her "face was known to millions of fans all over the world," they gave her stopover front-page coverage. As always, Anna May answered their many questions graciously. She declared herself delighted with her visit to China and marveled at how modern it was. She had come, she told reporters, to get some sunshine akin to that of her home in California. She admitted that she was not currently under contract for any movie, at the present, but did say she was considering an updated version of the play, *The Princess Turandot*. As in Shanghai, her presence set off a round of invitations, including a state dinner hosted by President and Mrs. Manuel Quezon at their palace. By Saturday, she sailed back to China.[19]

Wong Sam Sing told his daughter that the situation in Chang On was still tense, so before debarking in Hong Kong, Anna May and Lulu made a short trip to Macao. Although she traveled incognito, word soon spread of her arrival at the home of a locally famous teacher. Celebrities and reporters gathered for autographs and photos. Anna May now felt comfortable enough to visit a number of local sites.[20]

Anna May returned to Hong Kong on April 9. She took Warner Oland, who had just arrived in town, to a special Chinese lunch. Shortly after she went by car into Guangdong Province and arrived at her ancestral village of Chang On a day later. There are various reports of how she was received. Oral histories published in the 1980s state that villagers threw rocks at her as she approached. Other accounts, including some given directly to this writer, contend that she was well received. She spent over ten days in Chang On and slept some nights in the nearby village of Wing On, from which her clan originated. Old men recall that she regularly handed out candy and 40 *jiao* pieces (a small amount of currency, but sufficient to buy a *jin* [just over a pound] of meat). One villager remembered how a filmmaker (Newsreel Wong) who accompanied her shot Anna May and her father as they slowly walked apart while facing each other. Similar accounts say that Lee Shee, her father's first wife, and her son, Huang Dounan, welcomed Anna May and made her stay comfortable and happy. Chang On is about 5 kilometers outside of Taishan, the county seat. When Anna May went into town on occasion, she found the villagers perplexed by her presence. They had seen some of her films in a theater built in 1928 with money from overseas Chinese. Locals believed, Anna May later claimed, that she was a myth or a kind of machine, and not a real person.[21]

Anna May's response to Chang On reveals more of her personal character than the supremely self-possessed persona known across the Western world and in northern China. Chang On was much like dozens of other small villages that dot the Guangdong countryside. Located not far from a larger city (in this case,

Taishan), such villages are composed of a series of adjoining homes constructed of brown masonry. Walkways connect the front doors, and alleyways snake alongside each home. A large wall protects the homes, accessible only through a gate and gun tower designed to warn residents against roving bandits. Anna May found a wooden welcoming gate just outside the main entrance to the town. In her home movie, screened on American television twenty years later, she spoke with excitement about her approach to Chang On. She spoke fondly of the train trip from Guangzhou. Newsreel Wong filmed Anna May as her father greeted her and Richard, her brother, and they all walked up the path to Chang On. Richard was then sent on to school because, as Anna May explained, the Chinese have high regard for education. She then spent much time conversing with Wong Sam Sing on the steps of his home. Anna May surveyed the fish pond and fields around the village and noted how the residents helped each other out. Some of these moments were clearly staged and represent Anna May's immigrant nostalgia for a home she had never known and had envisioned many times in her mind. She concluded the television show by observing that this visit was easily the most satisfying event of her life.

Having satisfied a deep personal longing and her father's wishes, Anna May returned to Hong Kong, where a batch of photos from Van Vechten awaited her. The photographer had taken many of them late in 1935 in front of the Algonquin Hotel in New York City. Anna May then voyaged back north to Shanghai on March 23.[22]

During the next two months, Anna May stayed in and around Shanghai. Newspaper accounts continued to chart her daily progress. She traveled briefly to Suzhou, a noted seaside spa, where she and James wandered through the streets, then walked along the Suzhou River, watching boys herd water buffalo. On April 1, Anna May visited the beautiful city of Hangzhou, famous for its lakes and silk products. Her brother filmed her being fitted for a silk *qipao*. The tailor used the traditional measurement, using a string and knotting it in several places, a method that seemed never to fail. Afterwards, she went sightseeing along Hu-Hang Road, met the mayor, had dinner, and ordered more *qipaos*. She returned to Shanghai the next day.[23]

The Chinese media's relentless attacks on Anna May gradually softened. Part of the reason had to be her facility with reporters. Despite their provocative questions, she patiently sat through lengthy interviews, reciting the story of her life over and over again and defending her career while disclaiming roles she had been forced to take. She began to speak more freely in Mandarin. Invariably, even the most intrusive journalists asked for her autograph at the close of the session. She always complied. A second cause for this change was the open friendship that Mei Lanfang and Hu Die, China's best-known actors, showed toward Anna May. Equally celebrated after representing China at the Moscow International Film Festival and their subsequent tour of Europe, the star of the Peking Opera and the first lady of Chinese film each stood at the pinnacle of his or her profession. Mei Lanfang had graciously hosted Anna May at a dinner soon after her arrival. Hu Die, who had been distant to Anna May in London the year before, now publicly embraced her. Hu Die's popularity was at an all-time high after her sensational marriage in November 1935 to businessman Eugene Peng in the Most Holy Trinity Anglican Cathedral, an event that outdrew the ceremonies held for Chiang Kai-shek and Soong Meiling several years before. Now, newspapers and magazines portrayed Anna May alongside Hu Die and Peng. Reporters learned to be on the lookout for the Anna May and Hu Die pair strolling in the streets near Anna May's hotel. Newsreel Wong filmed the two while they walked around Shanghai, signed autographs, and strolled through the markets. He then sent the footage back to Hearst Publications in Los Angeles, where it quickly made its way into the movie theaters so that all of America could share in the China tour of one of its favorite actresses. One can cynically claim that Hu Die stood to benefit from friendship with the more famous American, but her courage in standing up to hostile journalists should be credited. By the summertime, the Hearst newspapers could report that their Chinese counterparts had accepted Anna May Wong.[24]

Hu Die took Anna May to the Mingxing Film Studio, the most famous in Shanghai, in late April. As Newsreel Wong filmed their arrival, Hu Die introduced Anna May to the leading figures of the company, who took them on a tour of the production studios. They also made a two-hour news film, sections of which appeared in the film made by Newsreel Wong. While in China, Anna May did not neglect her American friend. She wrote to Carl Van Vechten on May 8, sending him the menu from the best Chinese restaurant in Shanghai, and told him of her plans to study Mandarin and Chinese drama in Peking (Beiping).[25]

On May 9, Anna May began her trip to Peking by car. Her first stop was Nanking, the capital of the Kuomintang party. The government had invited her to a special reception, which she considered an honor. Present were Li Dijun, the head of the Foreign Intelligence Department; Lu Gang, the principal of the National Opera School; Yu Shangyuan, the chief of the Central Film Industry Office; and other top officials. Anna May arrived respectfully dressed in a black silk *qipao* with red fringe and a navy blue coat. There were differing reports of this event. In one, published in *Diansheng* (Movietone News), Anna May received warm applause and spoke in English with a Chinese translation about her joy at being home in China. She mentioned her desire to spend several months in Peking studying Chinese and gathering "scripts of history dramas, so they can be performed in London, Paris, and New York," and to help the rest of the world understand China's extraordinary historical culture. Afterward she signed autographs as Ye Qianyu, a famous artist, drew some sketches. The writer concluded that she seemed to regret the disgraceful roles she had performed in the past. Another account was less sympathetic. In this version, her hosts used Anna May's inability to speak or understand Mandarin to heap insults upon her. Later, after she heard of this deception, Anna May claimed that she had successfully debated the pitfalls of her career with the bureaucrats. Unfortunately, the loss of historical documents after the Nationalist party defeat in 1949 keeps a true account of the event hidden.[26]

Rather than going directly to Peking, Anna May stopped first to climb Mount Tai in Shandong Province and visit its famous temples. In the port city of Tianjin, she went to the Goddess Palace, kowtowed before the deity, burned joss sticks, and sought divine guidance by drawing lots. As she drew the best lots, onlookers concluded that the goddess would bless her and give her a bright future. Later she went to a fortune-teller in Peking and asked whether it was better for her to marry a foreigner or a Chinese man. According to her birthday, she was told that a Chinese man would be better. She smiled and left.[27]

On May 14, Anna May arrived in Peking, where she stayed at the city's best hotel. As Newsreel Wong recorded her movements, she wandered about and rode in streetcars, rickshaws, and sedan chairs, and shopped on trading streets. Later, she visited the Old Summer Palace and took a ride on the famous concrete barge. She went to a drama school and took Chinese lessons. Meanwhile, the daily and weekly journals endlessly described her dresses, hairstyles, makeup, and handbag, on which was knitted HUANG LIUSHUANG.[28] Anna May followed her Shanghai itinerary by visiting the city's greatest celebrities. *The Pei-Yang Pictorial News*, which had so derided her in previous years, printed a picture of her standing with John Leighton Stuart, the founding president of Yenching University, easily the most important Christian educational institution in China. Anna May and Stuart shared a Presbyterian upbringing. He was born in China and was among the most respected westerners. The photograph of the two of them added much to her stature among ordinary Chinese. As well, Stuart was an important advisor of Chiang Kai-shek and an open supporter of the Kuomintang. His endorsement of Anna May gave her political luster. Later, Stuart was the special negotiator between the warring Kuomintang and the Communist parties. Anna May got to know luminaries on all sides of the political spectrum. She also spent time with Frank Dorn, an American military aide in Peking. Newsreel Wong introduced her to Edgar Snow and his wife, Helen, who were good friends of the cameraman.[29]

As in Shanghai, Chinese newspaper accounts combined breathless accounts about her clothing with digs at her appearance, her status as a tourist, and her rejection of a private residence in favor of the grand Peking Hotel. Anna May spent time at famed tourist spots. Accompanied by a visiting American senator, she went to Nankou. There a group from the Tianjin Beiyang College of Industry noticed her and surrounded her with requests for photos and autographs. She signed over fifty autographs in the next hour. After that she and her party went to Badaling, where she was thunderstruck by the Great Wall.[30]

Anna May had an especially pleasant time on June 8, when the first lady of Peking, Wu Tang, and her brother, Wu Tanjun, welcomed Anna May to their home for dinner and to see the famous Taiping Flowers in their garden. Anna May came accompanied by a man named Ai. She was dressed in a yellow *qipao*, and carried the handbag with her name in Chinese and her Leica. Present at the dinner were a number of Peking's intelligentsia including Li Wanchun, the famous opera singer, and Wang Shaoqing, a violinist, both of whom briefly performed for the honored guest. During the dinner, Anna May expressed high praise and gratitude for their musical gifts. As reporters watched, Wu Tang picked two flowers and placed them in Anna May's hair band. It was a moment of tender, feminine affection reserved for those held in the highest esteem. As Anna May departed from the dinner, reporters heard her say that she was "Very, Very happy." The same evening she watched a performance by Li Wanchun. After the show, they dined together at the Liu Guo Restaurant. Clearly moved, Anna May took the singer's hand tightly as they departed. She thanked him for the evening and remarked: "What a pity we have to depart! We will be so far away from each other and I don't know when we will have a chance to meet again." Such associations with kindred spirits lifted Anna May's morale. Unlike Europe, where her moments with artists and intellectuals entailed a search for meaning, or Hollywood, where racial exclusion generally pushed her to the margins, such evenings as the one at the Wu home combined affectionate regard, culture, and national solidarity.[31]

As Peking's relentless summer weather began to exhaust her, Anna May traveled to Beidaihe, the favorite ocean spa for China's elite. She arrived there with several Americans on July 2. Soon, photos of her in bathing suits began to adorn the newspapers. She stayed at the beach resort until the end of July.[32] After four months in Peking (with a month vacationing at Beidaihe), Anna May returned to Shanghai. She had learned to speak a fair amount of Mandarin and could play a little on the mandolin. She now prepared to leave China for home. A reporter visited her on the last day. She proclaimed the visit a success and hoped that she could return once a year. She contended that "even two or three months can still provide me with a little new knowledge." China was making great progress, she noted. Her favorite place was Peking, where she could see the real China, though the villages were also worthy of attention. Initially she sailed to Hong Kong, where she received a telegram from an English movie studio offering her a job. She accepted and decided to go home first for a short visit, then to Paris by plane and then back to London by ship. She sailed from Shanghai for America on October 23. She arrived in Honolulu on November 5 and in San Francisco on November 28. The great visit was over.[33]

Anna May's visit to China did not turn her into a Chinese citizen. She stayed primarily in internationally acclaimed hotels, mingled with the nation's elite, spent sizable sums of cash on clothing, and traveled to major cities. With the exception of her brief sojourn in Chang On, she rarely mingled with ordinary Chinese people. There were no trips to more remote spots where she was unknown. She did study Mandarin but seemed to have dropped her plans for a traveling troupe of Peking actors and had no thoughts of films made in Chinese.

Still, Anna May returned to the United States filled with resolve to help improve her ancestral nation's image, to alleviate its poverty, and to support its intensifying struggle against Japan. Anna May wanted to identify herself with China and to see herself as Chinese. She had moved closer to this position since the late 1920s and now seemed prepared to align herself with the Nationalist Party, Chiang Kai-shek, and the urban intellectuals. If hers was a fragmented comprehension of China, Anna May was, as always, sincere, warm, and determined to help her adopted nation.

Six

In the Service of the Motherland

In China, Anna May was generally an honored guest. In the United States, she was just another "alleged Chinese citizen." Immediately upon her arrival in San Francisco, Anna May was greeted with a reminder of her family's status. On her return to the United States, Anna May had to report to the Immigration and Naturalization Service to retrieve her certificate of identity. Part of the interview required informing inspector Boyd Reynolds of the whereabouts of the rest of her family. She told him that her father was living in Chang On and that she "never saw him looking better." Richard was still with him; Lulu was still living in Hong Kong; and James was living at the Shanghai YMCA and teaching a commercial course at St. John's and at the Shanghai University Commercial College. Telling the immigration officer these facts was especially important because an imposter had stolen James's identity in Chicago and advertised himself as the brother of Anna May Wong. The Immigration and Naturalization Service asked Anna May to distinguish James's photograph from the other man's in a lengthy interview. The sheaves of forms she had to wade through attest to the thoroughness with which the government kept tabs on Chinese American citizens. Eventually, Anna May was able to clear up the confusion. She told the inspectors as well that Lulu was living in Shanghai. Frank was staying in the new family home at 1200 North Fifty-Fifth Street in Los Angeles and studying aviation. Roger was living with him. Anna May had to vouch as well for her father when Wong Sam Sing returned to the United States without the required re-entry papers. Though he was native-born, a discrepancy in a past statement indicated that he was born in China. Although Anna May's fame and cool demeanor saved the day, she had to post a guarantee that he would not become a public charge.[1]

After accounting for her family, Anna May gave her friend Rob Wagner an interview about her trip. She talked about her joy in experiencing China. She spoke happily about the constant bargaining among shopkeepers and the hospitality of her landlady in Peking, who refused to accept two months' rent from her. Her voice turned fonder when she talked of the visit to Chang On and laughed as she recalled that her father was trying hard to make his fellow villagers American. She spoke more seriously about skin color in China and insisted that it was largely a function of geography and protection against the sun. She finished by talking about her home movie, which she promised to limit to private shows, unless "Colossal Pictures offers me a million dollars for it."[2]

Anna May was enthusiastic about cinema in China, telling the *Los Angeles Herald Express* that "The possibilities for motion pictures in China were infinite." All too aware of nationalist castigation of her past roles, she began canvassing the studios with projects that would feature favorable roles and themes about China. She found an appreciative audience at her old workplace. Listeners at Paramount were amazed when Anna May spoke in two Chinese languages, German, French, Italian, and other European languages. She admitted that she was "stumped" at first by Mandarin, but after a few months, she had learned enough to get along in the official language. Later in life, Anna May Wong recalled her visit to China as one of the great accomplishments of her life. In 1937 she could not foresee that wars, revolution, and Cold War politics would nullify any chance for her return. Her family had to come back to the United States. The first to return were James and Lulu, who arrived with graphic tales of the Japanese bombing of Shanghai. She had moved there from Hong Kong to work in the customs office. She fled with other American citizens when the Japanese bombings "killed hundreds of Chinese." She prayed that she would never have to see such scenes again and declared that Americans were fortunate not to be drawn into the conflict. As the Japanese army invaded southern China and full-scale war ensued, an aged Wong Sam Sing and Richard Wong were forced to flee to the United States in November 1938, leaving Chang On barely ahead of the Japanese land invasion and occupation of Guangdong Province. Staying behind was his first son, Huang Dounan. As the most educated person in Chang On village and the only Japanese speaker in the region, Huang Dounan was of special interest to the Japanese military. They beat him and ordered him to explain to his fellow villagers what their duties would be to their new masters. Initially, Huang Dounan refused, but eventually he had to accept this unpleasant role. He worked throughout the war to help the residents of Chang On and is remembered for his great heroism. Huang Dounan had three wives with whom he had fourteen daughters and eight sons. His mother, Lee Shee, died on May 7, 1942. Huang Dounan took his third wife, Kuang Yanrong, around this time, and in 1943 she gave birth to his third daughter, Wong Cuixian, who now lives in Guangzhou.[3] These personal connections and her own trip to China made Anna May far more patriotic about her ancestral country and more hostile to its Japanese invaders. A Paramount press release later that year told how Anna May moved from one residence to another to avoid looking down at a Japanese garden.[4]

As she arranged her life in Los Angeles, Anna May seemed ready for a permanent relationship with a studio. Her interaction with Hollywood film factories seemed to indicate that nothing had changed. There was talk that she might get a lead role in the MGM production of *The Adventures of Marco Polo*, but the studio, showing its usual wisdom, preferred newcomer Sigrid Gurie to play opposite Gary Cooper. Such laughable casting was hardly the only problem for the production, and the movie bombed. MGM did include Anna May in a variety show entitled *Hollywood Party*, a two-reel production released on April 9, 1937. Notable as the sole opportunity for Anna May and Clark Gable to appear in a film together, the compilation gave Anna May a chance to show off her new wardrobe. In the film's script, Anna May speaks to the camera about having just spent a "most marvelous year in China, my first visit to my ancestral country." Anna May continued by describing how all the Chinese ladies "look so smart and vivid in the beautiful modern *qipaos*." Anna May could not resist buying as many as she could afford. Two young Chinese girls appeared on the screen with her. She spoke Chinese to them, but they apologized that "they could only speak Cantonese." Anna May replied, "Oh, I thought I could brush up on my Mandarin," an indication that she had indeed learned the official language. Westernized versions of Chinese classics accompanied her fashion show.[5] While the Hollywood studios debated how to use Anna May's new skills, she was preparing for another kind of commitment. Eric Maschwitz and she had been close since 1931 and had seen each other frequently in London. Their first meeting inspired Maschwitz to pen the lyrics to one of the century's most unforgettable songs. He started the song on an ocean liner and finished it in London. The first few lines of "These Foolish Things" unmistakably evoke the romance of Anna May:

> A cigarette that bears a lipstick's traces
> An airline ticket to romantic places
> And still my heart has wings
> These foolish things remind me of you.

Maschwitz had enjoyed a great year. He was director of variety shows at the BBC and had been made a life peer. Then Hollywood beckoned. When Maschwitz took leave of his job at the BBC to visit California and contemplate a six-figure offer for his hit play *Balalaika*, Anna May picked him up at the Burbank airport in her car. Maschwitz was fretting over leaving his job in London. Anna May discussed his worries carefully and convinced him that Hollywood was the place for him. Maschwitz marveled at how "calmly, kindly, shrewdly, Miss Wong analyzed my situation for me." When she took him to the airport for his return to London, he philosophized that "everyone should know and love at least one educated Chinese person in their lives." Anna May did not tarry long after Maschwitz left. Soon she was sailing over to London to see him and take in the season's theater. They made a fast trip to Paris, where they saw Yvonne Printemps in *Trois Valses* and attended a performance of Paganini. She then went home to wait for Maschwitz's return.[6]

She arrived to face a terrible threat. In March 1937 Anna May became the victim of an extortionist who sent her a note threatening to throw acid in her face and disfigure her father (who was still in China) unless she contributed $20,000 toward a movie production. In the late 1930s, deranged fans with violent fantasies were not unusual. Initially the police did not take Anna May's terror seriously until the wife of producer David O. Selznick received the same demand. In the note, a doctor named E. J. Foote demanded cash from Selznick in order to finance a movie in which he would play Jesus Christ. Joining him would be Anna May and another actress named Aimee McPherson (not the evangelist). The note warned Selznick to pay up or else his children would be blinded. Anna May was shocked by the threats. She told the *Los Angeles Examiner* that she hadn't slept a wink since receiving the letters and had hired a bodyguard. Within days the situation became more complicated. A woman in Minnesota wrote McPherson a threatening note. A Minnesota housewife named Lydia Swenson was arrested and judged insane. J. Edgar Hoover, the director of the FBI, became interested in the saga and demanded almost daily reports. The bureau interviewed Anna May on March 25, 1937. She told its agents that she had no idea why she had been targeted by the extortionist and that she had never known any one who "possessed a desire to produce such a motion picture." As the agents listened, she then called Foote, who claimed he had also received threatening letters. This tactic helped Foote to avoid arrest though he remained under surveillance by the bureau. The FBI's attention also turned to one Cecil Reynolds, a former physician from Glendale and a former technical advisor to Selznick. Reynolds claimed to know Anna May and to have provided some services to her. Over the next six months, the FBI and the County District Attorney took little action on the case, except for screening Anna May's mail. By 1939, the local deputy attorney general even suggested that the entire thing was a hoax designed to keep Anna May in the public eye. Despite his willingness to slander Anna May, neither the attorney general's office nor the bureau managed to make any convictions, and eventually the case was dropped in 1941.[7]

Such nasty business did not keep Anna May from traveling, and she did not linger in Hollywood. She revisited the immigration offices and made arrangements for a trip to Europe in June, a voyage that she had to postpone until the fall. She first did some shows in Washington, DC, after which, in late May 1937, she did a week of cabaret at the Loew's State Theater in New York City. The show was similar to those she had performed in Europe. Dressed in a severe black *qipao*, she began the show with an old Cantonese folk song, followed by a dramatic sketch drawn from her life over the years, prefaced by Noel Coward's "Half-Caste Woman." Employing her famous sense of humor, she informed a reporter at the Algonquin, by now her New York home away from home, that waiters everywhere answer to "Oy" and "Hallo"; however, only a bell would work at the famous Manhattan hotel. After a quick return to the West Coast, she went back to New York and did summer stock theater in Westchester County, New York, and in Westport, Connecticut. Anna May seemed to enjoy the ambiance because she arrived over a month before her August appearance. She starred in *Turandot*, a dramatic adaptation of Puccini's opera. Anna May's first try at summer stock was a resounding success. The Westchester Playhouse was a gathering place for elite New Yorkers, many of whom crowded into the opening to cheer for Anna May. Later she was the honored guest at parties. The presence of the influential patrons guaranteed notices in the leading New York City newspapers as well as the adoring local press. Adjectives such as "glorious," "unique," and "delightful" were common. Many reviewers commented on the beauty of her costumes, which she had brought home from China. Only *Variety*, which referred to her acting as "awkward in action and expression," was negative. There were more kudos in Connecticut. Carl Van Vechten, who was a prominent member of the theater's board of trustees, came to take numerous photos of Anna May. On opening night, some of Broadway's greatest female stars, including Tallulah Bankhead, Ethel Barrymore, and Alla Nazimova, showed up. The presence at the opening of Bankhead and Nazimova is indicative of the high regard Anna May had among gay women.[8] According to his daughter, Anna May had a brief affair with costar Vincent Price. Price had recently married, a fact that casts some doubt on the rumor. Anna May did not return to Los Angeles after the summer. At the end of August 1937, Anna May was off for a brief trip to London where she saw *Porgy and Bess* at His Majesty's Theatre and *Before Sunset* at the Shaftesbury Theatre. She did not stay long.[9] The reason was Maschwitz. Leaving his wife behind in New York, Maschwitz flew out to Los Angeles. There he evaded MGM's studio greeters to meet Anna May at the airport. She found him a good hotel. Then they celebrated with several months of romance. She took him to eat with her family in Chinatown. They walked on the sands of Santa Monica beach, visited the "unreally beautiful" racetrack at Santa Anita, and relaxed at the "desert oasis of Palm Springs." She showed him around Hollywood. Soon he set up in a small bungalow that became a retreat for the English exiles in town.[10]

Val Gielgud, the older brother of John, and a distinguished writer as well as a friend of Maschwitz at the BBC, often rode along with Anna May and Maschwitz. Gielgud liked Anna May and found her "charmingly decorative" and "invariably sweet to me," rare praise from a man who found Hollywood generally character-less. Although Gielgud was appalled at the behavior of film producers and directors, whom he felt treated actors like "jars of jam at the grocery," he enjoyed the routine Anna May could offer. One afternoon, Gielgud and Maschwitz lunched at a benefit for Chinese and Spanish children that Anna May hosted at the "It" Café.

Later they drove out to meet Upton Sinclair and then made a visit to Forest Lawn Cemetery to observe Irving Thalberg's expensive vault and to marvel at how much money families paid to inter their loved ones near Jean Harlow's grave. A few days later, the English duo picked up Anna May at her apartment at the Park Wilshire and then dined at Perino's restaurant, after which they moved on to the Cocoanut Grove. After they watched the floor show of Edgar Bergen and Charlie McCarthy, Anna May took them to "a little downtown café on the way back, to see a boy do a turn which Anna May thought promising." Gielgud was most delighted when Anna May took him to the Paramount lot, where they lunched at the commissary. This was a treat Anna May reserved for her best visitors, including the Van Vechtens and Aldous Huxley. They lunched with Akim Tamiroff, and Anna May introduced Gielgud to John Barrymore, Dorothy Lamour, and Lloyd Nolan. A publicity man took pictures of Gielgud with George Raft and a terrific shot of the Englishman with Anna May at the Paramount Gate, which Gielgud put in his memoir of Hollywood days.[11]

While Maschwitz fooled around with his Hollywood and London buddies, Anna May kept busy at her career. She wanted to incorporate the experiences of her trip to China into every part she played. At the end of 1937, for example, she participated in a spontaneous sketch on the Royal Gelatin Hour on WCAF-NBC, New York, and played a "Chinese girl returning to her native country after spending all her life in America." Paramount helped her hone this new image. A press release, apparently penned by Wong, read: "Though I am American born of American born parents, I am a full-blooded Chinese and more Chinese than ever. When I returned from my first visit to China I found here an even more restless seeking for something that couldn't be found. The Chinese found it many centuries ago—a sort of serenity, an inner calm that comes from the understanding of life." The movie magazines helped in this regard, contending that Anna May's love of China helped her discover the serenity others might find in marriage or a career. Even though she understood that Chinese attitudes toward her were not always positive, she remained fulfilled by her visit. *Modern Screen* quoted her as saying, "I feel that the real Chinese should be shown to the audiences of the world, if only to correct film impressions of the past."[12]

Fortunately, Anna May's wishes coincided with a liberalized American policy toward China. The China lobby, led by Pearl Buck and Henry R. Luce

and supported by President Franklin D. Roosevelt, called for American respon-
sibility toward China and assistance in its struggle against Japanese imperialism.
Combining a paternalist belief drawn from several generations of missionary work and a secular sense of national benevolence, Americans began to
regard China more favorably. Despite the absence of Anna May Wong from its
marquee list, the film *The Good Earth* had done much to alter Americans' prejudice toward the Chinese. With the coming of World War II, aid to China rose
to the level of military necessity. American citizens and government favored
the nationalist regime of Chiang Kai-shek; of added importance was his wife,
Madame Chiang Kai-shek (Soong Meiling), whose beauty, intellect, and education (she graduated from Wellesley College) seemed to personify a westernized
Chinese woman.[13]

The principal vehicle for American citizens to aid China was United China
Relief (UCR). After her return to the United States from China, Anna May
pitched in to help the UCR in any way possible. Improved American attitudes
toward China meant that the studios initially gave her more attractive roles.
Eventually, however, the new attitudes toward China and the power of Madame
Chiang Kai-shek doomed Anna May's brave attempt to help her people. They
also convinced many that Anna May's film persona was dated and even insulting
to the Chinese, an attitude that would prove disastrous to her career.

Initially, Anna May had much to make her happy after her return to the
United States. A good contract with Paramount Pictures meant renewal of relations with their superb support staff. Edith Head, designer to the stars and an old
friend, created magnificent costumes for Anna May and was receptive to her use
of original Chinese gowns in the films. These two sources of costumes allowed
Anna May to wear full-length outfits that covered her legs and made her more
dignified to Chinese viewers. Her association with Head had mutual benefits
when the designer paid Anna May the ultimate compliment by adapting Anna
May's hairstyles with bangs for her own use. Val Gielgud left a nice description in
his memoirs of how Head worked with her stars. Each of them had a dressmak-
er's dummy that was an exact replica bearing "all the necessary measurements,"
which Head used to model the extravagant dresses she created for Anna May and
other stars. Gielgud also watched as Paramount's makeup artists adorned Anna
May "so that I could watch that highly skilled process at close quarters so that I

could admire—and thank God that there are other ways to make a living! Few things impress more than the discomfort of the film star's life."[14]

At Paramount, John Engstead headed a staff of first-rate glamor photographers, who maximized hair styling and makeup and understood Anna May's special needs and skills. Paramount seemed committed to Anna May's new conception of the role of the Chinese in American films. At the same time, the studio was unwilling to commit huge budgets to promote her stardom and regarded hers as "B" movies, which were intended to round out the double bills popular in American theaters.[15]

Anna May's first movie with Paramount was *Daughter of Shanghai*, which began production in the late autumn of 1937. Initially, Paramount wanted to call the film *Daughter of the Tong*, but decided against the title after a discussion with the Chinese consul. Studio insiders called it "The Anna May Wong Story," but the studio wanted an "action title." Anna May declared herself to be happy to be in the movie, because of its positive depiction of China: "I like my part in this picture better than any I've had before . . . This picture gives Chinese a break—we have sympathetic parts for a change." The studio boasted that T. K. Chang, the Chinese consul, had accepted the script. The film's director was Robert Florey, a skilled "B" movie artist and avid collector of Chinese furniture, which he used on the sets. Anna May's costars included Philip Ahn, J. Carrol Naish, and Buster Crabbe. Also starring in the film was a youthful Anthony Quinn, who had just married Katherine DeMille, Anna May's dance coach from London. Chingwah Lee had a small part in the film. Anna May received top billing for the film and earned $4,166.67 for her 25 days on the set. By comparison, Ahn, who worked 20 days, earned only $1,000. Anna May's pay was useful, but lagged far behind the immense sums Paramount was paying Marlene Dietrich, Claudette Colbert, Mae West, and others at the time.[16]

Anna May's character, Lan Ying Lin, was the focus of the narrative. The film begins with the murder of Lan Ying Lin's father, an importer of Chinese antiques, by smugglers angered by his refusal to help them bring illegal aliens into San Francisco. Enter Detective Kim Lee (Ahn) to crack the case. He first meets with Lan Ying and a family friend, Mrs. Mary Hunt (Cecil Cunningham). Lan Ying distrusts the officer and determines to solve the case herself. She travels to Central America in search of one Otto Hartman (Charles Bickford), who she believes ordered the killing. To observe him, she hires on at his nightclub as a dancer. Kim Lee spots her there and arranges for a private meeting. At question is a business ledger, evidence of the crime. Lan Ying arranges a disguise to smuggle the ledger herself aboard a departing ship of immigrants. When the immigrants discover that she is a woman, they attack her. Only by swimming ashore with Kim Lee can Lan Ying escape. On shore, the pair stumbles into Mrs. Mary Hunt's estate and realize that she is the real villain. Mrs. Hunt holds them hostage, but Kim Lee is able to escape, call the police, arrest Mrs. Hunt, and save Lan Ying. Kim Lee then proposes marriage to Lan Ying, who accepts. The duo then live happily ever after.[17]

Studio publicists spread the word of an impending "real" marriage between Wong and Ahn. She refused to acknowledge it, contending that kissing Ahn reminded her of kissing her own brother. Anna May said this because Ahn and she were pals and at times could be seen together helping Asian students register at the University of Southern California. Their friendship apparently overcame her comments, and the film did fairly well. The *New York Times*, no friend of Anna's, gave her good notices and generally approved of the movie. Paramount made a decent publicity effort for the film, but not as hefty as that for *Daughter of the Dragon* six years earlier.[18] Abroad, Anna May's journalist friends came through. In England, *Picturegoer* praised her and declared the movie "good rough stuff." *Kinetographic Weekly* applauded the reappearance of "her old charm." The Austrian *Das Kino-Journal* announced the coming of the new film with great anticipation.[19] A sign of Anna May's new popularity came from a favorable review of *Daughter of Shanghai* in the Chinese magazine *Guoguang Yingxun* (Cathay-Grand News). The reporter reminded readers of her earlier career, when her films were "estranged from the motherland." Now that she had visited China, Anna May had become "repentant of her errors." When she left China, she declared that from then on she would make films with only positive views of China. The new movie showed that she was keeping her promise. While that comment was encouraging, there were other signs that the Chinese film industry and media had not forgiven Anna May for her earlier roles. Chen Yunshang, the beautiful star of the hit movie *Mulan Joins the Army*, an anti-Japanese film, advertised herself as "not Anna May Wong" and stated that she would not play in racist movies that offended China.[20]

Anna May enhanced her representation of China in the film by wearing a number of gorgeous gowns she had purchased in Peking. One dress was made of blue Chinese crepe with a brocaded plum blossom pattern. Piping of three shades of blue satin accented the costume. The trousers were blue silk, with an oriental knot pattern applied over the net. Another dress from her collection featured white Chinese satin brocade with a gold butterfly pattern. Piping of gold braid was fastened with tiny gold butterflies and a gold lamé cape matched trousers of the same fabric. Significantly, all of her costumes during this period covered her legs, in compliance with Chinese standards. Anna May gained obvious pleasure in these garments and in the ones that her friend Edith Head designed for her Paramount productions. Her happiness is evident in stills from this period. Of the hundreds of photographs taken over several decades, images taken between 1937 and 1939 for Paramount reveal the brightest moments of Anna May's career. Whether in production stills or informal poses with other actors and studio executives, Anna May regularly beams with happiness and satisfaction. Paramount's staff photographers were good, but they could not match the artistry of the cameramen captivated by Anna May in the late 1920s. Rather, Anna May's contentment and the extraordinary clothing made the pictures brim with positive spirit.[21]

After completion of *Daughter of Shanghai*, Anna May was pleased with the flurry of activity. She wrote to Carl Van Vechten in early December 1937 about Lulu's return from war-torn Shanghai, about her new movie, derived from *On the Spot*, and that her work at the studio kept her so busy that "I don't get around socially much these days." She wrapped up *Dangerous to Know* a few days before Christmas and then quickly started on a new picture. Anna May and Gail Patrick were both listed as "featured players" in the film, though the latter was paid $14,437, far more than Anna May's $5,000 salary and even more than director Robert Florey. Anna May turned all her Christmas money over to Dr. Margaret Chung, the famous Chinese physician, who was collecting cash for China Relief. She did feel grateful to the Van Vechtens for sending a postcard commemorating her birthday on January 3. Anna May was thirty-three.[22]

Daughter of Shanghai did well at the box office, and a few months later Paramount released *Dangerous to Know*, the second "B" movie directed by Robert Florey and starring Anna May and Gail Patrick. Anna May's character was

Madame Lan Ying, the mistress of a powerful gangster, Stephen Recka, played by Akim Tamiroff. Anthony Quinn portrayed Recka's hoodlum associate, Nicky, and Lloyd Nolan performed as Inspector Brandon, determined to bring the trio to justice. The plot revolves around Recka's ambition to control city hall and court the socialite Margaret Van Kase (Gail Patrick). Recka and Brandon share the same birthday, a fact that the mobster commemorates annually with a bribe offer, which is promptly refused by the honest cop. More open to Recka's importuning is Van Kase's fiancé, Philip Euston (Harvey Stephens), who is delighted when Recka suddenly invests a colossal sum in bonds with him. This of course is a ruse to get rid of the inconvenient Euston, who innocently confounds the issue by telling Madame Lan Ying that Recka plans to wed Margaret Van Kase and leap up into high society. Recka plans to ensure the deal by robbing Euston of the bonds while pinning the loss on the gullible trader. Recka then forces an engagement from Van Kase in exchange for Euston's freedom. Despite his criminal career, Recka is a cultured man who enjoys playing Bach, Mozart, Tchaikovsky, and Handel on his pipe organ. Lan Ying confronts her lover about his infidelity while singing along to "Thanks for the Memories." While he performs Handel's *Largo*, Lan Ying stabs herself to death. Enter Inspector Brandon, who pins the crime on Recka. At the close, Van Kase and Euston ride off on a train to their honeymoon, blissfully unaware of the tragedy they have left behind.[23]

The dialogue amplifies the plot's standard injunctions against interracial sex. Such temptations cost Recka his career and indirectly push Lan Ying to suicide. Lan Ying tells Recka that Margaret Van Kase lives in a world he can never hope to enter. Better, she advises, that he accept her love. When he refuses, Lan Ying kills herself.[24]

In the United States the film gained scant critical recognition. The *New York Times* and *Variety* generally dismissed the film as unworthy of the talents of the actors. The *Hollywood Reporter* was a somewhat kinder, calling Anna May "beautiful" and hailing her acting for its "poise and restraint."[25] The impending war crisis in Europe cut down the number of screens open to American films. In England, however, critics gave it much broader approval. *Picturegoer Magazine* helped viewers by freely quoting the dialogue for the movie in a lengthy article. *Kinetographic Weekly* called it a "gripping, biographical gangster melodrama," with excellent acting from Anna May and Tamiroff. In France, Germany, and

Austria, the film got favorable reviews. The German reception is notable in that Nazi cultural ministries apparently accepted the film, despite Anna May's non-Aryan background. Publicity photos and reviews of *Dangerous to Know* in Germany carried a stamp of approval from the Nazi Ministry of Culture. As noted earlier, Hitler's party allowed Berliners to maintain a fragment of their earlier liberalism long into the 1930s. American film studios continued to send product to Germany, whose populace had always liked Anna May. Austrian magazines, not yet fully under the rule of the Third Reich, expressed their fondness of Anna May. Vienna's *Das Kino-Journal* reviewed *Dangerous to Know* with a headline referring to our "dear old acquaintance from the movies, Anna May Wong." This was one of her last-known mentions in Austrian or German magazines until after World War II.[26]

This flurry of activity could not hide the sadness in her heart. Maschwitz had tired of the "eternal sunshine" and was ready to go back to London and to his wife. His Korean chauffeur, hired for Maschwitz by Anna May, drove the pair out to the airport. Maschwitz later wrote that leaving Anna May was the hardest part of his departure because "she was somebody very precious to me, a friend, a counselor, a piece of porcelain too delicate for my rough hands to handle with any safety. The bell sounded, the confused farewells were said, and all of a sudden, knee-deep in chocolates and novels by Pearl S. Buck, with tears in my eyes," he was gone. There would be many transatlantic phone calls over the next few years, but distance and war fractured what Anna May later told a friend was "the love of her life."[27]

With her great love gone, Anna May concentrated on work. Anna May's third film within six months was the astrological thriller *When Were You Born?*, for which Paramount loaned her to Warner Brothers. The production credits listed the talents appearing with Anna May by their birth signs. Mary Lee Ling (Anna May) uses astrology to detect crimes. On a ship en route to San Francisco, she informs an antiques dealer, Philip Corey (James Stephenson), that he only has forty-eight hours to live. Onshore, Corey dies by an unknown hand. Mary Lee Ling is accused of the killing and must use astrology to prove that she is innocent. Through her significant questions to various people in Corey's life, she establishes that he was a blackmailer who forced his wife to marry him. Her further detection reveals that in fact Corey is not who he says he is; he is actually a drug smuggler in disguise. The real Corey has been killed to hide bad investment deals. In the end, Mary Lee Ling is acclaimed as a heroine of the stars. The film gathered scant reviews in the United States, but in England, Anna May's performance received strong support from trade critics.[28]

Anna May's next Paramount film, *King of Chinatown*, was intended as a tribute to the famous Chinese American surgeon, Dr. Margaret Chung. Paramount, pleased with the earnings of her last film, raised Anna May's salary to $9,790 for this production. Akim Tamiroff costarred in the film, joined by J. Carrol Naish, Philip Ahn, and Anthony Quinn. In the film, Frank Baturin (Tamiroff) controls the rackets in Chinatown. He loses $20,000 betting on a boxing match, a loss more damaging to his honor than his wallet. Baturin orders his hit man to kill his rival, Mike Gordon (Quinn). That worthy had already won the loyalty of a top Baturin aide nicknamed the "Professor" (Naish), who betrays his boss. Gordon shoots Baturin in front of a Chinese pharmacy owned by Dr. Chang Ling (Sidney Toler), who had previously refused protection from Baturin. The doctor is also the father of a famed female physician, Dr. Mary Ling (Wong). At the hospital, she treats Baturin during his extended convalescence. Later, he convinces her to forego a trip to China intended to raise funds for Red Cross relief and become his personal physician. Unsurprisingly, the racketeer falls in love with her, despite her engagement to Dr. Bob Li (Ahn). Out in the mean streets, Gordon is running amok and terrorizing Chinatown. Gunning to finish off Baturin, he threatens to kill Dr. Chang Ling unless his daughter helps in the execution of the wounded crime boss. Enter the police, who extract a confession from Gordon. After his arrest, the drama focuses on the Professor, who turns out to be an escaped convict. At Baturin's home, the Professor kills the reformed gangster just before the police arrive. Baturin's will includes a healthy endowment for Dr. Mary Ling's nursing unit in China. Soon, she marries Dr. Li and they sail away to China.[29]

Anna May prepared for the role by observing a dangerous kidney operation at Los Angeles Hospital. While in the operating room, Anna May donned a surgeon's gown and mask and carefully watched the surgical methods. Her visit was fully covered by *Click Magazine*, which devoted several pages of photographs to it.[30] Despite its good intentions, the film received unenthusiastic reviews. *Variety* gave Anna May a favorable notice amidst a generally condescending summary of the film; the *Daily Variety*'s reviewer saw more hopeful signs in her energy, which he felt could lead to better roles. The *Hollywood Reporter* gave the film better notices and credited Anna May for a "well-shaded performance." The *New York Times* once more blamed Paramount for cheating its actors with such a script.[31] Abroad, reactions were more favorable. *Boy's Cinema* of England devoted ten pages to the film's dialogue, spiced with numerous pictures of Anna May. *Kinetographic Weekly* called her "distinctive as usual." *King of Chinatown* was the last Anna May film to appear in Austria as the coming of World War II curtailed further screenings of American films.[32]

Anna May sought other projects as well. Pearl Buck's agent contacted her about a possible lead role in a play entitled *Flight into China*. Anna May responded warmly but said she was more interested in the film rights. At the same time, Anna May's agent contacted Buck's people about doing *The Good Earth* as summer stock in 1938. The first stage run of the famous novel had bombed, and Buck should have been grateful for any interest. As the two sides negotiated over several possibilities and a deal loomed, the talks were cut short suddenly by Pearl Buck's terse rejection of Anna May for any part. Anna May finally worked with Pearl Buck through the intercession of Orson Welles. The famed actor produced *The Campbell (Soup) Playhouse*, and on April 14, 1939, he featured Anna May in a radio version of Buck's novel *The Patriot*.[33]

Anna May's last movie for Paramount was *Island of Lost Men*, filmed in the spring of 1939 and released in the summer of that year. Anna May shared featured player status with J. Carrol Naish. She played Kim Ling, who is searching for her father, who was kidnapped by a motley crew headed by Gregory Prin (J. Carrol Naish) and located in the jungle somewhere north of Singapore. The father, General Ling (Richard Loo), has been unjustly accused of embezzling money from the Chinese government. Kim Ling meets Prin in a Singapore nightclub, nicknamed Claridge's bar, after one of her favorite London hotels. There she performs "Music on the Shore," a song written for her by Frederick Hollander, lyricist for many of Marlene Dietrich's film songs, and Frank Loesser. Her lyrics described feelings that occasionally must have flowed through her heart:

> With a beach for my bed,
> And the palms overhead,
> And the waves making Music on the Shore,

> Leave me there, Leave me there,
> Getting sand in my hair,
> Watching boats drift by from Singapore,
> I'll leave this crazy world to fight things out,
> And I'll never shout, "What's the Score?"
> With a beach for my bed,
> And the palms overhead,
> And the waves making Music on the Shore.[34]

Kim Ling agrees to travel with him to his jungle headquarters. There Kim Ling meets Chang Tai (Anthony Quinn), who is an undercover agent searching for General Ling. Prin soon discovers Tai's true identity and orders him killed. Fortuitously, Tai is saved by a Professor Sen, who is plotting with the locals to overthrow Prin. Tai then finds the general and the lost cash and tries to flee downriver with the Lings. Prin, believing that the natives will kill them, allows them to escape. Prin is betrayed by one of his henchmen, played by a young Broderick Crawford. When rebellious natives close in on Prin, he finds he has only one bullet left. They reward his trust in them with a spear through the chest. Chang Tai and the Lings then arrive safely in Singapore.[35]

Reviewers were more enthusiastic this time. *Variety* hailed the acting, atmospheric sets, and general production. Though the reviewer considered the plot trite, Anna May was described as "dignified, capable." The *Daily Variety* called her singing "pleasing." The *New York Times* had nice things to say about J. Carrol Naish. In England, *Kinetographic Weekly* dismissed the film but noted that Anna May played her part with conviction.[36]

The film's production ran into a few problems. Adolph Zukor originally called the film *Guns for China*, but that title offended war officials in Washington; eventually *Island of Lost Men* seemed the most innocuous. Additional nights were needed to shoot jungle scenes, and the water tub used for the river cost more than expected. Overall, cost overruns amounted to $22,500, a sizable share of the budget of $165,000, which, judging by the production notes, created friction between the staff and the home office. Anna May's salary for the film was $6,000 for thirty-seven days. She was on the set for twelve hours a day and earned an additional $1,000 for overtime. Paramount also spent about $1,000 creating or renting her wardrobe. Tamiroff, who had earned a fraction of her pay two years earlier, now made $8,125. Quinn earned only $750.[37]

Anna May's earnings for her Paramount films in the late 1930s are indicative of a pattern in her career. Her weekly salary for the four films averaged just under $1,000 per week; her starring roles, however, ensured that she earned about $5,000 to $6,000 per film, which placed her in the upper-middle-earnings level for Hollywood actors. Her "B" movies usually took only a few weeks to produce, making it possible for the studio to film many a year. Despite her competitive salary, Hollywood's conception of her as an Asian actress curtailed her earnings. While her weekly salary placed her earnings among the top twenty percent of Hollywood acting talent, her annual earnings from her films reduced her to the bottom half of the industry's moneymakers. As the only Chinese American actor of any fame, she was a high-exposure talent whose career was consciously limited by the studios. The prejudices and limited visions of the production units blocked Anna May's access to the big money. She was notably absent from the roster of the top one hundred Hollywood salaried actors, published in 1938.[38]

The extra costs of production may have been a factor in Paramount Pictures' decision not to renew Anna May's contract after the completion of four pictures. Always prepared, she had saved enough money from her contract to buy an attractive apartment house at 326 San Vicente Boulevard, which remains one of the loveliest streets in Los Angeles. Part of the Palisades development, Anna May's lot was located right on the corner of Fourth Street and San Vicente, just a few blocks from the Pacific Ocean. She converted her two lots into four separate units and promptly named them the Moongate Apartments. Long before the coming of the Santa Monica Freeway, Santa Monica offered succor to Hollywood actors, directors, and writers. The part of Santa Monica where Anna May bought her home had long had a bohemian flair. Nearby lived photographer Edward Weston and his sons as well as painter Nicolai Fechin, writer Christopher Isherwood, and Salka Viertel, Greta Garbo's lover. The Palisades was located not far from Rustic Canyon, where Anna May had sported with Charles Rasher more than a decade before. The Uplifters Club was now in decline, and much of the canyon was taken up by what became Will Rogers Park. Not far away from Anna May's new home was the German émigré village of Pacific Palisades with its architectural marvels. Malibu was a few miles further up the Pacific Coast Highway. The immediate neighborhood was spectacularly beautiful. San Vicente Boulevard sported stately coral trees all the way to Brentwood. Palm trees divided Fourth Street down to

Broadway. Anna May's new home featured a small pond in front of the residence, in the custom of Taishanese villages. Pictures of her sitting with Lulu circulated through China. Anna May is adorned with a *ji*—a married woman's hairstyle—combined with a Child Flower forehead. Chinese readers, knowing that she was not married to a man, could understand that Anna May considered herself "married to China." Her youngest brother, Richard, only sixteen and without a mother, moved in with Anna May. The pair enjoyed working hard in the garden, cultivating Anna May's collection of exotic plants, including an orchid that had been named after her. She also found companionship in a series of cats and dogs. Anna May luxuriated in entertaining international guests. On November 23, 1939, she threw an elaborate reception for Lin Yutang and his wife. Anna May decorated her home with fuschia and bird of paradise blossoms.[39]

Anna May paid $18,000 cash for two lots in the apartment complex. Hers were the two most expensive lots in the development, which was about ten years old. Her tax assessments valued the property at $3,680. A month after her purchase, she sold shares to her sisters Lulu and Mary for ten dollars, thus ensuring that the property would stay in the family.[40]

Anna May enjoyed being back in Los Angeles, though much had changed downtown. After the city government had condemned the old Chinatown and forcibly evicted its residents to make way for a railway terminal, a group of Chinese businessmen cooperated to create a new Chinatown, complete with a massive gate and many shops and restaurants catering to tourists. Anna May joined Consul T. K. Chang and his wife along with fellow actors Keye Luke and Soo Yong at the opening ceremony on June 25, 1938; Anna May dug the first shovelful of earth for planting a ceremonial willow tree. She graciously rode in the queen's carriage as the Mistress of Ceremonies at the start of the Moon Festival three years later. There, she set up a booth at the corner of Ferguson Alley and North Los Angeles Street in Chinatown, where she signed autographs for a fundraising effort for China Relief. Anna May demanded and received other preferential treatment at the festival, including a limousine and driver. Generally, other Chinese American actors did not resent the entitlements Anna May claimed. Swan Yee, an aspiring actor at the time, admired her: "Anna May Wong was a pretty good actress. She did not have any competition from other Asian actresses." Keye Luke, who appeared in a number of movies during this period, and Bessie Loo, an actress and casting agent, agreed that Anna May was treated far better in Europe than in the United States. According to her sister Lulu, Anna May was respected and liked for her devotion to her family and generous support of their education. Anna May's style and talents influenced other Chinese Americans. Around this time, troupes of entertainers dressed in a neo-Shanghai style loosely derived from Anna May's movies danced and sang in theaters and clubs in Chinatowns across the United States.[41]

During idle evenings Anna May relaxed at Eddy See's tavern and restaurant, The Dragon's Den, in the new Chinatown. See's establishment boasted murals of the Eight Immortals and of a dancing dragon done by artists Benki Okubu, Tyrus Wong, and Marian Blanchard. The Den soon became a popular hangout where Hollywood notables including Walt Disney and the Marx Brothers dined on fried shrimp and almond duck. Anna May had her own table where she held court. Even if customers talked about her behind her back, they gaped in awe before her. She usually dressed in a silk *qipao* cut on the bias, with a full-length ermine coat draped over her shoulders, and welcomed admirers with a seductively outstretched hand. She loved to share dumb jokes with Eddy See. One of her favorites was about a fisherman who caught a beautiful mermaid with long blonde hair. After he reeled her in, he examined her all over and then tossed her back into the sea. A fellow fisherman asked him, "Why?" The first fisherman replied, "How?"[42] In another act emphasizing her Chinese identity, Anna May refused a contract clause put in by the studio, which required that she bob her hair. The studio envisioned her characters in the three movies as Americanized. Anna May countered that her roles had to appeal to women in many countries, not just the United States. The studio acceded to her wishes, though its method of reporting the dispute was through a publicity sheet, indicating that the struggle was not bitter. The incident was reported in China as an example of her patriotism. One magazine told its readers that Anna May defied the studio in memory of her mother, who was an old-fashioned woman and would never approve of short hair on her daughter. She did have to cut her fingernails for the first time in twenty years because of the physical demands of her role in *Daughter of Shanghai*; as soon as her nails grew back, she donned ornamental nail guards. Newspapers in China applauded her staunch defense of traditions.[43]

As a sign of improved public attitudes toward China, American magazines now viewed Anna May's embrace of her national culture with approval. *Better Homes and Gardens* devoted a full-page layout to her Chinese-influenced interior decoration and flower arrangements. While readers' ogling of the furniture of a star contributed to Hollywood mystique, the article on Anna May's home combined exoticism with comfort, enabling her fans to accept a Chinese American as a glamorous figure. The only jarring note was that the article was in black and white, while surrounding it were more mundane stories in glorious color. There were other reminders of the limitations of the American press. *Look* put Anna May on the front cover of its second issue. While the magazine identified her as the "World's Most Beautiful Chinese Girl," the image showed Anna May brandishing a dagger. Inside, the story featured a tamer photo with her brother Roger; the text stated that she was a single woman. The following month, the magazine took another racial slant by reprinting the Alfred Eisenstadt picture of Anna May, Marlene Dietrich, and Leni Riefenstahl with the caption, "Hitler Wouldn't Like This One—It can never be taken again."[44]

Anna May attempted to give a Chinese glow to every publicity shot. She brought an extraordinary Chinese costume complete with an elaborate headdress from her collection to a photography shoot by legendary cameraman George Hurrell. The photographer recalled her as completely businesslike. One of the surviving photos makes the Chinese headdress appear almost prosaic by comparison. In this second image, which Hurrell later printed in expensive, limited editions, the photographer portrayed the beautiful actress with her dress slipping off her shoulder and baring a nipple. That image became a collector's item, and Hurrell capitalized on such interest by printing numerous limited editions of it over the years. Other shots from this sitting were published in the June 1938 issue of *Photoplay*.[45]

This reminder of the wild days of the late 1920s was generally eclipsed by Anna May's deeper conviction to better the world. Anna May kicked off a drive in June 1938 to send money and medical supplies to China by auctioning off her collection of gowns. She had collected the gowns over a period of years in Paris, New York, China, and Hollywood. A year earlier she spoke of a desire to sell some of them because she was running out of closet space. She made an earlier sale in March 1937 to benefit the Assistance League. Now she was ready to sell all of them to help out China Relief. The collection included many costumes that had never been worn and several that she had worn on screen for her Paramount films. She was also able to peddle a $5,000 necklace for Mrs. Wellington Koo, with the proceeds going to China Relief. At the auction, Anna May showed five reels of her home movie shot during her visit to China in 1936. She deposited the proceeds of the auction into a Chinese bank fund designated to help Chinese war refugees.[46]

Anna May's pursuit of her career and her simultaneous devotion to the cause of China kept her on the road. In April 1939, she was in New York for a private party at the Van Vechtens, which honored Lin Yutang and her.[47] War prevented any thoughts of traveling to either China or Europe, so Anna May signed on to a vaudeville tour of Australia. Her intention was to lecture and host subscription campaigns for China aid. She sailed out of San Francisco to Honolulu for Melbourne, Australia, on May 4. Publicity photos showed her wearing one of her signature fur coats, because, as she explained, winter had arrived in Australia. She arrived on June 5 in Melbourne, where the Tivoli Theater Company had scheduled a series of variety shows. Anna May was the featured player in the show, titled *Highlights from Hollywood* and which featured Sonny Lamont and Betty Burgess along with minor acts of two brothers playing a mandolin, tightrope dancers, and some ballet sketches. Anna May stood out among this motley talent. She opened her performance with a Chinese folk song, followed by a Basque love song, a satirical tribute to the Australian woman, and closed with her familiar rendition of "Half-Caste Woman." This song had been her signature piece for eight years, reflecting how well it fit her personality. Critics hailed the quality of her dramatic ability and laughed at her gentle satire of Australians.

She combined these popular presentations with several Chinese plays depicting Japanese aggression. On July 1, Anna May suddenly revamped her program to introduce a more stinging critique following a tense standoff between Japanese forces and international residents of Tianjin. The new drama reflected a crisis that had developed in late July over protection in the international community of four Chinese men accused of murdering a Japanese official. The occupiers retaliated by barricading the British settlement, denying it access to food and fuel, and publicly strip-searching anyone who tried to enter. Anglo-Japanese relations deteriorated sharply. Anna May's contribution, "At the Barricade," used dramatic effect to portray the suffering within these international settlements and of the Chinese generally. She did so despite harsh criticism from the program director who denounced her as a "has-been," and "a faded old bag." She responded to his insults by bowing low and thanking him before walking off the stage, to the applause of the company.[48]

While in Melbourne, Anna May made several appearances at screenings of *The King of Chinatown*, which was playing at the Tivoli Theater. While Anna May was pleasant to all, she did have some bitter words about Hollywood. She informed reporters that she was tired of playing sinister parts and wanted new roles. Variety performances might mean less pay, she acknowledged, but "I do get something out of life." After several successful months in Melbourne, Anna May returned to the United States on September 3, 1939. She told Van Vechten how "happy and delighted she was to be home again." On the trip from Honolulu, she kept company with Adolph Zukor and his wife and Artur Schnabel, the pianist. All felt the cold wind of the new war, which Anna May prayed would be a "brief business."[49] She made two quick inconsequential pictures, appearing in *Chinese Garden Festival* for Republic Pictures in 1940. This single-reel film was part of the *Harriet Parsons Meet the Stars* series and included such luminaries as Rosalind Russell, Dorothy Lamour, Rita Hayworth, Walter Pidgeon, and Mary Pickford. Anna May's next role was a bit more substantial. She took second billing to Ralph Bellamy in the latest installment of the popular series *Ellery Queen's Penthouse Mystery*, produced by Columbia Pictures in 1941. The plot involved a scheme to transport a fortune in jewels from the Orient to the United States for sale to get cash for the Chinese war against the Japanese. Gordon Cobb (Noel Madison), a wealthy jewel collector, is involved in the transaction and soon disappears with the jewels. In the convoluted plot, Ellery Queen (Bellamy), the famous detective, is called in to unravel the mystery. Among the characters is Lois Ling (Anna May), who is acting as an agent for the Chinese government. Murder is afoot and, by use of secret messages, Ellery Queen is able to find the murderer, recover the jewels, and assist the Chinese.[50] The film was the most inconsequential of the Ellery Queen series and few critics recommended it. *Variety* noted that Anna May "handled a minor role with ease" while the *Hollywood Reporter* acknowledged that she was "pleasantly effective."[51]

Gradually, film work dried up for Anna May. She complained to Van Vechten that the studios were not hiring and "one wonders if one is going to work again." Anna May went frequently to the theater and usually went backstage to visit friends and collect autographs. She entertained the wealthy Sir Victor Sassoon from China and took him and other friends to the studio. A few months later, she lamented that "professional life is quiet on all fronts." While she wished for something to happen, she conceded that "at least I am learning what makes a house tick." She and a tenant discovered new plants in her garden at the house at 326 San Vicente Boulevard.[52] As her film career seemed to fade, Anna May became more stoical, thrifty, and concerned about her time. In a remarkable interview that appeared in the *Seattle Daily Times* in April 1939, Anna May questioned the value of possessions, speculating whether one should clean house twice a year and get rid of unused things, especially those needed by others. Aware of the plenty at her disposal, Anna May dismissed the need to store things for future use, wondering if she would ever live long enough to use them. She had just proven this adage by donating her Chinese gowns for the benefit of China Relief. Friendship also needed to be reviewed. Anna May noted "we outgrow people, or they outgrow us; we are useless to each other." Anna May had experienced many disappointments in life and love and doubtless wished to push away time-wasters. To do so, she used a ten-cent telephone service that discouraged all except those who truly had something to say to her. Dull people were unworthy of her time: "It's not unkind to shed such people as they are easily content with someone else, but if we let them consume our time, we lose and they gain nothing." Regret was another useless emotion. Perhaps she regretted her time as a flapper, but recognized that "We can't go back . . . We can do nothing about it, but we vow not to repeat a mistake to devote ourselves to the ones who really matter to us," in her case, her family. One does not have to accept Anthony Chan's argument that Anna May was a Daoist Butterfly to realize that Anna May was carefully contemplating the aging of her life and career. Much of her wisdom derived directly from experience. After twenty years in the film business, she had learned the hard way the fleeting nature of love and friendship. She would soon call upon her stoicism about life and death. [53]

In the summer of 1940, tragedy struck the family. Mary Wong, perhaps distraught over her negligible acting career, of which the sole credits were *Daughter of the Dragon* and *The Good Earth,* hanged herself in the garage at the family home on July 25. Wong Sam Sing said that Mary had been employed intermittently as a stenographer and had not been despondent. Anna May was planning to do summer stock of *On the Spot* in Pennsylvania, but she quickly had to postpone her plans. She wrote to the Van Vechtens on August 12, thanking them for their telegram and appreciating their kindness "when we most needed the understanding of friends." In characteristic fashion, she told them that the suicide was so "recent and tragic it is difficult to refer to it so I will leave the subject alone." She rescheduled her performance in Pennsylvania to open on August 26. She was bringing Richard with her and expected to arrive at the Algonquin in New York around September 1.[54]

Anna May and Richard spent about a month in New York. He was now eighteen, slightly more than half the age of his famous sister. With their mother dead and with no child of her own, Anna May increasingly acted as a surrogate mother for the young man. A few years earlier, she had taken him to Europe and met him in China. Now they hit New York, and the Van Vechtens escorted Richard to a series of Broadway plays and to meet the actors. He wrote that, having heard so much from his sister about the Van Vechtens, he was so glad to find that they were "two of the kindest people" he had met in New York. Then sister and brother returned to their home at 326 San Vicente Boulevard.[55]

Upon her return, Anna May quickly did a fundraiser for the China Aid Council. China Relief work was now becoming a full-time job for Anna May. She became the head of the motion-pictures division of the Bowl of Rice drive, which was intended to provide medical aid to China and the China Aid Council. On October 26, she flew from Los Angeles to New York to be the Queen of the Bowl of Rice Ball, held on November 1 at the Waldorf Astoria. Right after that, she hosted a fashion show featuring a parade of "eight lovely Chinese girls . . . followed by fourteen American women, chosen from the ranks of society's loveliest, who modeled modern evening gowns . . . all inspired by traditional Chinese dress, but skillfully adapting Chinese color combinations, motifs, and patterns to suit the American face and figure." What Anna May had initiated in England a decade before was finally hitting the United States. Her adaptations of Chinese clothing were now acceptable to American audiences. Anna May traveled to Boston for a Bowl of Rice benefit, then toured the rest of New England, doing more fundraising parties and shows. She returned to her "pet hotel," the Algonquin, on December 15 to collect her things and take the train to Los Angeles.[56]

Her travels and Mary's death took their toll on Anna May. She was grateful to Richard for handling Christmas "as I just did not have the pep." Van Vechten sent her a batch of new photos, his third of the year, which gave her pleasure. She told him that in the future, "I shall just sit for you exclusively," and was thinking of "interesting costumes for you to photograph." In a touching close to the letter, she thanked her friends for the "many kind thoughts and deeds" over the past year.[57]

Anna May did more radio shows, appearing on Fred Allen's *Texaco Star Theater* on November 12, 1941. Despite the war in Europe, her friends abroad did not forget Anna May. *Theatre World* in London published a full-page photo of her having lunch in her Santa Monica home. The editors pointed out a lovely caricature of Anna May by the opera singer Autori, which adorned the wall. The photo was captioned "Hollywood's Friend of Democracy."[58]

With no regular studio contract, Anna May was free to support the Chinese effort in the war against Japan in any way she chose. One method was film. She starred in *Bombs over Burma*, produced by the Poverty Row Studio Producers Releasing Corporation (PRC). Joseph H. Lewis, who had a number of westerns under his belt and regularly worked for big and small studios, directed *Bombs over Burma*. Production began on March 30, 1942, and the film opened on May 28, 1942.

Bombs over Burma is a curious piece. Generally derided as a sign of Anna May's drooping reputation, the film was an effective propaganda film designed to support the Chinese cause, much like several films put out by the China Relief Agency. Anna May performs as Lin Ying, a schoolteacher in Burma, who is secretly spying for the Chinese army. She is assigned to ensure the passage of a secret food supply convoy along the Burma Road. In the first ten minutes of the film, Anna May speaks only Chinese to her class of young students. No English is heard until Japanese bombs start dropping on the schoolhouse. Lin Ying moves all of the children to safety, but she realizes too late that a young boy has been left behind. Just as she enters the classroom to retrieve him, Japanese gunners shoot the boy. Leaving the village on a bus, Lin Ying is accompanied by a Chinese priest and spy, Me-Hoi (Noel Madison), and an undercover German spy, Sir Roger Howe (Leslie Dennison). Howe soon recognizes the true intent of his passengers, and orders them arrested and held by the bus driver (Nedrick Young). Lin Ying is able to convince the driver that Howe is the true villain. Villagers attack Howe with hoes and kill him, after which the Burma Road is safe for the convoy.[59] Less safe was the critical reception. *Variety* referred to it as a "wartime programmer of very minor grade"; the *New York Times* dismissed it as a "dud." Anna May's overseas fans were more receptive. The English critics called her work "sincere and at times moving."[60]

Anna May spent much of 1942 working on Red Cross, USO, and China Relief activities. In January, she went to New Orleans for a Red Cross fundraiser. In New Orleans, she appeared alongside Lee Ya Ching, whom Anna May referred to as "our female aviatrix." Lee Ya Ching was a major fundraiser for China during her barnstorming tour that year. Ching sometimes received more credit than Anna May, but the latter kept doggedly working for the national good. On August 19, she made a national radio broadcast to rally for the war chest workers. She joined Gregory Peck, Charles Boyer, and Akim Tamiroff for a benefit on September 23 and with several other Asian actors in a fundraiser for the war effort in Santa Ana, California, on October 14. Anna May showed her patriotism on the first anniversary of the Pearl Harbor attack by being sworn in as an air raid warden. She contended that as an American-born Chinese, she felt it a privilege to help defend the advantages bestowed on her in a free democracy.[61]

She also returned to writing to support the cause. In 1942 Anna May contributed the preface to a cookbook, *New Chinese Recipes*, a project intended to raise money for the United China Relief. Authored by Mabel Stegner, a home economics consultant, and Fred Wing, a young Chinese restaurateur, the cookbook contained about sixty Cantonese recipes, many of which became familiar staples for American enthusiasts of Chinese food. Surprisingly, it was among the first Chinese cookbooks printed in the United States, preceded by only three imprints, two of which were academic reports. Chinese restaurant owners had long adapted to local food ways but had rarely codified their methods. The book had a less subtle intention. It was attempting to make Chinese cooking more mainstream at a time of reaction against ethnic foods in general. Anna May's plans were prescient. Despite the turn against ethnic foods, Americans recognized the Chinese as allies. Just as they attended many "rice bowl" parties, where Anna May was often the star attraction, Americans flocked to Chinese restaurants, which enjoyed boom times during the war. Anna May had contributed to a celebrity cookbook a decade earlier, but this was her first chance to talk about Chinese food extensively. In her preface, she wrote that she hoped Chinese culture would become assimilated into the American mainstream. In the two-page essay, Anna May invented "an American housewife" who wanted to cook Chinese food at home but could not comprehend its mysteries. After visiting the kitchens of many Chinese restaurants, she realized that Chinese cooks measured by "feel" and judged temperature and cooking time by experience. Their answers to her many questions were vague and bewildering. She wanted desperately to find a way to translate Chinese cooking methods into American food customs. Fortunately, she encountered Stegner and Wing, who set about translating Chinese artistry into "definite measurement and scientific cookery terms any American housewife could follow." An added benefit was that all ingredients were readily available in any supermarket. The result, Anna boasted, was a book that brought interesting, healthy food to the table and saved time and money. Best of all, the recipes appealed to children and husbands, "who have never enjoyed vegetables." Offering recipes was a staple method used by stars to promote their wholesomeness. Anna May's book had stronger ideological overtones. Rather than selling just an individual image, she strove to make Chinese American food a part of the American diet. Her insistence on easily found ingredients and the simplicity of preparation, as well as her admonition that eating Chinese food was good for the war effort, all contributed to Chinese cuisine's appeal to the American palate.[62]

Despite reports that she had retired, Anna May was always in pursuit of a good role. She negotiated in June 1942 with Bertolt Brecht about the possibility of her acting as Shen Te in *The Good Woman of Setzuan* on Broadway. Anna May soon lost interest in working with the German playwright.[63] Later that summer, she started work on a second film for PRC. Called *Lady from Chungking,* and released in December 1942, the film detailed Chinese resistance to the Axis powers. This time, Anna May played Kwan Mei, a noble woman in charge of guerrilla actions. Kwan Mei works surreptitiously among the peasants in a rice paddy to observe Japanese troop movements. She and her co-workers rescue two American pilots who crash land in the region and kill the Japanese overseer who tried to arrest the Yanks. The local Japanese commander forces her to hand over one of the pilots, while local peasants hide the other American flyer. Worse, the Japanese commander takes a liking to Kwan Mei and makes her his hostess. For her part, she wants to learn more about troop movements. Their tryst is interrupted by news of the discovery of the body of the Japanese soldier killed by the peasants. Kwan Mei is able to convince him not to kill the peasants. Later she is exposed as "Madame Kwan Mei, the famous guerrilla leader." There are hints of interracial romance with one of the flyers. Kwan Mei has to kill General Kaimura, the Japanese commander, to convince the peasants that she is not his mistress. As the Japanese execute her, Kwan Mei proudly describes the inevitable Chinese victory over their conquerors. The film received respectful but not strong notices. At the same time, she had to feel good about the positive portrayal of a Chinese woman. She was the heroine, a role often lacking in films featuring Euro-American actresses. Rarely did Hollywood make wartime female characters into heroines, preferring to ridicule them.[64]

Anna May was pleased about the film, which she felt helped the war effort. The conflict seemed very close that summer as war planes droned above Los Angeles and she heard spasmodic firing. Richard had to drive her at night because they lived in a "dim-out" area and her eyes were not what they had been; she plied him with vitamin A and carrots. Anna May was very excited about Richard's fledgling acting career. As Kim Wong, he appeared in *The Amazing Mrs. Holiday* (1943) starring Deanna Durbin and directed by Bruce Hanning. His career was interrupted by a call by the military. Perhaps his sister's connections helped, because he was assigned to the elite intelligence services. After a few dull months in camp, he was transferred to London. Later, he worked in Paris and Brussels.[65]

Anna May continued her work for United China Relief and for the war effort. Events beyond her control would compromise appreciation of her work. During the winter of 1942 and spring of 1943, Madame Chiang Kai-shek made a highly successful propaganda visit through the United States. Speaking before Congress, and billed as the star attraction at massive rallies in New York, Chicago, San Francisco, and Los Angeles, Madame Chiang impressed Americans with the notion that she could be an effective leader and that her role as supportive homemaker did not deter her from valiant patriotism. She spoke extremely well, wowed Americans with her beauty and grace, and in every way seemed the best combination of Western, Christian educated, and Chinese womanhood.

Hollywood pulled out all its resources for her visit. Henry R. Luce and David O. Selznick hosted a special tea for her with 200 Hollywood stars and later had a party attended by 1,500 celebrities. Madame Chiang Kai-shek's speech before 30,000 people at the Hollywood Bowl about the destruction of her homeland brought tears to everyone's eyes. Many found themselves humming the Chinese national anthem for days afterward. On stage at the Hollywood Bowl, she was placed with a group of glamorous female actresses including Ingrid Bergman, Barbara Stanwyck, Ginger Rogers, and Loretta Young. Conspicuously absent from the stage was Anna May Wong.[66] Many in Hollywood were outraged by this snub. Anna May's faithful friend Rob Wagner pointed out that "There wasn't a single representative of the Chinese colony, except for the Consulate staff." He noted that Madame Chiang Kai-shek had requested a private meeting with studio executives even before the gala with specially picked stars. Wagner contended that "there has been no more faithful worker for the cause of United China than Anna May Wong. Was she asked to greet Madame at the film reception? She was not!" Wagner's wife pointed out that the absence of Anna May was the only "bum note" in the proceedings. Selznick, anxious over such criticism, countered that "there were reasons why Anna May Wong was not asked." Further investigation revealed that a Mr. Hsung from Madame Chiang's delegation had specifically requested that Anna May should not be included.[67]

In fact, many Chinese Americans were absent from the podium and from the events. That omission doubtless stemmed from the historic Chinese disdain for their overseas countrymen. For centuries, the Chinese government had regarded overseas Chinese as traitors and criminals. In the United States the situation was further complicated by the fact that most Chinese Americans hailed from southern China and spoke Cantonese, a language and culture that were in disfavor in Mandarin-speaking Republican China. Madame Chiang Kai-shek had made strong statements in the past about the image of Chinese Americans. During this visit, she observed that she wished that Americans could see Chinese Americans as more than coolies and laundrymen, a reference that had to cause pain to Hollywood's daughter of a laundryman. Anna May's film career created problems. Madame Chiang Kai-shek was known to dislike Hollywood's presentation of Chinese characters and she let the studio executives know of her displeasure. In her eyes, Anna May stood for the bad old days. Others shared this view. Before her script was amended for a radio program made for China Relief, Pearl Buck referred to a character as a "slangy Anna May Wong-type." Madame Chiang Kai-shek had written about the role of Chinese women in the struggle against Japan. While she considered Chinese women highly patriotic and a determined force, she clearly did not envision actresses as productive models. In a section of her book *China Shall Rise Again*, Madame Chiang Kai-shek discussed cultural workers. That term to her described people who provided mass education for women, not actresses. Anna May Wong could do all the benefits she wanted for United China Relief, but she had no place in the Nationalist ideology. Finally, Madame Chiang Kai-shek simply lacked the democratic ability to accept Anna May as an equal. Earlier in the trip, Madame had raised a controversy by insisting that Winston Churchill at least meet her halfway between her residence in New York and Washington, where he was visiting. Asked to compromise by her brother, Madame responded that her rank was much higher than the English prime minister and that he should come to her. While her brother and Ambassador Wellington Koo were appalled by this insistence of protocol over national security, the meeting never occurred. Madame Chiang's dismissal of Anna May was in the same spirit. Madame Chiang was of Chinese nobility, and to expect her to share a podium with a laundryman's daughter was beyond imagination. The snub was not resolved. Anna May tried to make the best of it, arguing that the important thing was the cause. The long-term effect of the incident was the injection of elitist Chinese Republican attitudes about Anna May into American thought. Soong Meiling's ill regard of Anna May was later adopted by left-wing scholars in the United States and is largely responsible for the eclipse of her reputation in America. Anna May's fate was overshadowed by the positive effects of Madame Chiang Kai-shek's visit, which did much to improve American attitudes about China. The success of her visit inspired President Franklin D. Roosevelt to push successfully for the abolition of the Chinese Exclusion Act.[68]

Anna May put the best face on things and continued with her career and cause. In August 1943, she starred in *The Willow Tree*, by J. H. Benrimo and Harrison Rhodes, at the Cambridge Summer Theater in Cambridge, Massachusetts. Anna May reported to Fania Marinoff that the critics did not like the play at all but were kind about her performance. After the run of the play, she traveled to New York, staying at the Hotel Elysée and spending happy times with the Van Vechtens.[69]

Anna May spent the Christmas holidays touring military bases in Nebraska, where she found the soldiers appreciative. Two of the camps were segregated, and Anna May used her memories of the parties held by the Van Vechtens to entertain Black soldiers with stories about their "well-known favorites."[70] After that experience she visited USO headquarters, hoping for an overseas tour. What she got was Alaska and Canada. Anna May spent part of the summer of 1944 working for the USO camp shows arranged by the Hollywood Victory Committee and touring American bases from Edmonton, Canada, almost to the Arctic Circle. She sounded fervently patriotic when she stated that "many of the boys I met fought the Japs in the Aleutians" and were very anxious to fight them again. She boasted that all of them think of the Japanese only "in terms of extermination." By late May she was in Minneapolis, where she disrupted the mess hall by pulling out a pair of chopsticks.[71]

Anna May was agitating for a tour abroad. She lobbied her friends in England to help get her a role. After Anna May wrote him a charming note, Eric Jones in London's *Theatre World* recommended that someone in the West End theaters create a stage vehicle for her. He suggested a revival of *Turandot*. Jones argued that such a production would be a success because she "inevitably casts her spell by merely slipping out of the wings on to the stage, whether to sing, dance, or speak." He recalled one pleasurable evening when she appeared at a London cocktail party with a cornflower blooming at each earlobe. He contended that her presence in London would help lift the sadness of five years of war.[72]

In September 1944, in the aftermath of D-Day, Anna May was a regular at the Stork Club in New York. Her presence there seems to have raised few eyebrows. Only a few years later, Josephine Baker would have to sue owner Sherman Billingsley after the staff refused her service. Billingsley's famous racial intolerance toward African Americans apparently did not extend to America's most illustrious Chinese American actress.[73]

The close of the war found Anna May with time on her hands. No movie roles surfaced, and with cutbacks in national transport, theatrical parts were scarce. She started to sell the house on San Vicente but did not like the potential buyers. Then a windstorm blew down the *For Sale* sign, which she took as an omen. She encouraged her agent to get her a role someplace. She went with a friend to watch the Peace Conference parley in San Francisco. She had hoped to go to

New York to greet Richard and take part in a benefit sponsored by Van Vechten, but could not because of "transportation difficulties." Finally, in October, she took a train by the southern route to New York, writing the Van Vechtens that her progress was so slow that she expected to have a southern accent when she arrived.[74] Anna May could look back on her war efforts with pride. She had worked hard and long to aid China and to defeat Japan. At the same time, her toil did not bring her closer to the Chinese American community. She had tried to build bridges, but the snub during Madame Chiang Kai-shek's trip hurt. At the same time, the wartime experiences of most Chinese American women were distinctly different from hers. They worked in factories, served in the military, and formed lives outside of the home. They were able to create a gender solidarity based upon mutual experiences. For most, it was doubtless hard to relate to Anna May's travels and highly publicized events. Ordinary women established a working-class solidarity, while Anna May's allure was based on Hollywood and its transient loyalties.[75] Anna May had to wonder if her era had passed.

Seven

Becoming Chinese American

Anna May's enforced leisure continued in the postwar years. Los Angeles offered gatherings with her old friends and some vague promises of work at start-up studios, but she missed traveling and especially longed to be in New York City. She jumped at the chance for an arduous tour in the fall of 1947, which would take her through smaller cities in the northeast. When she got to New York City, she lectured on Chinese beauty customs for Lentheric's Shanghai Perfume at the Plaza Hotel and at Stern's Department Store. During the trip she took time for relaxation on board cartoonist Robert Ripley's Chinese yacht on the Long Island Sound. Ripley had the excursion filmed. The footage shows Anna May surrounded by younger women, all emulating her classic looks and dress.[1] After the New York show Anna May went on a thirty-city tour to give her lectures on Chinese health and beauty, events that established her notoriety as an authority on Chinese female beauty. Publicity for the tour included a lavish program with linen pages. Surviving notes of the lectures tell of her emphasis on home remedies. She told her audiences, for example, that the best methods for protecting a woman's hair were to dress it once a week and to sleep on leather pillows so as "not to disarrange the coiffure." Hair should be combed rather than brushed. Washing should be done with care because it removes the natural oils; "instead it is rinsed with vegetable oil." Sections of the hair should be tied close to the scalp with strands of silk. Plenty of lacquer imparted luster. Flowers and jewels adorned a woman's hair. Opium packs help keep the skin's texture. Anna May recommended the use of nail guards "either of precious metals for those who could afford them or of bamboo. A woman should keep a box of mirrors and vanity boxes filled with cosmetics, brushes, and perfumes." Sandalwood adds flavor to the entire ensemble. Anna May recommended keeping goldfish because watching them exercises the eyes.

The following summer she again hit the road, working in the Pocono mountain resorts. While she could enjoy these fleeting moments of renewed fame, greater consolation came from her brother Richard's climb through college at USC and then UCLA. She wrote to the Van Vechtens with pride about his efforts in geometry and engineering but noted his real ambitions lay in photography. Could the Van Vechtens help get him a job in New York? It seemed nothing was forthcoming, and certainly Anna May needed his presence in the lonely house.[2]

Moongate needed her attention. As any homeowner knows, a house has its ups and downs. A fire, which started in the fireplace in her bedroom study, spread to other rooms and caused substantial damage. In the yard, she had to have thirty old trees removed to keep peace with the neighbors. At one point she nearly sold the place, but hard social realities forced her to reconsider. Hedda Hopper, the gossip columnist and one of the most feared people in Hollywood, agreed upon a price with Anna May and put up the escrow money. Anna May then set out to find a new home, only to learn that racial restrictive covenants applied to all Chinese, even the famous and beautiful. Faced with a sale but without a new home, she sent Hopper a telegram begging her to cancel the deal, which Hopper, a friend, was willing to do. As her film work dried up, the extra apartment at 246 San Vicente Boulevard became a useful cash source from short- and long-term renters. Generally Anna May stayed aloof from her tenants, but occasionally she befriended them. Conrad Doerr, a student at Santa Monica City College, rented a room above the garage for forty dollars per month. The apartment, originally planned as a home for her brothers, was roomy and comfortable. Planning to stay only a short while, Doerr remained there for eight years. After a few months, Anna May became friendly.

She invited Doerr into the main house. He noted that the interior was largely Western in style with little ostentation. Inside the door was a private apartment for Richard, whom Doerr found difficult to know. Anna May was easier. She enlisted Doerr as a driver after Richard refused the position. On such occasions, Doerr and Anna May visited Edith Head, or drove to Santa Monica to see Anthony Quinn's performance in a touring version of *A Streetcar Named Desire*. They would go out on evening crawls to local theaters or just shop for groceries.

One other night, at a recital of *Turnadot*, she mounted the stage at intermission and sang a Puccini song. Doerr noticed that she still caused a sensation whenever she appeared in public. Plus, she was an excellent cook who often invited him over to share a meal. Anna May bought the ingredients in Chinatown, and Doerr learned not to ask about each dish's components.[3]

Friends became more important than ever. As always, Anna May reported her comings and goings to the Van Vechtens. Many of the names are forgotten now but were illustrious literary and Hollywood people in their day. She entertained frequently at her home, dressed in striking Chinese outfits. Doerr recalled that for formal evenings, Anna May took elaborate care with her appearance. Regular guests included the See family members; James Wong Howe and his wife, Sanora Babb Howe; Dorothy Jeakins, the Oscar-winning costume designer; and Katherine DeMille, the adopted daughter of Cecil and wife of Anthony Quinn, friends of more than a decade. On one such occasion, James Wong Howe screened his short film about his time in China after World War II, reviving Anna May's memories about her fateful trip a decade earlier. Lin Yutang and his wife stopped by whenever they were in town, as did the writer Ivy Wilson. Norman Foster, director of the Charlie Chan, Mr. Moto, and Davy Crockett films, lived nearby and was reported to be a lover of Anna May's. Another frequent guest was photographer Nikolas Muray, whom she had known since the late 1930s in New York. One of her famed neighbors, the painter Nicolai Fechin, did a portrait of her. Anna May knew her limits. She was offered a chance to join a new nightclub in Malibu sponsored by Joan Crawford, but declined because memberships cost $1,100 annually. She preferred casual moments, sitting around with the boys from the Dragon's Den, smoking, drinking, and playing poker. On these occasions and other casual times, Anna May, dressed in black slacks and sweater, her hair just as dark as in *The Thief of Bagdad*, a distant two decades before, would mutter, "You know, fifty million Chinamen can't be Wong." Everyone would laugh at her corny humor. Her jokes were the Chinese equivalent of ironic, self-deprecating, African American blues tales. Most of the time, she seems just to have enjoyed home life with Richard. In one sweet instance, she told Van Vechten on the back of a postcard that Richard and she were starting a fashion shoot at home when Duke the dog intervened and sent master and mistress sprawling on the floor. So the trio sent the Van Vechtens a card with their everlasting love, along with a tie enclosed in an envelope.[4]

But the road still beckoned. Sometimes these trips presented hardship. She accompanied Ray See, of the famous family, on a trip across country to a Chicago convention to help push his Chinese furniture. The work was tough, standing on high heels all day and shaking hands. See later claimed that Anna May wanted to make love to him and get him to divorce his wife and marry her. By the end of the exhibit, they were sick of each other. After one such occasion, Anna May collapsed on her return to Santa Monica. The years of traveling, heavy food, alcohol, career disappointment, and racism took their toll. In December 1948, she entered Santa Monica Hospital and was diagnosed with Laennec's cirrhosis, a liver ailment generally caused by excessive alcoholic intake. Her doctors considered an operation, but instead sent her home with some stern warnings.[5]

Finally, Hollywood paid her some attention. In 1949, after a five-year absence from the screen, Anna May took a part in a Brian Donlevy film noir entitled *Impact*. In the film, Anna May played Su Lin, a Chinese maid to a wealthy industrialist. While not a large part, Su Lin's role was pivotal to understanding the attempted murder of the industrialist Walter Williams (Donlevy) by his faithless wife Irene (Helen Walker). *Daily Variety* called her return "excellent," and The *Hollywood Reporter* praised Anna May's acting for its "conviction and authority." However limited her role was, Anna May perceived it as a small revival of her career. She talked with Hal Wallis at Paramount Pictures about a major role in the remake of *Shanghai Express*, to be called *Peking Express*. In this version, Anna May is married to the warlord and has two sons, one of whom is a Nationalist and the other a Communist. Though the film, which starred Joseph Cotten, included many Chinese characters, Anna May's role did not make the final cut when *Peking Express* was released in 1951.[6]

Family milestones preoccupied Anna May over the next few years. After a long illness, Wong Sam Sing's brave heart finally failed at the Homestead Lodge in Eagle Rock, California, on October 11, 1949; he was eighty-nine years old. Services were held at the graveside in Rosedale Cemetery and were conducted by Reverend Philip Lee of the Chinese Presbyterian Church. Lulu made all the arrangements and determined that Wong Sam Sing's body would be cremated and the ashes placed in a grave apart from his wife's. Cremation was rarely used by the Chinese at this time but had remained popular from earlier eras in Guangdong Province. Through his interment, Wong Sam Sing sustained his cultural traditions. Attending the services were his two surviving daughters, Lulu and Anna May, and his sons, James, Frank, Roger, and Richard. Anna May was so overcome by grief that she collapsed and spent two days in the Queen of Angels Hospital. Though the battle for China may have prevented the American family from learning of his death, Huang Dounan had predeceased his father, dying on February 29, 1948, in Chang On. He left behind four sons and four daughters.[7]

Two years later, Anna May celebrated happier occasions. Richard graduated from UCLA and Lulu married Howard Kwan, a local businessman, at the end of 1951. Anna May gave her siblings a reception at the Assistant League Tea Room on September 10, 1952. Lulu, according to Anna May, "adhered to the Chinese customs," and so everybody "teased the heck out of her." Now Lulu seemed much happier, and no longer had to look after all the Wongs, and, wrote Anna May to the Van Vechtens, "Thank God, she is out of our hair." Lulu, as the eldest, had taken charge of her siblings. Even though Anna May thought her new husband would preoccupy Lulu in the future, the eldest sister would make all the major family decisions.[8]

The favorable reviews she received for *Impact* did help Anna May make a career change. Television was hiring veteran actors to give it respectability and fill up airtime. Anna May understood that the new format was a degraded version of the movie industry, but she was eager for work. She traveled to New York for several weeks in the summer of 1950. There was talk of a radio and television combination series that never materialized. Then the Dumont Network, which was associated with Paramount Pictures, gave Anna May her own show, a Chinese detective series entitled *The Gallery of Madame Liu Tsong*. Anna May had to live in New York for the fall of 1951 for the filming of the show, an aspect of the work she enjoyed thoroughly. Unfortunately, the film archives of Dumont were tossed away long ago and no scripts survive. The first season of the half-hour show, which debuted on August 27 and ran until November 21, 1951, involved the experiences of Madame Liu Tsong, a beautiful Chinese proprietress of an art gallery, as she ventured forth in search of treasured art objects. The first episode lacked a title. The titles for the nine remaining episodes were "The Golden Women" (9/3), "The Spreading Oak" (9/10), "The Man with a Thousand Eyes"

(9/17), "Burning Sands" (9/24), "Shadow of the Sun God" (10/1), "The Tinder Box" (10/31), "The House of Quiet Dignity" (11/7), "Boomerang" (11/14), and "The Face of Evil" (11/21). There was talk of a second series for the spring of 1952. This new series would include features of *Fu Manchu* and *Daughter of the Dragon*. No prints of the first or second series survive. Given subsequent events in her life, it is unlikely the spring 1952 schedule ever happened. In any event, Dumont canceled the series.[9]

Personal issues emerged. After returning from New York, where she had filmed the television show, Anna May began to go through menopause, uncertain each day how she was going to feel physically and emotionally. Doerr observed that she was often tipsy during the day, frequently buying bottles of vodka. Sometimes they spent hours drinking and talking about the past. Doerr recalled that Anna May was proud of her career but lamented the bad roles Hollywood had imposed upon her. MGM's rejection of her for *The Good Earth* still rankled. Of all her films, she seemed fondest of *Java Head*, a fairly minor effort, but the sole movie in which she kissed her leading man on screen.

Doerr recalled that Anna May was never satisfied unless she had a part. Nothing else would suffice. Bennett Cerf, an old friend for years and now a major editor at Random House, constantly sent her books that she promptly devoured. He proposed that she write her autobiography, but nothing came of it. She could distract herself with Richard's job at Douglas aircraft in Santa Monica and his dreams of opening a gift shop. Richard maintained his work in photography and started a side business making coolie coats with silkscreen butterfly designs. But she enjoyed playing the mama. Inside, she suffered and longed to travel to New York City, visit the Van Vechtens, and do some work. There were plans afloat to do plays in Germany or a picture in England, but nothing was certain. Hollywood was busily converting many of its studios to television production and Anna May worried that the "film business . . . is rapidly vanishing." Richard and she "broke down" and bought a small television set; she found that watching it could "become a disease and encourages laziness."[10]

Suddenly, Anna May's health broke. She suffered a stroke and an internal hemorrhage in early December 1953. Richard blamed the breakdown on a number of factors including a bad liver, self-isolation, menopause, and financial worries stemming from unemployment, all of which culminated in disregard of life and friends. Anna May's cheery, brave demeanor had hidden terrible suffering. Again, her physicians blamed Laennec's cirrhosis. The disease is irreversible, creating tough scar tissue on the liver, inhibiting removal of waste from the bloodstream, and causing hypertension of the body's ports. The doctor at Santa Monica Hospital pumped eight pints of blood into her to tide her over and sternly warned her "he wasn't going to dig me out of the grave again." After her hospital stay, Anna May transferred to the Sierra Madre Lodge in Pasadena for two months' convalescence. The lodge was a small, pleasant place where she was placed under doctor's orders to "eat like a pig, as that it is exactly what I am doing." Her brave humor helped her get through this cruel patch of life. Richard asked the Van Vechtens to help Anna May get some work back east, believing that "that will be the best medicine." The hospital and nursing home expenses were high, so Anna May placed some jewelry on consignment locally and asked the Van Vechtens to help sell it in New York. By February she felt well enough to spend time in Palm Springs and later to visit Paramount Studios. Nothing was cooking there, but Anna May did have lunch with Cecil B. DeMille, Adolph Zukor, and other executives. Even though there was little work for her, their kind reception was testament to her sterling reputation in Hollywood. To help her mood, she read Dale Carnegie's book, *The Power of Positive Thinking.*[11]

The next year, Anna May worked on her house, complained about carpenter's fees, and tried to lose ten pounds "so I can get into some of my evening clothes." She spent ten days in New York, then returned to Los Angeles to oversee the sale of one hundred square feet of property on San Vicente to pay for her medical costs and maintain herself and Richard. The apartments were getting too expensive; tax assessments had jumped to $18,800 by 1954 and seemed ready to go higher. She related to Fania Marinoff how it broke her heart to see the beautiful old trees torn up; she felt that "every time a breeze comes up, a tired palm frond waves reproachfully." Guiltily, she thought of wearing blinders when she went into the garden so that she would not see the majestic trees lying on their sides. She wondered if her own time on San Vicente was nearly finished. Richard continued to work on the apartments, which brought in more than enough to pay for taxes and upkeep on the home. Anna May's guilt feelings were exacerbated by the noise of the construction as developers put up eighteen units of housing on her old land; she had to ask the workmen to move their privy away from her house. Others joined in her nostalgia for better days. She ran into Jesse and Bessie Lasky of Paramount at a museum; Jessie told her: "We made pictures in happier days."[12]

By August 1955, Anna May felt well enough for travel and planned a trip to England and the Continent. Her idea was to first go to London, then Paris, and possibly Munich, where "they are making quite a few good films in English and German." By early September she was in London for the first time in eighteen years. Although she told reporters that the trip was just for pleasure, she brought an extensive Chinese wardrobe with her and asked so many questions about the English studios and the current film scene that many were convinced that she would sign up quickly for any decent production. Strange events ensued. Someone named Anna May took a small part as Peach Blossom in MacLean Rogers's farce, *Just Joe*. Rogers, best known for his direction of *The Goon Show* with Spike Mulligan and Peter Sellers, was a master of low-budget comedies and pulp-novel melodramas. In this film, Joe, played by Leslie Randall, works at a detergent factory and is generally ignored by his bosses. When a case of industrial espionage occurs, Joe proves heroic. Another notable in the film was Jon Pertwee, later known as the third Doctor Who in the British science fiction television show. Rogers put out several programs like this each year and waited until 1958 to issue it in England and until 1960 to a distributor in the US ATV, an English television network, offered Anna May a small role in a series entitled *The Voodoo Factor* about a hard-driven scientist named David Whitaker who found himself battling for the survival of the world against a disease spreading from a tropical island caused by a legendary 2,000-year-old spider-goddess. *The Voodoo Factor* was a six-part series starring Maxine Audley and Maurice Kaufman. Anna May had a role in one episode of this science fiction classic. She played a Malayan girl, not the ancient goddess. Her part may have been in a pilot for the series, which did not appear in England until the end of 1959.

However bizarre her roles were, London was a tonic for Anna May. She stayed at the Westbury Hotel near Berkeley Square, enjoyed wonderful weather, and had lunch with Somerset Maugham at the Dorchester. After reviewing her budget she decided to forego Paris and Munich and returned to America on October 12. Her return flight was exhausting, but Richard presented her with a pleasant surprise upon arrival by painting her apartment. At the door were real estate agents eager to grab the rest of her property, one of the last desirable corner lots left. Her old investments had left her with a trump card or two. Before she could contend with them her medical problems flared up and she spent two days in the Santa Monica Hospital.[13]

Finally, Anna May could no longer resist the entreaties of the real estate agents. In the spring of 1956, she sold her home on San Vicente Boulevard and moved into an apartment at 308 Twenty-first Place in Santa Monica. As she described the sale to Fania Marinoff, she dismissed most of the proposals straight off, and then the right person came along and bought the place over a weekend. The new owner allowed Anna May to take many of her rare plants to her next home. She quickly ordered new personal stationery with her characteristic HUANG LIU TSONG in block characters at the top. Richard handled most of the transfer of eighteen years of living, wallpapered the apartment, and tried to teach his sister how to use the fancy new appliances. Friends helped out by inviting them over for dinner; during idle moments sister and brother went to the movies to see *The King and I* and *Picnic*. The sale of the San Vicente home closed an important era in Anna May's life, but notable about the episode is that many years after her heyday and several years after a severe illness, she had a devoted brother and many friends to care for her. Even though Anna May had never married or had children, there remains a powerful sense that she was deeply loved by those close to her. The Van Vechtens were doubtless the most attentive. Her birthday never went unnoticed; appearances on television always received praise and support. The New York couple sent her copies of books or news clippings that mentioned her. Carl and Fania celebrated holidays by sending her flowers and cards. They were not the only ones. Her friends were often members of old Hollywood, and the names of DeMille, Lasky, Knopf, and Vidor are sprinkled through her correspondence with the Van Vechtens. In turn, Anna May sent out Easter, Christmas, and Chinese New Year cards as well as quick postcards from the road. Her warmth, cheer, and courage inspired many to reach out to her as she moved into the later stages of her life. They also made her someone delightful to have at a dinner party or to visit unannounced. Unlike many former stars, who fell into self-destruction or isolation, Anna May possessed those qualities Walter Benjamin had observed in Berlin more than a quarter century before. They were helping her pull through some hard times. There is something admirable, too, in her financial wisdom. She was not wealthy, but she was not needy, either. She had lived and planned well.[14]

The trip to London and the visit to Somerset Maugham paid off when director William Wyler hired her for his NBC Producer's Showcase version of Maugham's *The Letter* in 1956. Wyler had directed an earlier version in 1939 and had considered Anna May for the same part. In his autobiography, he noted that he did not use her in the first version because she "was kind of a sex kitten and too young." Now she had a featured role. Anna May adapted her part to give herself more dignity and power. At the conclusion of the story, Anna May, whose character is the "other woman," requires that the European American woman who wants a letter implicating her husband, kneel in front of her and beg for it. While she does, Anna May stands impassively above her, in a method not prescribed in the original version.[15]

Anna May continued to take small parts. She appeared in two episodes of *The Climax Series* on CBS; the first was entitled "The Chinese Game" and appeared on November 22, 1956. Costarring with Anna May were MacDonald Carey, Rita Moreno, and Constance Ford. The show received good reviews; the *Los Angeles Herald Express* called it the best dramatic show in two years. Such praise gave Anna May renewed confidence; she told Fania Marinoff that she was now going to take a relaxed attitude toward life and consign tension to the past.[16] Her next television show did not require any acting. A series called *Bold Journey*, which screened on ABC, decided to use footage from her 1936 home movie of her China trip. Anna May was invited to New York again to introduce and narrate the film, which was now entitled *Native Land*. Anna May told the Van Vechtens that *Bold Journey* was using her movie to kick off its new season. By now, she was getting used to transcontinental flights, even as she complained of how tiring they were. To her delight, Richard, who had just had his gallbladder removed, greeted her at the door with her prized cat, Smoky.[17]

Richard's hard work and devotion to his sister helped her climb back to life. He had painted the entire apartment and developed a "most interesting garden in our new wee home." Anna May rewarded her brother's devotion by helping him open a small gift shop, first at Brentwood Market and then his own store. Local newspapers printed photos of the "beautiful actress Anna May Wong coming into Kim Wong's Oriental Novel Décor shop" and bargaining for "a brass lotus lamp." Anna May helped her brother in the shop, doubtless helping make it a bigger attraction. Richard gained some private commissions to photograph and design home interiors. While he was out, Anna May "minded the store." Now she had the small job she had described in her article for her French fans in 1929. If any of her old audience were to come, they "might well see me running around the shop with a Chinese feather duster." Another improvement in her life came when she "broke down" and bought a new 1957 gray and red Oldsmobile, so that she and Richard could drive around and enjoy California sunshine.[18] Richard's willingness to chauffeur his older sister was an improvement on his earlier refusal to perform such a duty.

Anna May's renewed health made her more attractive to the television studios. There was talk of a running part in a twenty-six-week series, but nothing finally materialized. On May 1, 1958, she had another small role in a Climax production entitled *Deadly Tattoo*. Anna May delighted in rushing around the television studio and going to Los Angeles tattoo shops, "as I know I am going to have one made and between us we know nothing about the procedure." Always the professional, she worked with a voice coach to help her deliver her lines in "pidgin English." Anna May had to wear an eyepatch as well, which greatly amused her. She was featured in a fun advertisement in *Holiday Magazine* with Stan Freberg for Qantas Airlines. In October 1959 she was hired "to pep up" a new series, entitled *Adventures in Paradise*, starring newcomer Gardner McKay. Also starring in the first episode, called "The Lady from South Chicago," were Paulette Goddard, Suzanne Pleshette, and Simon Oakland. The show aired on November 2, 1959. Anna May enacted the role of Lu Yang, an international moneychanger. Despite the minor part in only one scene, Anna May seemed to be enjoying herself, perhaps because she was not playing a housekeeper or forced into a doomed part, casting decisions Hollywood usually chose for her. She did a second guest star stint a month later in an episode entitled "Mission to Manila," which also featured Julie London. These shows were not glamorous, but they did keep her name and face alive for the public.[19]

Next, the *Wyatt Earp Show* hired her for "China Mary" on March 15, 1960. The "China Mary" episode of the *Wyatt Earp Show* gave Anna May ample exposure and a good, challenging role. Set in Tombstone, a mining town with large Anglo-American and Chinese-American populations (a combination that the narrator assured viewers created conflict), the story's plot featured Anna May as the leader of the Chinese community as well as its illegal operations, most notably gambling. Because he suspects that some Chinese were attacking white drunks staggering through the streets late at night, Earp (Hugh O'Brien) goes to China Mary's headquarters, where "no white men were allowed." Television watchers could glimpse Anna May's past beauty in profile shots, but full face views revealed the ravages of disease. China Mary insists that she will investigate the sheriff's concerns and handle the matter herself, thereby maintaining the separation of the races. While Earp listens respectfully to her and leaves, another beating results in the arrest of a young Chinese man, named Li Kung. China Mary then goes to the jail and asks for his release, arguing that she will mete out the punishment. Back at the gambling den, the young man and China Mary argue fiercely. He contends that she is a disgrace to her people and that he and his gang are avenging the past crimes of the whites. Soon viewers can recognize that China Mary is the mother of the rebellious youth. She reluctantly frees him. Determined to solve the muggings, Earp disguises himself as a drunk. Just as Li Kung attacks Earp, his mother steps out of the shadows and shoots him. Earp later returns to her, bringing a ring found on Li Kung's finger. Earp walks into her room as China Mary is singing a sad lament before a Buddha. Earp acknowledges that as a white man, he will never fully understand the dynamics of the crime, but asks her to make sure Li Kung's mother gets the ring. She accepts the ring sadly and promises to do so. Despite her frail figure, Anna May's acting is strong and vibrant. The plot, with its references to second-generation gang conflicts, is fascinating and tragic. The subplot includes her character's relationship with the child Anna May never had.[20]

Next Anna May was the featured guest for the *Mike Hammer* detective series in an episode called "So That's Who It Was." The show starred Darren McGavin and, on this occasion including Keye Luke in the cast, was a noirish crime series. Anna May's episode, in which she played Madame Chu, is located in the Los Angeles Chinatown. The cinematography features nighttime street scenes and the interiors of *fan-tan* casinos, disguised as community clubs. Hammer is investigating the murders of Lee Chu, the husband of Anna May's character, and a small-time hood named Joey. After some snooping around, Hammer visits Madame Chu in her home, which features a lovely collection of Chinese antiques. Anna

May's acting is presentable if a little wooden, made more evident by the heaviness of her lower lip, still askew from her near-fatal stroke two years before. In the plot, Madame Chu hires Hammer to find her husband's killer. His prowling takes him to the *fan-tan* club, where Sam Wong (Luke) presides. The show, which so far has maintained some dignity, now descends into oafish racism. Hammer has to fight some burly "yellow face" guards to get inside. He pushes one of them over the fire escape, snarling "Happy landings!" At the *fan-tan* game, the Chinese players speak gibberish disguised as Mandarin. Hammer is openly contemptuous of them. As he leaves, Hammer tells Sam Wong to stop clowning. He asks Wong which college he graduated from: Cornell or Columbia? Wong grins and replies, "the University of California at Berkeley." The exchange reflects brutal sarcasm about the inability of Chinese American college graduates to get real jobs.

A brief visit to the police gives Hammer all the information he needs. While Lee Chu's murderer used a knife, Joey was killed with a 22-gauge pistol. Hammer returns to Madame Chu and easily extracts her confession that she had killed Joey after he murdered her husband. Hammer takes Madame Chu to the police, assuring her that they will be understanding about her need to avenge her husband's death. As they leave her home, she points out the symbols of yin and yang to Hammer, explaining their meaning as life and death. Though her part was dignified, Anna May could not have been too happy with this return to the themes of the 1920s. Chinatown as a locale for murder, her own character as a doomed woman, and the crude racism of Hammer's character must have seemed like bad dreams. Unsurprisingly, she did not alert the Van Vechtens to watch the show, as she often did with better productions.[21]

Anna May was organizing her spiritual life. Raised in a combination of Presbyterian and neo-Confucian faiths, she had embraced the Christian Science theology as an adult. Perhaps her breakdown in 1953 convinced her that the teachings of Mary Baker Eddy were insufficient. Now Anna May started classes at the Unity School of Christianity, where a number of her female friends were also members. She reported to the Van Vechtens that Dr. Sue Sikking, the pastor of Unity Church, led the classes, which gave Anna May "a happy and joyful outlook on life. I look forward to it every day." Anna May credited the church with pulling her through a medical crisis. In early 1960 she tried to pick up a stray cat that had wandered into her yard. The cat scratched her across the face, closing her right eye, making her forehead swell, and giving her a high fever. Anna May took medicine from a doctor but credited the healing class at Unity Church for her cure, calling its work miraculous. She included her New York friends in her prayers. Anna May gained spiritual contentment from literature as well. Fania Marinoff sent her a copy of Lin Yutang's new book, *The Importance of Understanding*, which Anna May loved. She described it as "practically a Chinese dictionary" (though Lin had produced a real dictionary three decades earlier) and found its message so important in "times of stress and strain caused by the misunderstanding of other nations."[22]

Emboldened by her successes on television, Anna May announced a comeback in June 1960. Her movie career seemed to be reviving as old friends helped get her parts. First, she had a small part in *Portrait in Black*, starring Lana Turner and Anthony Quinn, Anna May's friend since the 1930s. The film was billed as her return to the screen after seventeen years (conveniently overlooking *Impact* in 1949); Anna May had to play another maid's role that *Variety* contended was a "thankless vehicle" for her comeback. The film was released that June, so Universal Studios asked her to fly to New York for interviews and personal appearances. It was a big step up from television, and Anna May clearly relished the opportunity to be in New York and spend time with the Van Vechtens and other friends. From New York, the film tour took her to Boston, Washington, Baltimore, Cleveland, Detroit, and Chicago, where the world premiere was celebrated. She got back to Santa Monica in early July, exhausted but happy. Even better, Ross Hunter, the producer of *Portrait in Black*, purchased the rights to *Flower Drum Song* and asked her to play the aunt, one of the lead roles, when production began in February 1961. The fact that Hunter, one of Hollywood's premier commercial directors, considered Anna May strong enough for a rigorous role with several spectacular song and dance numbers indicates that he felt she was ready for a big comeback. Hunter befriended Anna May and made sure that she was invited to premieres where fans could see she was on the comeback trail.[23]

Anthony Quinn and his wife, Katherine, then announced that Anna May had a role in his new film, *The Savage Innocents*, directed by Nicholas Ray. Likely, the actress was again Marie Yang, who in England had played minor roles as Anna

May. The real Anna May was fortunate she was not involved, as the deception could not hide the film's major flaws. If she ever saw it, Anna May would have felt she was back in the early 1920s. The only redeeming factor was the extraordinarily beautiful cinematography.[24]

Anna May returned from Alaska in the autumn of 1960 intent on securing more roles and helping Richard with the shop. In addition to *Flower Drum Song*, there were rumors that she might get a part in *The World of Suzie Wong*, another major production. Anna May told the Van Vechtens that things were fine except that Christmastime was marred by "some kind of a virus," which kept her mostly in bed. By January, however, she reported to friends that she was feeling better and making plans for Chinese New Year and the possible new movies. She announced that her part in *The Barbara Stanwyck Theater* would air on NBC on January 30, 1961, and an episode of *Danger Man*, entitled "The Journey Ends Halfway," would appear on May 24. Other work seemed to be in the offing.[25]

In fact, Anna May was struggling for her life. The virus was actually a return of her liver disease, which required weekly injections from her physician, Dr. Robert F. Steele. He had to check her daily. Those she encountered noticed the strain. Ross Hunter reluctantly had to replace her with Juanita Hall in *Flower Drum Song*. Her old tenant, Conrad Doerr, ran into her at a bank early in the New Year and thought that she looked ill.[26] Still, her letters to the Van Vechtens remained cheery and optimistic about the future. Suddenly, on February 3, while taking an afternoon nap at home, Anna May died of a heart attack at 3:00 PM. Richard found her and called Dr. Steele, who rushed over and pronounced her dead at the age of fifty-six. Her passing was reported in many newspapers across the country and in England, with her age erroneously stated as fifty-four.[27]

In her will, Anna May bequeathed furs, jewelry, and some cash to her sister Lulu. The bulk of her estate, which included the apartment and about $80,000 in cash, went to Richard. Anna May specifically left out James, Frank, and Roger, saying that she had already provided enough for them during her lifetime. Had he lived, Wong Sam Sing would also have been denied a share. These exclusions are curious. Richard, to be sure, had lived with Anna May for over twenty years. Still, had he contributed that much more to her welfare than her other brothers? James, Frank, and Roger had not received that much of Anna's largesse; Richard had gained enormously from her generosity. Her death from a disease stemming from alcoholism had to cause anguish within her family, and undoubtedly there were deep tensions among them. Her estate was sizable, and a tribute to Anna May's careful management of her property and expenses. Considering that she had not had a major studio paycheck in over two decades, she had prospered. Despite the many prejudices that had limited her career, Anna May had a twilight far pleasanter than those of many of her contemporaries, some of whom died broke or dependent.[28]

Services were held on February 8 at the Unity in the Sea Church in Santa Monica, with the Reverend Sikking officiating. Years before, in her tour of the United States promoting Chinese beauty customs, Anna May described the funeral of a significant figure. Traditionally, Anna May's remains would be accompanied to the cemetery by hired mourners "with burning incense to purify the air." Paper money was burned en route. Refreshments were given to mourners along the road. One hopes that her family observed such customs. In a sign that she followed Taishanese custom, in her will Anna May asked to be cremated. Following these instructions, Lulu had Anna May's body interred at the Chapel of the Pacific at Woodlawn Cemetery. Her ashes were then placed near her mother's coffin in Rosedale Cemetery. The headstone names her mother with Anna May's on the side only in Chinese characters and no date or epitaph. Buried nearby, ironically, are Marshall Neiland and Tod Browning, two men who contributed much to her suffering.[29]

Epilogue

After Anna May's passing, Richard took a month off from the shop. Among the first contacts he made were with the Van Vechtens, whom he thanked for their kindness in a letter on April 14. Richard said that he was tired of inactivity and was ready to get back to work. He consoled them by saying that both Anna May and he believed in eternal life and that "we will all meet again and have a real happy reunion." Sometime later that year, Richard closed the shop and took a job at the nearby Veterans' Administration building. The new job was regular, had little stress, and paid better than selling Oriental knickknacks. He kept in touch with the faithful Van Vechtens over the next few years. In 1964, he told them happily that he had gotten married and that his wife Carol was expecting a child, which was to be the first grandchild of Wong Sam Sing and Lee Gon Toy. There were no others.

The family of Huang Dounan in China fared far better. Although only three of the daughters are still alive, collectively, there are fourteen granddaughters and seven grandsons, descended from Huang Dounan. The family lasted through the immense political changes in China. A family photo in the 1970s shows four of Huang Dounan's daughters in peasant clothing and sporting "liberation hairstyles," cut sharply just below the ears. By the 1980s, Huang Dounan's daughters began their migration to North America, living in Detroit and Toronto. The gaps of many decades meant that Anna May's memory diminished to a few yellowing pages from movie magazines filled with stories about her 1936 visit. Huang Dounan and his father fared better. Each year, those descendants still living in China gather in Chang On to honor Liangren, as Wong Sam Sing is known in the village, and Huang Dounan.[1]

Over the next decades, Anna May's other siblings passed away. James, who had been teaching for many years at St. John's University in Los Angeles, succumbed to a heart attack on April 10, 1971. By Lulu's orders, he was cremated and the ashes placed near his father's in Rosedale Cemetery. Roger, who was retired from his job as a warehouseman at McDonnell Douglas Aerospace, died on December 26, 1993, at the age of eighty-eight. He was not buried with the family but in the Forest Lawn Memorial Park in Hollywood Hills. Lulu died on October 31, 1995, two months shy of her ninety-third birthday. Richard died on December 14, 2007, at the age of 85. Her family's general longevity is testament to the hard life Anna May suffered chasing her Hollywood dreams.[2]

Anna May's legacy extends far beyond her immediate family. She is recognized as the great Asian American star of early cinema and pointed the way for later actors and actresses. As Helen Zia points out, Anna May's typecast roles evolved easily into the Suzie Wong–prostitute characters of later decades. But Anna May's death came during a brief golden era for Asian-themed films in the United States. *The World of Suzie Wong,* starring Nancy Kwan and William Holden, explored mixed-race love with greater openness and sensitivity than in any of Anna May's movies. Ross Hunter's 1961 production of *Flower Drum Song* had an actual Asian cast in an American setting. Handling issues of acculturation and gender stereotypes with subtlety and intelligence, Hunter's production, for which Anna May had originally been cast, was the kind of film she had longed for during her career. Instead, Nancy Kwan stepped forth in the high-powered dance number, "I Enjoy Being a Girl" and flourished. After those two sensational films, however, in general, roles for Asians in films remained rare and restrictive. In 1967, Tsai Chin played a Chinese sex nymph opposite Sean Connery in the James Bond epic, *You Only Live Twice.* Other Chinese American actors, including Beulah Quo, Chao Li-Chi, James Hong, and Lisa Lu, gained brief stardom in secondary roles, but were never able to crack Hollywood's casting limitations.

More often than not, Chinese and other Asian actors watched as "yellow faces" took roles from them even into the 1990s. Nancy Kwan herself found that only through travel to Europe and to Hong Kong could she break out of ethnic typecasting. Following a decade outside of the United States, she returned to Hollywood to learn that her star role as Suzie Wong had garnered more resentment than acclaim. Kwan remains more optimistic than other Asian actors, many of whom contend that their access to roles is rigidly bounded by race and ethnicity. Their limitations are not so narrow as those Anna May faced in her career, but the bitterness about stereotypes that she expressed continues to the present day.[3]

Anna May's memory lies primarily in her films. Her posthumous career fared little better than those of other Asians in film and television. The presence of Marlene Dietrich in *Shanghai Express* sustained interest in that film, but few of Anna May's other movies received much critical attention for decades: in the United States, Anna May might be seen occasionally on late-night television; in Europe, especially in England, her movies were feature attractions at film festivals; but in China, unsurprisingly, she has fallen nearly into complete oblivion.

Her memory in the Asian American community is mixed. Embarrassed by her roles and recollections of her wild years, she became a "No-Name Woman." Writers would occasionally identify her—negatively—as a Dragon Lady or Butterfly but did not move beyond the castigations of her career used by Nationalists in the 1930s. Gradually, there came recognition that Anna May's reputation had to be more than "cheesecake sexiness to exotic assimilation to droll camp." Still, despite the interest in her career, few writers have done much with Anna May's legacy. There has been a smattering of poems, plays, and critical pieces, but no sustained efforts.[4]

There have been occasional bright spots. In 1973, the Asian Fashion Designers named their annual award after her, citing her influence on fashion throughout her career. In that small way, her name stayed alive. Dresses, cosmetics, and dolls were produced in Anna May's honor.[5]

Her memory stayed strong in less tangible ways. One culture that understood the feelings of marginality kept her name alive. Gay people revered her memory and her film career and often claimed her as their own. Often they took from her what they needed for their own creations. Early in his career, Andy Warhol paid tribute to Anna May, among many other celebrities, designing a camp collage of "crazy golden slippers" in a gesture of admiration for her. Warhol's accolade for Anna May differed markedly from his other shoe drawings, which tended to be light and fanciful. This particular image is filled with tragedy and brutality. The shoe has an extremely high arch that would force a woman's foot into a curled position, precisely like the bound feet Chinese women endured for many centuries. While Anna May escaped this tragic fate, Hollywood studios "bound" her talent with restrictive, demeaning roles that accentuated a Western, often sadistic eroticizing of Chinese women. The colors of the leg encased by the shoe are an earthy brown streaked with blackened veins, suggesting the pains that Anna May endured in her career. Such colors are rare in Warhol's 1950s work and anticipate his deadly images of tabloid newspapers, execution chambers, and race riots of the 1960s. While it is doubtful that Warhol and Wong ever crossed paths, his unique genius permitted him to make powerful insights into Anna May's career.

Warhol's contemporary and sometime associate, collage and Pop artist Ray Johnson, created an imaginary Anna May Wong Fan Club, fabricated meetings between fantasy enthusiasts, and fashioned lovely pieces of art devoted to Anna May. Johnson, who was awkward with women, wrote once that "Anna May Wong is a hand that clearly says 'Go That Way.'" Years after Anna May's passing, she was a central figure in a Johnson fantasy club called the New York Correspondence School, a somewhat frivolous and ironic denomination for a circle that included artists around the nation. Johnson used mail art as a conceptual medium to entrance others into his network. Once hooked, participants took part in his fantasy Correspondence School. Within this world of subtle connections, Johnson obsessed about such figures as Marcel Duchamp, designer Paloma Picasso, and actresses Shelly Duvall and Anna May. On June 3, 1972, Johnson organized the imaginary Anna May Wong Fan Club, which met in the auditorium of the New York Cultural Center. Naomi Sims, the model and wife of a curator, Michael Finney, played the part of Anna May. Sims, an attractive, highly stylish African American woman, fit into Johnson's eccentric vision of Anna May's beauty. Johnson set these meetings in motion simply with the intention of learning what chance participants could create within his fantasy obsession with celebrity. Serendipitously, Johnson kept Anna May's name alive among a sizable group of influential artists and intellectuals.[6]

Other homosexuals were attracted to Anna May for "camp" reasons. Though not entirely a gay aesthetic, as Susan Sontag memorably pointed out, camp enthusiasm and homosexual aesthetics share a "peculiar affinity and overlap." Sontag wrote a book on camp sensibility. In Sontag's perspective, gays and camp followers viewed Anna May's movies and public persona as style more than substance; marginal, highly artificial, and extravagant; and filled with double meaning and signals. Often her work was seen as "so bad that it's good." In this view, Anna May's sincerity worked against her, because she had a seriousness that failed.[7]

Gay men also perceived Anna May as "too much" in her costumes. Although, as we have seen, her dress often held political and national associations, gay men considered her Peking Theater costumes overdone. As one example, Paul, a character in the hit Broadway musical *A Chorus Line*, recounts his past experiences as a drag dancer in the "Jewel Box Revue," where no one "had any dignity and most of them were ashamed of themselves." During one stint, the troupe appeared at the Apollo Theater on One Hundred Twenty-fifth Street "doing this Oriental number." Paul remembers that "I looked like Anna May Wong. I had these two great big chrysanthemums on either side of my head and a huge head-dress with gold balls hanging all over it." On his way to the stage Paul ran into his parents who had come unexpectedly for the show. His mother looked at Paul and exclaimed "Oh my God!" Anna May's costumes became even more shocking on a man.[8]

Part of this gay sensibility coalesced with another emerging view in the art of Martin Wong, a talented painter whose milieu was the Lower East Side of New York City. Wong combined his gritty urban realism with homoerotic imagery and reverence for Chinese and Chinese American forebears. Wong used archetypical Chinese American images such as the storefronts and signs of laundry shops, restaurants, and street vistas. Immersed in the pop imagery of Andy Warhol, Wong created admiring portraits of Mei Lanfang and Anna May in the late 1980s and early 1990s. In so doing, he reinvigorated serious intellectual interest in Anna May among Asian American intellectuals.[9]

Although they too were interested in the mysteries of her sexuality, emerging practitioners of Asian American history generally did not share such playfulness. For them, Anna May was a dilemma that had to be solved. She could be restricted to contributor status, much like pioneering Asian American figures in medicine, politics, education, sports, and other socially significant fields. One can find in encyclopedias and guides to Asian American history capsule biographies of her alongside other Asian American innovators. But because Anna May's legacy is Janus-faced, with meaning inside and outside of Asian American society, recasting her memory requires more breadth and subtlety than is needed for the worthy men and women who were pathbreakers in other fields.

One playwright who faithfully includes Anna May in his work is David Henry Hwang. His award-winning play *M. Butterfly* uses themes and motifs from Puccini's *Madame Butterfly*, which was also the basis for Anna May's Toll of the Sea. David Cronenberg's film of Hwang's play incorporates a brief glimpse of Anna May. As noted by Cynthia Liu, the character Song, whose name recalls the title of one of Anna May's best films, grasps a fan magazine with the late star on the cover to seize the irony of the elements of tragedy and glamor surrounding Anna May. At that moment, the movie suggests an understanding of how Anna May epitomized the melancholic, feminine star.[10]

Chinese American stars have yet to move from under Anna May's shadow. Joan Chen, who starred in the blockbuster hit *The Last Emperor* in 1987, found herself in the 1990s in roles akin to Anna May's. In the television miniseries "Tai-Pan," she played a China Doll harlot. Lucy Liu, who presently is the biggest Chinese American star, may be typecast as an Asian action hero. Other Asian Americans have found similar artistic inspiration in Anna May's persona and career. Poet John Yau entitled one of his verses "No One Ever Tried to Kiss Anna May Wong." The poem muses over Anna May's loneliness as she traveled around Europe, her dignified aloofness, and the cinematic tortures she endured, all without the happiness of love. Jessica Hagedorn's 1971 poem "The Death of Anna May Wong" identifies Anna May as the birth mother of Asian American screen females. Just as Martin Wong used his aunt to summon up an understanding of Anna May, so Hagedorn sees Anna May's remote glamor in her mother. Recently the play *China Doll*, by Elizabeth Wong, presented vignettes from Anna May's life. As Liu notes, such imaginings help Asian American artists move beyond negative perceptions of Anna May as solely the product of Orientalism.[11] There is evidence that other artists are incorporating Anna May into their work. Artist Mike Kelley used the wishing well in Los Angeles's Chinatown to express his fascination with Anna May. Kelley reworked the famous sculpture, which was partially a gift of Paramount Pictures to Chinatown, to include screen stills of Anna May. Anna May's influence is seeping into fashion design, as well. As this biography has endeavored to tell, as Asian Americans artists coalesce to tell their peoples' story, Anna May's example and spirit will blaze and enlighten the pathways.

Filmography

1. *The Red Lantern* (The Nazimova Productions for Metro Pictures, 1919). Directed by Albert Capellani. Scripted by June Mathis and Albert Capellani. Based on the novel *The Red Lantern: Being the Story of the Goddess of Lantern Light* by Edith Wherry. 7 reels. Cast: Alla Nazimova, Edward J. Connelly, Noah Beery, Frank Currier, Yukio Ao Yamo, Darrell Foss, Mrs. McWade, Virginia Ross, Winter Hall, Amy Van Ness, Harry Mann. AMW uncredited as a lantern bearer.

2. *Outside the Law* (Universal Pictures, 1920). Presented by Carl Laemmle. Directed by Tod Browning. Scenario by Lucien Hubbard and Tod Browning. Photography by William Fildew. 8 reels. Cast: Priscilla Dean, Ralph Lewis, Lon Chaney, Wheeler Oakman, E. A. Warren, Stanley Goethals, Melbourne MacDowell, and Wilton Taylor. AMW as extra.

3. *Dinty* (Associated First National Pictures, 1920). Directed by Marshall Neilan and John McDermott. Scenario by Marion Fairfax. Story by Marshall Neilan. Cinematography by David Kesson, Charles Rocher, and Foster Leonard. 7 reels. Cast: Wesley Barry, Colleen Moore, Tom Gallery, J. Barney Sherry, Marjorie Daw, Noah Beery Sr., Walter Chung, Pat O'Malley, Kate Price, Tom Wilson, Aaron Mitchell, Newton Hall, Young Hipp, and Hal Wilson. AMW as "Chinatown Resident."

4. *A Tale of Two Worlds* (Goldwyn Pictures Corp., 1921). Directed by Frank Lloyd. Scenario by J. E. Nash. Story by Gouveneur Morris. Cinematography by Norbert Brodin. Photographed by Harry Weill, assistant director. Cast: J. Frank Glendon, Leatrice Joy, Wallace Beery, E. A. Warren, Margaret McWade, Togo Yamamoto, Jack Yutake Abbe, Louie Cheung, Chow Young, Etta Lee, Ah Wing, Goro Kino, Arthur Soames, Edythe Chapman, Dwight Crittenden, and Irene Rich. AMW in uncredited role.

5. *The White Mouse* (Selig-Roark, 1921). Directed by Bertram Bracken. Cast: Wallace Beery, Willard Louis, Margaret McWade, Lewis Stone, Ethel Grey Terry, and Bessie Wang. AMW uncredited as Chinese Wife.

6. *The First Born* (Hayakawa Feature Play Co. for Robertson-Cole Distributing Corp., 1921). Directed by Colin Campbell. Scenario by Fred Stowers. Based on the novel

The First Born by Francis Powers. 6 reels. Cast: Sessue Hayakawa, Helen Jerome Eddy, "Sonny Boy" Warde, Goro Kino, Marie Pavis, Wilson Hummel, Frank M. Seki. AMW unbilled as servant.

7. *Bits of Life* (Marshall Neilan Productions for Associated First National Pictures, 1921). Directed by Marshall Neilan. Scenario by Lucita Squire. Additional story by Marshall Neilan. 6 reels. Cast: Wesley Barry, Rockliffe Fellowes, Lon Chaney, Noah Beery Sr., John Bowers, and Anna May Wong. AMW as Toy Sing, wife of Chaney character.

8. *Shame* (Fox Film Corp., 1921). Directed by Emmett J. Flynn. Scenario by Emmett J. Flynn and Bernard McConville. Cinematography by Lucien Androit. Based on the story "Clung" by Max Brand. 9 reels. Cast: John Gilbert, Mickey Moore, Frankie Lee, George Siegmann, William V. Mong, George Nichols, Anna May Wong, Rosemary Theby, Doris Pawn, and "Red" Kirby. AMW as Lotus Blossom.

9. *The Toll of the Sea* (Technicolor Motion Picture Company for Metro Pictures, 1922). Directed by Chester M. Franklin. Script and story by Frances Marion. Camera: J. A. Bell. 5 reels. Cast: Anna May Wong, Kenneth Harlan, Beatrice Bentley, Baby Marion, Etta Lee, and Ming Young. AMW as Lotus Flower, main character.

10. *Drifting* (Universal Pictures, 1923). Directed by Tod Browning. Scenario by Tod Browning and A. P. Younger. Cinematography by William Fildew. Based on the play *Drifting* by John Colton and Daisy Andrews. 7 reels. Cast: Priscilla Dean, Matt Moore, Wallace Beery, J. Farrell MacDonald, Rose Dione, Edna Tichenor, William V. Mong, Anna May Wong, Bruce Guerin, William Moran, Marie de Albert, and Frank Lanning. AMW as Rose Li, daughter of sinister doctor, played by Mong.

11. *Thundering Dawn* (Universal Pictures, 1923). Directed by Harry Garson. Scripted by Lenore Coffee and John Goodrich. Story by John Blackwood. 7 reels. Cast: Winter Hall, Thomas Santschi, J. Warren Kerrigan, Anna Q. Nilsson, Charles Clary, Anna May Wong, Georgia Woodthrope, Richard Kean, Edward Burns, and Winifred Bryson. AMW as "Honky-Tonk girl."

12. *The Thief of Bagdad* (Douglas Fairbanks Pictures for United Artists, 1924). Directed by Raoul Walsh. Cinematography by Arthur Edeson. Scenario by Lotta Woods. Story by Elton Thomas. 14 reels. Cast: Douglas Fairbanks Sr., Snitz Edwards, Charles Belcher, Julanne Johnston, Anna May Wong, Winter-Blossom, Etta Lee, Brandon Hurst, Tote G. Du Crow, Sojin, K. I. Nambu, Sadakichi Hartmann, Noble Johnson, Mathilde Comont, Charles Stevens, and Charles Sylvester. AMW as the Mongol slave girl.

13. *The 40th Door* (Pathé Exchange, 1924). Produced by C. W. Patton. Directed by George B. Seitz. Cinematography by Vernon Walker. Scenario by Frank Leon Smith. Based on the novel *The Fortieth Door* by Mary Hastings Bradley. 6 reels. Cast: Allene Ray, Bruce Gordon, Frank Lackteen, Anna May Wong, Bernard Seigel, Lillian Gale, Eli Stanton, Frank Mann, Scott McGee, and Omar Whitehead. This was a feature version of a serial also released in 1924. AMW as Zira.

14. *The Alaskan* (Famous Players-Lasky for Paramount Pictures, 1924). Directed by Herbert Brenon. Scenario by Willis Goldbeck. Based on the novel *The Alaskan* by James Oliver Curwood. 7 reels. Cast: Thomas Meighan, Estelle Taylor, John Sainpolis (later St. Polis), Frank Campeau, Anna May Wong, Alphonz Ethier, Maurice Cannon, and Charles Ogle. AMW as Keok, an Eskimo.

15. *Peter Pan* (Famous Players-Lasky for Paramount Pictures, 1924). Directed by Herbert Brenon. Scenario by Willis Goldbeck. Based on the novel *Peter Pan, or The Boy Who Wouldn't Grow Up* by James Matthew Barrie. 10 reels. Cast: Betty Bronson, Ernest Torrence, Cyril Chadwick, Virginia Brown Faire, Anna May Wong, Esther Ralston, George Ali, Mary Brian, Philippe De Lacey, and Jack Murphy. AMW as Tiger Lily.

16. *Forty Winks* (Famous Players-Lasky for Paramount Pictures, 1925). Directed by Frank Urson and Paul Iribe. Cinematography by Peverell Marley. Scenario by Bertram Millhauser. Based on the novel *Lord Chumley* by David Belasco and Cecil B. DeMille. 7 reels. Cast: Viola Dana, Raymond Griffith, Theodore Roberts, Cyril Chadwick, Anna May Wong, and William Boyd. AMW as Annabelle Wu, an adventuress.

17. *His Supreme Moment* (Samuel Goldwyn Productions for First National Pictures, 1925). Directed by George Fitzmaurice. Cinematography by Arthur Miller. Scenario by Frances Marion. Based on the story "World Without End" by May Edginton. 8 reels. Cast: Blanche Sweet, Ronald Colman, Kathleen Myers, Belle Bennett, Cyril Chadwick, Ned Sparks, Nick De Ruiz, and Anna May Wong. AMW as Harem Girl.

18. *Fifth Avenue* (Belasco Productions for Producers Distributing Corp., 1926). Produced by A. H. Sebastian. Directed by Robert G. Vignola. Cinematography by James C. Van Trees. Scenario by Anthony Coldeway. Based on the story "Fifth Avenue" by Arthur Stringer. 6 reels. Cast: Marguerite de la Motte, Allan Forrest, Louise Dresser, William V. Mong, Crauford Kent, Lucille Lee Stewart, Anna May Wong, Lillian Langdon, Josephine Norman, Sally Long, and Flora Finch. AMW as Nan Lo, a prostitute.

19. *A Trip to Chinatown* (Fox Film Corp., 1926). Directed by Robert P. Kerr. Cinematography by Barney McGill. Scenario by Beatrice Van. Based on the story by Charles Hoyt. 6 reels. Cast: Margaret Livingston, Earle Foxe, J. Farrell MacDonald, Anna May Wong, Harry Woods, Marie Astaire, Gladys McConnell, Charles Farrell, Hazel Howell, Wilson Benge, and George Kuwa. AMW as Ohtai.

20. *The Silk Bouquet* (a.k.a. *The Dragon Horse*, Fairmont Productions for Hi Mark Films and the China Educational Film Company, 1926). Directed by Harry Revier. Script and story unknown. 8 reels. Cast: Jimmy Leong, Anna May Wong, Fay Kam Chung, Marie Muggley, K. Namian, and Ernie Viebare.

21. *The Desert's Toll* (a.k.a. *The Devil's Toll*, MGM, 1926). Directed by Clifford Smith. Cinematography by Jack Roach. Titles by Gardner Bradford. 6 reels. Cast: Kathleen Key, Chief Big Tree, Anna May Wong, Tom Santschi, Lew Meehan, Francis McDonald, and Guinn "Big Boy" Williams. AMW as Oneta.

22. *Driven from Home* (Chadwick Pictures, 1927). Directed by James Young. Cinematography by Ernest Miller. Scenario by Enid Hibbard and Ethel Hall. Story by Hal Reid. 7 reels. Cast: Ray Hallor, Virginia Lee Corbin, Pauline Garon, Sojin, Anna May Wong, Melbourne MacDowell, Margaret Seddon, Sheldon Lewis, Virginia Pearson, Eric Mayne, and Alfred Fisher. AMW as Cho-San.

23. *Mr. Wu* (MGM, 1927). Directed by William Nigh. Cinematography by John Arnold. Scenario by Lorna Moon. Based on the play *Mr. Wu* by Harry Maurice Vernon and Harold Owen. 8 reels. Cast: Lon Chaney, Louise Dresser, Renée Adorée, Holmes Herbert, Ralph Forbes, Gertrude Olmstead, Mrs. Wong Wing, Anna May Wong, Sonny Loy, and Claude King. AMW as Loo Song.

24. *The Honorable Mr. Buggs* (Pathé/Hal Roach, 1927). Directed by Fred Jackman. Script by Barry Barringer and Ted Burnsten. 2 reels. Cast: Anna May Wong, Matt Moore, Sojin, and Oliver Hardy. AMW as Baroness Stoloff.

25. *Old San Francisco* (Warner Bros., 1927). Directed by Alan Crosland. Cinematography by Hal Mohr. Scenario by Anthony Coldeway. Story by Darryl F. Zanuck. 8 reels. Cast: Warner Oland, Dolores Costello, Charles E. Mack, Josef Swickard, John Miljan, Anders Randolf, Sojin, Angelo Rossitto, and Anna May Wong. AMW as "a Chinese girl."

26. *Why Girls Love Sailors* (Pathé Short, 1927). Directed by Fred C. Guiol. Scenario by Hal Roach. Cast: Stan Laurel, Oliver Hardy, Bobby Dunn, Anna May Wong, Sojin, and Eric Mayne. AMW as Delamar.

27. *The Chinese Parrot* (Universal Pictures, 1927). Directed by Paul Leni. Cinematography by Ben Kline. Scenario by J. Grubb Alexander. Based on the novel *The Chinese Parrot* by Earl Derr Biggers. 7 reels. Cast: Marian Nixon, Florence Turner, Hobart Bosworth, Edmund Burns, Captain Albert Conti, Sojin, Fred Esmelton, Ed Kennedy, George Kuwa, Slim Summerville, Dan Mason, Etta Lee, Jack Trent, and Anna May Wong. (Considered to be the forerunner to the "Charlie Chan" series.) AMW as "Nautch Dancer."

28. *The Devil Dancer* (Samuel Goldwyn, Inc. for United Artists, 1927). Directed by Fred Niblo, Alfred Raboch, and Lynn Shores. Cinematography by George Barnes and Thomas Brannigan. Scenario by Alice D. G. Miller. Story by Harry Hervey. 8 reels. Cast: Gilda Gray, Clive Brook, Anna May Wong, Serge Temoff, Michael Vavitch, Sojin, Ura Mita, Ann Schaeffer, Clarissa Selwynne, Martha Mattox, Kalla Pasha, James B. Leong, William H. Tooker, and Claire Du Brey. AMW as Sada.

29. *The Streets of Shanghai* (Tiffany-Stahl Prod., 1927). Directed by Louis Gasnier. Cinematography by Max Dupont and Earl Walker. Story by John Francis Natteford. 6 reels. Cast: Pauline Starke, Kenneth Harlan, Eddie Gribbon, Margaret Livingston, Jason Robards, Mathilde Comont, Tetsu Komai, Sojin, Anna May Wong, Toshiye Ichioka, and Media Ichiokal. AMW as Su Quan.

30. *Across to Singapore* (MGM, 1928). Directed by William Nigh. Scenario by Ted Shane. Based on the novel *All the Brothers Were Valiant* by Ben Ames Williams. 7 reels. Cast: Ramon Navarro, Joan Crawford, Ernest Torrence, Frank Currier, Daniel

Wolheim, Duke Martin, Edward Connelly, and James Mason. AMW as barroom prostitute.

31. *The Crimson City* (Warner Bros., 1928). Directed by Archie Mayo. Cinematography by Barry McGill. Script and story by Anthony Coldeway. 6 reels. Cast: Myrna Loy, Conrad Nagel, John Miljan, Leila Hyams, Anders Randolf, Richard Tucker, Anna May Wong, Matthew Betz, and Sojin. AMW as Su.

32. *Chinatown Charlie* (First National Pictures, 1928). Produced by C. C. Burr. Directed by Charles Hines. Cinematography by Al Wilson. Scenario by Roland Asher and John Grey. Story by Owen Davis. 7 reels. Cast: Johnny Hines, Louise Lorraine, Harry Gribbon, Fred Kohler, Sojin, Scooter Lowry, Anna May Wong, George Kuwa, and John Burdette. AMW as The Mandarin's Girl.

33. *Song* (a.k.a. *Wasted Love, Schmutziges Geld*, Gennan-British International Co. Production, 1928). Directed by Richard Eichberg. Based on the story "Dirty Money" by Karl Volmoeller. Running time unknown. Cast: Anna May Wong, Hans Adalbert Schlettow, Heinrich George, Paul Hörbiger, Mary Kid, and Julius E. Hermann. AMW as Song, a Malaysian dancer.

34. *The City Butterfly* (a.k.a. *Grossstadtschmetterling*, British International Pictures, 1929). Directed by Richard Eichberg. Running time unknown. Cast: Alexander Granach, Anna May Wong, Tilla Garden, Fred Louis Lerch, Gaston Jacquet, and E. E. Bostwick. AMW as "Sideshow Dancer."

35. *Piccadilly* (BIP Wardour, 1929). Directed by E. A. Dupont. Script and story by Arnold Bennett. 74 minutes. Cast: Jameson Thomas, Charles Laughton, Cyril Ritchard, Anna May Wong, King Hou Chang, Hannah Jones, Ellen Pollock, Harry Terry, Charles Paton, and Debroy Somers and His Orchestra. AMW as Shosho, performer and mistress to Thomas character.

36. *The Road to Dishonour* (a.k.a. *The Flame of Love* [US release], BIP Wardour, 1930). Directed by Richard Eichberg. Script and story by Monckton Hoffe and Ludwig Wolff. 82 minutes. Cast: John Longden, George Schnell, Anna May Wong, Mona Goya, Percy Standing, Fred Schwartz, and Ley On. AMW as Hai-Tang, a dancer.

37. *Hai-Tang* (BIP, 1930). Directed by Richard Eichberg. Script and story not credited. Running time unknown. Filmed at the British Elstree studios, this was the German version of *The Flame of Love*. Cast: Franz (Francis) Lederer, Anna May Wong, Hermann Blass, G. H. Schnell, Hugo Werner-Kahle, Edith D'Amara, Ley On, and Hai Young. AMW as Hai-Tang, a dancer.

38. *L'Amour Maitre des Choses* (1930). Directed by Richard Eichberg and Jean Kemm. Script and story not credited. Running time unknown. This was the French version of *The Flame of Love*. Cast: Robert Ancelin, Anna May Wong, Marcel Vibert, Helene Darly, Gaston DuPray, Francois Viguier, Armand Lurville, Clair Rowan, and Mona Goya. AMW as Hai-Tang, a dancer.

39. *Sabotage* (1930). Directed by Erno Metzner. Cast: Liselotte Schaak, Grace Chiang, Bob Stoll, Nien Son Ling, and Anna May Wong. AMW as car mechanic.

40. *Elstree Calling* (BIP Wardour, 1930). Directed by Alfred Hitchcock, André Charlot, Jack Hubert, and Paul Murray. Script and story by Adrian Brunel, Val Valentine, and Walter C. Mycroft. 86 minutes. Cast: Will Fyffe, Lily Morris, Teddy Brown, Anna May Wong, Gordon Harker, Hannah Jones, The Charlot Girls, The Berkoff Dancers, The Three Eddies, The Adelphi Girls, and The Kasbek Singers. AMW as herself.

41. *Daughter of the Dragon* (Paramount, 1931). Directed by Lloyd Corrigan. Cinematography by Victor Milner. Scenario by Lloyd Corrigan and Monte M. Katteijohn. Based on the novel *Daughter of Fu Manchu* by Sax Rohmer. 70 minutes. Cast: Anna May Wong, Warner Oland, Sessue Hayakawa, Bramwell Fletcher, Frances Dade, and Holmes Herbert. AMW as Princess Ling Moy, daughter of Fu Manchu.

42. *Shanghai Express* (Paramount, 1932). Directed by Josef von Sternberg. Cinematography by Lee Garmes. Screenplay by Jules Furthman. Original story by Harry Hervey. 80 minutes. Cast: Marlene Dietrich, Clive Brook, Anna May Wong, Warner Oland, Eugene Pallette, Lawrence Grant, Louise Closser Hale, Gustav von Seyffertitz, and Emile Chautard. AMW as Hui Fei, a prostitute.

43. *A Study in Scarlet* (KBS Productions for World Wide Pictures, Inc. and Fox Film Corp., 1933). Directed by Edwin L. Marin. Cinematography by Arthur Edison. Screenplay by Robert Florey. Based on the novel A *Study in Scarlet* by Sir Arthur Conan Doyle. 71 minutes. Cast: Reginald Owen, Anna May Wong, June Clyde, Allan Dinehart, John Warburton, J. M. Kerrigan, Alan Mowbray, Doris Lloyd, Billy Bevan, and Cecil Reynolds. AMW as Mrs. Pyke, a crook.

44. *Tiger Bay* (Wyndham, 1933). Directed by J. Elder Wills. Script and story by J. Elder Wills and Eric Anselol. 70 minutes. Cast: Henry Victor, René Ray, Lawrence Grossmith, Anna May Wong, Victor Garland, Ben Soutten, Margaret Yarde, Brian Buchel, Wally Patch, and Ernest Jay. AMW as Lui Chang, a café owner.

45. *Chu Chin Chow* (Gaumont British / Gainsborough Pictures, 1934). Directed by Walter Forde. Screenplay by Sidney Gilliat. Based on the musical by Oscar Asche and Frederick Norton. 95 minutes. Cast: Sir George Robey, Fritz Kortner, Anna May Wong, John Garrick, Pearl Argyle, Dennis Hoey, Sydney Fairbrother, Lawrence Hanray, Frank Cochrane, and Thelma Tuson. AMW as Zahrat, a slave girl.

46. *Limehouse Blues* (Paramount, 1934). Produced by Arthur Hornblow Jr. Directed by Alexander Hall. Cinematography by Harry Fischbeck. Screenplay by Cyril Hume and Arthur Phillips. Original story by Arthur Phillips. 65 minutes. Cast: George Raft, Jean Parker, Anna May Wong, Kent Taylor, Montagu Love, Billy Bevan, Louis Vincenot, E. Alyn Warren, Robert Loraine, John Rogers, and Wyndham Standing. AMW as Tu Tuan, mistress to Raft character.

47. *Java Head* (ATP, 1934). Directed by J. Walter Ruben. Screenplay by Martin Brown and Gordon Wellesley. Story by Joseph Hergesheimer. 85 minutes. Cast: Elizabeth Allan, John Loder, Edmund Gwenn, Anna May Wong, Ralph Richardson, Herbert Lomas, George Curzon, and Roy Emerton. AMW as Taou Yuen, the doomed wife of Loder character.

48. *Hollywood Party* (MGM, 1937). Produced by Lewis Lewyn. Directed by Roy Rowland. Screenplay by John Krafft. 2 reels. Cast: Clark Gable, Elissa Landi, Joan Bennett, Anna May Wong, Joe E. Brown, Freddie Bartholomew, Leon Errol, Joe Morrison, Betty Rhodes, Charlie Chase, and Leon Janney. AMW as herself.

49. *Daughter of Shanghai* (Paramount, 1937). Produced by Edward Lowe. Directed by Robert Florey. Cinematography by Charles Schoenbaum. Screenplay by Gladys Unger and Garnett Weston. 67 minutes. Cast: Anna May Wong, Charles Bickford, Larry "Buster" Crabbe, Cecil Cunningham, J. Carrol Naish, Anthony Quinn, John Patterson, Evelyn Brent, Philip Ahn, Fred Kohler Sr., Guy Bates Post, and Virginia Dabney. AMW as Lan Ying Lin, who seeks the murderer of her father.

50. *Dangerous to Know* (Paramount, 1938). Produced by Edward Lowe. Directed by Robert Florey. Cinematography by Theodor Sparkuhl. Screenplay by William R. Lipman and Horace McCoy. Based on the play *On the Spot* by Edgar Wallace. 70 minutes. Cast: Anna May Wong, Gail Patrick, Lloyd Nolan, Akim Tamiroff, Harvey Stephens, Anthony Quinn, Roscoe Karns, Porter Hall, Hedda Hopper, Hugh Sothern, Ed Pawley, and Pierre Watkin. AMW as Madame Lin Ying, mistress to Recka.

51. *When Were You Born?* (Warner Bros., 1938). Directed by William McGann. Cinematography by L. William O'Connell. Screenplay by Anthony Coldeway. Original story by Manley Hall. 65 minutes. Cast: Margaret Lindsay, Lola Lane, Anthony Averill, Anna May Wong, Jeffrey Lynn, Eric Stanley, Leonard Mudie, Olin Howland, Maurice Cass, Frank Jaquet, and Jack Moore. AMW as Mary Lee Ling, an astrological detective.

52. *King of Chinatown* (Paramount, 1939). Directed by Nick Grinde. Cinematography by Leo Tower. Screenplay by Lillie Hayward and Irving Reis. Story by Herbert Biberman. 60 minutes. Cast: Anna May Wong, Akim Tamiroff, J. Carrol Naish, Sidney Toler, Philip Ahn, Anthony Quinn, Bernadene Hayes, Roscoe Karns, Ray Meyer, and Richard Denning. AMW as Dr. Mary Ling.

53. *Island of Lost Men* (Paramount, 1939). Produced by Eugene Zukor. Directed by Kurt Neumann. Cinematography by Karl Strauss and Charles Lang. Screenplay by William R. Lipman and Horace McCoy. Based on the play *Hangman's Whip* by Norman Reilly Raine and Frank Butler. 63 minutes. Cast: Anna May Wong, J. Carrol Naish, Anthony Quinn, Eric Blore, Broderick Crawford, Ernest Truex, Rudolph Forster, William Haade, and Richard Loo. AMW as Kim Ling, a daughter of a general.

54. *Chinese Garden Festival* (Republic, 1940). Part of the Harriet Parsons "Meet the Stars" Series. 1 Reel. Cast: Rosalind Russell, William Bakewell, Dorothy Lamour, Rita Hayworth, Cesar Romero, Walter Pidgeon, Anna May Wong, Patricia Morrison, Beulah Bondi, Mary Martin, Gertrude Niesen, Rose Hobart, Charles "Buddy" Rogers, Mary Pickford, Vera Vague, Jane Withers, Susan Peters, and Ona Munson. AMW and other celebrities attend a party.

55. *Ellery Queen's Penthouse Mystery* (Darmour for Columbia, 1941). Produced by Larry Darmour. Directed by James Hogan. Cinematography by James S. Brown Jr. Screenplay by Eric Taylor. Story by Ellery Queen. 69 minutes. Cast: Ralph Bellamy, Anna May Wong, Margaret Lindsay, Charles Grapewin, James Burke, Edward Ciannelli, Frank Albertson, Ann Doran, Noel Madison, Charles Lane, Russell Hicks, Tom Dugan, Mantan Moreland, and Theodore Von Eltz. AMW as Lois Ling, a diplomat.

56. *Bombs over Burma* (Producers Releasing Corp., 1942). Produced by Arthur Alexander and Alfred Stern. Directed by Joseph H. Lewis. Cinematography by Robert Cline. Screenplay by Milton Raison and Joseph H. Lewis. 67 minutes. Cast: Anna May Wong, Noel Madison, Leslie Denison, Nedrick Young, Dan Seymour, Frank Lackteen, and Judith Gibson. AMW as Lin Ying, a schoolteacher.

57. *Lady from Chungking* (Alexander-Stern Productions, Inc. for Producers Releasing Corp., 1942). Produced by Alfred Stern and Arthur Alexander. Directed by William Nigh. Cinematography by Marcel Le Picard. Original story by Sam Robins and Milton Raison. 71 minutes. Cast: Anna May Wong, Harold Huber, Mae Clarke, Rick Vallin, Paul Bryar, Ted Hecht, Ludwig Donath, James Leong, Archie Got, and Walter Soo Hoo. AMW as Kwan Mei, a guerrilla leader.

58. *Impact* (Cardinal Pictures for United Artists, 1949). Produced by Leo Popkin. Directed by Arthur Lubin. Cinematography by Ernest Laszlo. Scripted by Dorothy Reid and Jay Dratler. 111 minutes. Cast: Brian Donlevy, Ella Raines, Helen Walker, Charles Coburn, Anna May Wong, Robert Warwick, Art Baker, Mae Marsh, Erskine Sanford, and Philip Ahn. AMW as Su Lin, a maid.

59. *The Savage Innocents* (Grayfilm-Pathé for Paramount, 1961). Produced by Maleno Malenotti. Directed by Nicholas Ray. Cinematography by Aldo Tonti and Peter Hennessy. Screenplay by Nicholas Ray. Based on the novel *Top of the World* by Hans Ruesch. 110 minutes. Cast: Anthony Quinn, Yoko Tani, Anna May Wong, Francis de Wolff, Andy Ho, Peter O'Toole, Kaida Horiuchi, Yvonne Shima, Lee Montague, Marco Guglielmi, Anthony Chin, Michael Chow, Ed Devereaux, and Carlo Giustini. AMW as Hiko, Anthony Quinn's mother-in-law. Although attributed to Anna May Wong, this was probably Marie Yang, acting under the famous star's name.

60. *Portrait in Black* (Universal Pictures, 1960). Directed by Michael Gordon. Screenplay by Ivan Goff and Ben Roberts. 112 minutes. Cast: Lana Turner, Anthony Quinn, Sandra Dee, John Saxon, Anna May Wong, Richard Basehart, Lloyd Nolan, Ray Walston, Virginia Grey, Dennis Kohler, Paul Birch, John Wengraf, Richard Norris, James Nolan, Robert Lieb, John McNamara, Charles Thompson, George Womack, Henry Quan, Elizabeth Chan, Harold Goodwin, Jack Bryan. AMW as Tani, a housekeeper.

61. *Just Joe* (Parkside [Archway], 1960). Directed by MacLean Rogers. Screenplay by Donald Bull and Raymond Drewe. 73 minutes. Cast: Betty Huntley-Wright, Anna May Wong, Howard Pays, Jon Pertwee, Leslie Randall, Joan H. Reynolds, Bruce

Seton, and Martin Wyldeck. AMW as Peach Blossom. Although attributed to Anna May Wong, this was probably Marie Yang, acting under the famous star's name.

Sources: Tom and Sara Pendergast, *International Dictionary of Films and Filmmakers 3 Actors and Actresses*, 4th edition; *Moving Pictures Stories*, 21 January, 11 February 1921; Denis Gifford, *The British Film Catalogue*, 3rd edition; Barrie Roberts, "Anna May Wong: Daughter of the Orient," *Classic Images*, 1997; Patricia King Hanson and Alan Gevinson, eds., *American Film Institute Catalog of Motion Pictures Produced in the United States*, 1st edition; IMDB (Internet Movie Data Base).

Television Appearances

The Gallery of Madame Liu Tsong and Madame Liu Tsong (After October 10) Lead Actor. Dumont Network, 1951. Episodes: 1. (Unknown Title), August 27, 1951; 2. "The Golden Women," September 2, 1951; 3. "The Spreading Oak," September 12, 1951; 4. "The Man with a Thousand Eyes," September 17, 1951; 5. "Burning Sands," September 24, 1951; 6. "Shadow of the Sun God," October 1, 1951; 7. "The Tinder Box," October 31, 1951; 8. "The House of Quiet Dignity," November 7, 1951; 9. "Boomerang," November 14, 1951; 10. "The Face of Evil," November 21, 1951

"The Letter," *Producer's Showcase*, NBC, 1955

"Native Land," on *Bold Journey*, ABC, February 14, 1956

"The Chinese Game," *Climax*, CBS, November 22, 1956

"Deadly Tattoo," *Climax*, CBS, May 1, 1958

"So That's Who It Was," *Mickey Spillane's Mike Hammer*, CBS

Adventures in Paradise with Gardner McKay, "The Lady from South Chicago" aired November 2, 1959 and "Mission to Manila," aired December 7, 1959, ABC

"Voodoo Factor," ATV-UK TV, 1959. Although attributed to Anna May Wong, this was probably Marie Yang, acting under the famous star's name.

"China Mary," *Wyatt Earp*, ABC, March 5, 1960

"Dragon by the Tail," *Josephine Little*, a pilot spin-off of *Barbara Stanwyck Show*, NBC, January 30, 1961

"The Journey Ends Halfway," *Danger Man*, CBS, May 24, 1961

Source: Vincent Terrace, *Encyclopedia of Television Series, Pilots, and Specials*. 3 vols. New York: New York Zoetrope, 1986.

Notes

Preface to Third Edition

1. Rebecca Sun, "Gemma Chan, Nina Yang Bongiovi Developing Anna May Wong Biopic with Working Title Films (Exclusive)," *Hollywood Reporter*, March 24, 2022, https://www.hollywoodreporter.com/movies/movie-news/anna-may-wong-biopic-gemma-chan-1235118243/.

2. In addition to major databases such as ProQuest and NewsBank, see the sources at the New York Public Library (https://www.nypl.org) and the UC Berkeley Library (https://guides.lib.berkeley.edu/history/latinamerica/news). Proquest's Entertainment Industry Magazine Archive database has ample material on Wong's films and travels.

3. *New Journal and Guide* (Norfolk) June 20, 1942; *Call & Post* (Cleveland) April 29, 1944; *Baltimore Afro-American*, April 29, 1944.

4. For English language skills, see *Chung Hwa English Weekly* (Shanghai, 1931), Nankai University Library. Zou Taofen, *Guoji wenming de Huang Liushuang* (Shanghai: Dazhong ji, 1937), 75–77. For Hu Die, see "Huang Liushuang Hu Die chuci huijian ji," *Chunse* 2, no. 11 (1936): 20. For cablegram, see *Chicago Defender*, July 16, 1938.

5. For estate sale, see https://estatesales.org/estate-sales/ca/los-angeles/90049/grand-asian-estate-sale-in-706481, though the larger link is no longer active. For Harvard collections, see http://id.lib.harvard.edu/alma/990149367510203941/catalog and http://id.lib.harvard.edu/alma/99155842462303941/catalog. For *Island of Lost Men*, see 173–174, 219. On Lambert, see Andrew Motion, *The Lamberts: George, Constant and Kit* (New York: Farrar Straus & Giroux, 1986), 161.

6. Susan Blumberg-Kason, "The Movie Star and Madame Salon: The Friendship of Anna May Wong and Bernardine Szold Fritz," *Ms.*, March 3, 2022.

7. Shirley Jennifer Lim, *Anna May Wong: Performing the Modern* (Philadelphia: Temple University Press, 2019), 154.

8. For overseas payments, see Madeline Y. Hsu, *Dreaming of Gold, Dreaming of Home: Transnationalism and Migration Between the United States and South China, 1882–1943* (Palo Alto: Stanford University Press, 2000), 90–114. For Lee Shee, Austin Yu to author, June 3, 2022, in author's possession. Classic understanding of women's roles can be found in Cao Xueqin and Gao E, *The Story of the Stone, or The Dream of the Red Chamber*, trans. David Hawkes and John Minford, 5 vols. (New York: Penguin Classics, 1974–1986).

9. Family information comes from emails from Austin Yu to author, May 22 and 25, June 2, 2022, in author's possession.

10. *Hollywood*, created by Ryan Murphy and Ian Brennan, May 1, 2020, on Netflix, https://www.imdb.com/title/tt9827854/?ref_=nm_flmg_act_7.

11. *Searching for Anna May Wong*, directed by Denise Chan and Z. Eric Yang, November 26, 2020, can be found on Amazon. PBS screened a short biography in 2020 of Wong in its American Masters series; see https://www.pbs.org/wnet/americanmasters /anna-may-wong-first-asian-american-movie-star-bfnigk/13978/.

12. Yiman Wang, "'Speaking in a Forked Tongue': Anna May Wong's Linguistic Cosmopolitanism," in eds. Sabrina Qiong Yu and Guy Austin, *Revisiting Star Studies: Cultures, Themes and Methods* (Edinburgh: Edinburgh University Press, 2017), 65–83.

13. Lim, *Anna May Wong*. Her earlier book *A Feeling of Belonging: Asian American Women's Public Culture, 1930–1960* (New York: New York University Press, 2006), describes my book as "heavily dependent" on the work of Karen Leong. I first read Leong's dissertation while composing this book. In the second edition of this book, I cited her published book chapter on Wong. While I respect Leong's scholarship, her perspective is very different from mine and my research is far broader. See Karen J. Leong, *The China Mystique: Pearl S. Buck, Anna May Wong, Mayling Soong, and the Transformation of American Orientalism* (Berkeley: University of California Press, 2005), 57–105.

14. Gao Yunxiang, "Chinese American Actresses Soo Yong and Anna May Wong: Contrasting Struggles for Recognition in Hollywood," the *Conversation*, April 25, 2021, https://theconversation.com/chinese-american-actresses-soo-yong-and-anna-may-wong-contrasting-struggles-for-recognition-in-hollywood-159174. Gao is completing a biography of Soo Yong.

15. On Chan and Met Gala, see Emily Chan, "Gemma Chan Pays Homage to Hollywood's First Chinese-American Star with her Prabal Gurung Met Gala Look," *Vogue* (UK), September 14, 2021, https://www.vogue.co.uk/fashion/article /gemma-chan-met-gala-2021-prabal-gurung. On makeup, see "I Transformed Myself into a 1920s Hollywood Star, Beauty with Mi," Refinery29, uploaded May 27, 2019, YouTube video, 10:22, time code 4:54, https://www.youtube.com /watch?v=0rLetpQy43o&t=294s.

16. Anne Anlin Cheng, "Shine: On Race, Glamour, and the Modern," *PMLA/ Publications of Modern Language* 126, no. 4 (2011): 1022–1041.

17. Sally Wen Mao, "Poetry Feature: Sally Wen Mao," *Missouri Review* 38, no. 1 (Spring 2015); Sally Wen Mao, *Oculus* (Minneapolis: Graywolf Press, 2019). Peter Ho Davies, *The Fortunes* (Boston: Mariner Books, 2017). Amanda Lee Koe, *Delayed Rays of a Star* (New York: Nan A. Talese, 2019).

18. Katherine L. Neff, Dr. Stacy L. Smith, and Dr. Katherine Pieper, *Inequality Across 1,500 Popular Films: Examining Gender and Race/Ethnicity of Leads/Co Leads from 2007 to 2021*, USC Annenberg Inclusion Initiative, March 2022, https://assets .uscannenberg.org/docs/aii-study-inequality-popular-films-20220311.pdf; on

actor statistics, see "Actor Demographics and Statistics in the US," Zippia, April 18, 2022, https://www.zippia.com/actor-jobs/demographics/ and *Honolulu Star-Register*, July 12, 2017. For James Hong see "James Hong: Filmography," IMDB, accessed May 2022, https://www.imdb.com/name/nm0393222/?ref_=tt_cl_i_4.

Introduction

1. Kingston, *The Woman Warrior*, 3–16. I am using this controversial term precisely. For a good collection of the disputes raised by Kingston's work and her myths, see the many arguments in Skandera-Trombley, *Critical Essays on Maxine Hong Kingston*. For discussion of the difference between fame and status, see Chang, "The Good, the Bad and the Beautiful," in Zhang, *Cinema and Urban Culture*, 133. For recent history, see Chang, *The Chinese in America*, 208–10. The one article surveying the effects of Wong's career on contemporary literature has notably few examples to discuss. See Cynthia W. Liu, "When Dragon Ladies Die, Do They Come Back as Butterflies? Re-Imagining Anna May Wong," in Hamamoto and Liu, eds., *Countervisions*, 23–40. For quote on difference of fame and achievement, see Yunxiang Gao, "Sex, Sports, and National Crisis," 96–161. The other statues are of Mae West, Dolores Del Rio, and Dorothy Dandridge.

2. Said, *Orientalism*, 2–9; Spence, *Chan's Great Continent*; Hardt and Negri, *Empire*; Mulvey, *Visual and Other Pleasures*, 14–29. I admit to redacting these complex works but contend that I am using them as their authors intended. For creation of the Oriental, see Yu, *Thinking Orientals*.

3. On such people, see Hodes, "The Mercurial and Abiding Power of Race," 84.

4. For recent evaluations of Anna May's status as a Modern Girl, see Leong, *The China Mystique*, 77–83, and Lim, *A Feeling of Belonging*, 75–80. For Anna May as a "yellow yellow face," see Wang, Yiman, "The Art of Screen Passing: Anna May Wong's Yellow Yellowface Performance in the Art Deco Era," *Camera Obscura*, 20: 3 (2005), 159–61. Two other books on Anna May appeared at the same time as the original edition of my biography. Philip Liebfriend and Chei Mi Lane's *Anna May Wong* is a useful, non-analytical compilation, packed with useful tidbits about her work with many rare images. A good, searchable compliment to it is the Internet Movie Database. For her entry, see http://www.imdb.com/name/nm0938923/. A second biography is Anthony B. Chan's *Perpetually Cool: The Many Lives of Anna May Wong (1905–1961)*. I have used two pieces of evidence from this book for this new edition.

5. Chan, "Race, Ethnic Culture, and Gender in the Construction of Identities Among Second-Generation Chinese Americans," in Wong and Chan, *Claiming America*, 127–64.

6. For an excellent discussion of transnationality with particular reference to Anna May's regional background, see Wang, *Chinese Overseas*, 31–32, 38–40, 57.

7. See *On Gold Mountain*.

Chapter One Childhood

1. "The True Life Story of a Chinese Girl, by Anna May Wong," *Pictures Magazine*, August, September 1926; Statements of Wong Sam Sing and Lee Gon Toy, US Department of Labor, Immigration Service, February 13, 1925, in National Archives, Pacific Region, Laguna Niguel, California; Leong, *The China Mystique*, 3; Shevsky and Williams, *The Social Areas of Los Angeles*, 54; Chow, "Sixty Years."

2. Aarim-Heriot, *Chinese Immigrants, African Americans*, 10–11, 25–44, 52, 68–69, 82–83.

3. Wang, *Chinese Overseas*, 62–65; Hing, *Making and Remaking*, 19–22; Chang, *Chinese in America*, 110–12. Chang points out that many interracial marriages were successful.

4. Hing, *Making and Remaking*, 21–28; Aarim-Heriot, *Chinese Immigrants, African Americans*, 172–214; Chang, *Chinese in America*, 130–56; Lee, *At America's Gates*.

5. Spence, *The Chan's Great Continent*, 118–43.

6. Smith, *The Lonely Queue*, 21; Lou, "The Chinese-American Community," 23–27; Chang, *Chinese in America*, 121.

7. Greenwood, *Down by the Station*, 20–29, 140–42; Wild, *Street Meeting*, 23–24.

8. *Sanborn Insurance Maps of Los Angeles*, 3: 268; Wild, *Street Meeting*, 124–26; on Chinatowns, see Benton and Gomez, *Chinatown*, 5–7.

9. Zorbas, *Fiddletown*, 30–36. Huang Family Genealogy, Chang On. For the mining camps, see Randall Rohe, "Chinese Camps and Chinatowns: Chinese Mining Settlements in the North American West," in Lee, et al., *Re-Collecting Early Asian America*, 31–54.

10. Wong, "The True Life Story of a Chinese Girl"; Statements of Wong Sam Sing and Lee Gon Toy, US Department of Labor, Immigration Service, February 13, 1925, in National Archives, Pacific Region, Laguna Niguel, California; Huang Family Genealogy, Chang On; Hsu, *Dreaming of Gold*, 40–42; Johnson, *Roaring Camp*, 243–46.

11. Statements of Wong Sam Sing and Lee Gon Toy; Lou, "The Chinese-American Community," 43–49, 64; Interview with Huang Cui-Xiang, 2001, Guangzhou; Lee, *At America's Gates*, 92–95.

12. "The True Life Story of a Chinese Girl"; Interview with Huang Cui-Xiang, 2001.

13. Hsu, *Dreaming of Gold*, 11–13.

14. Statement of Lee Gon Toy, February 20, 1925; Yung, *Unbound Feet*, 166–67; Chen, *Chinese San Francisco*, 67; Aarim-Heriot, *Chinese Immigrants, African Americans*, 68–69.

15. Gyory, *Closing the Gate*, 242–61; Peffer, *If They Don't Bring Their Women Here*, 7–15; Hing, *Making and Remaking*, 203–7.

16. Liu, *Inside Los Angeles Chinatown*, 185–92; Siu, *The Chinese Laundryman*; Lou, "The Chinese-American Community of Los Angeles," 64; Barbagallo, "Changing with the Rhythm," 9; Chang, *Chinese in America*, 168–69. For number of people working at the laundry, see *Los Angeles Times*, July 24, 1921.

17. Liu, *Inside Los Angeles Chinatown*, 33.

18. For her conviction, see How, "Between Two Worlds," 26. For the account of another Chinese family practicing the same deception, see Larson, *Sweet Bamboo*, 62.

19. "Statement of Lee Gon Toy to J. C. Nardini," April 26, 1925, National Archives, Pacific Region, Laguna Niguel Office (Lulu and Jimmy); County of Los Angeles, Health Department, Birth Certificates 18768 (Anna May); 9927 (Mary); 1843 (Frank); 3133 (Roger); 3044 (Marietta); 8573 (Richard).

20. Sucheta Maxumdar, "In the Family," in *Linking Our Lives*, 36–40, and Barbagallo, "Changing with the Rhythm," 10.

21. Greenwood, *Down by the Station*, 92, 119–32; *Hua Tzu Jih Pao* (Hong Kong), February 22, 1936.

22. Smith, *The Lonely Queue*, 39–40.

23. See *On Gold Mountain*; for photo, see statement of J. C. Nardini, February 24, 1925, US Department of Labor, Immigration Service, 25200/105, National Archives, Pacific Region, Laguna Niguel Office. See also Smith, *Lonely Queue*, 39–40.

24. Wong, "The True Life Story of a Chinese Girl."

25. Leong, *The China Mystique*, 60; *The New Movie Magazine* (London), July 1932, 26; Wong, "The True Life Story of a Chinese Girl," "Anna May Wong," New York Public Library (NYPL). For similar incidents, see Larson, *Sweet Bamboo*, 69–71; and Lou, "Chinese-American Community," 112.

26. Greenwood, *Down by the Station*, 20–21; Lou, "Chinese-American Community," 259–66; Wong, "Childhood of a Chinese Screen Star," 34; Wong, "The True Life Story of a Chinese Girl"; Leong, *The China Mystique*, 60; Liu, *Inside Los Angeles Chinatown*, 64; Jesperson, *American Images*, 2.

27. Chen, *Being Chinese*, 112–26.

28. See *On Gold Mountain*, 228; Yung, *Unbound Feet*, 108–9; Gebhart, "Jazz Notes on Old China"; "Anna May Wong," NYPL.

29. Chu, *Chinese Theater in America*, 9–41, 56–65, 75, 91, 96–108. For recollections, see *London Era*, February 27, 1929.

30. Wong, "Bamboo, or China's Conversion to Film"; for using lunch money, see *Mein Film*, June 4, 1930.

31. Spears, *Hollywood: The Golden Era*, 373; Sklar, *Film*, 70; Koszarski, *An Evening's Entertainment*, 271; Wong, "My Film Thrills"; Wong, "The True Life Story of a Chinese Girl"; and *Screen Play Secrets*, October 1931. For Alma Rubens, see *Time*, October 1, 1934. For Peking Theater, see Lou, "Chinese-American Community," 58. For another Chinese girl going to the movies at the same time, see Larson, *Sweet Bamboo*, 123. For spectatorship, see Hansen, *Babel and Babylon*, 16; and Barbas, *Movie Crazy*, 9–15, 61. For crying scenes, see de Silva, *These Piquant People*, 51–52. On Wu Fang, see Eugene Wong, "The Early Years: Asians in the American Films Prior to World War II," in Feng, *Screening Asian Americans*, 53–71.

32. De Cordova, *Picture Personalities*, 55–90; Fuller, *At the Picture Show*, 133–68.

33. Sabine Haenni, "Filming 'Chinatown' Fake Visions, Bodily Transformations," in Feng, *Screening Asian Americans*, 21–53. On such slumming in other Chinatowns, see Heap, *Slumming*, 144–46.

34. Spence, *The Chan's Great Continent*, 165–67.

35. Brownlow, *The Parade's Gone By*, 31.

36. *Moving Pictures Stories*, February 4, 1921. For comment, see Marchetti, *Romance and the "Yellow Peril,"* 4.

37. Lambert, Nazimova, 211–13; *AFI Catalog F1* (Feature Films, 1911–1920), 760–61.

38. For an unintentionally revealing story about this practice, see *Picture Show*, January 20, 1923. For the Chinese government's criticism of Hollywood at this time, see Leyda, *Dianying*, 32–33.

39. Wong, "My Film Thrills"; Wong, "My Story"; Wong, "Bamboo, or China's Conversion to Film"; *London Era*, February 27, 1929; and *Screenplay*, October 1931. For Reverend Wang comments, see *Ciné Miroir*, November 27, 1931, and *Films in Review*, 12 (1960), 129–30. For actions by Carr and Ye, see *Rob Wagner's Script Magazine*, September 1935, 13. For the influenza epidemic in Los Angeles, see Crosby, *America's Forgotten Pandemic*, 92.

40. Wong, "Bamboo, or China's Conversion to Film."

41. Andrew W. Field, "Selling Souls in Sin City: Shanghai Singing and Dancing Hostesses in Print, Film, and Politics, 1920–49," and Michael G. Chang, "The Good, the Bad and the Beautiful: Actresses and Public Discourse in Shanghai, 1920s–1930s," in Zhang, *Cinema and Urban Culture*, 100–59; Brownlow, *The Parade's Gone By*, 31, 39; Wong, "The Childhood of a Chinese Screen Star," Wong, "Bamboo, or the Conversion of China to Film"; Leong, *The China Mystique*, 57. On racial grief, see Cheng, *Melancholy of Race*, 8–16. On the hazards of breaking into Hollywood, see Barbas, *Movie Crazy*, 68–77.

42. See the brilliant commentary on immigrants and the movies in Hansen, *Babel and Babylon*, 111–13.

43. Wong, "The True Life Story of a Chinese Girl."

44. See the discussion of Kingston's novel in Cheng, *The Melancholy of Race*, 64–67.

45. Stills Collection, the Wisconsin Center for Film and Theater Research.

46. Harris, "Silent Speech," 132–37, 140–42; Field, "Selling Souls in Sin City: Shanghai Singing and Dancing Hostesses in Print, Film, and Politics, 1920–49," in Zhang, *Cinema and Urban Culture*, 99–127.

47. *Motion Picture Stories*, July 28, 1922.

48. See the brilliant commentary on this process in Cohen, *Silent Film*, 139–41.

Chapter Two Seeking Stardom

1. Klepper, *Silent Films*, 215–17; *AFI Catalog*, 1921–1930 (Feature Films), 580.

2. *AFI Catalog*, 1921–1930 (Feature Films), 784–85.

3. Carlisle, "A Chinese Puzzle," *Movie Classics*, May 1925, and *Pictures and Picturegoer*, February 1925; *Pantomine*, December 10, 1921; *AFI Feature Films Catalog, 1911–1930*, 689, for *Outside the Law*. For her comments on the Beery film, see *Picture Show*, September 7, 1929; for *Lilies of the Field*, see *Picture Show*, January 12, 1935.

4. *AFI Feature Films Catalog, 1911–1930*, 215; *Moving Pictures Stories*, January 21, 1921. For *Dinty* in Austria, see *Der Filmbote*, July 23, 1921; *Das Kino-Journal*, August 6, 1921 and September 15, 1923; Wong, "Bamboo, or China's Conversion to Film."

5. *AFI Feature Films Catalog, 1921–1930*, 248; *Moving Pictures Stories*, February 11, 1921; *Der Filmbote*, August 6, 1921. For teacup scene, see *Time*, October 1, 1934.

6. For articles on Hayakawa and his wife, see *Picture Show*, May 7, June 4, November 5, December 2, 1921. For summary of his career, see Sklar, *Film*, 80–81. For his home and entertaining, see Hayakawa, *Zen Showed Me the Way*, 147–50.

7. *AFI Catalog, F1 R* (Feature Films, 1921–1930), 62; *Variety*, October 21, 1921; *Motion Picture Classic*, March 1922, 46; *Picture Show*, January 27, 1923; *Bits of Life*, Pressbook; Koszarski, *An Evening's Entertainment*, 230–32; Rainsberger, *James Wong Howe*, 15–16.

8. Winship, 'The China Doll"; Spear, "Marshall Neilan," in his *Hollywood: The Golden Era*; *Kinema Junpo* (Tokyo), November 5, 1924. For cross, see Louella Parsons column in the *Los Angeles Examiner*, August 12, 1934. Sex with Anglo-Americans was frowned upon in the Chinese community as well. See Lou, "Chinese-American Community, 333–34. For laws, see Pascoe, *What Comes Naturally*, 90–92; for mixed marriages, see Wild, *Street Meeting*, 136–44.

9. *AFI Catalog F1 R* (*Feature Films, 1921–1930*), 702–3; *Variety*, August 5, 1921; *Moving Picture World*, October 29, 1921; *Das Kino-Journal*, June 9, 1923.

10. For a lengthy discussion of the story, see Nick Browne, "The Undoing of the Other Woman: *Madame Butterfly* in the Discourse of American Orientalism," in Daniel Bernardi, ed., *The Birth of Whiteness*, 227–51; and Marina Hueng, "The Family Practice of Orientalism: From Madame Butterfly to Indochine," in Bernstein and Studlar, eds., *Visions of the East*, 158–83; and Yoshihara, *Embracing the East*, 77–101; on acting, see Naremore, *Acting in the Cinema*, 48–49.

11. McCaffery and Jacobs, *Guide to the Silent Years*, 269–70; Sklar, *Film*, 105, 109; Basaten, *Glorious Technicolor*, 31. For crying, see *Picture Show*, May 6, 1922, and the commentary in Cohen, *Silent Film*, 155. For Harlan's career, see *Picture Show*, May 26, 1923. For Anna May's recollections, see *Los Angeles Examiner*, August 29, 1960.

12. *AFI Catalog F1 R* (*Feature Films, 1921–1930*), 818; *Variety*, December 8, 1922; *New York Times*, December 2, 1922; Beauchamp, *Without Lying Down*, 143; Barbas, *Movie Crazy*, 72.

13. *Kinetetographic Weekly*, April 26, 1923; *Picture Show*, September 22, 1923; *Kinema Junpo* (Tokyo), February 1, 1924; *Screen and Stage* (Tokyo), March, 1924; *Teano Film Gesellschaft Berlin*, July 5, 1924.

14. Pan, *Encyclopedia of the Chinese Overseas*, 334.

15. *Chinese Students Monthly*, December 1922, 74–77.

16. "Anna May Wong," NYPL; Smith, *Lonely Queue*, 36, 49; Chen, "Exclusion of Chinese Women," 128; Lee, *At America's Gates*, 100, 238; Zhao, *Remaking Chinese America*, 15, 17, 37–39; Hing, *Making and Remaking*, 44–48, 206–8. On mixed-race marriages in Los Angeles, see Chang, *Chinese in America*, 196. On preferences of American-born Chinese men, see Sucheng Chan, "Race, Ethnic Culture and Gender," in Wong and Chan, *Claiming America*, 127–64. For differences between Chinese students and Chinese Americans, see Yu, *Thinking Orientals*, 115–16.

17. Anna May remembered this story so well that she related it ten years later in *Mein Film*, August 5, 1932.

18. *Wilmington* (Florida) *Journal*, December 4, 1923, Clipping File, AMPAS; Kingsley, "I Shall Marry a Man of My Own Race." On kiss in O'Neil's play, see Mumford, *Interzones*, 121–32.

19. Gebhart, "Jazz Notes on Old China." See also *Screenland*, January 25, 1922.

20. On the American flappers, see Chang, *Chinese in America*, 195–96. For China, see Koo, *No Feast Lasts Forever*, 98, 180–84; Sergeant, *Shanghai*, 271; Hansen, *Babel and Babylon*, 120; "East is West," *Screen Snapshots*, ca. 1924. On Li Hongzhang, see Spence, *The Search for Modern China*, 213–35.

21. *Wilmington* (Florida) *Journal*, December 4, 1923, Clipping File, AMPAS; *Motion Picture Classic Magazine*, August 1923.

22. Hirschorn, *The Universal Story*, 42; *Kinema Junpo* (Tokyo), February 1, 1924.

23. *AFI Catalog F1 R* (*Feature Films, 1921–1930*), 203; *Variety*, August 23, 1923; Skal and Savada, *Dark Carnival*, 72–74.

24. Winship, "The China Doll." For picture of Anna May and her car, see *Theatre*, September 26, 1925, 48. See also *Motion Picture Magazine*, July 1923; *Movie Weekly Magazine*, November 1, 1924; *Photoplay*, June 1923, March 1924, April 1925, August 1927. See also *Das Kino-Journal*, July 7, 1923. For Cliffords, see Program Notes for *Tschun-Tschi*, Neuen Wiener Schauspielhaus, Vienna, 1930.

25. *AFI Catalog F1 R* (*Feature Films, 1921–1930*), 811; *Variety*, December 8, 1923.

26. Sklar, *Film*, 108–10.

27. *AFI Catalog FI R* (*Feature Films, 1921–1930*); *Variety*, March 26, 1924; Fonoroff, *Silver Light*, 1–2; Youngblood, *Movies for the Masses*, 20, 51–52, 183n27; McCaffery and Jacobs, *Guide to the Silent Years*, 265–66; Pratt, *Spellbound in Darkness*, 298–99; "Anna May Wong," NYPL; *Kinetographic Weekly*, October 2, 1924; *Pictures and Picturegoer*, November, December 1924; *Picture Show*, November 29, 1924; Mannock's recollections are printed in *Picturegoer*, February 23, 1950, 23. In France, see *Ciné-Miroir*, April 15, May, June, September 1924. For cover, see *Cinémonde*, July 30, 1924. For German, see also *Das Kino-Journal*, August 14, 1926; *Mein Film*, 35, 36, 42 (1926). For South America, *see Cinelandia*, May 1928. Portuguese critics also believed that Anna May was Japanese. See the cover of *Cinéfilo*, October 1, 1928.

28. For *Across the Pacific*, see *Herald* (Australia), January 2, 3, 9, 10, 17, 19, 24 and February 2, 6, 1925; *The Movie Times* (Tokyo), February 1, 1925; *Play and Movie* (Tokyo), February 1924; In Austria, see *Der Filmbote*, March 20, April 24, August

14, 15 (*The Toll of the Sea*) 1924 and *Paimann's Filmlisten*, March 9 and August 27, 1926. For upstaging, see Carey, *Doug and Mary*, 146.

29. *Diangying Zazhi* (Movie Magazine), November 1925; *Diangying Huabao* (Screen Pictorial), May 1925. For affair, Mrs. Douglas Fairbanks Jr. interview with author, 2004.

30. For date with Romney, see Nolan, *Lorenz Hart*, 62.

31. *Variety*, September 24, 1924; *Motion Picture Magazine*, November 1924; *Motion Picture Classic Magazine*, December 1924; for British reviews, see *Pictures and Picturegoer*, June 1925, October 1925; *Picture Show*, June 14, 1925; for Japanese reviews, see *The Movie Times* (Tokyo), October 1, November 5, 1925.

32. *AFI Catalog F1 R* (*Feature Films, 1921–1930*), 600; Koszarski, *An Evening's Entertainment*, 222; Rainsberger, *James Wong Howe*, 151–54; *Variety*, December 17, 24, 31, 1924; Seagrave, *American Films Abroad*, 25; *Kinetographic Weekly*, January 22, 1925; *Picture Show*, March 7, 1925; *Der Filmbote*, January 1924.

33. For forms, see Wong Lew Song File 14036/236A, Immigration and Naturalization Service, National Archives, Pacific Region, Laguna Niguel, California. For the convoluted rights of American-born Chinese women, see Chan, "Exclusion of Chinese Women," 118–20, 125. For suits, see How, "Between Two Worlds," 26. For inspectors, see Lee, *At America's Gates*, 47–75.

34. "Anna May Wong File," NYPL. For Wong Sam Sing's lease, see Los Angeles Recorder's Office, Norwalk, California, Book 5129, 1–3. On the 1924 law, see Hing, *Making and Remaking*, 32–34; 213–14; on Mexico and ease of entrance, see Lee, *At America's Gates*, 158–59, 179–87.

35. *Xinyingxing* (Silverland), September 1, 1928.

36. "The True Life Story of a Chinese Girl, by Anna May Wong," *Pictures Magazine*, August, September 1926.

37. Leong, *The China Mystique*, 68–70.

38. Sklar, *Film*, 183; Fowles, *Starstruck*, 66, 78–9, 86.

39. For contract and San Francisco shows, see *San Francisco Chronicle*, July 18, 1924 and January 22, 1925. For St. Dennis, nautch girls and trials, see *Los Angeles Times*, January 21, 1915; for trial, see among others *Los Angeles Times*, January 14, 1925.

40. Slide, *Encyclopedia of Vaudeville*, 181; *Der Filmbote*, July 25, 1925. Her playbills are gathered in the Anna May Wong Gift Collection at New York Public Library. For this period, see Book 8408.

41. *AFI Catalog F1 R* (*Feature Films, 1921–1930*), 269; *Variety*, February 4, 1925; *Films in Review*, 16 (1965), 569; *Kinema Junpo* (Tokyo), September 21, 1925; *Movie Times* (Tokyo), October 11, 1925; *Der Filmbote*, March 3, 1924; *Paimann's Filmlisten*, March 12, 1926; *Mein Film* 2, 4 (1926).

42. *AFI Catalog F1 R* (*Feature Films, 1921–1930*), 181, 235, 719.

43. *Motion Picture World*, December 5, 1925. Fairmont Productions completed *Silk Bouquet*, later renamed *The Dragon Horse*, on February 26, 1926. It was licensed to play in New York State on June 26, 1926, and renewed on January 4, 1927. See License Applications for Silk Bouquet, Film Script Collection, Manuscript Division,

New York State Archives. For comment on rich Chinese people and their intentions, see *Mein Film* 10 (1926).

44. For *The Desert's Toll*, see *Bioscope*, January 27, 1927, and *Picturegoer*, November 1927. For pay, see Anna May Wong File, "Contract for *The Desert's Toll*," September 4, 11, 1926, USC Film Archives. For Swanson, see Parish, *Paramount Pretties*, 22–26.

45. *Variety*, May 25, 1927; *Screen Secrets*, May 1928; *China Doll*, 3; *Screen and Stage* (Tokyo), April 1927, and *Mein Film*, 45 (1927). For salary for *Mr. Buggs*, see Anna May Wong File, *Honorable Mr. Buggs*, University of Southern California Film Archives. There is some debate whether Anna May appeared in *The Dove* (United Artists, 1927), with Wallace Beery and Norma Talmadge. See *Films in Review*, 38:10 (1987), 510.

46. *Los Angeles Times*, June 30, 2002; Young, *Rustic Canyon*, 83; Pendergast and Pendergast, *Writers and Production Artists*, 738–40.

47. *Mein Film*, 100 (1927).

48. *Mr. Wu*, MGM Production Notes, USC Archives.

49. *Variety*, April 20, 1927; for Jannings and for *Photoplay* article, see AMPAS Clipping File; in London, see *Bioscope*, February 9, 1928; *Kinetographic Weekly*, February 9, 1928; *Picturegoer*, September 1927; *Picture Show*, March 12 and 26, 1927. For South America, see *Cinelandia*, April, May 1927. In Austria, see *Paimann's Filmlisten*, June 24, 1927. For Japanese reviews, see *Movie Times* (Tokyo), September 21, October 21, 1928, and *Kinema Junpo* (Tokyo), November 2, 1928. Chaney's encouragement is reported in the *St. Louis Post-Dispatch Daily*, July 25, 1931, and reprinted in *Shanghai Express*, 1:1 (1999). For discussion of "yellow faces," see Fuller, "Hollywood Goes Oriental."

50. *AFI Catalog F1 R* (*Feature Films, 1921–1930*), 562; *Variety*, June 29, 1927; Moy, *Marginal Sights*, 90–92; *Kinema Junpo* (Tokyo), January 10, 1930; *Das Kino Journal*, August 29, 1928, January 5, 1929, and *Picturegoer*, August 1928. For emphasis on the face, see Cohen, *Silent Film*, 107–31. On use of voice, see Crafton, *The Talkies*, 74, 172, 218.

51. For examples of magazine coverage, see *Picture Play*, September 1, 1924, November 1927; *Photoplay*, March 1924, August 1926; *Picture Show Supplement* (London), July 27, 1925; *Movie Weekly*, November 1, 1924; *Theater*, August 1924, August 26, 1927. See *Picturegoer* (September 1927) for direct comment on the limitations of her roles.

52. Chu, *Chinese Theater*, 173. For quote, see Xiao, "Film Censorship," 246.

53. For Jannings, see Carlisle, "Velly Muchee Lonely," 94. Sojin, *The Unpainted Face of Hollywood*, 60–61.

54. Endres and Cushman, *Hollywood at Your Feet*, 23, 27–34; Film Clip, Sekani Moving Ideas, Film Archive.

55. Anna May Wong Gift Collection Book 8409, NYPL; Pepper and Kobal, *The Man Who Shot Garbo*, 32; *Theatre Magazine*, 1927; *Vanity Fair*, 93 (May 1928), 91; Pepper, *Camera Portraits*, 26; Beaton, *Photobiography*, 46–7.

56. See, for example, in England, *Picture Show*, January 2, 1926. In Japan see *Kinema Junpo* (Tokyo), January 21, 1924; March 1, 11; October 21, 1925; October 21, 1927; February 11, 1929. Swimsuit photo appears in *Stage and Screen (Tokyo)*, August 1927; the other in the March 1927 issue.

57. *Liang You Huabao*, July 30, 1927; Lee, *Shanghai Modern*, 64–65. On Li Lillli, see Gao, "Sports, Gender, and the Nation-State," chapter 4.

58. *Pei-Yang Pictorial Weekly* (Tianjin), November 30, 1927; May 8, August 29, 1928. For an English review, see *Picturegoer*, March 1928; for France see *Ciné-Miroir*, December 2, 1927; for Austria see *Paimann's Filmlisten*, August 10, 1927, and *Das Kino-Journal*, October 8, 1927. For Germany see *Mein Film*, March 25, 1927. On Gray see *Screen Secrets Magazine*, December 1927, January 1928. For censorship see *Chinatown Charlie* and *Devil Dancer* Files, Censorship Board Scripts, New York State Library.

59. *Variety*, February 5, March 28, 1928; Ellenberger, *Ramon Novarro*, 83–4; *Bioscope*, May 17, 1928; *Movie Times (Tokyo)*, November 5, 1929. For Bull photos, see Pepper and Kobal, *The Man Who Shot Garbo*, 32, and Anna May Wong file at the Wisconsin Center for Film and Theater Research. For South American advertisements, see *Cinelandia*, June, July, August 1928.

60. *Across to Singapore*, MGM Files, USC Film Archives.

61. Carlisle, "Velly Muchee Lonely," 94; *Hollywood Magazine*, February 1932; *Ciné Miroir*, November 27, 1931; *Mein Film*, May 5, 1928; Anna May Wong File, June 7, 1927, National Archives, Pacific Region, Laguna Niguel, California; "Anna May Wong File," NYPL; AMPAS Clippings and *Screen Secrets Magazine*, July 1928.

62. Segrave, *American Films Abroad*, 19–23, 34–35, 41–44, 69–70.

Chapter Three Europe

1. Rotha, *The Film Till Now*, 230; Palmer and Neubauer, *The Weimar Republic*, 263; Ritchie, *Faust's Metropolis*, 350–54, and Elsaesser, *Weimar Cinema and After*, 33–37; AMPAS Clippings.

2. Willet, *The Weimar Years*, 89; Jelavitch, *Berlin Caberet*, 167–74; Gordon, *Voluptuous Panic*; Rose, *Jazz Cleopatra*, 83–88; Schrader and Schebera, *The "Golden" Twenties*, 142, and Ritchie, *Faust's Metropolis*, 343–45.

3. Flemming Christiansen, "Chinese Identity in Europe," and Erich Guttinger, "A Sketch of the Chinese Community in Germany Past and Present," in Benton and Peike, *The Chinese in Europe*, 42–67, 197–211.

4. Bergfelder, "Negotiating Exoticism," in Higson and Maltby, *Film Europe*, 305–8; Kreimeier, *The UFA Story*, 134; Vincendeau, *Encyclopedia of European Cinema*, 125; *Mein Film*, May 5, July 6, September 14, November 23, 1928.

5. Bergfelder, "Negotiating Exoticism," in Higson and Maltby, *Film Europe*, 302–5. Bruno, *Atlas of Emotion*, 294–95.

6. *Film Photos Wie Noch Nie*, 131–32, 159, 170, 237; Pepper, *Camera Portraits*, 26; *Tänzerinnen Der Gegenwart*, 47; Weiss, "Heads and Tales." For Menasse, see Faber,

ed., *Divas and Lovers*, 49. For later use of Jacobi's images, see *Tolnai Vilaglapja*, June 21, 1939, 42. For availability of magazines in China, see Lee, *Shanghai Modern*, 18–20, 34.

7. Benjamin, "Gesprächt mit Anna May Wong," in Witte, *Walter Benjamin*, 105–16; Broderson, *Walter Benjamin*, 164–66. For similar reactions, see Guttinger, *Köpfen Sie Mal ein Ei in Zeitlupe*, 23, and Hubert, *Hollywood: Legends and Reality*, 106–9. For café society, see Ritchie, *Faust's Metropolis*, 345–46; and for theater and opera, see the many programs in Anna May Wong Gift Collection, Books 8401, 8402.

8. Spence, *The Chan's Great Continent*, 144–46.

9. Anna May Wong Gift Collection, Book 8414, NYPL; *Pour Vous*, July 18, 1929; *BN L'Arsenale*, February 1929. For population figures, see Pan, *Encyclopedia of the Chinese Overseas*, 311–12.

10. Live Yu-Sion, "The Chinese Community in France: Immigration, Economic Activity; Cultural Organization, and Representation," in Benton and Pieke, *The Chinese in Europe*, 96–125.

11. Anna May Wong Clipping File, AMPAS; *Screenplay Secrets*, June 1929, May 1930.

12. *Ciné Miroir*, June 14, 1929; *Cinémonde*, January 24, 1929. For her life in London, see *Picturegoer*, September 1928 and Anna May Wong Gift Collection, Book 8405. For Lulu's departure, see *Los Angeles Examiner*, May 30, 1929; *Picture Show*, July 27, 1929. For discussion of the impact of Anna May on English fashion, see Rivers, "Anna May Sorry She Cannot Be Kissed."

13. de Silva, *These Piquant People*, 49–54. See also *Picture Show*, September 7, 1930 and *Cinémonde*, January 16, 1930.

14. David Parker, "Chinese People in Britain: Histories, Futures, and Talents," in Benton and Pieke, *The Chinese in Europe*, 67–96.

15. *Ciné Miroir*, November 15, 22, 1929.

16. Jager, "Song," *FilmKritik*. The fullest French review was in *Ciné Miroir*, November 22, 1929. *Song* is dramatized in *Picture Show*, August 17, 1929.

17. Bergfelder, "Negotiating Exoticism," 308–30; Jager, "Song," *FilmKritik*; *Paimann's Filmlisten*, August 31; *Film-Kurier*, August 18, 29, 25; September 1, 8, 10, 1928; *NYT*, August 22, 1928.

18. *Cinémonde*, May 23, 1929; *Close Up*, 3:6 (December 1928), 9–14; *Variety*, November 14, 1928; *New York Times*, August 22, 1928 and December 30, 1929.

19. Wong, "The Chinese Are Misunderstood."

20. McLellan, *The Girls*, 62; Spoto, *Blue Angel*, 38–39; Ritchie, *Faust's Metropolis*, 355; Eisenstadt, *People*, 22; Palmer and Neubauer, *The Weimar Republic*, 12, 151, 272. For Baker's appearances in Berlin, see *Film-Kurier*, September 12, 1928.

21. *Pour Vous*, February 14, 21, 1929.

22. *BN de L'Arsenale*, February 1929.

23. For her statement that she was twenty-three years old in 1930, see *Paris-Midi*, May 1930. For wrong birthday, see *Die Filmwoche*, 35 (1932).

24. *Pour Vous*, March 7, 1929.

25. *Pour Vous*, July 27, 1933 and November 14, 1930.

26. *Pour Vous*, May 26, 1932.

27. *Pour Vous*, March 23, 1933.

28. *Ciné-Miroir*, March 8, 1929; *Pour Vous*, March 16, 1933; *Cinémonde*, October 10, November 2, 1928.

29. *Screen and Stage*, August, October, 1928; *Xinyingxing* (Silverland), September 1, 1928; *Pei-Yang Pictorial News*, August 31, December 26, 1929, March 18, 20, April 1, November 22, 1930.

30. *Film Weekly*, December 17, 1928; February 11, 1929; *Das Magazin*, 63:6 (November 1929); *Filmjournalen*, 5 (1930); See also *Illustrated Sporting and Dramatic News*, November 20, 1929; *Picture Show*, August 28, 1928; *Ciné-Miroir*, November 15, 1929. For German and Austrian reviews of *Piccadilly* and reruns, see *Paimann's Filmlisten*, February 15, 1929, April 11, 1930, January 11, 1929, and *Mein Film*, January 30, 1930. For Portugal see *Cinéfilo*, November 17, 1928.

31. Brodi, *Der verbotene Blick*, 297.

32. *Kinetographic Weekly*, February 7, 1929; *Close Up* 5 (July 1929), 45–47; *Picture Show*, August 17, 1929; January 12, 18, 1930; February 8, 1930; March 1, 29, 1930; July 12, 1930. For France, see *Hebdo-Cinema*, January 25, 1929. For Austria, see *Das Kino-Journal*, February 16, 1929. For the United States, see *New York Times*, July 14, 1929.

33. This description and the following paragraphs are taken from the review in *Ciné Miroir*, June 20, 1930, from *Picture Show*, March 12, August 18, 25, 1928; October 20, December 29, 1929, and from my own reading of the film. For Thomas's sketch, see *Piccadilly* Pressbook, LOC LP559.

34. Rivers, "Anna May Sorry She Cannot Be Kissed"; Bennett, *Piccadilly*; Doerr, "Reminiscences of Anna May Wong," *Social Magazine*, February 1932.

35. Rivers, "Anna May Sorry She Cannot Be Kissed."

36. There are more than fifty clippings and reviews in the Rose Quong Collection, Pennsylvania Historical Society. None favors Anna May and all commonly argue that Rose Quong trumped the movie star. For transition to talkies and effect on stars, see Sklar, *Film*, 172–75.

37. Dean, *Mind's Eye*, 67–71. For American coverage, see *Los Angeles Examiner*, February 12, 1929, March 10, 1929. For anecdote about the luncheon, see *Los Angeles Examiner*, August 12, 1934. For 100 pound fee, see *Time*, October 1, 1934.

38. *Filma*, March 13, 1930; *Ciné Miroir*, June 27, 1930; *Hebdo-Film*, March 15, 29, 1930; *Mein Film*, March 15, 1929; *Das Kino-Journal*, March 16, May 4, 1929; *Variety*, May 8, 1929.

39. AMW to VV, September 26, 1929.

40. Klaus, *Deutsche Tonfilme* 2 (1931); Guy, "Calling All Stars: Musical Films in a Musical Decade," in Richards, ed., *The Unknown 1930s*, 102, 104; *Cinémonde*, January 16, February 13, 1930; *Mein Film*, October 7, 1930.

41. *Ciné Miroir*, May 2, September 19, 1930; *Illustrieter Film-Kurier* (Berlin), 59 (n.d.); *Mein Film*, October 16, November 27, 1929.

42. Rivers, "Anna May Sorry She Cannot Be Kissed"; *Los Angeles Examiner*, November 23, 1929; for appearances see *Film Weekly*, April 5, 1930.

43. *Variety*, November 5, 1930; AMPAS Clipping File; *New York Times*, November 4, 1930, April 2, 1931; *Cinémonde*, September 18, 1930; *Hebdo-Cinéma*, October 4, 1930. For German films, see *Die Filmwoche*, January and February 1930. For German indifference to Dietrich, see Ritchie, *Faust's Metropolis*, 358.

44. *Mein Film*, July 22, 1930.

45. On *Sabotage*, see *Hebdo-Film*, June 7, July 5, 1930. *Sabotage* is not listed among Metzner's credits that are detailed in *Film Dope* 42 (1989), 40–43. He left Europe for Hollywood in the mid-1930s to escape Hitler. See also Kracauer, *From Caligari to Hitler*, 194–95.

46. *Ciné Miroir*, June 13, 1930; *Cinémonde*, July 24, 1930.

47. Rivers, "Anna May Sorry She Cannot Be Kissed."

48. *New York Times*, April 20, 1930.

49. Martin Duberman, "Robeson and Othello," in Stewart, ed., *Paul Robeson*, 123–35. For program of this night, see Anna May Wong Gift Collection, Book 8405.

50. *Ciné Miroir*, November 11, 1929; *Mon Ciné*, March 11, 1930; *Carnet*, September 28, 1930; *Cinémonde*, May 18, 1933. The German journalists agreed; see *Mein Film*, February 27, 1929. For French resentment, see Blower, *Becoming Americans*, 55–93, esp. 78–79.

51. *Ciné Miroir*, June 13, 14, 1930; *Paris-Midi*, May 1930.

52. *Ciné Miroir*, June 13, 14, 1930. For many theatrical evenings, see Anna May Wong Gift Collection, Book 8401.

53. *BN de L'Arsenale*, February 1929.

54. *Mein Film*, June 4, 1930.

55. Kracauer, *From Caligari to Hitler*, 6–10, 135; Eisner, *The Haunted Screen*; Berfelder, "Negotiating Exoticism."

56. *Wiener Handelsblatt*, July 5, 15, 19, 24, August 4, 5, 12, 30, 1930; *Der Tag*, June 22, July 2, 6, 15, 20, 28, 30, 1930; *Neue Freie Presse*, July 10, 1930; *New York Times*, October 18, 1930; *Los Angeles Examiner*, August 22, 1930; *Mein Film*, August 19, 1930. On Feldkammer and Preminger, see Prikopa, *Der Wiener Volksoper*, 83–87.

57. *Der Tag*, August 14, 1930.

58. *Wiener Zeitung*, August 17, September 10, 1930; *Wiener Handelsblatt*, September 16, 17, 1930; *Der Tag*, August 16, 1930. For German remarks, see *Mein Film*, August 17, 1930.

59. For homesickness, see *Los Angeles Examiner*, October 19, 1930.

60. *Screenplay Secrets*, October 1931. I could not find much on Grace Wilcox. She wrote a one-act play involving a flapper and her lover, which was published in *Poet Lore: World Literature and the Drama* (Boston: Richard G. Badger, 1930), 251–60.

61. *New York Times*, October 18, November 16, 1930.

62. Smith, *Life in a Putty Knife Factory*, 25.

63. Anna May Wong, AMPAS Clipping File; *Motion Picture Magazine*, October 1931; Lim, *A Feeling of Belonging*, 55–56.

Chapter Four Atlantic Crossings

1. *New York Times*, April 20, 1930; October 30, 1930; Wong, "My Film Thrills," *Cinegraf*, July 1932. Botto, *At this Theater*, 205.
2. On the death of Lee Gon Toy, see Clippings File, AMPAS; *Los Angeles Examiner*, November 12, 1930, February 3, 1931.
3. *American Photography* (Boston), November 1931, 573.
4. For arrival, see *Los Angeles Examiner*, June 2, 1931, and Anna May Wong Clipping File, AMPAS. For Oland quote, see Bob Thomas article, December 22, 1959, reprinted in *Shanghai Express* 1:1 (1999). For salaries, see *Daughter of the Dragon*, Production Notes, Box 32, Paramount Pictures File, AMPAS.
5. *AFI Feature Films, 1931–1940*, 467. Paramount also included a photo of Anna May in a twenty-year anniversary film, which was not released to the public. Ibid., 970.
6. Berenstein, *Attack of the Leading Ladies*, 39–40, 221n10.
7. *New York Times*, August 25, 1931; *Variety*, August 25, 1931; *Los Angeles Examiner*, August 28, 1931; *Screenplay Secrets*, October 1931; *Film Fun*, October, November 1931.
8. *Cinéfilo*, March 1932.
9. "Daughter of the Dragon Pressbook," LP2444, LOC; *Cinelandia*, December 1931.
10. Berry, *Screen Style*, 95–119.
11. Willis, "Famous Oriental Stars Return to the Screen"; see also *Los Angeles Examiner*, May 13, June 2, 3, 1931. For Mary see *Picture Show*, December 19, 1931. Anna May's "return" even received play in Europe. See *Picturegoer Weekly*, October 17, 1931.
12. Winokur, *American Laughter*, 212; Berry, *Screen Style*, 136–40.
13. Parish and Leonard, *Hollywood Players*, 535; Anna May Wong Gift Collection, Book 8408, Book 8409. Van Vechten Scrapbook, 24; *Los Angeles Examiner*, August 25, 1931; *Los Angeles Times*, October 30, 1931.
14. Wong, "Manchuria," 7.
15. Wong, "Manchuria," 6–7. For passive resistance, see Fu, *Passivity, Resistance and Collaboration*, 21–68.
16. *AFI Feature Films, 1931–1940*, 1904; Rainsberger, *James Wong Howe*, 19; *Cinelandia*, March 1932.
17. For a similar reading, see Marchetti, *Romances*, 65. For dialogue, see "Shanghai Express Censorship Dialogue Script," New York State Archives.
18. Program for Anna May Wong, La Scala, Rome, 1934, Anna May Wong Gift Collection, Book 8402.
19. *Shanghai Express*, Production Notes, Box 116, Paramount Pictures File, AMPAS; on clothing, see Rosten, *Hollywood*, 193–95. For comments on von Sternberg's use of Dietrich, see Naremore, *Acting in the Cinema*, 132–36.
20. *Picturegoer Weekly*, October 1, 1932, and *New York Times*, February 18, 1932.

21. *Pei-Yang Pictorial Weekly*, December 5, 1931; *Radio Movie Daily News* (Shanghai), June 17, 1932; Jones, *Portrayal of China*, 37–41. See translation of the Pei-Yang article and several letters between Paramount executives in the Anna May Wong Clipping File, AMPAS. For Hong Shen, see Leyda, *Dianying*, 82; Zhao, "Film Censorship in China," 194–96; Xiao, "Anti-Imperialism and Film Censorship during the Nanjing Decade, 1927–1937," in Lu, *Transnational Chinese Cinemas*, 38–40; Zhang, *Encyclopedia of Chinese Film*, 188; Pickowicz, "The Theme of Spiritual Pollution," and Sergeant, *Shanghai*, 248–50. On students, see Spence, *Search for Modern China*, 283. On Hong Shen, see Ye, *Seeking Modernity*.

22. See the complete discussion of censorship around this time and Hong Shen's reputation building in Xiao, "Film Censorship in China," 178–200. For suspension, see Vasey, *The World According to Hollywood*, 155.

23. "*Shanghai Express* Censorship Dialogue Script," New York State Archives.

24. *Mein Film*, 330 (1932).

25. Riva, *Marlene Dietrich*, 127; Dietrich, *Marlene*; Wollstein, *Vixens, Floozies and Molls*, 25–31; Parish, *Paramount Pretties*, 186–93.

26. *The New Movie Magazine* (London), March 1932, 42. For French magazines, see *Cinémonde*, April 21, 28, 1932; for Portuguese see *Imagem*, January 21, 1932.

27. Marchetti, *Romance and the "Yellow Peril,"* 61–68.

28. For the chill in the air, see Lim, *A Feeling of Belonging*, 60.

29. For comments on studios, gossip columnists, travel, and gays, see Ehrenstein, *Open Secret*, 46–52. For conservative attitudes toward lesbians, see Faderman, *Odd Girls and Twilight Lovers*, 93–118.

30. AMW to VV, September 21, 1932.

31. *Picture Show*, September 10, 1932; May 20, 1933.

32. *AFI Feature Films, 1931–1940*, 171, 1996; Wollstein, *Vixens, Floozies and Molls*, 25–31; Rosten, *Hollywood*, 252.

33. *Screenplay Magazine*, November 1931, January 1932; *Film Fun*, March 1932; *Imagem*, January 1932; *Mein Film*, 286, 317, 320 (1931–1932). For Baker show, see Anna May Wong Gift Collection, Book 8402.

34. *Los Angeles Examiner*, March 30, 1932; *Los Angeles Times*, March 29, 1932.

35. AMW to VV, May 5, July 31, 1932; Kellner, *Carl Van Vechten*, 260; Huston, *Dust Tracks*, 243; on meetings and parties, see Kellner, ed., *The Splendid Drunken Twenties*. On the bicycle races, see Ritchie, *Faust's Metropolis*, 357. For Maschwitz, see Miall, *Inside the BBC*, 31–40, and Maschwitz, *No Chip on My Shoulder*, 59–60, 62. For tolerance, see Mumford, *Interzone*.

36. Paramount Press Clippings, January 13, 1938, Anna May Wong File, AMPAS. On actors and their pretensions, see Rosten, *Hollywood*, 163–68. On her reading habits, see *Screenland Magazine*, October 1931.

37. Woolf, *Hindsight*, 140–46; Woolf, *On the Way to Myself*, 123–25.

38. Woolf, *Studies in Hand-Reading*, 130–33.

39. Application for Form 430, Local File #14036/120, dated December 16, 1935, Los Angeles.

40. Case, *Do Not Disturb*, 267; Case, *Tales of a Wayward Inn*, 209; Van Vechten Scrapbooks, 25, 26, NYPL; Kellner to Author, November 11, 2002; *Diansheng* (Movietone News), October 23, 1936.

41. Parker, "Anna May Wong's Chinese Love Code."

42. *Revue Mondiale* (Paris), June 1, 1932; AMW to VV, September 21, 1932; Zhao, *Remaking Chinese America*, 39. On Chinese students, see Ye, *Seeking Modernity*, 81–113. For another article affirming Wong's unwillingness to give up career for marriage, see *Times of India* (New Delhi), May 30, June 10, 1933.

43. *Der Wiener Tag*, September 12, 13, 14, 15, 1932; *Neues Wiener Journal*, September 12, 13, 1932; *Neues Wiener Tagblatt*, September 12, 13, 1932; *Mein Film*, June 23, 1932; *New York Times*, September 11–17, 1932; AMW to VV, September 21, 1932. Anna May Wong, AMPAS Clipping File; Gielgud, *Years of the Locust*.

44. For family photo, see *Cinema Illustrazione* (Rome), September 5, 1934. For trips, see Newnham, "Chinese Puzzle"; Anna May Wong Clipping File, AMPAS; Immigration File 14036/120 and 84021/345 (Roger), NARA, Laguna Niguel, California; *Royal Pictorial*, February 1935.

45. *Los Angeles Examiner*, May 11, 1933; *Mein Film*, June 5, 1933; Anna May Wong Gift Collection, Box 8407, 8414, Immigration File 14036/120, NARA, Laguna Niguel, California. On Berlin, see Ritchie, *Faust's Metropolis*, 426–30, 452–57.

46. AMW to VV, July 5, 1933.

47. Anna May Wong Gift Collection, Box 8401, 8407; Anna May Wong AMPAS Clipping File; *Shanghai Express* 1:2 (1999), 6. For Dublin, see *Dublin Evening Mail*, October 3, 1933, *Irish Press*, October 3, 1933, *Irish Times*, October 3, 1933. For Ellington Show, see Nicholson, *Duke Ellington*.

48. Balio, *Grand Design*, 321.

49. *AFI Feature Films Catalog, 1931–1940*, 2085; *Variety*, June 6, 1933; *New York Times*, June 1, 1933; *Kinetographic Weekly*, August 10, 1933; *Picturegoer Weekly*, January 27, 1934. For studio change, see Pitts, *Poverty Row Studios*, 353–56; for strange quality of film, see Balio, *Grand Design*, 340.

50. Richard, *The Age of the Dream Palace*, 112.

51. Print viewed at BFI.

52. US Department of Labor Statement of Wong Lew Song, Local File 8402/117, Los Angeles, April 4, 1933 at NARA, Laguna Niguel, California; Parish and Leonard, *Hollywood Players*, 535; Edwards, *The DeMilles*, 131.

53. *Film Star Weekly* (London), October 13, 1934; *Picturegoer Weekly*, October 6, 13, 1934; *Picture Show*, October 13, 1934; *Film Weekly* (London), October 3, 1934; *Variety*, September 25, 1934; *Los Angeles Examiner*, November 28, 1934; Souvenir Program in author's possession; Anna May Wong, AMPAS Clipping File; Low, *Film Making in 1930s Britain*, 138. For Austria, see *Das Kino-Journal*, October 6, 1934. For an example of American reviews, see *Time*, October 1, 1934.

54. *Variety*, August 7, 1935; *Los Angeles Examiner*, January 9, 1934; *Picturergoer*, October 13, 1934; *Film Weekly*, August 24, 1934; *Kinematograph Weekly*, June 8, July 26, 1934; *Today's Cinema*, June 2, 1934.

55. *Variety*, May 29, 1934; *New York Times*, July 31, 1935.

56. *Limehouse Blues*, Production Notes, Box 76, Paramount File, AMPAS.

57. For lyrics, see "*Limehouse Blues* Censorship Dialogue Script," New York State Archives. Anna also had a rough time on the set. Perhaps the broken middle fingernail, reported in the *Los Angeles Examiner* as a tragedy, was minor, but by September, Anna May was suffering from an impacted tooth. *Los Angeles Examiner*, August 17, 1934.

58. *AFI Feature Films Catalog, 1931–1940*, 1200. For reviews, see *Cinema Illustrazione* (Rome), July 31, 1935; *Piccolo* (Belgium), November 16, 1934. For Wagner, see *Rob Wagner's Script Magazine*, September 1, 1934, 13.

59. *Variety*, December 18, 1934; *Modem Screen Magazine*, February 1934; *New York Times*, December 12, 1934; *Los Angeles Examiner*, November 9, 1934; *Kinetographic Weekly*, January 3, 1935; *Picturegoer Weekly*, April 6, 1935; *Picture Show*, August 13, 1935; *Cinema*, January 3, 1935. For Spanish language reviews, see *Cinegraf*, January 1935.

60. *Diansheng*, January 1, 11, February 29, July 19, December 6, 1935.

61. *Los Angeles Examiner*, August 5, 12, 1934; *Xinning Magazine*, October 1934.

62. *Diansheng*, July 20, 1935; *Revista Del Hagar*, November 17, 1935; Anna May Wong Gift Collection, Box 8402, 8403, 8408; *Pour Vous* (Paris), June 2, 1932; Newnham, "A Chinese Puzzle"; *Shanghai Express* (1999), 6. On the rarity of Chinese in Scandinavia, Spain, Italy; and Switzerland, see the relevant essays in Benton and Pieke, *The Chinese in Europe*.

63. Day, ed., *Noel Coward*, 141–43.

64. "Recollections of Hu Die," 14; *Diansheng*, July 19, 1935; *Dianying Huabao*, July 15, 1935; Fania Marinoff to Carl Van Vechten, May 21, June 3, 8, 13, 16, Van Vechten Papers; *Los Angeles Examiner*, January 9, 1936. For photos, see Box 162, Van Vechten Papers; Duberman, *Robeson*, 192–93, 198.

65. Paul Robeson, *Here I Stand* (Boston: Beacon Press Reprint of 1958 edition), 30.

66. *Rob Wagner's Beverly Hills Script Weekly*, 13:326 (July 13, 1935), 21; *Los Angeles Examiner*, August 9, 1934. For prestige of studios, see Rosten, *Hollywood*, 177. For studios' relationship with Chinese officials, see Vasey, *The World According to Hollywood*, 175–79. On Buck, see Spence, *The Chan's Great Continent*, 180–82.

67. See Leong, *The China Mystique*, 75, and Wollstein, *Vixens, Floozies, and Molls*, 254. For comments on miscegenation, see *AFI Feature Films Catalog, 1931–1940*, 808.

68. "*The Good Earth* Production Notes," Folders 2, 10, MGM Collection, USC Film Archives. Wong, "My Story"; Jew, "Metro Goldwyn Mayer."

69. On Buck's homogenization of Chinese people, see Yoshihara, *Embracing the East*, 152–64. For the European reaction, see *Das Kino-Journal*, October 2, 1937. The other comments are my own.

70. *Los Angeles Examiner*, March 8, 1936.

71. *Gua Hua Bao*, February 23, 1936; *Dianying Huabao* (Shanghai Screen Pictorial), March 1, 1936; Pizzitola, *Hearst over Hollywood*, 315; AMW to VV, December 16, 1935. For Chinese American migration to China, see Gloria H. Chun, "Go West . . . to China," in Wong and Chan, *Claiming America*, 165–90; Immigration

File 14036/120, NARA, Laguna Niguel, California. For Mary, see MGM Legal Department Records, Folder 73, AMPAS. Mary received sixty dollars, which was the minimum for the Chinese actors used in the production. MGM fired all of the Chinese actors right after the picture was finished. For Mei-Mei Sze, see *Los Angeles Examiner*, January 28, 1936.

Chapter Five China

1. AMW to CVV, January 7, 1936; *New York Times*, January 26, 1936; *Rob Wagner's Script Magazine*, January 25, 1936, 27; *Los Angeles Examiner*, January 9, 17, 24, 26, March 8, 1936. For theater, see Anna May Wong Gift Collection, Book 8408.
2. *Los Angeles Examiner*, March 8, 1936; Chu, *Chinese Theaters*, 209.
3. Lin, *My Country and My People*, 140–53.
4. *New York Herald Tribune*, May 14, 1936; AMW to VV, February 22, 1936.
5. AMW to VV, February 22, 1936; *Ashahi Shimbun*, February 4, 1936; *Tokyo Nichi Nichi*, February 9, 1936; *Osaka Mainichi*, February 9, 1936; *New York Herald Tribune*, May 24, 1936; Spence, *Search for Modern China*, 420–21, on the pamphlets.
6. For brother's defense, see *Diansheng* (Shanghai Movietone News), November 27, 1935; January 24, February 14, 1936. For questions about accepting her, see *Diansheng*, January 1, 1936; *Dianying Huabao* (Screen Pictorial), March 1, 1936; *Shidai Dianying* (Film Age), February, March 1936; *Lian Huabao* (United Chinese Pictorial), February 1936; *Yisheng Dianying* (Voice of Art Film), February 1936.
7. Spence, *Search for Modem China*, 415–16.
8. See Harris, "Silent Speech," chapter 10, for full analysis of this fascinating controversy. See also Zhang and Xiao, *Encyclopedia of Chinese Film*, 284–86, and for Ruan Lingyu, 292–93.
9. Harris, "Silent Speech," 354–58.
10. On the Leftist perspective, see Lee, *Shanghai Modern*, 99–101.
11. Lee, *Shanghai Modern*, 83–110; *All About Shanghai*, 75–77; Jones, *Yellow Music*, 3–8; Clayton, *Buck Clayton's World*, 66–79.
12. For interview, see *Hua Tzu Jih Pao* (Hong Kong), February 22, 1936. For other accounts of her arrival, see *Diansheng* (Shanghai Movietone News), February 14, 1936; *Dianying Huabao* (Screen Pictorial), March 1, 1936; *Gua Hua Bao* (Guangzhou), February 23, 1936; *Pei-Yang Pictorial Notices* (Tianjin), February 12, 1936; *Peking and Tientsin Sunday Times*, February 16, 1936. *North-China Daily News*, February 10–15, 1936; *North-China Herald* (Shanghai), February 19, 1936; *Shun Pao* (Peking), February 10–12, 1936. For her home movie, see Scene List of Wong, "Where the Wind Rocks the Bamboo," AMPAS.
13. *North-China Daily News*, February 12, 14, 15, 16, 1936; Koo, *No Feast Lasts Forever*; *New York Herald Tribune*, May 31, June 7, 1936; Wong, "Where the Wind Rocks the Bamboo." AMW to VV, February 22, 1936; *ANB*, 13: 659–61.
14. *Rob Wagner's Script Magazine*, December 12, 1936, 11.

15. *Liang You Huabao*, February 1936; *New York Herald Tribune*, June 7, 14, 1936.

16. Emily Hahn, *China to Me: A Partial Autobiography* (New York: Doubleday, Doran, 1944), 38.

17. *Hua Tzu Jih Pao* (Hong Kong), February 18, 1936; *Diansheng* (Shanghai Movietone News), February 21, 1936; *Ming Xin*, February 1936; *Yisheng Dianying*, February 1936. On flaneurs and tourists, see Gleber, *The Art of Taking a Walk*, 132–35. On Shanghai, see Bruno, *Atlas of Emotion*, 290–3. For satire, see *Manhua Jie* (Modern Puck), April 1936.

18. *Diansheng* (Shanghai Movietone News), March 27, 1936; Spence, *Search for Modern China*, 426.

19. *Manila Bulletin*, March 4–8, 1936; *Manila Tribune*, March 4, 1936; AMW to VV, March 14, 1936.

20. *Diansheng* (Shanghai Movietone News), April 3, 1936.

21. *Shun Pao* (Shanghai), March 10, 1936; *North-China Herald* (Shanghai), April 1, 1936; interviews of villagers by author, June 2001; Austin Yu to author, March 12, 2002, in author's possession. For myth of villagers, see *Birmingham (Al) News*, August 22, 1937, Clipping File, Wisconsin Center for Film.

22. AMW to CVV, March 23, 1936.

23. *Shun Pao*, March 27, April 1, 1936; *Diansheng* (Shanghai Movietone News), May 15, 1936.

24. *Los Angeles Examiner*, August 20, 1936; Sergeant, *Shanghai*, 258–59.

25. AMW to CVV, May 8, 1936. Beiping was used as the name for Peking between 1928 and 1949.

26. *Shen Pao* (Peking), May 1, 5, 1936; *Diansheng* (Shanghai Movietone News), May 8, 1936.

27. *Diansheng* (Shanghai Movietone News), August 28, September 18, 1936.

28. *Da Gong Bao* (Peking), May 17–21, 1936; *Pei-Yang Pictorial* (Tianjin), May 16, 1936; *Shun Pao* (Shanghai), May 10, 1936. On Stuart, see West, *Yenching University*, 23–27, 177–83.

29. *Pei-Yng Pictorial* (Tianjin), May 23, 1936; Spence, *The Chinese Century*, 102.

30. *Da Gong Bao* (Peking), May 17–21, 1936; *Diansheng* (Shanghai Movietone News), June 5, 1936

31. *Pei-Yang Pictorial* (Tianjin), June 9, 1936; *Diansheng* (Shanghai Movietone News), June 19, 1936; *Mei Shu Sheng Huo* (Arts and Life), June 1936.

32. *Diansheng* (Shanghai Movietone News), July 10, 1936.

33. *Diansheng* (Shanghai Movietone News), August 7, 14, October 2, 9, 23, 30, 1936; Anna May Wong File 14036/97. Immigration and Naturalization Service, NARA, Laguna Niguel, California.

Chapter Six In the Service of the Motherland

1. There are numerous forms dealing with the imposter in 1935 and 1936 in the Anna May Wong File 14036/297, November 30, 1936, Immigration and Naturalization Service. For incident with father, see Leong, *The China Mystique*, 96.

2. *Rob Wagner's Script Magazine*, December 12, 1936, 11.

3. File 14036/1459-A. November 17, 1938, National Archives, Pacific Region, Laguna Niguel Office; Huang Family Genealogy. For Huang Dounan family, see Family Genealogy supplied to Author by Huang Cui-Xian.

4. *Los Angeles Examiner*, November 23, 30, 1936; *Los Angeles Herald Express*, November 30, 1936; Spence, *Search for Modern China*, 437–50; Paramount Press Clippings, AMPAS.

5. *AFI Film Catalog, Feature Films, 1931–1940*, 12–13; Wollstein, *Vixens, Floozies and Molls*, 256. For *Hollywood Party*, see "*Hollywood Party* Dialogue Censorship Script," New York State Archives.

6. Anna May Wong Gift Collection, Book 8401; Maschwitz, *No Chip on My Shoulder*, 87–88. Maschwitz told both Anna May and his wife Hermione Gingold that he had written the song with each in mind. See Gingold, *How to Grow Old Disgracefully*, 54.

7. *Los Angeles Examiner*, March 24, 25, 26, 27, 29, April 3, 4, 1937; Anna May Wong File 390596/190-H.Q. Federal Bureau of Investigation. On deranged fans, see Barbas, *Movie Crazy*, 165–72.

8. For stage show, see *New York Herald Tribune*, May 21, 1937, and *New York Times*, May 23, 1937. For *Turandot*, see Price, *Renaissance Man*, 77; see also programs for the productions in the Anna May Wong Gift Collection, Books 8408, 8410, and Clipping File, NYPL. For her trip preparation, see the numerous forms in US Department of Labor, Immigration and Nationalization Service File 14036/120, NARA, Laguna Niguel, California.

9. Anna May Wong Gift Collection, Book 8403; US Department of Labor, Immigration and Nationalization Service File 14036/120, April 23, 1937, NARA, Laguna Niguel, California.

10. Maschwitz, *No Chip on My Shoulder*, 104–7.

11. Gielgud, *Years of the Locust*, 156–60.

12. Leong, *The China Mystique*, 88.

13. Jesperson, *American Images*, 45–58.

14. Gielgud, *Years of the Locust*, 158; Chierichetti, *Edith Head*, 54.

15. Engstead, *Star Shoots*, 114, 97–229.

16. *Daughter of Shanghai*, Production Notes, Box 32, Paramount Pictures, AMPAS. On Florey, see Balio, *Grand Design*, 320, and Spear, *Hollywood: The Golden Era*, 333–61. On pay, see Parish, *Paramount Pretties*, 154, 197, 302.

17. *AFI Film Catalog, Feature Films, 1931–1940*, 466; Marrill, *Films of Anthony Quinn*, 49; Edwards, *The DeMilles*, 143–47.

18. *New York Times*, December 25, 1937; *Paramount Service Magazine*, November 13, 1937.

19. *Picturegoer*, July 16, 1938; *Kinetographic Weekly*, July 3, 1938; *Film Weekly*, March 20, 1938; *Das Kino-Journal*, October 30, 1937.

20. *Guoguang Yinxun* (Cathay-Grand News), June 22, 1938. For Chen Yunshang, see Fu, "Selling Fantasies at War: Production and Promotion Practices of the Shanghai Cinema, 1937–41," in Cochran, ed., *Inventing Nanjing Road*, 199. For registration at

USC, I rely on the recollections of Joseph B. Comstock Jr., father of Ned Comstock, curator of the film collection at USC.

21. *Des Moines Register* Stills Collection, LOC.

22. AMW to VV, December 4, 1937; January 3, 1938.

23. *AFI Feature Films Catalog, 1931–1940*, 456; Marrill, *Films of Anthony Quinn*, 52; Production Notes, *Dangerous to Know*, Paramount Pictures, AMPAS.

24. *Picturegoer*, August 21, 1938.

25. *New York Times*, March 12, 1938; *Variety*, March 16, 1938; *Daily Variety*, February 24, 1938; *Hollywood Reporter*, February 24, 1938; *Movie Story*, April 1938.

26. *Kinetographic Weekly*, March 17, 1938; *Paimann's Filmlisten*, October 7, 1938; *Cine Mundial*, April 1938; *Mein Film*, 666 (1938); Ritchie, *Berlin*, 455. For Vienna, see *Das Kino-Journal*, August 6, 1938.

27. Maschwitz, *No Chip on My Shoulder*, 112–17, Doerr, "My Years with Anna May Wong."

28. *AFI Institute Catalog, Feature Films, 1931–1940*, 2400; *New York Times*, June 9, 1938; *Kinetographic Weekly*, July 7, 1938.

29. *King of Chinatown*, Production Notes, Box 69, Paramount Picture Files, AMPAS; *AFI Institute Catalog, Feature Films, 1931–1940*, 1106–7; Marrill, *Films of Anthony Quinn*, 61.

30. *Click Magazine*, December 1938, 8–10; Smith, *Lonely Queue*, 47, 91–93.

31. *Variety*, March 22, 1939; *Daily Variety*, March 15, 1939; *Hollywood Reporter*, March 15, 1939; *New York Times*, March 16, 1939.

32. *Boy's Cinema* (London), May 20, 1939; *Kinetographic Weekly*, March 30, 1939; *Paimann's Filmlisten*, September 25, 1939.

33. *Campbell (Soup) Playhouse*, "The Patriot," episode 19, April 14, 1939.

34. *Island of Lost Men File*, AMPAS Library.

35. *AFI Feature Films Catalog, 1931–1940*, 1041. Fine Arts Pictures also sought to use Anna May's talents that spring for their production of *Panama Patrol*, but she could not fit the film into her schedule. *AFI Feature Films Catalog, 1931–1940*, 1615–16.

36. *Variety*, August 25, 1939; *Daily Variety*, August 2, 1939; *New York Times*, August 18, 1939; *Los Angeles Examiner*, August 16, 1939; *Hollywood Reporter*, August 2, 1939; *Kinetographic Weekly*, October 5, 1939.

37. *Island of Lost Men*, Production Notes, Box 65, Paramount Pictures, AMPAS.

38. I used the data in Rosten, *Hollywood*, 342, 382, to bolster my argument in this paragraph.

39. *Pei-Yang Pictorial Weekly*, February 23, 1937; Anna May Wong Clipping File, WCFTA; Young, *Rustic Canyon*, 131–42; for her party, see *Los Angeles Examiner*, November 23, 1939.

40. Los Angeles Recorder's Office, Document 446, 447, Books 16095, 26, and 16005, 268. For sale to her sisters, see Document 1467, Book 17003, 21.

41. *Paramount News*, Film Clip, August 7, 1941. *Chinatown, Los Angeles*. Souvenir Program of the Chinese Moon Festival, 1941. For interviews with Chinese actors, see Lim, *A Feeling of Belonging*, 73. For troupes of entertainers, see the videotape by

Dong, *Forbidden City*. On Chinatown restaurants and tourists, see Gabaccia, *We Are What We Eat*, 102–5.

42. See, *On Gold Mountain*, 215.

43. Paramount Press Release, 1938, AMPAS Clipping File; *Shanghai Movie Star*, January 1, 1939, and *Diansheng Weekly*, November 20, 1928.

44. *Better Homes & Gardens*, 20 (September 1941), 28; *Look*, March 1, April 1, 1938. On furniture and glamor, see Thorp, *America Goes to the Movies*, 91.

45. Stine, *The Hurrell Style*, 113; *Photoplay*, June 1938.

46. *New York Times*, June 22, 1938; Paramount Publicity Sheets, December 28, 1937; January 13, 1938, Anna May Wong Clippings File, AMPAS; AMW to VV, May 9, 1940. For earlier auction, see *Los Angeles Examiner*, January 7, March 9, 1937. See also *Das Kino-Journal*, March 5, 1938.

47. Van Vechten Scrapbook, 27, NYPL.

48. Derham Groves, *Anna May Wong's Lucky Shoes*, 16–19.

49. File 14036/236-A. April 13, September 3, 1939, National Archives, Pacific Region, Laguna Niguel Office; AMW to VV, September 11, 1939, *Los Angeles Examiner*, May 3, 5, September 5, 1939. For Australian coverage, see the *Melbourne Age*, June 3, 10, 13, 1939, and the *Sydney Morning Herald*, June 3, 5, 10, 1939.

50. *AFI Feature Films Catalog, 1931–1940*, 681; Marrill, *Films of Anthony Quinn*, 64.

51. *Variety*, March 21, 1941; *New York Times*, March 7, 1941; *Daily Variety*, February 21, 1941; *Hollywood Reporter*, February 21, 1941.

52. AMW to VV, February 20, April 2, 4, May 10, 1940. Anna May Wong Gift Collection, Book 8411.

53. *Seattle Daily Times*, April 9, 1939, as quoted in Chan, *Perpetually Cool*, 147–56. For Chan's description of Anna May as a Daoist Butterfly, see *idem*, 145–59.

54. *New York Herald Tribune*, July 25, 1940; AMW to VV, August 12, 1940.

55. Richard Wong to VV, October 10, 1940.

56. *New York Times*, September 17, 1940; Anna May Wong Clipping File, WCTA; AMW to VV, October 12, December 12, 1940.

57. AMW to VV, December 30, 1940.

58. *Theatre World* (London), December 1941.

59. *AFI Institute Catalog, Feature Films, 1941–1950*, 275; Mundy, "Joseph H. Lewis."

60. Jesperson, *American Images*, 66, 78; *Variety*, August 19, 1942; *New York Times*, August 10, 1942; *Kinetographic Weekly*, November 19, 1942; *Bombs Over Burma* Censorship Script, New York State Archives.

61. *Los Angeles Times*, December 8, 1942; *Shanghai Express*, 1:1 (1999); AMW to VV, January 20, February 10, 1942; Office of Talent Committee Reporting Activities of Hollywood Victory Committee, USC Film Archives.

62. Wong, "Preface" to Wing, *New Chinese Recipes*. A second, expanded edition came out the following year. On importance of recipes for stars, see Thorp, *America at the Movies*, 91–94. On Chinese food, local influences, and cookbooks, see Gabaccia, *We Are What We Eat*, 102–5, 140–50, 176. For Anna May's previous cookbook

participation, see *Milady's Style Parade and Recipe Book for 1935*. For recipe books, see Roberts, *China to Chinatown*, 152, 188.

63. Volker, *Brecht Chronicle*, 114; Hayman, *Brecht*, 263.

64. *AFI Institute Catalog, Feature Films, 1941–1950*, 1311; *Variety*, January 20, 1942; *Los Angeles Examiner*, December 24, 1942; *Hollywood Reporter*, November 4, 1942; *Daily Variety*, November 4, 1942; *Screen Romances*, March 1943; AMW to VV, August 31, 1942. On Hollywood, women, and the war, see Koppes and Black, *Hollywood Goes to War*, 93–101. See also "*Lady from Chungking* Censorship Script," New York State Archives.

65. AMW to VV, August 31, September 10, 1941, October 5, 1943, March 17, 1944.

66. Jesperson, *American Images*, 98–102.

67. Quotes are from Leong, *The China Mystique*, 113; Pan, *Encyclopedia of Chinese Overseas*, 98–99; Wang, *Chinese Overseas*, 42–47.

68. Jesperson, *American Images*, 105–6; for comment on laundrymen, see Lin, *Biography of Mayling Soong*, 225; for cultural workers, see Chiang, *China Shall Rise Again*, 326–27.

69. Anna May Wong Clipping File, AMPAS; AMW to VV, August 9, 1943.

70. AMW to VV, March 17, 1944.

71. AMW to VV, May 10, 22, 1944, January 6, 1945; *Los Angeles Times*, July 25, 1944, in Anna May Wong Clipping File, AMPAS; *Los Angeles Examiner*, March 30, 1944.

72. *Theater World* (London), July 1944, 24–25.

73. Blumenthal, *Stork Club*, 27.

74. AMW to VV, January 6, April 9, September 28, October 31, 1945.

75. See Zhao, *Remaking Chinese Americans*, 48–78, for Chinese American women in wartime.

Chapter Seven Becoming Chinese American

1. AMW to VV, September 11, November 14, 1946; *Shanghai Express* (1999). For another opportunity at this time, which Anna May apparently rejected, see H. A. Spanuth to AMW, January 31, 1946, Herrick Library. The Ripley film can be found at the UCLA film archives.

2. AMW to VV, August 18, 1947; February 25, 1948; October 17, 1950.

3. AMW to VV, February 25, 1948; Robert Payne Papers; Doerr, "Reminiscences of Anna May Wong," 660; Chow, "Sixty Years."

4. See, for example, AMW to VV, September 11, 1946; February 25, 1948; See *On Gold Mountain*, 284. For Howe screening, see Richard See interview with Yunah Hong, May 2003.

5. Doerr, "Anna May Wong," 661. See *On Gold Mountain*, 293–95; *Los Angeles Examiner*, December 23, 1948.

6. *AFI Feature Films Catalog, 1941–1950*, 1148–49; *Variety*, March 16, September 21, 1949; *Daily Variety*, March 15, 1949; *Hollywood Reporter*, March 15, 1949; *Los*

Angeles Examiner, April 18, 1949. For her attitude, see Conrad Doerr to author, March 24, 31, 2003.

7. Los Angeles City Department of Health Internment Order 52015; AMPAS Clipping File; for cremation rituals, see Brook, "Funerary Ritual," Huang Family Genealogy, and *Los Angeles Examiner*, October 15, 1949. For AMW's hospital stay, see *Los Angeles Examiner*, October 26, 1949.

8. *Los Angeles Times*, September 10, 1952; AMW to VV, December 31, 1951; February 17, 1952.

9. Parish, *Actor's Television Credits*, 852; Gianarcis, *Television Drama*, 211; Terrance, *The Complete Encyclopedia of Television Programs*, 295; AMW to VV, February 17, 1952. For the saga of Dumont's files, see Zimmerman, "Archiving Television."

10. AMW to VV, May 29, 1952; October 3, 1952; July 28, 1953. Conrad Doerr to Author, March 24, 2003.

11. Richard Wong to VV, December 19, 1953; AMW to VV, December 28, 1953; January 31, March 6, 1954.

12. AMW to VV, October 29, 1954; January 3, 1955; August 22, 1955.

13. AMW to VV, February 28, August 26, September 8, October 6, 1955; January 7, 14, 1956; *London Star*, September 9, 1955; *London Morning Chronicle*, September 28, 1955 in BFI Clipping Files. For hospital stay, see *Los Angeles Examiner*, October 20, 1955. For Rogers, see Bushnell, *Directors and Their Films*, 287. For *The Voodoo Factor*, see www.us.imdb.com/Title?0191746.

14. AMW to VV, July 15, 31, 1956. Van Vechten cards are almost too numerous to list, but a good example is described in AMW to VV, August 11, 1958.

15. Masden, *William Wyler*, 203; AMW to VV, November 5, 1956.

16. Parish, *Actor's Television Credits*, 852; AMW to VV, January 2, 1957.

17. AMW to VV, January 2, February 27, 1957; Giarnarcis, *Television Drama*, 409.

18. AMW to VV, November 5, 1956; August 15, 1957; August 1, 6, 11, October 27, 1958; January 12, 1959; RW to VV, October 25, 1958.

19. AMPAS Clippings, May 1, 1958; Parish, *Actor's Television Credits*, 852; Giarnarcis, *Television Drama*, 409; AMW to VV, April 15, August 11, 1958; January 15, June 6, 1959; *Holiday Magazine*, 1957.

20. Print viewed at the UCLA and Television Center.

21. Giarnarcis, *Television Drama*, 409.

22. AMW to VV, June 6, October 26, 1959; April 4, August 14, 1960; *Los Angeles Examiner*, July 29, 1960.

23. For comeback, see *Time*, June 20, 1960. For reviews, see *Variety*, June 15, 1960; Marrill, *Films of Anthony Quinn*, 186–87; AMW to VV, February 1, June 1, July 17, 1960; *Time*, June 20, 1960, and *Hollywood Reporter*, June 6, 1960, in AMPAS Clippings; AMW to Ward Morehouse, July 16, 1960; *Los Angeles Examiner*, December 4, 1959; June 30, 1960.

24. *Variety*, June 29, 1960; *New York Times*, May 25, 1961; Wollstein, *Vixens, Floozies and Molls*, 258. There is some dispute over whether Anna May's part made it past the final cuts. She is listed among the players in the *Variety* review, however.

25. AMW to VV, January 4, 1961; Parish, *Actor's Television Credits*, 852; Giarnacis, *Television Drama*, 45.
26. Doerr, "Reminiscences of Anna May Wong," 662.
27. County of Los Angeles, Certificate of Death, 7080/2660; *Los Angeles Examiner*, February 4, 1961.
28. Her will is #439787 in the Hall of Records, City of Los Angeles. For a useful evaluation of the post-fame status of a number of stars, see McCann, *Silent Screen*, 97–114. For amount of estate, see *Los Angeles Herald*, March 1, 1961, and *Los Angeles Examiner*, March 1, 1961.
29. Ellenberger, *Celebrities in Los Angeles Cemeteries*, 192–94. For obituaries, see the many notices in the AMPAS Clipping file.

Epilogue

1. RW to VV, April 14, October 17, 1961; February 12, May 7, 26, 1962; April 26, 1964; Yu Jinyan to Author, March 12, 2002.
2. County of Los Angeles, Certificate of Death 7097–015690 (James); County of Los Angeles, Certificate of Death 39519046194 (Lulu); County of Los Angeles, Certificate of Death 39319056008 (Roger). Roger's remains were placed in Interment Space 1, Lot 9778, Murmuring Trees, Forest Lawn Memorial Parks and Mortuaries. I have been unable to locate Frank's death certificate.
3. For reviews of the plight of Asians or Asian Americans in American cinema, see *The Village Voice*, December 5, 1989; Zia, *Asian American Dreams*, 109–39; Nga, "The Long March from Wong to Woo." On "yellow faces," see *USA Today*, September 10, 1985; *New York Post*, August 10, 1990. For views of Nancy Kwan and other actors, see Lee, *Asian American Actors*. Recently, an Asian American activist group forced Fox Network Television to abandon screenings of Warner Oland's Charlie Chan movies on the grounds that they were unpleasant reminders of the yellow face era. See *Los Angeles Times*, July 1, 2003.
4. See the discussion of these in Liu, "When Dragon Ladies Die, Do They Come Back as Butterflies? Re-Imaging Anna May Wong," in Hammamoto and Liu, *Countervisions*, 23–40.
5. *Life Magazine*, December 10, 1971; Chu, "Anna May Wong," 288.
6. For Warhol, see Meyer, *Outlaw Representation*, 114; for Johnson, see De Salvo, *Ray Johnson*.
7. Sontag, *Against Interpretation*, 275–93; Meyer, *Outlaw Representation*, 108–9.
8. Bennett, *A Chorus Line*, 103.
9. Scholder, ed., *Sweet Oblivion*.
10. Liu, "When Dragon Ladies Die," 35.
11. Liu, "When Dragon Ladies Die," 31, 37.

Selected Bibliography

Primary Manuscript Sources and Archives

Anna May Wong File 390596/190 H.Q.-1121432. Federal Bureau of Investigation, Washington, D.C.

Anna May Wong Gift Collection and Clipping Files. Billy Rose Theater Collection. New York Public Library.

Anna May Wong Clipping and Still File. The Wisconsin Center for Film and Theater Research, Wisconsin Historical Society.

British Film Institute Clipping Files, London.

Carl Van Vechten and Fania Marinoff Letters. Beinecke Library, Yale University.

Carl Van Vechten and Fania Marinoff Papers. Manuscripts Division, New York Public Library.

"Censorship Dialogue Script" Collection. New York State Archives, Albany, NY.

City of Los Angeles Department of Deeds and Assessments.

Copyright Register Files. Library of Congress. Motion Picture Division, Washington D.C.

Fourteenth Census of the United States, 1920, Population, Los Angeles County. National Archives.

Hearst Newsreels Collection. UCLA Television and Motion Picture Archives.

Los Angeles Public Library.

Margaret Herrick Library. Academy of Motion Pictures, Arts, and Sciences, Los Angeles.

Mercedes de Acosta Papers. Rosenbach Museum & Library, Philadelphia.

Paramount Production Notes and Stills Collection. Academy of Motion Pictures, Arts, and Sciences, Los Angeles.

Registrar's Records. Angelus Rosedale Cemetery, 1831 West Washington Boulevard, Los Angeles.

Segregated Chinese Files, RG 85. Immigration and Naturalization Service. National Archives. Pacific-Laguna Niguel Office, Los Angeles District.

Thirteenth Census of the United States, 1910, Population, Los Angeles County. National Archives.

UCLA Theater Arts Library.
University of Southern California Film Archives.
Ward Morehouse Papers. Billy Rose Theater Collection. New York Public Library.
Warner Brothers Productions Archives. University of Southern California Film/TV
    Archives.

Articles by Anna May Wong

"Bad Luck That Helped Me." *Picture Show*, September 7, 1929.
"Bamboo, or China's Conversion to Film." *Mein Film* 222, 1930.
"The Chinese Are Misunderstood." *The Rexall Magazine*, May 1930.
"Foreword." *New Chinese Recipes Using Ingredients Easily Obtainable in Neighborhood
    Stores*. By Fred Wing and Mabel Stegner. New York: United China Relief, 1942.
"'I Am Very Happy' by Anna May Wong." *Mein Film*, May 5, 1928.
"Manchuria." *Rob Wagner's Beverly Hills Script Magazine* (January 16, 1932), VI: 153.
"Mein Erstes Wort in Sprechfilm" (My First Word in Talking Movies). *Mein Film*, July 27,
    1930.
"My Film Thrills." *Film Pictorial* (London), November 11, 1933.
"My First Words in a Talkie." *Mein Film*, July 22, 1930.
"My Life by Huang Liushang." *Liang You Huabao* (Shanghai), February 1936.
"The Orient, Love and Marriage." *Revue Mondiale* (Paris), June 1, 1932.
"The True Life Story of a Chinese Girl." *Pictures* (Hollywood), September/October,
    1926.

Selected Interviews and Articles

Carlisle, Helen. "Velly Muchee Lonely." *Motion Picture Magazine*, March 1928, 41,
    94, 101.
Howe, Herb. "Between Two Worlds." *The New Movie Magazine*, July 1932, 25–27, 74.
Leung, Louise. "East Meets West." *Hollywood Magazine*, January 1939.
Newnham, John K. "Chinese Puzzle." *Film Weekly*, June 17, 1939.
Parker, Ralph. "Anna May Wong's Chinese Love Code." *Hollywood Magazine* 21:2
    (February 1932).
Rivers, Audrey. "Anna May Wong Sorry She Cannot Be Kissed." *Movie Classics*, November
    1929.
Tiklesley, Alice L. "Why Waste Your Time?" *Settle Daily Times*, April 9, 1939.
Willis, Betty. "Famous Oriental Stars Return to the Screen." *Motion Picture*, October
    1931, 44–46.
"The World's Most Beautiful Chinese Girl." *Look Magazine*, March 1, 1938, 36–37.

Magazines

Austria
Der Filmbote

Das Kino-Journal

Paimann's Filmlisten

United States
American Photography (Boston)

Beverly Hills Script Weekly (Los Angeles)

China Doll (Baltimore)

Chinese Students' Monthly

Cinelandia (Los Angeles)

Film Fun (New York)

Hollywood Magazine

Life Magazine (New York)

Look Magazine (New York)

Modern Screen

Motion Picture (New York)

Movie Classic (New York)

Movie Story (New York)

Movie Weekly

Pantomime

Photoplay (New York)

Pictures (New York)

Picture Show (New York)

Saturday Evening Post

Screenland

Screenplay Secrets

Screen Romances

England
Cinema (London)

Close Up (London)

Kinematograph Weekly (London)

Film Pictorial (London)

Film Weekly (London)

New Movie Magazine (London)

Picturegoer (London)

Picture Play (London)

Royal Pictorial (London)

Today's Cinema (London)

China
Liang You Huabao (Shanghai)

Ming Xing (Shanghai)

Shidai Jie (Modern Puck) (Shanghai)

Radio Movie Daily Times (Shanghai)

Xinning Magazine (Taishan)

Xinyingxing (Silverland) (Shanghai)

France
Ciné-Miroir (Paris)

Cinémonde (Paris)

Filma (Paris)

Hebdo-Cinéma (Paris)

Pour Vous (Paris)

A-Z (Paris)

Other Nations
Cinefilo (Portugal)

Cinema Illustrazione (Italy)

Filmjournalen (Sweden)

Geillustreerd Stuiversblad (Holland)

Het Weekblad (Holland)

Imagem (Portugal)

Mein Film (Germany)

Revista del Hogar (Spain)

Social Magazine (Cuba)

Tolnai Vilaglapja (Hungary)

Newspapers

Australia
Melbourne Age   Sydney Morning Herald

Austria
Der Morgen (Vienna)   Wiener Handelsblatt (Vienna)
Der Tag (Vienna)   Wiener Zeitung (Vienna)

China
Da Gong Bao (Beijing)   North China Herald (Shanghai)
Guo Hua Bo (Guangzhou)   Pei-Yang Pictorial News (Tianjin)
Hua Tzu Jih Pao (Hong Kong)   Shen Bao (Shanghai)
North-China Daily News (Shanghai)   Shi Pao (Shanghai)

England
London Era

Ireland
Dublin Evening Mail   Irish Times (Dublin)
Irish Press (Dublin)

Philippines
Manila Bulletin   Manila Tribune

United States
Daily Variety   New York Post
Hollywood Reporter   New York Times
Los Angeles Times   USA Today

Fiction and Poetry

Hagedorn, Jessica. "The Death of Anna May Wong." In *Danger and Beauty*. San Francisco:
    City Lights Books, 2002.
———. "Film Noir." In *The Gangster of Love*. Boston: Houghton Mifflin, 1996.

Printed Primary Sources

All About Shanghai: A Standard Guidebook. Shanghai: University Press, 1934.
Benjamin, Walter. "A Chinoiserie from the Old West." In *Walter Benjamin Gesammelte
    Schriften*. 5 vols. Frankfurt am Main: Surkamp Verlag, 1990.
Bennett Arnold. "*Piccadilly*": *The Story of the Film*. London: The Readers' Library
    Publishing, Ltd., 1929.
Bennett, Michael. *A Chorus Line*. New York: Applause Books, 1995.
Case, Frank. *Do Not Disturb*. New York: Frederick A. Stokes Company, 1940.

————. *Tales of a Wayward Inn*. New York: Garden City Publications, 1938.

Chiang, Kai-shek, Madame. *China Shall Rise Again*. New York: Harper & Brothers, 1941.

Clayton, Buck. *Buck Clayton's Jazz World*. New York: Oxford University Press, 1987.

Correspondence: An Exhibition of the Letters of Ray Johnson. N.p.: North Carolina Museum of Art, 1976.

Dean, Basil. *Mind's Eye: An Autobiography 1927–1972, The Second Volume of Seven Ages*. London: Hutchinson of London, 1973.

De Silva, Annesley. *These Piquant People: Being a Collection of Conversations*. London: Cecil Palmer, 1932.

Doerr, Conrad. "Reminiscences of Anna May Wong." *Films in Review* (December 1968).

Gielgud, Val. *Years of the Locust*. London: Nicholson &Watson, 1947.

Gingold, Hermione. *How to Grow Old Disgracefully*. New York: St. Martin's Press, 1988.

Hahn, Emily. *China to Me: A Partial Autobiography*. New York: Doubleday, Doran, 1944.

Hayakawa, Sessue. *Zen Showed Me the Way . . . to Peace, Happiness, and Tranquility*. New York: Bobbs-Merrill, 1960.

Hubert, Ali. Hollywood: *Legende und Wirklichkeit*. Leipzig: Verlag E.A. Seeman, 1930.

Hurston, Zora Neale. *Dust Tracks on a Road: An Autobiography*. 2nd edition. Urbana: University of Illinois Press, 1984.

Kingston, Maxine Hong. *The Woman Warrior: Memoirs of a Girlhood Among Ghosts*. New York: Knopf, 1977.

Koo, Madame Wellington with Isabella Taves. *No Feast Lasts Forever*. New York: Quadrangle Books, 1973.

Larson, Louise Leung. *Sweet Bamboo: A Memoir of a Chinese American Family*. Berkeley: University of California Press, 1989.

Lin, Yutang. *My Country and My People*. New York: John Day, 1935.

Maschwitz, Eric. *No Chip on My Shoulder*. London: Herbert Jenkins, 1957.

Milady's Style Parade and Recipe Book for 1935 with Photos of Favorite Movie Stars. N.p., 1935.

Price, Victoria. *Vincent Price: A Daughter's Biography*. New York: St Martin's Press, 1999.

Robeson, Paul. *Here I Stand*. Boston: Beacon Press. Reprint of 1958 edition.

Smith, H. Allen. *Life in a Putty Knife Factory*. Garden City: Doubleday, Doran & Company, 1945.

Snow, Helen Foster. *My China Years: A Memoir*. New York: William Morrow and Company, 1984.

Sojin, Kamiyama. *The Unpainted Face of Hollywood*. Tokyo: Jitsugyo no Nihonsha, 1930.

Souvenir Program of the Chinese Moon Festival: Ancient China's Greatest Festivity. Sponsored by The Chinese Consolidated Benevolent Association Benefit of United China Relief, Los Angeles, California. August 7, 8, 9, 1941.

Weiss, Felix. "Heads and Tales." *Christian Science Monitor*.

Woolf, Charlotte. *Hindsight*. London: Quartet Books, 1980.

————. *On the Way to Myself: Communications to a Friend*. London: Methuen & Co, 1969.

————. *Studies in Hand-Reading*. New York: Knopf, 1938.

Photography Collections

Beaton, Cecil. *Photobiography*. Garden City: Doubleday and Company, 1951.

Eisenstadt, Alfred. *People*. New York: Viking Press, 1973.

Engstead, John. *Fifty Years of Pictures and Stories by One of Hollywood's Greatest Photographers*. New York: E.P. Dutton, 1978.

Faber, Monica, ed. *Divas and Lovers: The Erotic Art of Studio Manasse*. New York: Universe Publishing, 1998.

Film Photos Wie Noch Nie. Berlin: Kindt & Bucher, 1929.

Pepper, Terence. *Camera Portraits by E. O. Hoppé*. London: National Portrait Gallery, 1978.

Pepper, Terence, and John Kobal. *The Man Who Shot Garbo: The Hollywood Photographs of Clarence Sinclair Bull*. New York: Simon and Schuster, 1989.

Spence, Jonathan, and Annping Chin. *The Chinese Century: A Photographic History of the Last Hundred Years*. New York: Random House, 1996.

Stine, Whitney. *The Hurrell Style: Fifty Years of Photographing Hollywood*. New York: John Day Company, 1976.

Tänzerinnen Der Gegenwart: 57 Bilder Erläutert Von Fred Hildenbrandt. Leipzig: Orell Fussli Verlag, 1931.

Secondary Sources

Aarim-Heriot, Najia. *Chinese Immigrants, African Americans, and Racial Anxiety in the United States, 1848–82*. Urbana: University of Illinois Press, 2003.

Acker, Ally. *Reel Women: Pioneers of the Cinema, 1896 to the Present*. New York: Continuum, 1991.

The American Film Institute Catalog of Motion Pictures Produced in the United States. 12 vols. to date. New York and Berkeley: R. R. Bowker (until 1988) and University of California Press, 1988.

Asian American Studies Center. *Linking Our Lives: Chinese American Women in Los Angeles*. Los Angeles: Chinese Historical Society of Los Angeles, 1984.

Balio, Tino. *History of American Cinema*. Vol. 5. *Grand Design: Hollywood as a Modern Business Enterprise, 1930–1939*. New York: Charles Scribner's Sons, 1993.

Barbagallo, Tricia. "Changing with the Rhythm: Anna May Wong—the Essence and Transformation of Identity." Unpublished Manuscript, 2003.

Barbas, Samantha. *Movie Crazy: Fans, Stars, and the Cult of Celebrity*. New York: Palgrave, 2001.

Basinger, Jeanne. *Silent Stars*. New York: Knopf, 1999.

Basten, Fred E. *Glorious Technicolor: The Movies' Magic Rainbow*. London: A. S. Barnes, 1980.

Benton, Gregor, and Frank N. Pieke, eds. *The Chinese in Europe*. New York: St. Martin's Press, 1998.

Benton, Gregor, and Edmund Terence Gomez. *Chinatown and Transnationalism: Ethnic Chinese in Europe and Southeast Asia*. Canberra: Centre for the Study of the Chinese Southern Diaspora, 1998.

Berenstein, Rhona J. *Attack of the Leading Ladies: Gender, Sexuality, and Spectatorship in Classic Horror Cinema*. New York: Columbia University Press, 1996.

Bernardi, Daniel. *The Birth of Whiteness: Race and the Emergence of U.S. Cinema*. New Brunswick: Rutgers University Press, 1996.

Bernstein, Matthew, and Gaylyn Studlar, eds. *Visions of the East: Orientalism in Film*. New Brunswick, NJ: Rutgers University Press, 1997.

Berry, Sarah. *Screen Style: Fashion and Femininity in 1930s Hollywood*. Minneapolis: University of Minnesota Press, 2000.

Blower, Brooke L. *Becoming Americans in Paris: Transatlantic Politics and Culture between the World Wars*. New York: Oxford University Press, 2011.

Botto, Louis, and Robert Viagas. *At this Theater: 100 Years of Broadway Shows, Stories, and Stars*. New York: Applause Books, 2002.

Broderson, Momme. *Walter Benjamin, A Biography*. London and New York: Verso, 1996.

Brodi, Michaela, et al. *Der verbotene Blick: Erotisched aus zwei Jahrtausenden*. Wien: Ritterbooks für Österreichiste Nationalbibliotek, 2002.

Brook, Timothy. "Funerary Ritual and the Building of Lineages in Late Imperial China." *Harvard Journal of Asiatic Studies* 49 (1989): 465–500.

Bruno, Giuliana. *Atlas of Emotion: Journeys in Art, Architecture, and Film*. New York: Verso, 2002.

Bushnell, Brooks. *Directors and Their Films: A Comprehensive Reference*. Jefferson and London: McFarland & Company, 1993.

Carey, Gary. *Doug and Mary: A Biography of Douglas Fairbanks and Mary Pickford*. New York: E.P. Dutton, 1977.

Chan, Anthony B. *Perpetually Cool: The Many Lives of Anna May Wong (1905–1961)*. Lanham: Scarecrow Press, 2003.

Chan, Sucheng. *Entry Denied: Exclusion and the Chinese Community in America, 1882–1943*. Philadelphia: Temple University Press, 1991.

Chang, Iris. *The Chinese in America: A Narrative History*. New York: Viking Press, 2003.

Chen, Shehong. *Being Chinese: Becoming Chinese American*. Urbana: University of Illinois Press, 2002.

Cheng, Anne Anlin. *The Melancholy of Race: Psychoanalysis, Assimilation, and Hidden Grief*. New York: Oxford University Press, 2001.

Cheng Chi-hua. *History of the Development of Chinese Cinema*. 2 vols. Peking, 1963.

Chierichetti, David. *Edith Head: The Life and Times of Hollywood's Celebrated Costume Designer*. New York: HarperCollins, 2003.

Chow, Crystal. "Sixty Years on the Silver Screen," *Rice*. September 1988.

Chu, Judy. "Anna May Wong." In Emma Gee, ed., *Counterpoint: Perspectives on Asian America*, 284–89. Los Angeles: Asian American Student Center of the University of California, 1976.

Chu, Peter, et al. *Chinese Theater in America*. N.p.: Bureau of Research, Federal Theater Project, 1936.

Cochran, Sherman, ed. *Inventing Nanjing Road: Commercial Culture in Shanghai, 1900–1945*. Ithaca: Cornell East Asia Series, 1999.

Crosby, Alfred W. *America's Forgotten Pandemic: The Influenza of 1918*. New York: Cambridge University Press, 1989.

Day, Barry, ed. *Noel Coward: The Complete Works*. Woodstock, NY: Overlook Press, 1998.

DeCordova, Richard. *Picture Personalities: The Emergence of the Star System in America*. Urbana: University of Illinois Press, 1990.

De Salvo, Donna. *Ray Johnson: Correspondences*. Paris: Flammarion Press, 2000.

Dong, Arthur. *Forbidden City, USA*. Videotape. Los Angeles: Deepfocus Productions, 1989.

Duberman, Martin Bauml. *Paul Robeson*. New York: Knopf, 1988.

Edwards, Anne. *The DeMilles: An American Family*. New York: Harry N. Abrams, 1988.

Ehrenstein, David. *Open Secret: Gay Hollywood, 1928–1998*. New York: William Morrow, 1998.

Ellenberger, Allan R. *Celebrities in Los Angeles Cemeteries: A Directory*. Jefferson: McFarland & Company, 2001.

Endres, Stacey, and Robert Cushman. *Hollywood at Your Feet: The History of the World-Famous Chinese Theatre*. Los Angeles: Pomegranate Press, 1992.

Faderman, Lillian. *Odd Girls and Twilight Lovers: A History of Lesbian Life in Twentieth-Century America*. New York: Columbia University Press, 1991.

Feng, Peter X., ed. *Screening Asian Americans*. New Brunswick: Rutgers University Press, 2002.

Fonoroff, Paul. *Silver Light: A Pictorial History of Hong Kong Cinema, 1920–1970*. Hong Kong: Joint Publishing Co., 1997.

Fowles, Jib. *Starstruck: Celebrity Performers and the American Public*. Washington: Smithsonian Institution Press, 1992.

Fu, Poshek. *Passivity, Resistance and Collaboration: Intellectual Choices in Occupied Shanghai, 1937–1945*. Palo Alto: Stanford University Press, 1993.

Fuller, Karla Rae. "Hollywood Goes Oriental: CaucAsian Performance in American Cinema." Ph.D. diss. Northwestern University, 1997.

Fuller, Kathryn H. *At the Picture Show: Small-Town Audiences and the Creation of Movie Fan Culture*. Washington: Smithsonian Institution Press, 1996.

Gabaccia, Donna. *We Are What We Eat: Ethnic Food and the Making of Americans*. Cambridge: Harvard University Press, 1998.

Gao Yunxiang, "Sex, Sports, and 'National Crisis,' 1931–1945: The 'Athletic Movie Star' Li Lili (1915–2005)." *Modern Chinese Literature and Culture* 22, no. 1 (spring 2010): 96–161.

———."Sports, Gender, and Nation State during the War of Resistance Against Japan from 1931 to 1945." Ph.D. diss. University of Iowa, 2003.

Garraty, John, and Mark C. Carnes, eds. *American National Biography*. 25 vols. New York: Oxford University Press, 1999.

Gianarcis, Larry James. *Television Drama Series Programming: A Comprehensive Chronicle, 1947–1959*. Metuchen: Scarecrow Press, 1980.

Gleber, Anke. *The Art of Taking a Walk*. Princeton: Princeton University Press, 1999.

———. "Women on the Screens and Streets of Modernity: In Search of the Female Flaneur." In Dudley Andrew, *The Image in Dispute: Art and Cinema in the Age of Photography*. Austin: University of Texas Press, 1997.

Groves, Durham. *Anna May Wong's Lucky Shoes: 1939 Australia Through the Eyes of an Art Deco Diva*. Melbourne: Self-Published, 2011.

Guttinger, Fritz. *Köpfen Sie mal ein Ei in Zeitlupe!* München: Wilhelm Fink Verlag, 1992.

Gyory, Andrew. *Closing the Gate: Race, Politics, and the Chinese Exclusion Act*. Chapel Hill: University of North Carolina Press, 1998.

Hamamoto, Darrell Y., and Sandra Liu, eds. *Countervisions: Asian American Film Criticism*. Philadelphia: Temple University Press, 2000.

Hardt, Michael, and Antonio Negri. *Empire*. Cambridge: Harvard University Press, 2000.

Harris, Kristine Marie. "Silent Speech: Envisioning the Nation in Early Shanghai Cinema." Ph.D. diss. Columbia University, 1997.

Hayman, Ronald. *Brecht: A Biography*. New York: Oxford University Press, 1983.

Heap, Chad. *Slumming: Sexual and Racial Encounters in American Nightlife, 1885–1940*. Chicago: University of Chicago Press, 2009.

Higson, Andrew, and Richard Maltby, eds. *"Film Europe" and "Film America" Cinema, Commerce, and Cultural Exchange, 1920–1939*. Exeter: University of Exeter Press, 1999.

Hing, Bill Hong. *Making and Remaking Asian America Through Immigration Policy, 1850–1990*. Stanford: Stanford University Press, 1993.

Hirschorn, Clive. *The Universal Story*, 2nd ed. London: Hamlyn, 2000.

Hodes, Martha. "The Mercurial Nature and Abiding Power of Race: A Transnational Family Story." *American Historical Review* 108 (2003): 84–118.

Hsu, Madeline. *Dreaming of Gold, Dreaming of Home: Transnationalism and Migration Between the United States and South China, 1882–1943*. Stanford: Stanford University Press, 2000.

Jesperson, T. Christopher. *American Images of China, 1931–1949*. Stanford: Stanford University Press, 1996.

Jew, Victor. "Metro Goldwyn Mayer and Glorious Descendant: The Contradictions of Chinese American Employment in the Hollywood Studio System during the 1930s." Paper Presented to the 2003 Meeting of the American Historical Association.

Jones, Andrew F. *Yellow Music: Media Culture and Colonial Modernity in the Chinese Jazz Age*. Durham: Duke University Press, 2001.

Jones, Dorothy. *The Portrait of China and India on the American Screen, 1896–1955*. Cambridge: MIT Press, 1955.

Kazuko, Ono. Chinese *Women in a Century of Revolution, 1850–1950*. Palo Alto, CA: Stanford University Press, 1989.

Kellner, Bruce. *Carl Van Vechten and the Irreverent Decades*. Norman: University of Oklahoma Press, 1968.

———. ed. *"The Splendid Drunken Twenties": Selections from the Daybooks, 1922–1930, by Carl Van Vechten*. Urbana: University of Illinois Press, 2003.

Kirihara, Donald. "The Accepted Idea Displaced: Stereotype and Sessue Hayakawa." In Daniel Bernardi, ed. *The Birth of Whiteness: Race and the Emergence of U.S. Cinema*. 81–102. New Brunswick, NJ: Rutgers University Press, 1996.

Koppes, Clayton R., and Gregory D. Black. *Hollywood Goes to War: How Politics, Profits and Propaganda Shaped World War II Movies*. New York: Free Press, 1987.

Koszarski, Richard. *History of American Cinema. Vol. 3. An Evening's Entertainment: The Age of the Silent Feature Picture, 1915–1928*. New York: Charles Scribner's Sons, 1990.

Kracauer, Siegfried. *From Caligari to Hitler: A Psychological History of the German Film*. Princeton, NJ: Princeton University Press, 1947.

Kreimeier, Klaus, *The UFA Story: A History of Germany's Greatest Film Company, 1918–1945*. New York: Hill and Wang, 1996.

Lee, Anthony. *Picturing Chinatown: Art and Orientalism in San Francisco*. Berkeley: University of California Press, 2000.

Lee, Erika. *At America's Gates: Chinese Emigration: Chinese Immigration during the Exclusion Era, 1882–1943*. Chapel Hill: University of North Carolina Press, 2003.

Lee, Joann Faung Jean. *Asian American Actors: Oral Histories from Stage, Screen, and Television*. Jefferson, NC: McFarland, 2000.

Lee, Josephine. *Re-Collecting Early Asian America: Essays in Cultural History*. Philadelphia: Temple University Press, 2002.

Lee, Leo Ou-Fan. *Shanghai Modern: The Flowering of a New Urban Culture in China, 1930–1945*. Cambridge: Harvard University Press, 1999.

Leibfried, Philip. "Anna May Wong." *Films in Review* (March 1987): 147–53.

Leibfried, Philip, and Chei Mi Lane. *Anna May Wong: A Complete Guide to Her Film, Stage, Radio and Television Work*. Jefferson: McFarland, 2004.

Leong, Karen Janis. "The China Mystique: Mayling Soong Chiang, Pearl S. Buck, and Anna May Wong in the American Imagination." Ph.D. diss. University of California at Berkeley, 1999.

Leong, Karen J. *The China Mystique: Pearl S. Buck, Anna May Wong, Mayling Soong, and the Transformation of American Orientalism*. Berkeley: University of California Press, 2005.

Leyda, Jay. *Dianying Electric Shadows: An Account of Films and Film Audience in China*. Cambridge: MIT Press, 1972.

Lim, Shirley Jennifer. *A Feeling of Belonging: Asian American Public Culture, 1930–1960*. New York: New York University Press, 2006.

Lin Jiayou, and Li Jikui. *Song Meiling zhuan*. Zhengzhou: Henan renmin chuban she, 1995.

Lou, Raymond. "The Chinese-American Community of Los Angeles, 1870–1900: A Case of Resistance, Organization, and Participation." Ph.D. diss. University of California at Irvine, 1982.

Low, Rachael. *Film Making in 1930s Britain*. London: George Allen & Unwin, 1983.

Lu, Sheldon Hsaio-peng. *Transnational Chinese Cinemas: Identity, Nationhood, Gender*. Honolulu: University of Hawai'i Press, 1997.

MacCann, Richard Dyer. *The Silent Screen*. Lanham: Scarecrow Press, 1997.

Marchetti, Gina. *Romance and the "Yellow Peril."* Berkeley: University of California Press, 1993.

Marrill, Alvin H. *The Films of Anthony Quinn*. Secaucus: The Citadel Press, 1975.

Masden, Axel. *William Wyler: The Authorized Biography*. New York: Thomas Y. Crowell, 1973.

McClain, Charles, ed. *Chinese Immigrants and American Law*. New York: Garland Publishing, Inc., 1994.

Meyer Richard. *Outlaw Representation: Censorship and Homosexuality in Twentieth-Century American Art*. New York: Oxford University Press, 2002.

Miall, Leonard. *Inside the BBC: British Broadcasting Characters*. London: Weidenfeld and Nicolson, 1994.

Mitchell, Charles P. *A Guide to Charlie Chan Movies*. Westport: Greenwood Press, 1999.

Moy, James. *Marginal Sights: Staging the Chinese in America*. Iowa City: University of Iowa Press, 1993.

Mulvey, Laura. *Visual and Other Pleasures*. Bloomington: Indiana University Press, 1989.

Mumford, Kevin J. *Interzones: Black/White Sex Districts in Chicago and New York in the Early Twentieth Century*. New York: Columbia University Press, 1997.

Mundy, Robert. "Joseph H. Lewis Filmography." *Cinema* 7, no. 1 (1971).

Naremore, James. *Acting in the Cinema*. Berkeley: University of California Press, 1988.

Nga, Thi Thanh. "The Long March from Wong to Woo: Asians in Hollywood," *Cineaste* 21 (1995).

Nicholson, Stuart. *Duke Ellington*. London, Sidgwick & Jackson, 2000.

Pan, Lynn. *The Encyclopedia of the Chinese Overseas*. Cambridge: Harvard University Press, 1998.

Parish, James Robert. *Actor's Television Credits, 1950–1972*. Metuchen: Scarecrow Press, 1973.

Parish, James Robert, and William T. Leonard. *Hollywood Players: The Thirties*. New Rochelle: Arlington House Publishers, 1976.

Pascoe, Peggy. *What Comes Naturally: Miscegenation Law and the Making of Race in America*. New York: Oxford University Press, 2009.

Peffer, George Anthony. *If They Don't Bring Their Women Here: Chinese Female Immigration Before Exclusion*. Urbana: University of Illinois Press, 1999.

Pendergast, Tom and Sara Pendergast. *International Dictionary of Film and Filmmakers*, 4 vols. *Writers and Production Artists*. Detroit: St. James Press, 2000.

Pickowicz, Paul G. "The Theme of Spiritual Pollution in Chinese Films of the 1930s." *Modern China* 17, no. 1 (January 1991).

Pitts, Michael R. *Poverty Row Studios, 1929–1940: An Illustrated History of 53 Independent Film Companies with a Filmography for Each*. Jefferson: McFarland & Company, 1997.

Pizzitola, Louis. *Hearst over Hollywood: Power, Passion, and Propaganda in the Movies*. New York: Columbia University Press, 2002.

Prikopa, Herbert. *Die Wiener Voksoper: Die Geschichte eines notwendigen Theaters*. Vienna: Ibera, 1999.

Rainsberger, Todd. *James Wong Howe: Cinematographer*. San Diego: A.S. Barnes, 1981.

Richards, Jeffrey, ed. *The Unknown 1930s: An Alternative History of British Cinema, 1929–1939*. London: I.B. Tauris, 1998.

Ritchie, Alexandra. *Faust's Metropolis: A History of Berlin*. New York: Carroll and Graf, 1998.

Riva, Maria. *Marlene Dietrich*. New York: Knopf, 1992.

Roberts, J. A. G. *China to Chinatown: Chinese Food in the West*. London: Reaktion Books, 2002.

Rose, Phyllis. *Black Cleopatra: Josephine Baker in Her Time*. New York: Doubleday, 1989.

Rosten, Leo G. *Hollywood: The Movie Colony, the Movie Makers*. New York: Harcourt, Brace, and Company, 1941.

Rotha, Paul. *The Film Till Now*. London: Jonathan Cape, 1930.

Said, Edward. *Orientalism*. New York: Pantheon Books, 1978.

Scholder, Amy, ed. *Sweet Oblivion: The Urban Landscape of Martin Wong*. New York: Rizzoli Books, 1998.

Schrader, Bärbel, and Jürgen Schebera. *The "Golden" Twenties: Art and Literature in the Weimar Republic*. New Haven: Yale University Press, 1988.

See, Lisa. *On Gold Mountain: The One-Hundred-Year Odyssey of a Chinese American Family*. New York: St. Martin's Press, 1995.

Segrave, Kerry. *American Films Abroad: Hollywood's Domination of the World's Movie Screens*. Jefferson: McFarland, 1997.

Sergeant, Harriet. *Shanghai*. London: John Murray, 1998.

Shevsky, Eshref, and Marilyn Williams. *The Social Areas of Los Angeles: Analysis and Typology*. Berkeley: University of California Press, 1939.

Skandera-Trombley, Laura E. *Critical Essays on Maxine Hong Kingston*. New York: G.K. Hall, 1998.

Sklar, Robert. *Film: An International History of the Medium*. New York: Harry N. Abrams, 1993.

Slide, Anthony. *The Encyclopedia of Vaudeville*. Westport: Greenwood Press, 1994.

Smith, Icy. *The Lonely Queue: The Forgotten History of the Courageous Chinese Americans in Los Angeles*. Gardena: East West Discovery Press, 2000.

Sontag, Susan. *Against Interpretation and Other Essays.* New York: Noonday Press, 1966.

Spears, Jack. *Hollywood: The Golden Era.* New York: A.S. Barnes, 1971.

———. "Marshall Neilan Had a Natural Filmmaking Talent and a Character Flaw." *Films in Review* 13, no. 9 (1962): 517–48.

Spence, Jonathan D. *The Chan's Great Continent: China in Western Minds.* New York: W. W. Norton, 1998.

———. *The Search for Modern China.* London: Hutchinson, 1990.

Stamp, Shelly. *Movie-Struck Girls: Women and Motion Picture Culture after the Nickelodeon.* Princeton: Princeton University Press, 2000.

Stewart, Jeffrey C. *Paul Robeson: Artist and Citizen.* New Brunswick: Rutgers University Press, 1998.

Terrace, Vincent. *The Complete Encyclopedia of Television Programs, 1947–1976,* 2 vols. New York: A. S. Barnes, 1976.

———. *Encyclopedia of Television Series, Plots and Specials, 1937–1973.* New York: Zootrope, 2000.

Tong, Benson. *The Chinese Americans, Revised Edition.* Boulder: University Press of Colorado, 2003.

Vasey, Ruth. *The World According to Hollywood, 1918–1939.* Madison: University of Wisconsin Press, 1997.

Vincendeau, Ginette, ed. *Encyclopedia of European Cinema.* London: British Film Institute, 1995.

Volkre, Klaus. *Brecht Chronicle.* New York: Seabury Press, 1975.

Wang, Gungwu. *The Chinese Overseas: From Earthbound China to the Quest for Autonomy.* Cambridge: Harvard University Press, 2000.

Wang, Yiman. "The Art of Screen Passing: Anna May Wong's Yellow Yellowface Performance in the Art Deco Era." *Camera Obscura* 20, no. 3 (2005): 159–91.

West, Philip. *Yenching University and Sino-Western Relations, 1916–1952.* Cambridge: Harvard University Press, 1976.

Wide, Mark. *Street Meeting: Multiethnic Neighborhoods in Early Twentieth-Century Los Angeles.* Berkeley: University of California Press, 2005.

Winokur, Mark. *American Laughter: Immigrants, Ethnicity, and 1930s Hollywood Film Comedy.* New York: St. Martin's, 1996.

Witte, Bernd. *Walter Benjamin: An Intellectual Biography.* Detroit: Wayne State University Press, 1991.

Wollstein, Hans J. *Vixens, Floozies and Molls: 28 Actresses of the Late 1920s and 1930s Hollywood.* Jefferson: McFarland, 1999.

Wong, K. Scott, and Sucheng Chan, eds. *Claiming America: Constructing Chinese American Identities during the Era of Exclusion.* Philadelphia: Temple University Press, 1998.

Xiao, Zhiwei. "Film Censorship in China, 1927–1937." Ph.D. diss. University of California at San Diego, 1994.

Yau, Ching-Mei Esther. "Filmic Discourse on Women in Chinese Cinema (1949–65)." Ph.D. diss. UCLA, 1990.

Ye, Weili. *Seeking Modernity in China's Name: Chinese Students in the United States, 1900–1927*. Stanford: Stanford University Press, 2001.

Yoshira, Mari. *Embracing the East: White Women and American Orientalism*. New York: Oxford University Press, 2003.

Yu, Henry. *Thinking Orientals: Migration, contact, and Exocticism in Modern America*. New York: Oxford University Press, 2002.

Yung, Judy. *Unbound Feet*. Berkeley: University of California Press, 1994.

Zhang, Yingjin, and Xiao Zhiwei. *Encyclopedia of Chinese Film*. New York: Routledge, 1998.

Zhao, Xiaojian. *Remaking Chinese America: Immigration, Family, and Community, 1940–1965*. New Brunswick: Rutgers University Press, 2002.

Zia, Helen. *Asian American Dreams: The Emergence of an American People*. New York: Farrar, Straus and Giroux, 2000.

Zimmerman, Eric. "Archiving Television: The State of the Art." Paper Presented at the Annual Meeting of the Association for Education in Journalism, Seattle, 1979.

Zorris, Elaine. *Fiddletown from Gold Rush to Rediscovery*. Altadena: Mythos Press, 1997.

Index